THE
Avalanche
HANDBOOK

DAVID MCCLUNG AND PETER SCHAERER

THE MOUNTAINEERS/SEATTLE

5 4 3
5 4 3 2 1

Published by The Mountaineers
1011 SW Klickitat Way, Seattle, Washington 98134

Published simultaneously in Canada by Douglas & McIntyre, Ltd., 1615 Venables Street, Vancouver, B.C. V5L 2H1

Published simultaneously in Great Britain by Cordee, 3a DeMontfort Street, Leicester, England, LE1 7HD

Manufactured in the United States of America

Edited by Linda Gunnarson
Cover design by Lynne Faulk
Book design and typesetting by The Mountaineers Books
Book layout by Nick Gregoric

Cover photograph: Ice avalanche, Ultar, Pakistan. Photo © Greg Child

Library of Congress Cataloging-in-Publication Data
McClung, David.
        The avalanche handbook / David McClung and Peter Schaerer.
             p.   cm.
      Includes bibliographic references and index.
      ISBN 0-89886-364-3
      1. Avalanches--Handbooks, manuals, etc. I. Schaerer, P. A. (Peter A.) II. Title.
QC929.A8M39   1993
551.57'848--dc20   93-2027
                                                            CIP

CONTENTS

Chapter 6. Avalanche Prediction I: Elements of Stability Evaluation and Snowpack Observations   124

Chapter 7. Avalanche Prediction II: Avalanche Forecasting   151

Chapter 8. Safety Measures and Rescue   171

Chapter 9. Avalanche Protection   197

FOREWORD

The sequence of North American avalanche manuals over the past forty-five years, culminating in this present volume (*The Avalanche Handbook*), is a concise outline of the stages of development in avalanche science and practice during this time.

The pioneer period began when Monty Atwater assumed the position of snow ranger at Alta, Utah, immediately after World War II. With almost nothing in the way of prior information to guide him, Atwater used his keen observation skills and shrewd insights to lay the basis for avalanche forecasting and control. His earliest results appeared in 1948 as "Alta Avalanche Studies," written by Monty Atwater and Felix Koziol. Further rapid advances led to the earliest US Forest Service training programs and the need for a more comprehensive manual, which appeared in 1952 as the "Forest Service Avalanche Handbook."

The 1950s were the Golden Age of Forest Service avalanche studies. During this time, researchers systematically developed basic techniques of avalanche control. Using an extensive series of tests, they examined the effects of explosives on snow and tested a variety of hand charges and artillery weapons. By 1960 the techniques of control, the size of hand charges, and the most effective weapons had been identified, establishing the control methods still in use today. Drawing on Swiss techniques, researchers introduced the methods of snow pit analysis and time profiles, which became a routine part of snow observations. The Alta Avalanche School reached its heyday with expanded training programs and the preparation of instructional material and films. The Forest Service selected and designed new ski areas nationwide, using the knowledge they gained at Alta. Systematic observation programs at Stevens Pass in the Washington Cascades and at Berthoud Pass in the Colorado Rockies expanded the application of avalanche forecasting and control principles to other climates. When Atwater was assigned to apply all this developing knowledge at the 1960 Squaw Valley Winter Olympics, it fell to me to summarize the progress in the 1961 publication of USDA Handbook 194, "Snow Avalanches."

During the next fifteen years, avalanche work came of age in North America. The Alta research, long a stepchild of administrative studies, was transferred as a formal part of USFS research to the Rocky Mountain Experiment Station, and the Alta station was closed. In Canada, development of a major forecasting and control program at Rogers Pass launched considerable activity in avalanches. In the US, the National Avalanche School took over from the Alta training program. The Forest Service delegated much of the routine forecasting and control work in ski areas to an emerging cadre of trained professional patrolmen. The avalauncher air cannon was developed as a supplement to military weapons for control work. North American researchers played an increasing role in international affairs with participation in scientific conferences and research programs in Japan and Europe, while Handbook 194 was translated into foreign languages. In 1976 Ronald Perla and M. Martinelli, Jr. of the Rocky Mountain Station brought out a major revision and expansion of 194 under the resurrected title *Avalanche Handbook,* this time "USDA Handbook 489," which has remained the basic reference for the past seventeen years.

The years since 1976 have brought a flowering of mature and sophisticated activity to the avalanche scene. Central forecasting offices have been established in Western states supported by networks of field observers, remote-sensing instruments, and computerized data processing. Research and operational sophistication reached new levels under the guidance of a generation of investigators with advanced degrees and well-honed mathematical skills. Avalanche forecasting has advanced with new insights and theoretical analyses, supported by increasingly effective models for qualitative precipitation forecasts in mountain regions. The profession has been unified under the American Association of Avalanche Professionals and the Canadian Avalanche Association. The AAAP publication "Avalanche Review" and forums like the International Snow Science Workshop, with joint US-Canadian sponsorship, today assure rapid dissemination of ideas and methods among the avalanche community. A new generation of field workers brings a well-developed technology of avalanche control to public safety efforts.

In the 1980s the USFS research program at the Rocky Mountain Station was phased out. Such work continued in Canada, where both federal and provincial support contributed gains in science and engineering. It is therefore appropriate that this next *Avalanche Handbook* should be written by two leading Canadian researchers, David McClung and Peter Schaerer. McClung and Schaerer have set new and higher standards for scope and depth of treatment. This new book will be the basic reference of avalanche science for many years to come. If the increment of time between each new handbook and its predecessor continues to increase, this present one ought to serve well into the twenty-first century. I may not be around to see that next handbook, but I look forward with great anticipation to this one.

Ed LaChapelle
April 1993

PREFACE

With this publication, handbooks providing instruction on matters related to snow safety now have a 45-year tradition in North America. The last U.S. Forest Service publication in the series, *Avalanche Handbook* by R. Perla and M. Martinelli, Jr., was published in 1976 and revised in 1978. It represented a major expansion of material and was the most comprehensive publication on avalanche technology of its day. Our book is intended as the sequel to Perla and Martinelli's landmark publication.

Our work retains and enhances the technical flavor of previous handbooks. Also, we tried to make it as comprehensive as possible with a slightly more international flavor. For example, we pushed for use of the International Classification for Seasonal Snow on the Ground, and wrote the safety and rescue sections such that they are international in character.

Thematically, we elevated the "client base" of backcountry travelers to primary importance for potential readers of this book. Our chapters on avalanche prediction may be used by anyone trying to predict avalanches, but the use of backcountry forecasting analysis as the illustrative example in Chapter 7 is intentional. In addition, we included a major section on terrain, partially with the backcountry traveler in mind.

Other sections of the book have undergone major expansions compared to previous handbooks. Expanded subjects include snow metamorphism, characteristics of avalanches, the shear strength of alpine snow, mechanisms of avalanche release, characteristics of avalanche motion and effects, and avalanche prediction. In addition, there is an extensive set of appendixes, some of which document approaches to issues for which there are no clear international standards, for example, hazard rating scales and avalanche sizing.

In summary, we tried to produce a book about avalanches and the physical characteristics of snow that is as comprehensive as practical within the limits of one work. Simply stated, our goal was to produce the most comprehensive book on avalanches written from a technical yet non-mathematical framework. The writing, like battling avalanches, was a test of personnel, intellect, and equipment!

D. M.
March 1993

ACKNOWLEDGMENTS

The Avalanche Handbook is the result of input from many sources. We wish to thank Dr. Ron Perla and Dr. Pete Martinelli for contributing the foundation on which this book was built. We wish to thank all those who contributed photos. The art and graphic work of Alexis Kelner provided the base from which to work and this was expanded and enhanced by Evelyn McClung. Thanks to both of them.

The following people edited chapters and many others also gave extensive verbal input for which we are grateful: Betsy Armstrong, Dr. Richard Armstrong, Tim Auger, Dr. R. L. Brown, Dr. A. Burkhard, Dr. Sam Colbeck, Dr. Sue Ferguson, Doug Fesler, Jill Fredston, Dr. Hans Gubler, Dr. Bill Hotchkiss, Clair Israelson, Dr. Ed LaChapelle, Art Mears, Mark Moore, Dr. Ron Perla, Dr. Bruno Salm, Dr. Douw Steyn, John Tweedy, Ken White, Craig Wilbour, Knox Williams, and Norm Wilson.

Support for the writing of this book was provided by the National Research Council of Canada, Institute for Research in Construction. Without the sustained support of technical avalanche work for over three decades by the National Research Council, this book would not have been possible. We are grateful to George Seaden, director of the institute, for encouraging this work. Partial support for one of us (DMM) from the Natural Sciences and Engineering Research Council of Canada is also gratefully acknowledged.

INTRODUCTION

This book is designed to serve as a reference handbook on snow avalanches. It is aimed at anyone who may be involved with snow safety on a personal or professional level. The book can also serve as a text on avalanches and the physical properties of snow, knowledge of which is necessary to understand avalanche formation, movement, and effects. We expect our main readership will be people who wish to learn how to travel and operate safely in and near avalanche terrain. In addition, the book will serve those who wish to know about the physical characteristics of avalanches and snow in order to gain a background for deeper exploration of these subjects. We believe that the book will serve as a reference for instruction about snow and avalanches at all levels—from basic safety courses to university-level science and engineering courses if the latter are supplemented by appropriate mathematics and examples.

Our book is developed as a technical treatise, but it is not mathematical. Instead of equations, we use illustrations, photos, and examples to explain the concepts. Our retention of a technical flavor for the subject matter is intentional. Like any natural hazard mitigation, good avalanche safety does not just happen. It is the result of logical thinking and action. For example, safe backcountry skiing requires a logically sequenced risk reduction strategy, and proper rescue techniques require a well-organized approach so that precious time is used as efficiently as possible. It is our belief that if we had presented a superficial, nontechnical account of these subjects, the resulting effect on our readership would be superficial as well.

For snow avalanches, as with many of life's hazards, both education and experience are essential to provide the best survival chance. Our book is aimed at providing a solid building block for avalanche education in a readily understandable format. Experience cannot be learned from a book, but when supplemented by the logical framework of education, its true potential may be realized to provide the best protection available.

Figure 1.1. Flowing avalanche overtaking a road in New Zealand. (Photo by A. Dennis)

CHAPTER 1

EFFECTS OF AVALANCHES

We owe it to the victims of such catastrophes to overlook no avenue to understand and to more clearly foresee the reactions of nature to human interventions....

—Robert Haefeli

INDUSTRIES AFFECTED

Avalanches are falling masses of snow that can contain rocks, soil, or ice. The technology associated with avalanches has been developed with a view toward protecting people and property from the harmful and destructive effects of avalanches. In general, avalanches affect people directly by causing injury or death or by detaining them. Avalanches also cause property damage and they affect the environment. Some of the major industries affected by avalanches are:

- *Transportation:* Avalanches cause interruption of movement on (and placement of) highways and railways in mountain corridors. Companies and governments incur the costs of snow removal and repairs from avalanches. Deaths, injuries, and destruction of vehicles occur (Figures 1.1 and 1.2).
- *Construction:* Avalanches destroy buildings and kill or injure residents. Engineers must make informed decisions regarding the placement, design, and protection of facilities and operations in avalanche-prone mountainous terrain. Examples of facilities needing protection include houses, mines, telephone

Figure 1.2. Avalanche path crossing railway line, Rogers Pass, British Columbia. Three levels of vegetation damage are shown. (Photo by P. Anhorn)

Figure 1.3. Damage to the reinforced concrete base of a lift tower, Alyeska, Alaska April 14, 1973. (Photo by C. O'Leary)

and electric transmission towers and lines, and ski lift towers (Figures 1.3 and 1.4).

- *Tourism:* In mountainous recreational areas, avalanches can cause deaths, injuries, bad reputations from lawsuits, restrictions to services, or selection of alternate routes. Fear of avalanches causes anxiety for people traveling in avalanche terrain (Figure 1.5).

The true cost of avalanches to society is largely hidden and it would certainly be much higher without the dedicated cadré of professional individuals who are involved with avalanche technology.

EXAMPLES OF DESTRUCTIVE AVALANCHES

The term *avalanche hazard* refers to the exposure of people and property to the destructive effects of avalanches. Avalanche hazard is strongly related to the number of people exposed and the length of time they are exposed. For that reason, the hazard has always been very high in the heavily populated mountain ranges of Europe. For example, in 1951, 98 persons lost their lives in Switzerland and in 1954, 143 died in Austria. In both cases, avalanches destroyed numerous residences in several areas of the Alps.

The largest disaster by a single avalanche in recent European history occurred in 1970 at Val d'Isère in the French Alps when a hostel was struck and 39 inhabitants were killed. In the same winter, on February 24, a large avalanche destroyed six buildings at Reckingen, Switzerland; 30 people were found dead and 18 buried victims were rescued alive. The property damage was estimated at SFr 13 million (approximately U.S. $10 million). Avalanche defense earthworks built at Reckingen in the following years prevented another disaster when a large avalanche occurred at the site again in 1978.

Another example comes from northern India. On March 7, 1979, an avalanche moved through the village of Gusikar destroying several stone buildings and killing 35 residents. Widespread avalanche activity existed in the same week across the Indian Himalaya resulting in the deaths of about 200 people.

Figure 1.4. Transmission tower protected against avalanches. (Photo by H. Frutiger)

Figure 1.5. *Skier on steep avalanche terrain. (Photo by P. Anhorn)*

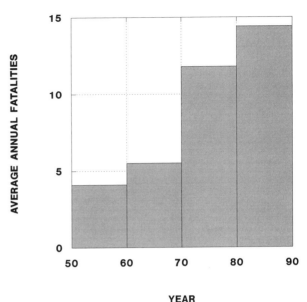

Figure 1.6. *Trend in avalanche fatalities in the United States.*

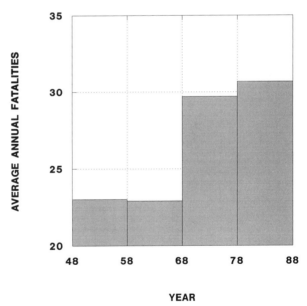

Figure 1.7. *Trend in avalanche fatalities in Switzerland.*

TREND IN AVALANCHE ACCIDENTS

Study of past disasters and accident trends indicates that the character of avalanche hazards has changed considerably due to human intervention in the past 20 to 30 years. Figure 1.6 shows the trend in avalanche fatalities in the United States based on 40 years of data. The rapid increase in the number of fatalities beginning in the early 1970s is a result of tremendous growth in backcountry winter mountain travel (skiing, mountaineering, snowmobiling). Data from Switzerland over 40 years show the same trend (Figure 1.7). Recent statistics show that the average annual number of fatalities is about 14 per year in the United States and 7 in Canada. In Switzerland, the total is nearly 30 per year and in Austria, France, and Japan the numbers are similar to those in Switzerland. In the Alps, approximately 120 people are killed each year by avalanches.

Data from North America, Europe, and Japan show that, beginning in the 1970s, a much larger percentage of the fatalities results from backcountry recreational activities rather than at worksites in buildings, at mine sites, or on transportation routes. The statistics from Canada shown in Table 1.1 indicate that the rate of occurrence of recreational fatalities has tripled (averaged over two 15-year periods).

Table 1.1 Avalanche Fatalities in Canada

	1959–1974	1974–1989
Fatalities during pursuit of recreational activities	33	97
Fatalities in buildings, on roads, at worksites	53	6

Two clear examples illustrating the reasons for the decline in nonrecreational deaths come from the worst avalanche disasters in the United States and Canada. Both occurred in March 1910 as a result of accidents on railways: 96 people were killed when two trains were bowled off the track near Stevens Pass, Washington; 62 workmen were killed at Rogers Pass, British Columbia, while attempting to shovel the track buried by an earlier avalanche. Neither accident would be possible at present because the tracks now run in tunnels bored through the

Figure 1.8. Avalanche overtaking mountaineering camp. In the Himalaya, incorrect camp placement accounts for the highest source of avalanche fatalities. (Photo by P. Anhorn)

mountains at each location. Even if the tunnels were not present, modern avalanche forecasting, control, and snow removal techniques would nearly eliminate the risk now in comparison to 1910. To provide a fair assessment of the cost of avalanches to society, a portion of the cost of the tunnels should be added to the costs (development and implementation) of modern forecasting and control methods. In a casual analysis, avalanches don't affect the railways at these and similar locations and the cost of the safety measures is hidden.

In North America, more than three-quarters of avalanche fatalities now occur during the pursuit of recreational activities. Of the total avalanche deaths in North America, data show that those in recreational activities are roughly stratified as follows: skiers, 40% to 50%; mountain climbers, 25% to 30%; others (including snowmobilers), 10% to 20%. The total fraction of recreational deaths is just as high in Europe, even though more villages are exposed to avalanches. In the Alps, an analysis of more than 1,200 fatalities during the 1975–1985 period showed that about 85% of the victims were engaged in skiing and mountaineering and only 10% were killed on roads and in buildings.

The number of backcountry fatalities would be rising even faster if not for the avalanche education programs and avalanche forecasting and warning services available from avalanche professionals. Quality education programs have a great effect in reducing avalanche accidents because they promote awareness and provide a survival strategy for people who are likely to be traveling in avalanche terrain. Warning services include recorded telephone messages, backcountry stability assessments posted in parks and recreational areas (or verbal messages), and occasional newspaper and radio bulletins. These forecasting and warning services should be used in combination, with perhaps more emphasis on education for the best overall safety: It is better to learn to do your own thinking (promoted by education) than to use someone else's (provided by warning services). Both education and warning services add to the general cost of avalanche safety (discussed in the next section). However, they target those people most likely to be involved with avalanches. Therefore, these services represent the best overall expenditure in terms of saving lives.

Expedition mountaineering in the Himalaya is one of the highest-risk human activities, and avalanches contribute greatly to the risk. At present, apart from falls, avalanches account for the greatest single source of fatalities in Himalayan mountaineering (Figure 1.8).

During the 1895–1989 period, there were 322 avalanche fatalities in Himalayan mountaineering. Of these, 56% occurred on the 14 peaks that exceed 8,000 m in height. Of the avalanche deaths on the 8,000-m peaks, 81% occurred on only five peaks: Everest (51), Nanga Parbat (30), Annapurna (25), Manaslu (21), and Dhaulagiri (20). Avalanche fatalities in Himalayan mountaineering have increased steadily since 1950 in agreement with a worldwide trend—from about three per year during the period from 1950 to 1969 to twelve per year from 1970 to 1989.

DIRECT COSTS

Property damage in North America from avalanches is relatively minor, but again the true costs are hidden. In the United States and Canada the average yearly estimated property damage cost is less than $500,000 in each country when averaged over 20 years from 1970 to 1990. Figure 1.9 shows five-year averages of property damage in the United States for the 1970–1990 period. When the costs are adjusted for inflation, the data show no increase in property damage values. These low figures are due to the efforts of engineers skilled in land-use planning in avalanche-prone terrain. For comparison, in the alpine countries of Europe (for example, Switzerland, Austria, and France) property damage costs are nearly 20 times higher.

Far more significant are the costs of protective defenses against avalanches (about four times the annual property damage cost) and the feasibility studies connected with land-use planning. On average, detailed engineering feasibility studies in Canada are carried out for about three times as many avalanche paths as those in which protection is actually undertaken.

Another hidden cost associated with avalanches is the rising insurance bill against liability for operations such as helicopter and snowcat ski companies and ski areas. Claims for liability directed at avalanche accidents are now increasingly common in both Europe and North America. The fear of lawsuits causes extreme uneasiness for companies operating in avalanche terrain.

Other costs (direct and indirect) are due to lengthy closures of rail and road routes and ski facilities during periods of high danger or during avalanche control operations. The uncertainty and complexity of forecasting and controlling avalanches is sometimes responsible for closures that can last for days. A closure costs people and companies money in terms of time and

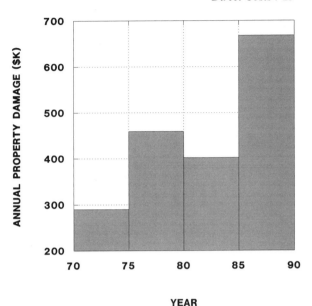

Figure 1.9. Property damage in thousands of dollars in the United States.

business lost and it exerts pressure on the governments and organizations responsible for avalanche forecasting and explosive control. In British Columbia, about 70 areas on highways have been identified as needing avalanche forecasting and/or control. Every major railway line in British Columbia is also threatened by avalanches. In western Canada, the bill for operational control and forecasting is about CDN $10 million per year.

Perhaps the greatest effect that avalanches have on most people is the anxiety they feel when traveling in avalanche terrain. Statistics show that most people caught in avalanches trigger the slides themselves. The risk of death for people once caught in avalanches is more than 100 times the risk for people engaged in ordinary mountaineering (which itself is a risky activity) and 10 times as high as that for people engaged in expedition climbing. Of those caught in avalanches, about 10% are killed, another 10% are injured, and overall about 40% are buried. These numbers show that education about avoidance and rescue techniques is essential for alpine travel.

The natural pattern of avalanching itself changes because climate and snowfall patterns vary. However, the hazard to humans is largely due to their own intervention. An example of this intervention that may be of future catastrophic importance in Europe is the potential

Figure 1.10. Mature trees with trunk diameters of 0.6 m broken by an avalanche. (Photo by H. Frutiger)

Item	1962–1963	1987–1988	Increase
Vehicles per day	400	2,069	518%
Avalanche paths with static defenses	23	36	156%
Avalanche paths with artillery control	47	68	145%
Number of targets for artillery control	70	170	243%
Number of artillery shells used per winter	300	805	265%

Note: Avalanche control by artillery is explained in Chapter 9.

The number of avalanches varies widely from year to year, but it is not increasing on average. However, people can change that too. Avalanche hazards, like other natural hazards, are increasing every year due to human influences. It seems clear that future mitigation will require greater human efforts.

for the death of forests caused by acid precipitation. In the Alps, forests protect villages and facilities from avalanches, but current evidence suggests that many stands of alpine forest are dying. This presents an ominous potential for disaster in the future if action is not taken. In Switzerland, it is regarded as the most serious avalanche-related problem.

Currently, more than 100 hectares of forest are destroyed in Switzerland annually and a similar amount of grazing and pasture land is damaged. These totals and the property damage and death tolls will surely rise as forests weaken and die due to the harmful effects of acid precipitation (Figure 1.10).

Avalanche hazards are tied to industries (including forestry), governments and the public, and environmental concerns. The number of times humans and their facilities are exposed to avalanches is increasing and there is rising demand for higher safety standards. At present, it is possible to protect buildings, worksites, and transportation corridors. However, the demand for this protection is becoming greater (see Table 1.2) with new developments and needs such as increases in traffic volume.

References

Fredston, J., and D. Fesler. 1991. Avalanche accidents in the United States, 1950–1991. National Avalanche School, November 5–11, 1991. Denver: National Avalanche Foundation, 11pp.

McClung, D. 1981. Avalanche Fatalities in Himalayan Mountaineering. *Amer. Alpine Journal.* 23(55): 138–145.

Schaerer, P. 1989. Studies on survival in avalanches. *Canadian Alpine Journal.* 71:55–56.

Schleiss, V. G. 1989. *Rogers Pass Snow Avalanche Atlas.* Glacier National Park, British Columbia, Canada. Revelstoke, B.C.: Environment Canada, Canadian Parks Service, 313 pp. + map.

Swiss Federal Institute for Snow and Avalanche Research. 1989. Schnee and Lawinen in den Schweizer Alpen Winter 1987/88. *Winterbericht No. 52.* Weissflujoch/Davos.

Valla, F. 1987. Accidents d'avalanches dans les Alpes au cours de la decennie 1975–1985. IAHS Publication No. 162: 647–652.

CHAPTER 2

ELEMENTS OF
MOUNTAIN WEATHER

The virtuous find delight in mountains, the wise in rivers.

—Confucius

MOUNTAIN WEATHER AND
SNOW CLIMATE TYPES

Snow layering that contributes to avalanche formation is due to a combination of weather elements interacting with the snowpack. Most destructive avalanche cycles are caused by direct loading of snowfall from large-scale (synoptic) weather systems. To understand how, why, and when avalanches form, it is necessary to have some background about basic mountain weather, the effects of weather parameters on snow, and the interaction of weather and topography, which influence the deposition and distribution of snow. The primary weather and atmospheric factors contributing to avalanche formation include precipitation patterns and intensity, wind direction and wind speed, sensible heat, and radiation heating or cooling on snow.

When avalanche formation is described in a broad, general sense it is useful to classify the snow climate of a given mountain range as either maritime or continental (Figure 2.1). This classification will not be useful in the individual situations encountered in avalanche prediction. However, in a general sense, the character of snow avalanching in a given range of mountains can be

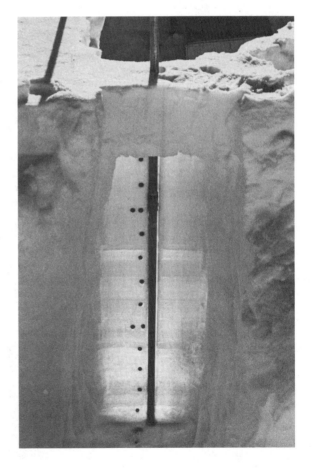

Figure 2.1. Illustration of snowpack structure. Structure usually depends on climate type in a general sense. (Swiss Federal Institute for Snow and Avalanche Research archive photo)

17

described as one of these two basic types or as transitional between maritime and continental. Since the character of avalanching differs between maritime and continental descriptions, the classifications provide a basis for discussing avalanche prediction in general terms.

Maritime Snow Climate

A maritime snow climate is characterized by relatively heavy snowfall and relatively mild temperatures. Snow covers are deep. While rain may fall at any time during the winter, cold arctic air can also appear several times per winter. Maritime snow covers are often very unstable with rapidly fluctuating instability. Typical examples of maritime ranges include the Cascade Range in the western United States, the Coastal Range of British Columbia, and the mountains of western Norway. The average annual snowfall in the maritime ranges of North America is 15 to 25 m.

Avalanche formation in maritime snow climates usually takes place during or immediately following storms, with failures occurring in the new snow near the surface. The prevalence of warm air temperatures promotes rapid stabilization of the snow near the surface once it falls, thereby limiting the time over which instability persists. A significant cause of major avalanching can be rain if it immediately follows deep, new snowfall. Rainfall may also cause formation of ice layers, which can act as future sliding layers when buried by subsequent snow storms. Due to the deep snow covers and warm snowpack temperatures, the persistence of buried structural weaknesses deep in the snowpack is not usually as common in maritime snow climates as in continental snow climates. Weather observations are primary tools for predicting avalanches in a maritime snow climate (Table 2.1).

Table 2.1 Characteristics of Maritime, Transitional, and Continental Snow Climates*

Type	Total Precipitation (mm)	Air Temperature (°C)	Snow Depth (cm)	New Snow Density (kg/m³)
Maritime	1,280	−1.3	190	120
Transitional	850	−4.7	170	90
Continental	550	−7.3	110	70

*Mean values compiled from 15 winters of U.S. data (Armstrong and Armstrong 1987).

Continental Snow Climate

A continental snow climate is characterized by relatively low snowfall, cold temperatures, and a location considerably inland from coastal areas. Snow covers are relatively shallow and often unstable due to the persistence of structural weaknesses. Typical examples of continental ranges include the Rocky Mountains (Canadian and Colorado), the Brooks Range of Alaska, and the Pamirs of Asia; the annual snowfall in the continental ranges of North America is usually less than 8 m.

Avalanche forecasting in continental ranges relies on observations of buried structural weaknesses in the snow cover as well as weather conditions that cause the failure of these layers. Many failures occur in new snow as well, but failure of old layers is a distinguishing feature of a continental snow climate. Extensive drifting in fair weather can cause heavy local accumulations to initiate failure in old snow layers. Due to the prevalence of thin snow covers, recrystallization weakens old snow in the presence of cold temperatures and high temperature gradients (see Chapter 3). The low temperatures also allow structural weaknesses to persist.

The two broad classes are useful as a framework for discussion of avalanche formation, but it must be stressed that considerable overlap occurs, with many areas exhibiting transitional features associated with both classes. That is, maritime conditions can occur in a continental range and vice versa. Examples of ranges that usually display transitional features are the Selkirk Range of British Columbia and the Wasatch Range of Utah.

MOUNTAIN WIND AND PRECIPITATION

Wind speed and direction and the resulting precipitation patterns are crucial elements in forecasting avalanches. In general, wind direction and speed depend on the balance of forces on the moving air. The horizontal component of the wind velocity is the most important element in terms of wind speed and direction in mountainous avalanche terrain; the vertical component is the key factor in determining the amount and pattern of snowfall.

Horizontal Wind Component: Direction and Speed

The character of the horizontal component of the wind field depends strongly on altitude because the

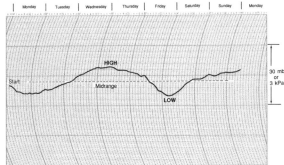

Figure 2.2. Left: microbarograph; right: chart with pressure ranges identified.

mountains act as huge roughness obstacles to the wind blowing over them (Figure 2.2). The atmospheric pressure is about 1,000 millibars (mb) at sea level (1,013 mb is one standard atmosphere), and near the earth's surface there is always a strong frictional component acting to slow the wind and alter the direction (Figure 2.3). Over flat terrain, this frictional effect on the wind is largely absent at about 1,000 m above the surface. The atmospheric pressure level of interest in avalanche forecasting depends on the height of the mountain tops (Figure 2.4). In the United States and Canada, the usual range of interest varies from 850 to 700 mb (excluding the highest ranges). This range is comparable to heights of 1,500 to 3,000 m. At avalanche starting zone elevations, frictional forces are still important in controlling the

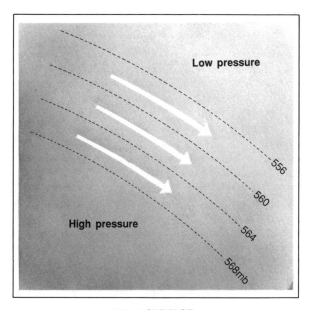

500mb SURFACE   **AT EARTH'S SURFACE**

Figure 2.3. At 500 mb the wind (free air speed) is parallel to pressure contours. At the surface, the wind flows across the contours.

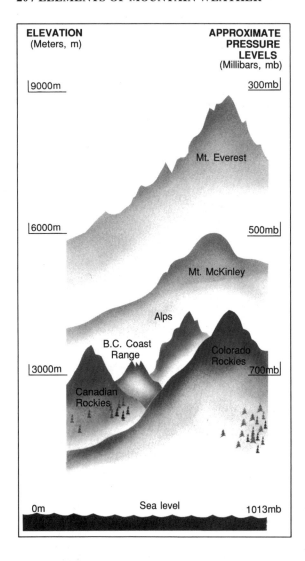

Figure 2.4. Atmospheric pressure variations with altitude.

balance of these forces causes the wind to blow at an angle to the isobars (lines of constant pressure) toward lower pressure at a speed determined by the exact balance of forces.

Free-air wind speeds are those well above rough mountain topography (for example, several hundred meters or more) so that frictional forces are absent. Most mountain weather and avalanche forecast operations predict either free-air wind speeds and directions (for high elevation sites) or surface winds (for example, at lower elevations such as mountain passes). It is then up to the forecaster or field practitioner to determine the influences of the topography on these winds at the local scale.

Wind speed sensors are placed on ridge tops, mountainsides, or in valleys. Therefore, they provide measurements influenced by frictional forces. Frictional forces have a strong influence on wind direction. In some cases when a mountain range forms a barrier between warm maritime air and cold continental air, free-air winds at upper levels can blow at 180° to the direction of surface pressure gradient winds, which have been strongly channeled through ground topography.

Vertical Wind Component: Amount, Rate, and Pattern of Precipitation

The vertical component of the wind causes precipitation; it determines how much, the rate, and the distribution. The precipitation rate is approximately proportional to the vertical component of the wind velocity. Therefore, the vertical wind speed is crucial for quantitative snowfall forecasts, which are an essential element of avalanche forecasting.

In general, processes that cause an upward component of the air motion result in cloud formation and precipitation; those with a downward component dissipate clouds and produce clearing skies. When moisture-laden air moves up a mountain, its temperature will decrease with height due to expansion as it moves through progressively decreasing pressure. In general, the amount of temperature decrease that an air parcel experiences with height depends on how much moisture is contained in it. Typical values are 1°C temperature change per 100 m of elevation (1°C/100 m) for dry air and about half that rate for moist air. Whether a vertically displaced air parcel is warmer or colder than the surrounding air will depend on the *average lapse rate* (that is, the temperature decrease with height in the

wind speed and direction in mountainous terrain. In North American ranges at the 700-mb level, for example, the forces controlling the wind speed and direction are (1) atmospheric pressure changes (gradients) associated with general (synoptic) weather conditions; (2) the frictional force due to drag from the earth's terrain features (directed opposite to the wind direction); and (3) an apparent force (Coriolis force) due to the earth's rotation that is at right angles to the wind (to the right in the Northern Hemisphere, to the left in the Southern Hemisphere). In high mountain terrain, the surrounding air). The average lapse rate in the lowest 10 km of the atmosphere is about 6.5°C/1,000 m. Since cold air is denser than warm air, an air parcel will sink when it is colder than the surrounding air. When a parcel is warmer than the surrounding air, it will rise, expand, and cool during ascent. Eventually the dew point will be reached, the air becomes moisture saturated, and further cooling will result in cloud formation through condensation of water vapor. The amount of moisture that air can hold *before* it condenses depends on its temperature: A parcel of warm air can potentially hold more water vapor prior to condensation than one with cold air. Further lifting causes water droplet growth around condensation nuclei (see Chapter 3) and then precipitation. In summary, the rate at which air rises, the amount of moisture it contains, and its initial temperature are crucial determining factors for the formation and amount of precipitation.

In general, four mechanisms cause air to rise, and the vertical rate of ascent strongly depends on which mechanism is responsible. These mechanisms are (1) cyclonic convergence—upward air motion around a center of surface low pressure; (2) frontal lifting—upward motion when one air mass is forced to rise over another; (3) orographic lifting—topographically induced, forced ascent; and (4) convection—thermally induced vertical motion. As a rough estimate, the following percentages apply to winter precipitation totals for the mechanisms: cyclonic, 10%; frontal, 30%; orographic, 50%; convection, 5%. These values will change with season, with mountain climate, and from year to year. In most cases,

more than one mechanism operates at a time to complicate precipitation forecasting. Table 2.2 gives typical characteristics of the mechanisms.

Table 2.2 Characteristics of Major Lifting Types (Typical Values)

Type	Vertical Wind Speed	Precipitation Rate (water equivalent) (mm/h)	Duration of Precipitation	Horizontal Scale (km)
Cyclonic	~1–10 cm/s	Up to 2	Tens of hours to several days	1,000
Frontal	~1–20 cm/s	~1–10	Up to tens of hours	100 for width 1,000 for length
Orographic	~1 cm/s to 2 m/s	~1–5	Up to tens of hours	10–100
Convective	~1– 10m/s	~1–30	Minutes to hours	0.1–10

CONVERGENCE: UPWARD MOTION AROUND A LOW-PRESSURE AREA

Convergence around a low-pressure area (cyclone) will result in a general vertical motion of the air (Figure 2.5). In the Northern Hemisphere, the air circulates counterclockwise and inward toward the center of the

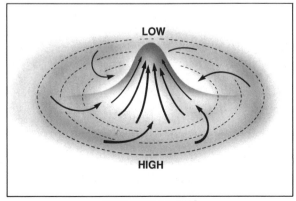

CYCLONIC LIFTING

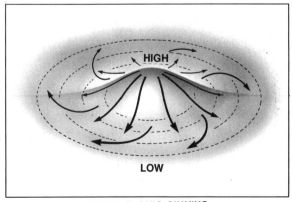

ANTICYCLONIC SINKING

Figure 2.5. Convergence around a low-pressure area (diameter of about 1,000 km) causes widespread precipitation. Divergence (sinking) around a high causes clearing skies.

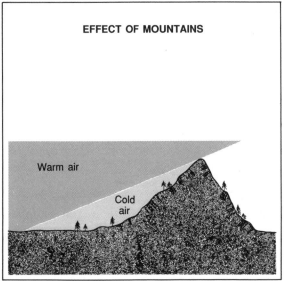

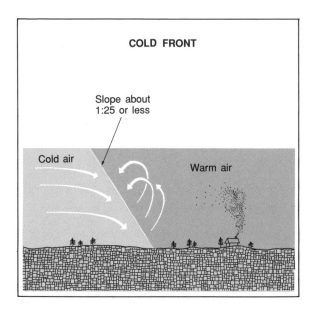

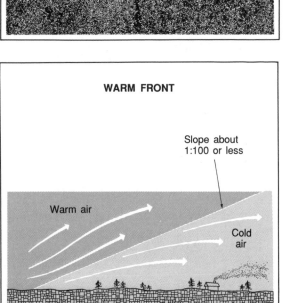

Figure 2.6. Frontal motion and the lifting effect of mountains on warm fronts. Top: due to differences in slope, precipitation is much more widespread during warm-front passage; left: mountains increase the lifting of warm fronts.

FRONTAL LIFTING

Another lifting mechanism is associated with the motion of an atmospheric front. A front is the boundary between air masses of different temperature (Figure 2.6). The boundary always slopes upward over the colder air. While the slope of the boundary is typically 1:100 or less for warm fronts, that for cold fronts is much steeper (as high as 1:25). The difference in frontal slopes leads to important variations in the rate, duration, and type of snow. Warm front precipitation may last 12 to 18 hours or more. Cold front precipitation typically occurs in a series of shower bands oriented almost parallel to the front with intense precipitation for about 4 to 6 hours.

When warm air moves against a wedge of cold air (warm front passage) or if a wedge of cold air pushes under warm air (cold front passage), forced lifting occurs, which causes cooling by expansion, leading to cloud formation and precipitation. In this case, the precipitation occurs over the frontal surface (typically 50 to 100 km wide). The occurrence is usually more widespread during warm front passage and more sharply defined during cold front passage.

storm (low pressure). To accommodate this inward flow, the air in the cyclone must then be forced up as the horizontal dimension of the air mass decreases (converges). The usual result is cloud formation over a large area and, in general, widespread precipitation over the mountains if they happen to be located near the low-pressure center. The opposite effect occurs in the case of divergence, resulting in sinking of the air downward and out from a region of high pressure, resulting in drying and cloud dissipation.

Mountain ranges can trap cold air masses on their windward sides or the pressure drop associated with the warm front may draw cold air over the mountains toward the front. Both of these mechanisms can intensify the lifting effect on warm fronts. The vertical wind velocity component induced by frontal lifting is usually small and comparable to lifting rates from convergence.

OROGRAPHIC LIFTING

When moist air is forced over a mountain range by horizontal pressure differences, it is forced to flow parallel to the slope of the mountain (Figure 2.7). This causes an upward (vertical) component of the velocity, which is a significant fraction of the incoming horizontal wind speed. The vertical wind speed produced is a factor of 10 to 100 greater than that for frontal lifting and convergence. This effect is of great importance for the avalanche forecaster and it is the primary consideration when forecasting snowfall amounts in mountain areas. Orographic effects are estimated to account for 50% to 70% of winter mountain precipitation. In general, the steeper the mountain slope that the wind strikes and the more directly perpendicular the wind hits the mountain, the greater the potential for producing precipitation. Maximum precipitation is achieved when the horizontal

wind is blowing perpendicular to the ridge crest so the vertical component of the velocity produced is a maximum.

CONVECTION

Convection results when air is heated near the earth's surface and is forced to rise because of its lower density relative to the surrounding air. Convection is a very local effect and its direct contribution to winter precipitation is small. However, convective instability following the passage of cold marine air over warm ocean water can contribute significantly to precipitation in coastal mountains. The resulting clouds and precipitation then contribute to the orographic component as the moisture is forced over the mountains. Convection can also be an important contributor to summer precipitation patterns in continental climates.

QUANTITATIVE PRECIPITATION FORECASTS

Avalanche and mountain weather forecasters operating out of weather offices produce quantitative precipitation forecasts to aid avalanche prediction. They have access to a host of models, mostly implemented on

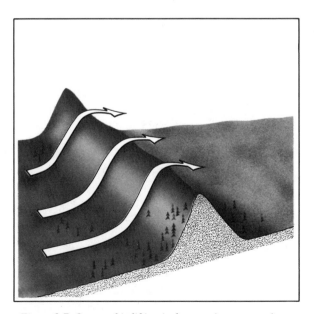

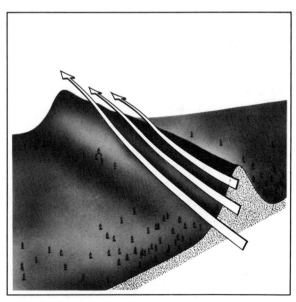

Figure 2.7. Orographic lifting is the most important winter precipitation mechanism; maximum effect is produced (left) when the wind is perpendicular to the mountain barrier.

computers, to determine vertical wind velocities due to fronts, convection, orographic effects, and general circulation. In addition, experience relevant to the mountain range in question is often integrated with other tools such as satellite imagery, climatology records, remote weather station output, radiosonde soundings, radar, and standard weather station products. In most cases, several precipitation mechanisms operate simultaneously to complicate the prediction scheme.

For avalanche forecasting, precipitation must be quantified on the scale of a mountain range width or less (mesoscale, 1 to 100 km), whereas precipitation amounts are normally forecast on a synoptic scale (storm width, 1,000 km) by conventional weather forecasters. Therefore, avalanche weather forecasters use *orographic precipitation models* to predict precipitation amounts as storms force moisture-laden air through the mountains.

OROGRAPHIC PRECIPITATION MODELS

Orographic precipitation models include the assumption that precipitation is produced at a rate that is directly proportional to the rate at which the air is lifted (vertical component of wind velocity) over the mountains. The first mountain struck will usually induce the most precipitation and subsequent barriers receive less as the moisture supply in the air mass diminishes.

Orographic models include computer-generated mountain terrain maps (155,000 km^2 in Colorado, for example) necessary to predict areas of lifting, subsidence, and shadowing. The procedure involves keeping track of the amount of condensation and precipitation as an air mass rises over the mountains. On the downwind side of the crest, much of the condensed moisture evaporates.

Orographic precipitation models require initial data from the forecaster before they are run. These data include wind direction, wind speed, a temperature profile (lapse rate), and an estimate of the thickness and width of the atmospheric layer capable of producing precipitation. These data are obtained from upper air soundings and standard weather forecast products. The duration of the precipitation is obtained by estimating the width of the moist layer and wind speed.

In addition to lifting mechanisms, other (local) effects are important in mountain precipitation forecasting:

- *Topographic convergence* refers to the flowing together and subsequent lifting of moist air downwind of a major mountain barrier. One well-known example is the Puget Sound convergence zone in Washington State. This phenomenon results from splitting and reconverging of the air flow around the Olympic Mountains west of Seattle. Subsequent forced lifting of the convergence-produced clouds and moisture results in enhanced snowfall in the Cascade Range east of Seattle. Topographic convergence can result in extremely variable precipitation patterns. Variations in snowfall amounts by a factor of 10 over a distance of less than 1 km have been observed. Local topographic convergence effects have also been noted behind the volcanoes of the Cascade Range.
- *Orographic convergence* refers to local convergence zones that can shift or form and disappear as the prevailing wind direction changes with respect to a given topographic feature.
- *Valley channeling* is the forced convergence of air by a gradually narrowing valley. The result is enhanced precipitation in the narrow portions of the valley over that expected for constant valley width.

All three of these effects can have major influences on the local distribution of snow. Local knowledge of all three is essential for good mountain precipitation forecasting. While an experienced forecaster may identify and partially quantify the expected precipitation patterns, success is not guaranteed.

In addition to orographic effects, other influences may cause snowfall to *decrease* with elevation, which can complicate the picture. Sometimes in coastal areas, an air mass can move slowly off the ocean with very little lifting to produce a band of precipitation at relatively low elevation. In addition, some observers cite evidence for enhanced snowfall near the freezing level, which may produce snowfall decrease with height.

LOCAL WINDFLOW OVER MOUNTAIN TERRAIN

Wind speed and direction in the mountains are crucial factors for determining whether or not avalanches will occur and the location and the character of avalanches that do form. In modern avalanche forecasting, wind speed and direction are considered essential input. On a local scale, wind effects are crucial for determining route selection in backcountry travel (Figure 2.8).

On an individual mountain, the characteristics of wind velocity change with both altitude and the local topographic features. Generally, in the middle and high

(Figure 2.9). On the world's highest peaks, however, there is a limit beyond which precipitation decreases with height because previous lifting has caused most of the available precipitation to fall out. In addition, near the tops of exposed peaks or ridges, the winds are often so strong that snow is blown off. This occurs because of general increases in wind speed with elevation and also because topographical frictional effects are greatly reduced.

On a given mountain, snowfall is generally greater on the windward side (lifting occurs) than the leeward side (subsidence occurs). In addition, as a storm passes over the mountain, snowfall is gradually subtracted from the total moisture available so that by the time the lee side is reached there is less moisture left to deposit. This same concept explains partly why continental ranges have less snowfall: Often a lot of snow has fallen in coastal ranges before the precipitating storm reaches inland destinations.

The *local* terrain features on a mountain have very important effects on snow deposition and wind patterns. A key concept for avalanche formation is that, in general, snow is picked up in places where the wind accelerates, and snow is deposited in deceleration zones (Figure 2.10). The vertical compression of airflow over a mountain causes acceleration. Deceleration is caused by zones of low pressure (high turbulent intensity) and dynamic wakes at the snow surface. All of these effects can occur simultaneously, but on the windward side of a ridge crest, the wind flow is compressed (the air pressure is higher) against the mountain and accelera-

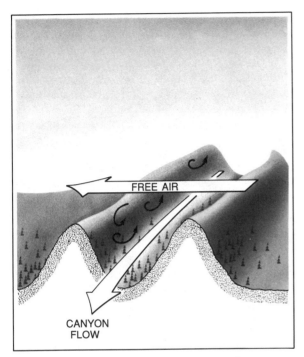

Figure 2.8. Deflection of flow in the direction of a canyon.

latitudes, wind speed increases with height due to the characteristics of the global westerly wind belts. The amount of snowfall generally *increases* with height on mountains of moderate height due to orographic effects

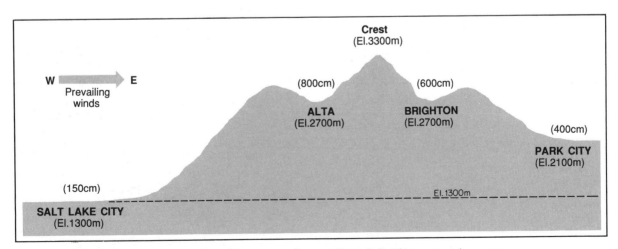

Figure 2.9. Snowfall varies with altitude and exposure to the prevailing wind within a mountain range.

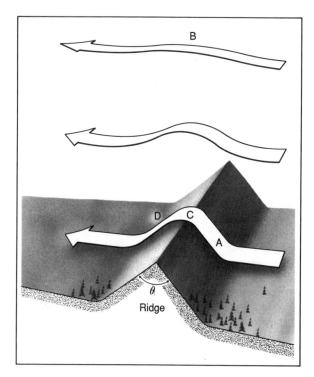

Figure 2.10. A: Airflow over a ridge; B: free-air motion; C: ridge crest; A, D: acceleration and deceleration zones.

compared to when a cornice forms. Field observations and measurements show that minor rolls or changes in slope angle may significantly affect the character and areal distribution of wind-deposited snow.

Intense mountain winds are sometimes encountered down mountain canyons oriented perpendicular to the free air flowing across a mountain range. This effect can produce cross-slope loading by drifting snow (see Figure 2.8).

When a large-scale low-pressure area is present in the lee of a mountain range, sometimes a dry, warm *foehn wind* (or *chinook*) will blow down the leeward side of the mountain. The foehn wind occurs when the prevailing winds in warm, moist air are directed upward against the mountains by the large-scale pressure differences between the windward and leeward sides (Figure 2.12). The ascent usually causes cloud buildup and sometimes precipitation on the windward side. The precipitation on the windward side can, of course, add load to the snowpack. However, the main feature of a foehn wind is the intense flow of air, which dries and warms due to compression as it descends the leeward side. The intense warming and drying is largely a result of loss of precipitation on the windward side and descent at the dry lapse rate on the leeward side.

tion (compressional effects) dominates. On the lee side of a mountain, the compressional effects are largely absent and deceleration dominates. Typically a pressure difference of 1 mb results in an increase in wind speed of 4 to 5 m/s over a ridge crest. It is common for the compression effect to cause winds on an exposed ridge crest to exceed the free-air speed. Sharp breaks of slope cause more turbulence in the air passing over them than if the slope change is gradual, due to greater pressure changes. This can cause the air flow to separate from the ground on the lee side; vertical eddies form and a reversal of flow direction at the snow surface takes place. These eddies are an important element in cornice formation, snow "dust" devils, and the determination of the distribution and character of deposited snow for avalanche formation (Figure 2.11).

The same logic applies to cross-loaded slopes when the slope breaks are not sharp enough to allow cornice formation. Wind deposition of snow will still be on the lee side of a ridge, but the prevailing wind direction is not as easy for an observer to determine from a distance

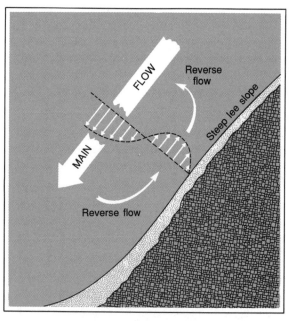

Figure 2.11. Reversal of flow on steep lee slopes. This pattern allows cornice and avalanche formation.

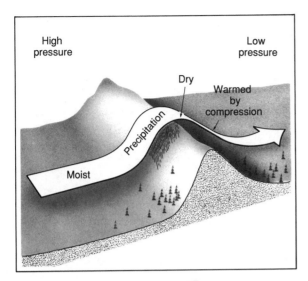

High pressure

Low pressure

Dry

Warmed by compression

Precipitation

Moist

Figure 2.12. Schematic of foehn wind.

Foehn winds can be important in avalanche work due to the warming that takes place during leeward descent. They are an important source of wet snow avalanching in the European and New Zealand Alps. In general, any snow temperature rise can adversely affect snow stability (see Chapter 7). However, since most avalanche starting areas are near the tops of peaks and since the warming takes place due to descent, little warming will be felt by the highest starting areas by foehn winds. Refreezing of the snow surface after melt from a foehn can cause crust formation, which might serve as a sliding surface if buried by later snowfalls.

BLOWING AND DRIFTING SNOW

Redistribution of snow by wind is a major feature of mountain snowpacks and it is essential for avalanche formation in some instances. In fact, redistributed snow can account for avalanche releases by loading even in clear weather. The term *blowing snow* is reserved to describe particles raised to a height of about 2 m or more. Blowing snow often obscures visibility. Drifting snow (about 90% of transported snow) is used to describe near-surface transport.

The critical wind speed (threshold wind speed) at which snow is picked up from the surface by turbulent eddies of wind is a complicated function of the physical conditions of the surface snow. No guidelines have yet been published to quantify the conditions in a manner

useful for avalanche workers. However, some useful general statements based on experimental information on the cohesion of ice and observation of blowing and drifting snow are possible: (1) Threshold wind speed increases with increasing temperature and humidity. (2) If the original deposition occurs with wind, the particles will be broken into small pieces and they will pack to a higher density to subsequently increase threshold wind speed. (3) Threshold wind speed will increase with time since deposition (due to bond formation between surface grains). The increase will slow with time and it is slower at colder temperatures. (See Chapter 3 for ice-bond physics.) (4) Threshold wind speed will be much lower if there is a source of particles such as new snowfall, a low strength layer at the surface (for example, surface hoar), or snow on trees.

For loose unbonded snow, the typical threshold wind speed (at a 10-m height) is 5 m/s. For a dense bonded snow cover, winds greater than 25 m/s are necessary to produce blowing snow. Blowing snow will occur with modest winds whenever snow is falling.

There are three modes of transport for wind-redistributed snow (Figure 2.13). *Rolling* involves the creeplike motion of dry particles along the surface (depth 1 mm). *Saltation* occurs as particles bounce along the surface in a layer about 10 cm deep, dislodging other particles as they hit the surface. Saltation is initiated with winds of 5 to 10 m/s over cold loose snow. Rolling is thought to account for about 10% of the mass when creep and saltation occur together. *Suspension* is caused by turbulent eddies lifting particles up to tens of meters above the surface. The transition from saltation to suspension occurs when the wind speed exceeds about 15 m/s. When turbulent upcurrents exceed the fall velocity of the snow particles (normally 0.2 to 2 m/s for newly fallen snow), experiments show that the majority of the mass is transported in the lowest meter above the surface. In general, turbulent suspension and saltation will both work to load avalanche slopes in regions of decelerating wind. With higher wind speed, saltation trajectories of particles will carry the particles higher and the proportion of the load carried by suspension will increase.

In the mountains, snow redistribution is uneven because it is strongly influenced by the local topography, including vegetation, rock outcrops, the "caps" of gullies, cols, notches, and gully walls (Figures 2.14 and 2.15). Hollows 10 to 100 m across tend to be filled in during the course of a winter until an equilibrium level of the snow surface is reached where erosion balances

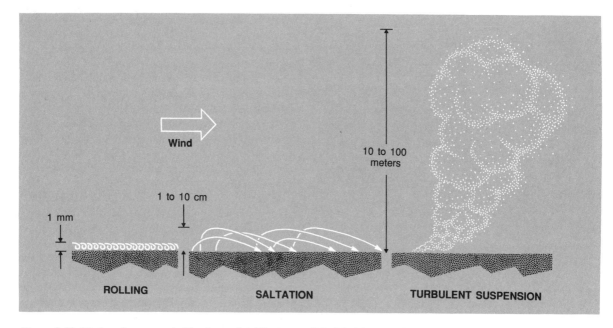

Figure 2.13. Modes of transport in blowing and drifting snow. (Modified from Mellor 1965)

deposition. Therefore, the amount of material blown past hollows increases during the winter as hollows are filled in and the snow surface topography changes.

Figure 2.14. Likely locations for cross-loading, gully, and notch deposition(shown by arrows) depend on prevailing wind direction.

Avalanche incidents (including at least one fatality) have been recorded that are attributed to avalanche formation in "blow holes" sculpted behind large terrain features. The minimum change of slope angle necessary to cause significant changes in drift development is about 10°. The choice of a safe route in mountainous terrain is often dependent on recognizing microscale features and their effects on drift development.

LEE SLOPE DEPOSITION: AVALANCHE AND CORNICE FORMATION

On the lee side of alpine ridge crests, where a sharp change in slope angle occurs, cornices and avalanche deposits may form due to formation of eddies by flow separation. The windward slope angle is thought to be critical in determining whether a cornice or snowdrift will form, but clearly the overall change in slope angle is important. In addition, as snow is redistributed, the particles become broken and abraded as they impact the snow surface. (Natural concentrations in blowing snow are thought to be generally too small for particle interactions above the surface.) These small fragments, upon deposition, become tightly packed and rapidly produce a slablike texture as they bond to their neighbors. This

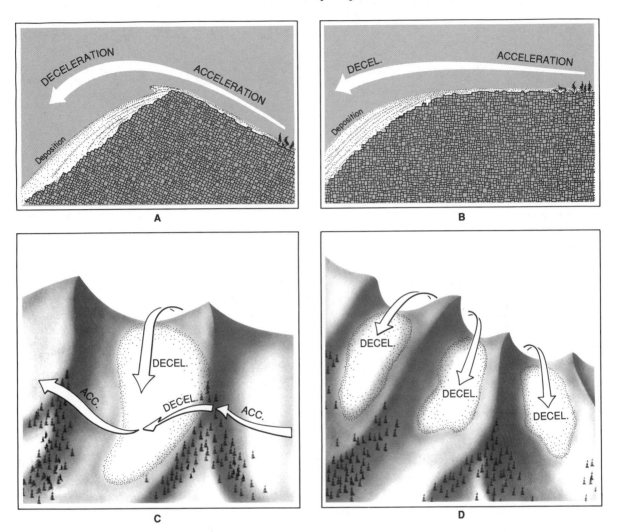

Figure 2.15. Snow is picked up in acceleration regions and deposited in deceleration regions (A, B). This produces lee zone deposition, cross-loading, and deposition in gullies and notches (C, D).

mechanism is therefore extremely important to avalanche formation (see Chapter 4). In addition to being favored places for producing slablike texture, lee zones usually collect greater amounts of snow than nearby wind-protected valley locations (factors of three to five times more and higher are not uncommon).

Cornices usually form on ridge crests but they can form at any place where a sharp change in slope angle is found (Figures 2.16 and 2.17). The threshold wind speed for cornice formation and growth is about the same as the threshold wind speed for transport over loose, cold snow (5 to 10 m/s). For winds in excess of 25 m/s, studies have shown that cornices can decrease in size due to windward scouring of the root. Because the snow in cornices is usually hard and dense (up to 500 kg/ m^3), the threshold wind speed for scouring may be greater than 25 m/s. Clearly, variations may result due to surface conditions, temperature, humidity, and other factors but it appears that cornice growth occurs for wind speeds in the range of 5 to 25 m/s. Also, for wind speeds in excess of 25 m/s, turbulent suspension is expected to be the mechanism for snow transport, so that

Figure 2.16. Blowing snow during cornice formation and lee zone deposition. (Photo by D. Fesler)

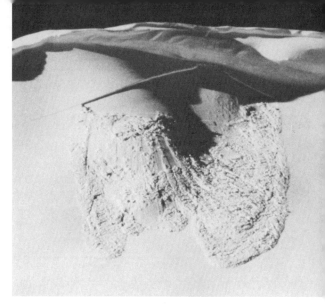

Figure 2.18. Slab avalanche formed under the lee of a cornice. (Photo by B. Jamieson)

snow particles may be transported far beyond the cornice scarp and perhaps beyond potential avalanche starting zones. In addition, such suspension can result in measurable amounts of snow being lost by sublimation as snow is transported through the air.

Cornices have three other features that are important to avalanche workers: (1) An overhanging cornice provides a quick assessment of the prevailing wind direction in a mountain range from a distance; (2) the steep, lee area below the face of a cornice is itself a prime area for unstable snow slabs to form (Figure 2.18); and (3) the overhanging face of a cornice on a ridge crest can and

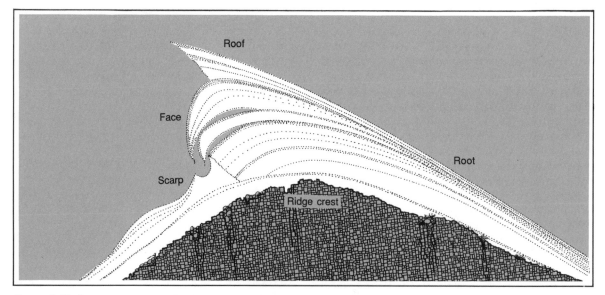

Figure 2.17. Cornice structure and nomenclature. Prevailing wind direction is from right to left.

often does collapse. Many serious and fatal accidents have resulted from cornice collapses. Avalanches are triggered by cornices, and occasionally falling cornices have damaged structures. Ridge crests are preferred as travel routes when unstable snow is expected, but the overhanging roofs of cornices are an exception (Figure 2.19). The steeper the face below the cornice and the greater the overhang, the more unstable the cornice. At times, cornices may form on both sides of a ridge causing further difficulty in travel.

HEAT EXCHANGE AT THE SNOW SURFACE

The exchange of heat between the snow surface and the atmosphere is important for avalanche formation for both wet and dry snow. Heat exchange can alter surface snow to produce weak snow there, which may fail or it may act as a future failure layer when subsequently buried.

Heat can enter or leave the snowpack surface by conduction, convection, or radiation. Heat flow by conduction in the air is negligible with respect to other mechanisms because of the inefficiency of passing heat by molecular collisions in air flow (the thermal conductivity of air is extremely low).

Heat may be transferred to and from the snowpack by turbulent exchange (called *sensible heat*) due to wind eddies. If the air is warmer than the snowpack, surface heat is added to the snowpack. If the surface is warmer than the air, heat is lost from the snowpack. Warm moist air flowing over a snowpack can result in significant surface warming by this mechanism (a foehn wind provides one example).

Heat may also flow to and from the snow surface by condensation resulting from diffusion of water vapor. In this case, the direction of heat flow is from regions of high water vapor concentration to regions of low concentration. Since saturated warm air can hold more water vapor than saturated cold air, the flux of heat (and water vapor) is from regions of high temperature to low temperature (Figure 2.20).

An important example with respect to avalanche formation is surface hoar formation. Surface hoar forms when relatively moist air over a cold snow surface becomes oversaturated with respect to the snow surface causing a flux of water vapor, which condenses on the surface. The result is feathery crystals (the ice/solid equivalent of dew) varying in thickness from 1 mm to

Figure 2.19. Cornice on a ridge crest. (Photo by A. Roch)

several centimeters. Once buried, the resulting weak layer is a serious consideration for avalanche formation. Surface hoar tends to form at night when the snow surface generally cools and the adjacent air becomes oversaturated (Figures 2.21 and 2.22). The amount of heat added by vapor deposition and subsequent refreezing is very small but the important element is the weak layer formed during the process. A detailed discussion of surface hoar is given in Chapter 3.

Falling precipitation can also warm or cool the snow surface, but the amount of heat exchanged is very small (for either snow or rain). Snow crystals will add heat if they are warmer than the snow surface and vice versa. However, more important than heat addition is the potential mismatch in layer properties. Rising temperatures in snowstorms can cause cold unstable layers to be buried (see Chapter 7). Rain can supply small amounts of heat to the snow surface, but more important is the added weight and the effect on the mechanical properties of layers below when water percolates downward. If rain freezes on the surface or below it, of course, additional heat will be released by the freezing process.

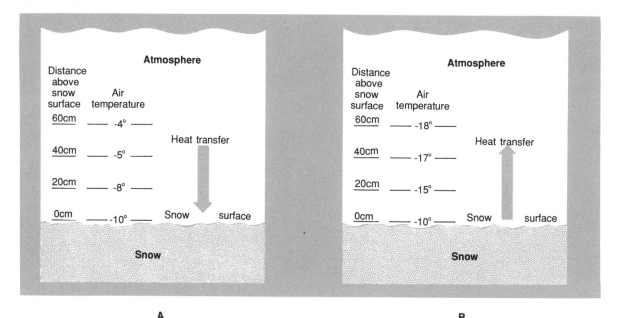

Figure 2.20. Examples of small-scale air temperature variations over a snow surface in calm conditions. A: temperature increases with height (inversion); B: heat transfer into the atmosphere.

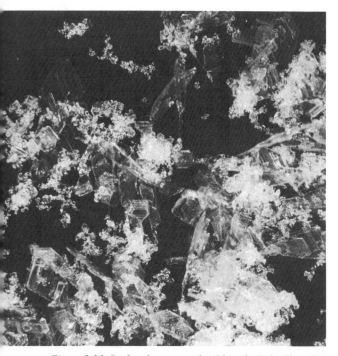

Figure 2.21. Surface hoar crystals. (Photo by E. LaChapelle)

Figure 2.22. Surface hoar crystals. (Photo by A. Roch)

PENETRATION OF HEAT INTO ALPINE SNOW

Once heat is applied or subtracted at the surface of a dry snow cover, it is transferred within the pack primarily by two mechanisms: (1) conduction through the network of ice grains and bonds and (2) vapor diffusion through the pore spaces (air spaces between snow grains). The effective thermal conductivity of low-density snow (100 kg/m^3) is about 1/25 that of ice. In low-density snow, heat is transferred mainly through the pore space due to the discontinuous nature of the ice (snow particle connections). At a density of 600 kg/m^3, the thermal conductivity increases tenfold to about half that of solid ice and heat is transferred mainly by conduction through the ice grains and bonds. Therefore, in the usual range of densities important for avalanche formation (100 to 400 kg/m^3), both mechanisms share the heat transfer.

An important fact about low-density snow is that heat is transferred less efficiently as the temperature decreases. This is *opposite* to what happens in ice and it shows that the diffusion mechanism (rather than conduction through the ice grains) is responsible for heat transfer in low-density alpine snow.

Heat can also be transferred in seasonal snow by convection in the pore space under very cold conditions (extreme temperature gradients) associated with a very thin snowpack. So far, the mechanism has been documented in thin arctic snowpacks, but it is not usually expected in mountain snowpacks where avalanches form. Convection does seem possible in low-density snow under the right conditions, but studies are lacking.

An important point about heat transfer with respect to avalanches is that it is very slow. For the low-density snow layers near the surface, temperature changes are brought about mostly by vapor diffusion through the pore space, which is an inefficient (and slow) mechanism to transport heat. For this reason, releases of avalanches in dry snow due to temperature changes are usually observed for thin slabs of snow only (less than 0.5 m thick). In one study, in a midwinter alpine snowpack, temperature measurements over 4 hours showed the snow surface temperature to increase from –13°C to near 0°C during the day. This resulted in increases of 5°C at 10 cm of depth, 2°C at 20 cm of depth, and negligible increases at 50 cm. Most of the increase in the surface layers (10 to 20 cm) may be attributed to direct solar radiation penetration rather than vapor diffusion or conduction (see the next section). This example confirms what measurements of thermal conductivity show: Heat transfer is slow in alpine snow.

INTERACTION OF RADIATION WITH THE SNOW COVER

Radiation interacting with the snow cover is primarily of two basic types: short-wave radiation (including visible light and other short-wavelength components) from the sun and long-wave or infrared radiation from the earth and sources near it such as clouds; 99% of solar energy is composed of short-wave radiation and 99% of terrestrial radiation is long-wave radiation (Figure 2.23). The changing balance between these two kinds of radiation is responsible for quick temperature changes near the surface of the snow cover. The result may be formation of weak layers, or it can cause avalanches directly by warming or cooling.

When short-wave radiation (sunlight) strikes a snow cover surface, up to 90% of it is reflected back into space when the snow cover is dry. This percentage decreases to at least 80% or less when the snow surface is wet.

The proportion of solar radiation that is not reflected can penetrate the snow cover, but the intensity of radiation decreases exponentially with depth (Figure 2.24). For dry alpine snow with a density typical of that found in slab avalanches (for example, 100 kg/m^3), it is estimated that less than 10% of solar radiation remains after a distance of 10 cm. For fresh fine-grained snow, this distance decreases to a few centimeters. For wet coarse-grained snow, the distance is also about 10 cm or more. In general, solar radiation penetration is deeper for snow with a larger grain size and higher density. Since wet, dense snow absorbs more of the incident radiation and that which is absorbed may penetrate further (because it usually has large grain sizes), it is easy to see how snow can become unstable quickly once it becomes wet.

While solar radiation provides heat input to the snow cover, long-wave radiation from terrestrial sources can either heat or cool the snow cover surface. The "balance" of these two sources of radiation can produce weak surface snow, which may serve as a sliding layer later when buried by snowfall.

The porous surface of a snow cover closely approximates a blackbody radiator (perfect absorber) with respect to long-wave radiation. It is estimated that at least 50% of incident long-wave radiation is absorbed right at the surface and it does not penetrate more than about 1 cm. Incident long-wave radiation comes from atmo-

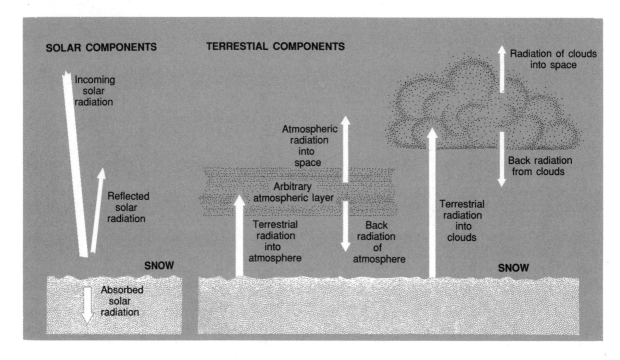

Figure 2.23. Radiation balance at snow surface. Incoming, absorbed, and reflected solar radiation is short wave (visible and ultraviolet). The other components from terrestrial sources are long wave (infrared).

spheric sources such as carbon dioxide and water vapor in clouds. (Clouds also approximate blackbody radiators with respect to long-wave radiation.) The snow cover surface also continuously gives off long-wave radiation, which contributes to cooling the snow surface. Thus, on a clear day in midwinter, it is expected that south-facing slopes can be warmed (solar radiation input exceeds long-wave radiation leaving), whereas the surface on a steep north-facing slope may be cooling (solar input is less than long-wave radiation leaving). During a clear night, almost all long-wave radiation leaving the snow cover surface can escape to space. In this condition, it is common to find the snow cover surface to be 5° to 20°C colder than the air above it.

An important example combining the effects of warming and cooling by solar radiation is what some avalanche workers call *radiation recrystallization*. Radiation recrystallization occurs preferentially on south-facing slopes at low latitudes and high altitudes. It is common in the San Juan Mountains of southwestern Colorado, but it is seen less often in the interior ranges of British Columbia. On south-facing slopes in clear weather, incoming radiation warms the first few centi-

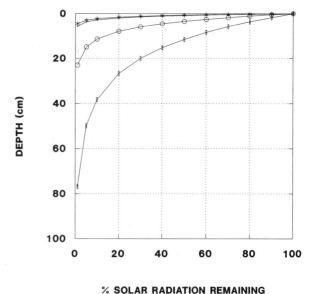

Figure 2.24. Penetration of short-wave radiation in the snow cover: ✳ = newly fallen snow; • = fine-grained snow; ○ = coarse-grained snow; ▢ = glacier ice.

meters of the snow cover. Daytime cooling by loss of long-wave radiation produces very cold temperatures near the surface. This combination of events gives rise to tremendous temperature differences in the top few centimeters of snow, which results in rapid recrystallization of the surface snow to form a weak layer of crystals. Sometimes the transmitted solar radiation can even produce a melt zone several centimeters below the surface, which later freezes to form an ice crust under the weak layer of recrystallized grains. This combination makes an ideal failure surface when buried by a later snow load. With or without the ice layer, an example is provided whereby the changing radiation balance can have a major influence on future snow stability.

Another important example of surface heat exchange is encountered during wet avalanche formation. Under thin fog or whiteout (low cloud) conditions, sunlight can penetrate through fog to warm the snow cover, but the long-wave radiation emitted by the snow cover cannot escape through the fog (the greenhouse effect). The result is tremendous heat input and melt water production at the snow cover surface, which can produce an optimum condition for wet snow avalanches assuming other snow properties are ripe for avalanching.

TEMPERATURE INVERSIONS

Temperature inversions are present when atmospheric temperatures increase with altitude. They can occur on a variety of scales from a microscale (for example, that

Figure 2.26. Valley fog during a temperature inversion. The cornice shows the prevailing wind direction from right to left, but riming on the post indicates recent wind direction from left to right. (Photo by A. Roch)

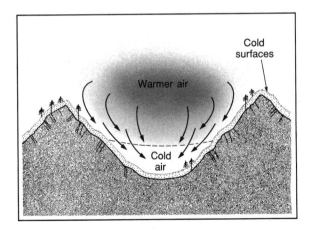

Figure 2.25. Temperature inversion formed between a mountain ridge and valley due to long-wave radiation cooling from the snow surface.

associated with surface hoar development) to the height of an individual mountain. Temperatures usually decrease with increasing altitude in the mountains. When temperatures increase with increasing altitude, the cause is usually loss of heat from the snow surface due to long-wave radiative cooling. In one common case, warm air from daytime heating is still present at the tops of the mountains but cold dense air created by cooling near the surface sinks to the valley floor (the cold air is denser than the warm air) (Figures 2.25 and 2.26). The air motion to set up this situation is usually too gentle to cause loading of avalanche slopes. The condition can confuse forecasters about temperature conditions at mountaintop levels if temperature information is available only from sensors in the valley bottoms. However, since this type of inversion usually occurs in fine weather, avalanche forecasters can concentrate on other aspects of the problem.

Mountain ranges (particularly coastal ranges) can sometimes act as a barrier between a mild, wet maritime climate and a colder, more continental climate characterized by extremes in temperature and intense nighttime radiational cooling. This situation can produce a reservoir of high-pressure cold air in valleys on the continental side which may be forced slowly to the maritime side through mountain passes. If a warm front then approaches, warm moist air is forced over the cold air below. The result can be rain in avalanche starting zone areas and sleet or freezing rain at pass levels, with extremely rapid shifts in both temperature and precipitation types over short time periods and distances. This effect is of considerable importance in maritime snow climates, but usually the mechanism is not considered important for avalanche prediction in continental climates because rain does not usually result.

References

Armstrong, R. L., and B. R. Armstrong. 1987. Snow and avalanche climates of the western United States: A comparison of maritime, intermountain and continental conditions. IAHS Publication No. 162, pp. 281–294.

Armstrong, Richard L., and Knox Williams. 1981. Snowfall forecasting in the Colorado mountains. *Second Conference on Mountain Meteorology,* Steamboat Springs, Colorado, November 9–12 (1981). Boston: American Meteorological Society, pp. 386–390.

Barry, R. G. 1992. *Mountain Weather and Climate,* 2nd ed. London and New York: Routledge, 402 pp.

Ferguson, S. A., M. B. Moore, R. T. Marriott, and P. Speers-Hayes. 1990. Avalanche forecasting at the Northwest Avalanche Center, Seattle, WA, U.S.A. *Journal of Glaciology* 36(122): 57–66.

Geiger, R. 1965. *The Climate Near the Ground.* Cambridge, MA: Harvard University Press, 611 pp.

Mellor, M. 1965. Blowing snow. Cold Regions Science and Engineering Laboratory. Part III, Section A3C. Hanover, NH: U.S. Army CRREL, 79 pp.

Mellor, M. 1977. Engineering properties of snow. *Journal of Glaciology* 19(81): 15–66.

Moore, M. 1988. Mountain precipitation mechanisms and their associated weather regimes. *The Avalanche Review* 6(4): 6–9.

Schmidt, R. A. 1980. Threshold wind speeds and elastic impact in snow transport. *Journal of Glaciology* 26(94): 453–467.

Speers-Hayes, P. 1986. A simple orographic precipitation model for the Pacific Northwest. *Proceedings of the International Snow Science Workshop*, Lake Tahoe, California, October 22–26, 1986. Homewood, CA: ISSW Committee, pp. 46–55.

Warren, S. G. 1982. Optical properties of snow. *Reviews of Geophysics and Space Physics* 20(1): 67–80.

CHAPTER 3

SNOW FORMATION AND GROWTH IN THE ATMOSPHERE AND SNOWPACK

You boil it in sawdust; you salt it in glue;
You condense it with locusts and tape;
Still keeping one principal object in view,
To preserve its symmetrical shape.

—Lewis Carroll

SNOW CRYSTAL FORMATION AND GROWTH IN THE ATMOSPHERE

Most avalanches occur as a result of newly fallen snow, perhaps more than 90% in some climates. Sometimes variations in type of new snow falling are responsible and experienced avalanche workers are alert to such changes.

Snow crystals begin their lives in atmospheric clouds. Clouds are composed of water droplets that form when the air is supersaturated with water vapor. The droplets form by condensation on small particles called *condensation nuclei* (salt, dust, or soil). These particles are very small with a typical diameter of 10^{-6} mm (1 μm), and they are always in abundant supply. Growth is by condensation of water vapor on their surfaces when the air is saturated with respect to the droplet (Figure 3.1).

When the air temperature at which the cloud becomes saturated is below 0°C, it is possible to form snow from tiny ice crystals. At these temperatures, small water droplets will remain as water droplets in a super-cooled state. Typically these droplets are about 20 μm in size with concentrations of several hundred per cubic centimeter.

To form a small ice crystal by freezing, foreign particles are also needed around which the ice crystallizes. However, these ice crystal nuclei (*freezing nuclei*) are much less common than the condensation nuclei needed for forming water droplets. The typical size of freezing nuclei is the same as for condensation nuclei, but they have a special character that promotes freezing. Not all small particles (including dust, soil, and other chemical particles) are suitable for freezing nuclei; they must have the correct molecular structure. Also, freezing nuclei are variable with respect to the temperature at which they allow freezing to take place. The number of "active" freezing nuclei increases as the air temperature decreases. At −10°C there are about 10 active nuclei per cubic centimeter. As the temperature in the cloud decreases, it becomes much easier for ice crystals to form by freezing and the number of ice crystals increases relative to the number of droplets. At a temperature of −40°C, droplets will freeze by themselves without the aid of freezing nuclei.

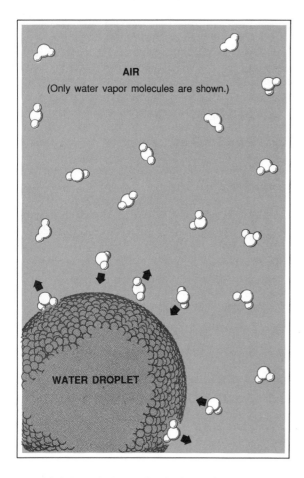

Figure 3.1. Growth of water droplets by condensation of water molecules when the air is supersaturated with respect to the droplet surface.

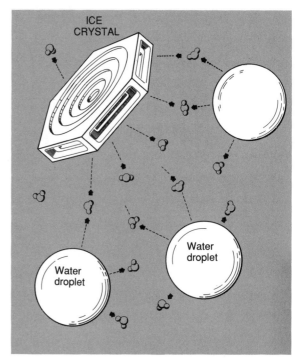

VAPOR

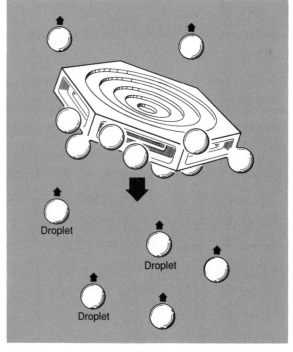

RIMING

Once a small ice crystal forms, its subsequent growth is determined by two processes (Figure 3.2). The process that determines the basic crystal form occurs by direct transfer of water vapor molecules from the supercooled water droplets in the cloud. It has been determined experimentally and theoretically that the vapor pressure over a water droplet is higher than over an ice crystal at a given temperature (Figure 3.3). Since the

Figure 3.2. Two mechanisms of ice crystal growth in the atmosphere: transfer of molecules from droplets (top) and riming resulting from collisions with droplets during their fall through the atmosphere (bottom).

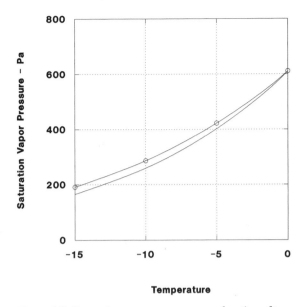

Figure 3.3. *Saturation vapor pressure as a function of temperature over flat ice (bottom line) and water (top line) surfaces.*

pressure is higher over the droplet, water vapor molecules diffuse toward neighboring ice crystals and they condense (deposit) from the vapor onto the ice crystal. Thus, ice crystals grow at the expense of supercooled droplets, due to vapor pressure differences between the droplets and the ice crystals.

The second growth mechanism occurs as the crystals move in the atmosphere. When the ice crystals attain a large enough size, they fall and gain mass by colliding with some of the larger supercooled droplets, which subsequently freeze onto the crystals in a second process called *riming*. The same process causes icing on an airplane wing moving through supercooled droplets in the atmosphere. When a crystal is rimed it usually falls faster because weight is added without much change in air resistance. In contrast, growth from the vapor usually increases air resistance by branch growth. Sometimes the crystal branches become entirely filled in by riming to form a rounded crystal called *graupel* in which the original type of crystal is usually unrecognizable (see Table C.1 in Appendix C). This requires a long growth period either from passage through thick clouds or repeated rides up and down in thermal convection updrafts in clouds that prolong the riming process. Graupel particles can also form hail if they ride updrafts involving freeze-thaw cycles.

The ultimate form that a snow crystal attains in the atmosphere depends on complicated conditions at and near the crystal surface, but temperature is the most important variable. In general, growth usually occurs in two basic directions: in the basal plane of the ice crystal or perpendicular to it. Ice crystals have three intrinsic axes in the basal plane (*a*-axes) separated by 120°, and an axis perpendicular to the basal plane (the *c*-axis) (see Figure 3.4). There is hexagonal symmetry in the basal plane and heat flows less efficiently in the basal plane

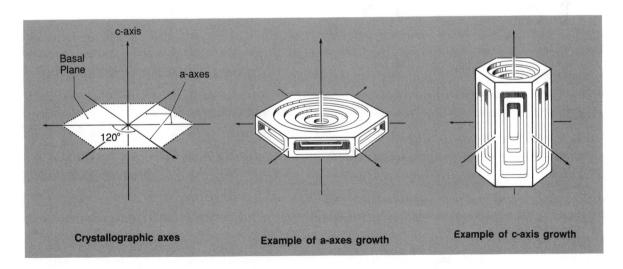

Figure 3.4. *Crystallographic axes and examples of* a-*axis and* c-*axis growth for ice crystals.*

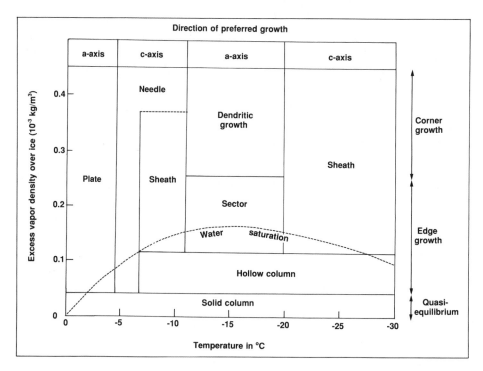

Figure 3.5. Snow crystal growth as a function of excess vapor density (at crystal surface) and temperature. Growth switches between the a- *and* c-*axes depending on temperature, the most important variable. Rounded forms are formed at low vapor density, edges and corners at higher vapor density.*

than in the *c*-axis direction. There is no hexagonal symmetry in the direction of the *c*-axis. Platelike crystals evolve from growth in the direction along the *a*-axes, while needlelike crystals are grown in the direction of the *c*-axis. Regardless of growth direction, snow crystals that grow from the vapor are six-sided due to the influence of basal plane. The rate of growth is also a strong factor in determining which shape a crystal takes. However, it is the excess vapor density (near the surface of crystals) over that which the ice can maintain at the surface that determines the form, along with the temperature. Figure 3.5 shows how growth direction (*a*-axes or *c*-axis) varies to produce the basic crystal forms as a function of temperature for typical atmospheric conditions.

At low excess vapor density, the shapes are basically columns at any temperature. At high growth rates (for example, higher excess vapor densities) growth occurs at edges and corners to produce more complicated crystals, such as dendrites. At these higher growth rates, the complex forms that result are due to transfer of water vapor molecules across the crystal surface. In general,

the molecules tend to be deposited at positions where the excess vapor density is highest such as edges and corners. The exact surface processes by which the growth direction switches from *a*-axis to *c*-axis growth as the temperature changes are not well understood. Figure 3.5 clearly shows that temperature is the primary variable determining the crystal form in the atmosphere, and the degree of supersaturation (growth rate) is second in importance.

Some of the complicated forms that arrive on the earth are produced because they pass through different temperature and water vapor density regimes as they pass through the atmosphere. For example, a solid column could be produced in cold air, but on entering a warmer regime, plates might grow on its ends to form a "capped" column.

The rate at which a crystal gains mass determines its size, which in turn depends on the temperature. In general, crystals that have fallen through a cold atmosphere are smaller than those that have been in a warm atmosphere. This is because the thermodynamic processes that govern growth occur faster at warmer temperatures and warmer air can potentially hold more moisture than cold air.

Experienced avalanche observers usually keep a close watch on snow crystals that fall. Observations of snow crystals provide clues about the condition of the atmosphere through which they have fallen. Changes in crystal types during storms, including changes in the amount of riming, can create conditions where one layer does not bond well to the next; this can be of significance in prediction of snow stability. Layers of graupel particles, for example, often do not bond well to their neighbors, which can set up the conditions for snowpack failure. In fact, it has been proposed that the amount of riming can be indirectly related to avalanche formation, including the type of avalanche and the degree of instability. However, at best, this is a second- or third-order effect, which must be integrated with other more important factors in evaluation of snow stability. Also, the breaking of branches of crystals by snow transport at the surface is generally of greater importance than riming for formation of dangerous avalanches. The integrated effects of crystal form, riming, and breakage can all contribute to instability in new snow and its bonding characteristics with old snow layers. However, because such a wide combination of these variables can produce unstable snow, no simple formula is available. Therefore, experienced snow stability analysts concentrate on the integrated effects of these variables as they relate to the mechanics of avalanche formation, rather than an emphasis on any one of these secondary factors in isolation (see Chapter 4).

CLASSIFICATION OF NEWLY FALLEN SNOW CRYSTALS

There are three levels of classification for newly fallen crystals depending on the degree of sophistication required in the work. The simplest and most commonly used method is to lump all newly fallen snow into one class with a note about the degree of riming. In most countries, the symbol + is normally used to denote new snow with +r designating rimed newly fallen snow. In Canada and the United States, a third class for a fully rimed group (graupel) with the symbol △ is also used.

A more sophisticated system is that of the International Commission on Snow and Ice (ICSI), as shown in Table 3.1. It includes five easily recognizable crystal types as well as a category for irregular crystals and classes for hail and ice pellets (see, for example, Figure

3.6). This system is not as commonly used by avalanche workers as the simple +, r, △ system. The reason is that, at best, new crystal forms are a secondary effect in avalanche stability evaluations. In avalanche work, snow is usually analyzed after deposition and a variety of types are mixed together, which complicates a decision. The ICSI system probably represents the most advanced system needed in operational avalanche work. Another even more complex system with 80 categories (including rimed categories) was proposed by Magono and Lee (1966) and is given in Table C.1 in Appendix C. Avalanche workers should be aware of the existence of this complete system, but when snow stability analyses are the objective, one's time may be used more profitably by concentrating on primary (see Chapter 6) rather than secondary effects of precision work in identifying new crystal types.

In classifying snow crystals near the surface of the snowpack, care must be exercised when identifying the predominant crystal form in a sample. It is easy to be distracted by one or two crystals that are easily identifi-

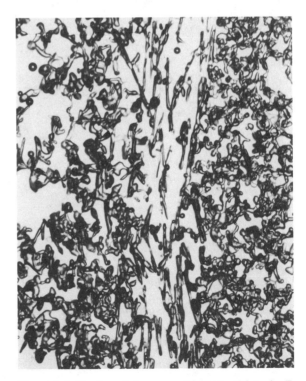

Figure 3.6. Needle and decomposed crystals. (Photo by E. Akitaya)

Table 3.1 ICSI Classification for Newly Fallen Snow Crystals

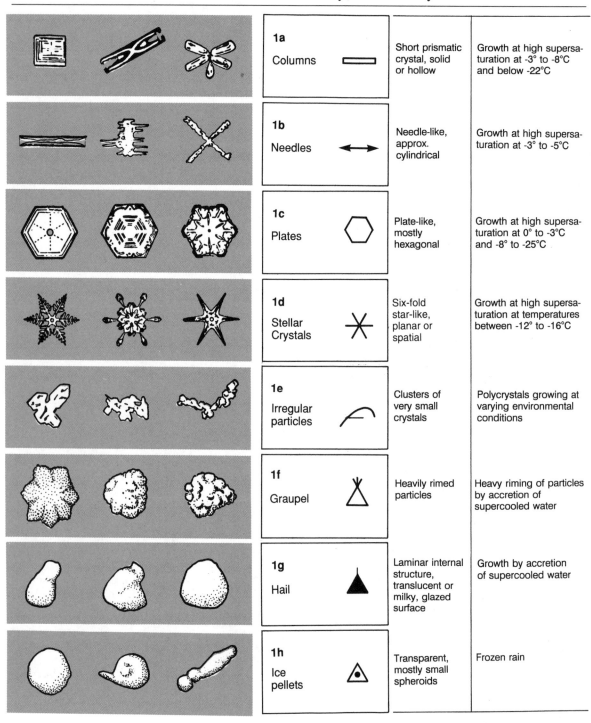

1a Columns	▭	Short prismatic crystal, solid or hollow	Growth at high supersaturation at -3° to -8°C and below -22°C
1b Needles	↔	Needle-like, approx. cylindrical	Growth at high supersaturation at -3° to -5°C
1c Plates	⬡	Plate-like, mostly hexagonal	Growth at high supersaturation at 0° to -3°C and -8° to -25°C
1d Stellar Crystals	✳	Six-fold star-like, planar or spatial	Growth at high supersaturation at temperatures between -12° to -16°C
1e Irregular particles	⌒	Clusters of very small crystals	Polycrystals growing at varying environmental conditions
1f Graupel	△	Heavily rimed particles	Heavy riming of particles by accretion of supercooled water
1g Hail	▲	Laminar internal structure, translucent or milky, glazed surface	Growth by accretion of supercooled water
1h Ice pellets	◬	Transparent, mostly small spheroids	Frozen rain

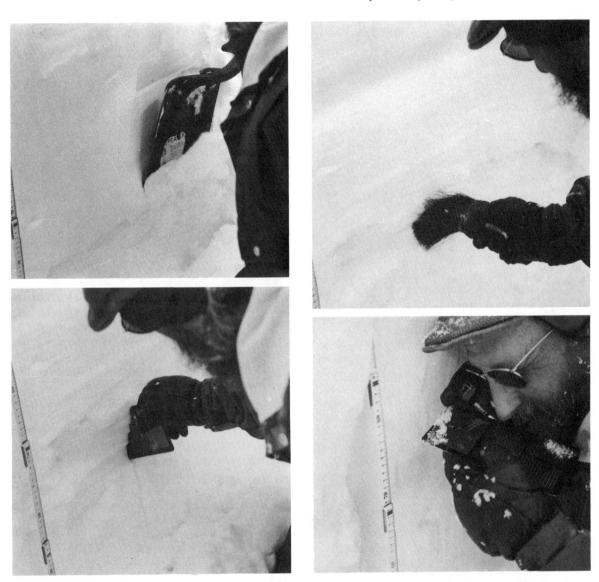

Figure 3.7. Definition of snow layers with shovel, brush, and edge of crystal screen. Use of a hand lens and millimeter crystal grid for examining snow crystals (bottom right). Magnification of 8 to 10X is recommended for field use.

able in a sample rather than the most prevalent form. For normal observations, a pocket or hand lens with about an 8X to 10X power is preferred (Figure 3.7). With higher magnification, the field of view narrows and there is a tendency to focus on the details of individual crystals rather than viewing a good portion of the sample to determine the predominant form. In scientific work, higher-powered lenses and microscopes are sometimes used.

The size of snow crystals is determined in the field by measuring the largest diameter (extension) of the average crystal. Usually avalanche observers quote a range of observed sizes seen on a crystal screen with a millimeter grid, for example, 0.5 to 1 mm. As with crystal forms, crystal size is of secondary importance with respect to avalanche formation. Table 3.2 gives the ICSI recommended size categories.

Table 3.2 ICSI Terms and Sizes for Grain Size Classification

Term	Size (mm)
Very fine	<0.2
Fine	0.2–0.5
Medium	0.5–1.0
Coarse	1.0–2.0
Very coarse	2.0–5.0
Extreme	>5.0

SURFACE HOAR: FORMATION AND GROWTH CONDITIONS

Surface hoar has been termed the solid equivalent of dew (Figure 3.8). The result is usually very weak, thin layers of snow that are extremely important in avalanche release. Surface hoar forms when the water vapor pressure in the air exceeds the equilibrium vapor pressure of ice (snow grains) at the surface. It usually grows rapidly

Figure 3.8. Surface hoar. (Photo by E. Akitaya)

provided two necessary conditions have been met: (1) A sufficient supply of water vapor must be available in the air and (2) a high temperature gradient (inversion) must be present above a snow surface that is chilled below the ice point.

Surface hoar usually forms on cold, clear nights with calm or nearly calm conditions in the lowest meter of air. Some investigators believe that slight air movement is necessary near the surface to replenish the supply of vapor deposited. However, if air movement is too rapid (i.e., turbulent), the near-surface air will be mixed, which can destroy the air temperature gradient near the surface. Temperature gradients (inversions) during surface hoar formation are commonly 100° to 300°C/m. Usually the relative humidity in the air is fairly high (>70%) but it is possible for surface hoar to form at lower values if the surface is losing heat by radiating to space. Surface hoar can occur in many forms depending mainly on the temperature. Since it grows from the vapor phase, the dependence of crystal form on temperature applies (Figure 3.5), as has been confirmed by field measurements.

Meteorological conditions favorable for surface hoar growth must set up the two conditions for formation described earlier. If a cold front passes after an overcast day, causing a clear night, surface hoar is likely. It has been reported that even a slight cloud cover, such as high cirrus clouds, can interfere with long-wave radiation cooling at the surface to inhibit growth. Another common situation for growth occurs when supercooled cloud decks (fog) at the surface are overlain by clear sky with low humidity. This allows strong long-wave cooling at the surface. It has also been reported that surface hoar growth is inhibited (or prevented) from forming in concave areas of the snow surface. Apparently, long-wave radiation from the side walls of a concavity strikes the opposite wall instead of escaping to space and the cooling mechanism is less efficient.

Surface hoar can form (and is observed) in any type of climate provided the necessary conditions for growth are met. Since it is extremely fragile, it is also easily destroyed. The agents of destruction include sublimation, wind, surface melt-freeze cycles, and freezing rain. Sometimes the wind destroys surface hoar above the tree line, making more sheltered locations below more hazardous than those near the tops of the mountains.

Buried surface hoar is extremely efficient in producing propagating shear instabilities (fractures) if it is disturbed. Fatal accidents have resulted when skiers on flat terrain precipitated propagating shear fractures in

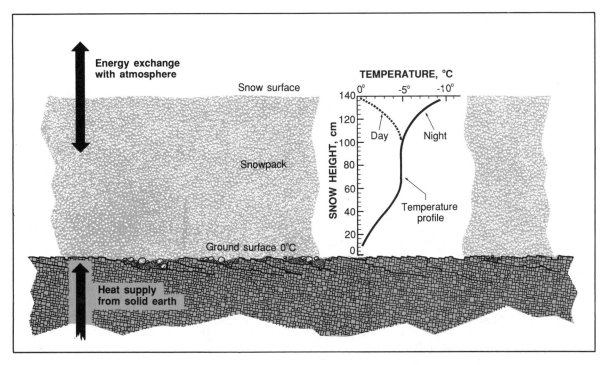

Figure 3.9. Illustration of the temperature variations in a snowpack. Diurnal variations occur in the upper portion. A temperature gradient of 10°C/m is strong enough to produce facets in the snowpack.

surface hoar, which ran upslope to undercut a slab. Such examples show that even though avalanches do not usually form at slope angles below 25° (see Chapter 5), it is not always safe to move on gentle slopes.

Surface hoar may gain strength by bond formation with adjacent layers (see Chapter 4). The persistence of instability depends primarily on the surface hoar layer thickness, which can vary from less than 1 mm to several centimeters. Thick layers can persist for months when buried. Persistence of instability is aided when the crystals are large and unlike their neighbors in form. The typical range of crystal sizes is from less than 1 mm to more than 1 cm in length.

SNOWPACK TEMPERATURES AND TEMPERATURE GRADIENTS

Snowpacks in which avalanches form are bounded by the atmosphere above and the ground surface below. There are circumstances in the high mountains where the lower boundary may be perennial snow or ice as well. Normally, stored heat in the ground from summer

warming (most important) and geothermal heat from the earth's center combine to warm the basal layer to 0°C (or close to 0°C). The upper snowpack surface is subjected to cold air during the winter, but snow temperatures at the surface fluctuate wildly in response to daytime and nighttime heating and cooling cycles (called *diurnal fluctuations*) and the prevailing synoptic conditions. Usually these effects combine to produce an upper surface that is cooler (on average) than the lower boundary, which is insulated from the diurnal fluctuations (Figure 3.9).

The long-term effect is a temperature gradient in the snowpack that is a vector quantity having both magnitude and direction. The magnitude of the temperature gradient is defined as the change in temperature (ΔT) divided by the distance (ΔX) over which the temperature changes. By convention, the direction of the temperature gradient is in the direction of increasing temperature (usually downward but sometimes sideways in the snowpack). In metric units, the temperature gradient is expressed in degrees Celsius per meter. When the temperature gradient is 0°C/m throughout, the snowpack is isothermal. The only common occurrence of this is when the snowpack is all at 0°C, which implies a wet snowpack throughout.

In a general sense, temperatures and temperature gradients in snowpacks are coupled together depending on the climate regime. In a maritime climate, prevailing air temperatures are usually mild and snowpacks are deep. These two effects combine to produce weak temperature gradients and warm snow temperatures. In continental climates, snowpacks are shallow and air temperatures are cold to produce strong temperature gradients and cold snow temperatures. The crystal forms that develop under these two scenerios differ, and this has profound effects on the *general* character and timing of avalanches that develop. In a rough, general sense, maritime snowpacks are characterized by relatively strong stable snow and there is a greater bias for avalanches to form in the new snow. Continental snowpacks are usually relatively weak, and often contain buried weak layers in old snow layers, which are susceptible to failures when loaded later. Snow metamorphism (changes in form due to heat flow and pressure), then, largely explains the difference in the character of avalanches in these climates. It must be remembered that crystal forms develop by physical processes (not climate characteristics) so that any crystal form can be found in any mountain range.

DISAPPEARANCE OF BRANCHES: INITIAL CHANGES IN NEWLY FALLEN SNOW

Once deposited, snow crystals begin to change form immediately. In some cases these initial changes are the direct cause of small avalanches (called *sluffs*). The changes in form also determine future snow strength. Newly fallen snow crystals have grown in an environment that is much more highly supersaturated with water vapor than that encountered once the snow crystals are deposited. Typical values of supersaturation in the atmosphere can be several tens of percent while they are typically less than 1% inside a snowpack. New snow crystals are unstable; they would need the highly supersaturated environment they came from to continue growth in the same form or to maintain their forms. In general, a large ratio of crystal surface area to volume is unstable once the atmospheric growth stops. In the snowpack, snow crystals with the largest surface-to-volume ratio (such as dendrites) are the most unstable and change

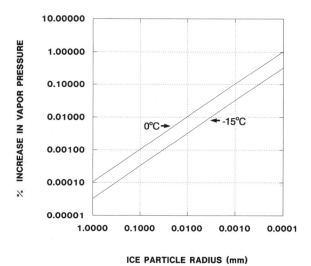

Figure 3.10. *Vapor pressure over a curved ice surface as a function of radius of curvature at –15°C and 0°C.*

form most quickly. The minimum surface-to-volume ratio form is theoretically a sphere, therefore rounded graupel particles are very stable (they persist for long periods of time).

The physical reason that the intricate branches of snow crystals initially disappear is because the vapor pressure over sharply curved branch features is very high (the pressure varies inversely with the radius of curvature of the surface). The vapor pressure is higher over a convex surface than it is over a concave surface. Thus, sharp branches promote sublimation by loss of molecules from the ice surface into the surrounding air.

The initial disappearance of branches by curvature does not last long. A key concept with respect to changes in form in dry snow is illustrated by comparing the vapor pressure changes due to curvature with the vapor pressure differences in the pore space as the temperature varies (for example, due to an applied temperature gradient; see Figure 3.9). The pressure changes due to curvature effects are very small. For example, the pressure due to curvature effects increases by about 0.03% for a branch point of radius 10^{-3} mm over that for a flat surface at 0°C and the increase is about 0.1% at –15°C. By contrast, the saturation vapor pressure (with respect to ice) in the pore space of a snowpack increases by more than 300% as air temperature increases from –15° to 0°C (Figure 3.10). This shows why overall temperature differences in dry snow due to snowpack temperature

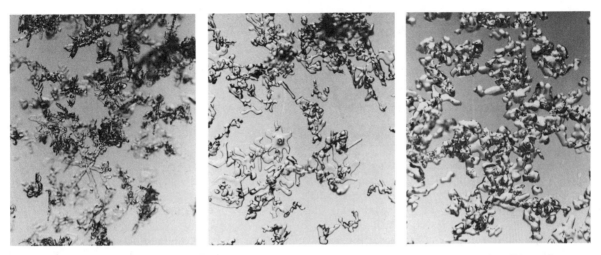

Figure 3.11. Transformation of newly fallen snow to rounded forms in three stages. (Photos by E. LaChapelle)

gradients provide the driving mechanism for snow metamorphism rather than curvature effects. Both grain curvature and overburden pressure due to the weight of overlying snow layers will also influence dry snow metamorphism because they are always acting (Figure 3.11).

The surface regions of the snowpack are those in which the temperature gradient is usually highest. In the general case, the metamorphism will be influenced by both the vapor pressure gradient (caused by the snowpack temperature gradient) in the pore space as well as curvature effects. However, the gradient effect usually drives the metamorphism in a snowpack unless the radius of curvature on branch surfaces is less than about 10^{-2} mm. Experimental data show that it takes more than 10 times as long for a dendritic crystal to decompose to a rounded form in a laboratory under constant temperature conditions than in the field where there is always a temperature gradient (see Figure 3.12). Curvature effects are important in that sharp branch points are preferential sites (high pressure) for sublimation to occur even with an applied temperature gradient. Curvature effects are therefore necessary to explain rounding of complex forms with a high surface-to-volume ratio. However, in general, the temperature and temperature gradient determine the rate of metamorphism of dry snow for either newly fallen snow or snow found at depth in the snowpack once initial rounding has taken place.

When branches disappear, the result is an initial decrease in the average particle size. This process has been called *destructive metamorphism*. However, in the snowpack, size begins to increase after the branches disappear. Sublimation supplies water vapor to increase the vapor pressure in the vicinity of the small particles or branches. Once the water vapor moves (due to the applied snowpack temperature gradient), it tends to condense on larger particles where the water vapor pressure is lower or vapor density is lower. This sublimation (condensation mechanism) encourages growth

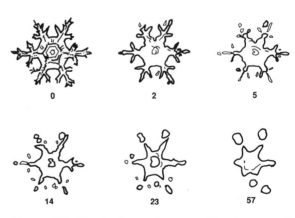

Figure 3.12. Sketch of crystal metamorphism (at constant temperature) by curvature effects. The numbers give the time in days. (After Bader, 1939)

of larger particles at the expense of the small ones. By this means (and perhaps heat flow paths within the structure), the average particle size eventually slowly increases when a mixture of sizes is present.

DRY SNOW METAMORPHISM IN THE SEASONAL SNOW COVER

Inside the snowpack the variety of forms is very limited because they are insulated by their neighbors and because the physical conditions around them vary slowly. In this section, the physical processes and changing crystal forms found within the alpine snowpack are described.

The term *metamorphism* includes changes in form due to temperature (heat flow) and overburden pressure. However, in seasonal snow in which avalanches form, the changes in crystal forms are due almost entirely to heat flow within the snowpack. Overburden pressure densifies alpine snow by rearranging the grains (see Chapter 4). It has a role in accelerating metamorphism (forming rounded grains). Overburden pressure *dominates* changes in form only in snow that has densified beyond the normal limits found for seasonal snow, such as firn snow on glaciers that is more than one year old.

A major difference between snow crystal formation in the atmosphere and snow metamorphism in the seasonal alpine snowpack is the degree of supersaturation in the air surrounding the crystals. In the alpine snowpack, the air in the pores is slightly supersaturated with values less than 1% being typical. In the atmosphere, supersaturation with respect to ice can vary from near 0% to 50% or more. For snow crystals forming in the atmosphere, temperature is the primary factor that determines the crystal form—the amount of supersaturation is secondary. For the alpine snowpack, the temperature gradient is the most important factor. There, heat flow and crystal growth rate are most strongly related to vapor diffusion through the pore space. This diffusion process is controlled by the temperature gradient.

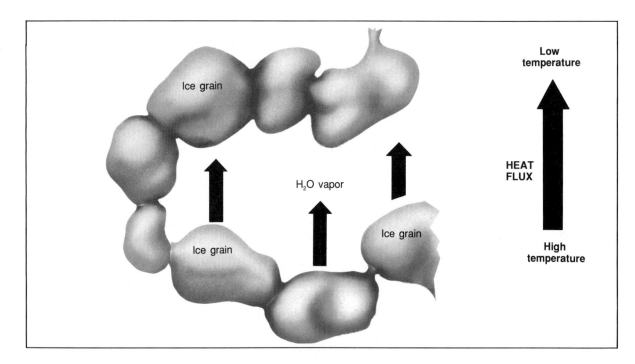

Figure 3.13. Heat flux (carried by the water vapor) occurs from the bottom to the top of the snowpack when temperatures increase with depth from the surface. Water vapor deposits on the underside of crystals and leaves the top in a "hand-to-hand" process.

The vapor diffusion process operates as follows. In a typical dry alpine snowpack, the temperature is near 0°C at the bottom due to stored heat from summer and geothermal heating. The snow temperature decreases toward the snow surface, which is exposed to the cold winter air. Since saturated warm air can hold more vapor than saturated cold air, a higher overall water vapor pressure exists in the pores of the snow at the bottom of the snowpack, and the water vapor is forced to move up. Water vapor moves up through the pore space by leaving the top of one crystal and condensing on a crystal somewhere above. Thus, the motion and heat flow are upward by a hand-to-hand process in dry snow. The rate of motion determines the crystal forms that develop under this recrystallization process (Figure 3.13).

CRYSTAL FORMS IN DRY SEASONAL ALPINE SNOW

For the low supersaturations found in the seasonal snow cover, a strong correlation exists between the overall growth rate and the crystal forms. (The terms *crystal* and *grain* are used interchangeably in this book to denote single ice particles.) The growth rate and crystal forms in a seasonal snow cover depend on three important variables: (1) temperature gradient, (2) the temperature, and (3) the pore space size. Of these three variables, the snowpack temperature gradient is the most important in determining the crystal form in the alpine snowpack. Crystal metamorphism in snowpacks is driven by the vapor density gradient therein. Since the equilibrium vapor pressure over an ice surface is a *nonlinear* function of temperature and temperature gradient, the discussion in this section immediately follows. The discussion here is based on temperature gradients (rather than vapor pressure gradients) since temperatures are normally measured by avalanche workers. In general, the highest crystal growth rates are found for large temperature gradients, high temperatures, and large spaces between the crystals. These conditions produce angular or faceted grains, which may later develop steps and striations on their surfaces, ultimately resulting in large cup crystals called *depth hoar*.

At the other extreme, low growth rates produce rounded forms. The lowest rates would occur with low temperature gradients, tightly packed crystals, and *lower* temperatures. In alpine snow covers, low growth rates are almost always associated with low temperature gradients and *high* temperatures because the tempera-

ture and temperature gradient are usually coupled in an average sense: Low temperature gradients and high temperatures usually occur together. The fact that both highly faceted crystals (depth hoar) and well-rounded crystals are found at high snowpack temperatures shows that the temperature gradient is more important than the temperature in controlling the crystal forms in alpine snow. The critical temperature gradient to produce faceted forms in alpine snow is about 10°C/m; below this value rounded forms tend to appear (Figures 3.14, 3.15, and 3.16).

As the temperature decreases in alpine snow, the degree of supersaturation adjacent to crystal surfaces increases rapidly. This should promote formation of facets and corners on snow grains similar to crystal formation in the atmosphere (see the right vertical scale of Figure 3.5). However, at lower temperatures, the growth rate must slow down. Therefore, in cold snow, facets form slowly; apparently under most conditions the growth rate is high enough to form large, cup-shaped (depth hoar) crystals only near the ground (where the temperatures are usually high).

Therefore, the unifying concept in alpine snow is the growth rate: At high growth rates, faceted crystals form; at slow growth rates, rounded crystals form. Higher growth rates imply high temperature gradients, larger crystals, and large pore spaces with the highest growth rates occurring at high temperatures (at the bottom of the snowpack). Lower growth rates imply lower temperature gradients (which imply high temperatures in an alpine snowpack) and small pore spaces.

In general, crystals that are produced under high growth rates form weak, unstable snow that is often responsible for serious avalanche conditions. Examples include surface hoar, radiation recrystallization, faceted snow, and depth hoar. The majority of these types form in cold climates characterized by high temperature gradients and a persistence of instability due to the cold. The class of crystals formed at high growth rates accounts for big avalanches and large numbers of fatalities. Backcountry travelers must pay close attention when such crystals are present in the snow cover. Unfortunately, the growth rate under which crystals are produced is not measured in avalanche work. Instead, avalanche workers look for the classes of crystals produced at rapid rates or they measure temperature gradients as a guide. High growth rate crystals form preferentially in cold, continental-type climates but not exclusively. In the United States, there is a mix of snow climates and people exposure but it comes as no surprise that the greatest

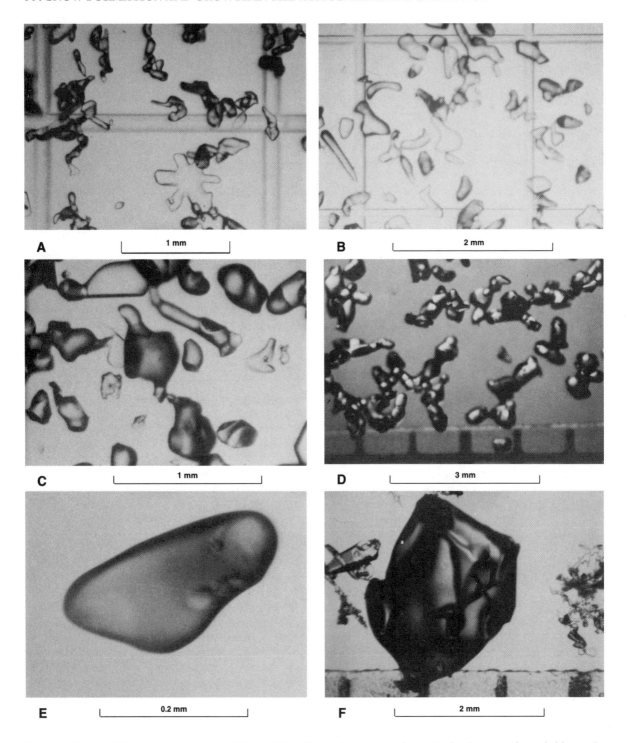

Figure 3.14. A: Initial metamorphism, original forms still visible; B: decomposing forms; C: development of rounded forms; D: rounded forms with bond formation; E: close-up of rounded form; F: faceted form with new snow particles. (Photos by R. Perla)

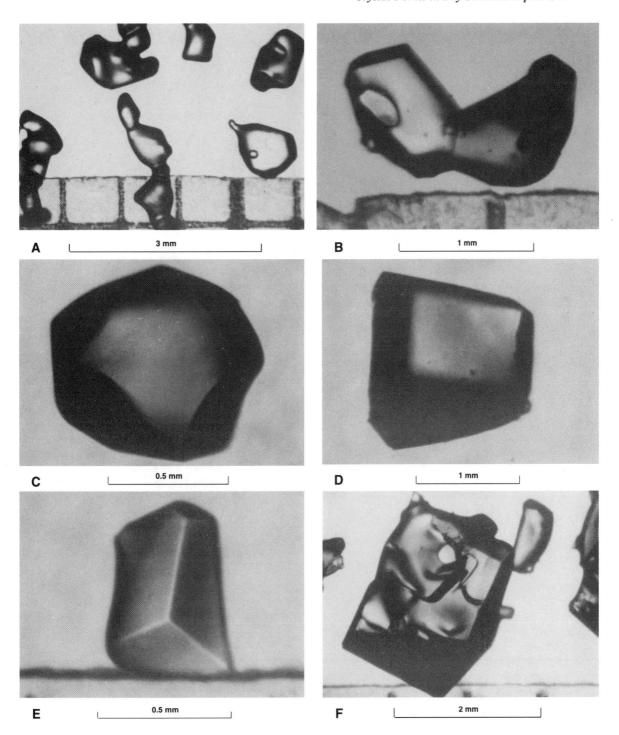

Figure 3.15. A: Faceted forms that have undergone rounding; B–F: examples of faceted forms. (Photos by R. Perla)

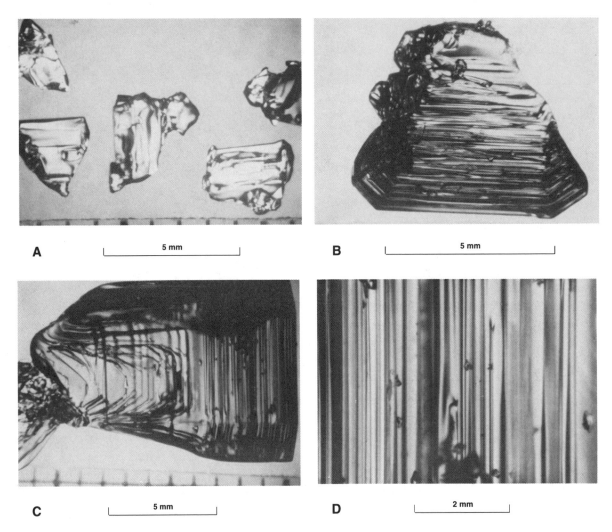

Figure 3.16. A–C: Depth hoar and hollow or cup-shaped crystals. Note the large sizes of crystals. D: Close-up of steps and layering on depth hoar. (Photos by R. Perla)

number of fatalities occurs in the continental climate of Colorado (Figure 3.17).

The pore space size and geometry is also important for determining crystal forms. Large pore spaces present favorable conditions for formation of facets and small pore spaces promote rounded crystals or at least prevent growth of large faceted crystals. It is possible to have faceted crystals growing in large voids when the surrounding crystals are growing as rounded crystals. In climates where depth hoar grows at the bottom of snowpacks, it is common to bootpack the slopes in early

season to pack the crystals more tightly. In reality, the pore space size is decreased by this process, which helps prevent depth hoar formation thereafter and, of course, the depth hoar present is compressed as well (see Chapter 9).

Depth hoar is not always weak. When fine-grained snow with density of about 350 kg/m³ or higher is subjected to a strong temperature gradient, tiny faceted crystals form in the pore spaces and actually "glue" the grains together to increase strength and hardness. It has also been observed that recrystallization in the presence

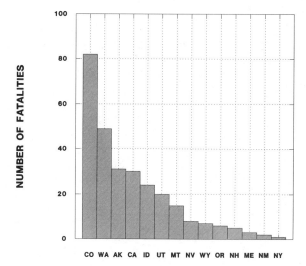

STATE

Figure 3.17. Thirty-five years of U.S. avalanche fatalities by state. Colorado has a continental snow climate that allows for the persistence of buried structural weaknesses.

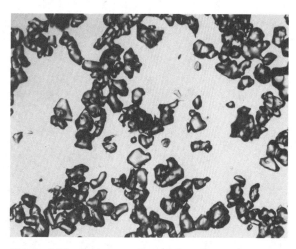

Figure 3.18. Grains transformed from facets to rounded forms. (Photo by E. Akitaya)

of strong temperature gradients appears to proceed more rapidly at high altitudes: Lower average air density in the pore space may allow more rapid diffusion of water vapor.

Mixed forms include rounded crystals with facets or faceted crystals with rounding; they develop at intermediate growth rates when the temperature gradient is near 10°C/m.

The preferred name for avalanche workers to describe crystals developing under the slowest growth rates is *rounded forms* or simply *rounds* (Figure 3.18). For faster rates, the term is *faceted forms* or *facets*. Crystal scientists also call these forms *equilibrium forms* and *kinetic forms,* respectively. However, laboratory studies of single-crystal growth show that the "equilibrium" form is actually a hexagonal (edged) plate at cold temperatures (below about −10°C) and rounded at higher temperatures. Therefore, it is felt that the term *rounded crystals* is a better descriptive label for the slow growth rate forms observed at warm temperatures in alpine snow.

In Appendix C, Table C.2 gives classifications for *dry* seasonal snow from the ICSI snow classification system including surface forms and crusts. Two levels

of classification are given. The basic system (first column) has classes for dry snow with three additional ones for surface forms and crusts—feathery (hoar) crystals, ice masses, and crusts—and one class for wet snow (Figure 3.19). The basic system is recommended for avalanche workers in snow profile work and is shown here in Table 3.3. The subclasses in column 3 of Table

Table 3.3 Basic ICSI system for classifying snow crystals

Decomposing and Fragmented Precipitation Particles	/
Rounded Grains (Monocrystals)	●
Faceted Crystals	□
Cup-Shaped Crystals; Depth Hoar	△
Wet Grains	○
Feathery Crystals	∨
Ice Masses	▬
Surface Deposits and Crusts	∨

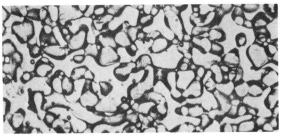

Figure 3.19. Thin sections of snow illustrating newly fallen snow, old dense snow (rounded forms), and a thin ice crust. (Photos by E. LaChapelle)

C.2 are also used by avalanche workers in some cases; sometimes a mixture of basic and subclasses is used. The level of complexity in the subclasses may not be necessary in avalanche work since crystal forms are usually a second-order effect in avalanche formation. Avalanche workers normally use the pictorial (graphical) symbols, but numerical and letter symbols are usually avoided except in computer plot packages.

In popular literature originating mostly from the United States, the term *equitemperature metamorphism* has been used to describe the process of generating rounded forms, and *temperature gradient metamorphism* has been used to describe development of faceted forms. Since temperature gradients largely determine the rate of growth, and therefore the form, in either case and since "equitemperature" conditions are nearly impossible to have in dry alpine snow, these terms are not recommended.

In general, the size of crystals found in the interior of a dry snowpack depends on their age and the physical conditions determining the growth rate at their location. The largest crystals are often depth hoar because they have been present the longest and they grow at the highest rates. The smallest crystals are usually found where growth is the slowest due to a low imposed temperature gradient and tightly packed condition (small pore spaces), for example, from wind effects creating small, fine-grained snow. The size of snow crystals is an important element in snow crystal identification in the field. Experienced observers often try to determine the size of crystals first when trying to identify crystals, because the size gives an important clue about the growth rate and hence the expected crystal form.

METAMORPHISM OF WET SNOW

When snow becomes wet, conditions with respect to heat flow and subsequent metamorphism change greatly. An added complexity is that wet snow can consist of air, ice crystals, and water (a three-phase system). Contrary to what might be thought at first glance, wet snow is not exactly at a temperature of 0°C. In fact, small differences in temperature within wet snow are responsible for the metamorphism of wet snow. Just as in dry snow, the pressure over the curved ice surfaces in wet snow particles is inversely proportional to the radius of curvature of the surface. This causes the melting temperatures of the particles to be size dependent—small particles have a lower melting temperature than large ones. The mechanism of metamorphism changes in wet snow as the mix of water, air, and ice contents changes.

SNOW WITH HIGH WATER CONTENT

Water-saturated snow is responsible for slush avalanches in the Arctic and it is commonly found at impermeable layers (including the ground) when large avalanches release due to water lubrication.

In water-saturated snow (slush), the particles are usually entirely separated from each other by water (Table 3.4). This is known to occur when the water content exceeds approximately 15% by bulk volume. Since small particles have a lower melting temperature than large ones, they melt first. The heat of melting comes from the larger particles, which undergo surface refreezing (release of heat) and an increase in size.

In water-saturated snow, the metamorphism or particle growth is caused by the heat flux through the water during the melting–refreezing process. The rate of growth is very rapid for any distribution of particles that includes sizes below about 1 mm. The rate of growth

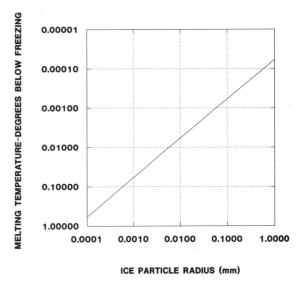

Figure 3.20. Melting temperature of ice particles in water as a function of particle radius.

(metamorphism) decreases and the average size of the particles increases with time. Since metamorphism proceeds as a result of temperature differences between particles, due to differences in size, theoretically metamorphism should stop if all particles were *spheres of the same size,* and the particles would slowly melt. However, such a situation would be virtually impossible to achieve in alpine snow and experimental evidence suggests that particles usually attain elliptical shapes.

The differences in melting temperature due to curvature of ice particles are very small in wet snow. It is estimated that the melting temperature of a 1-mm-radius particle is 10^{-4} °C below freezing and that for a particle 0.1 mm in size is 10^{-3} °C below freezing. However, due to the ease with which heat is transferred (by liquid water) among neighbors when the melting–refreezing process takes place, the cannibalism in which small particles melt to produce larger particles is very rapid in spite of these small temperature differences (Figure 3.20).

The term *very wet snow* (or funicular regime) is applied to snow with an intermediate water content (8% to 15%). The presence of air bubbles in this case is important in retarding the growth of particles in wet snow. Since heat conduction is much slower in air than water, the main effect of air bubbles is to reduce the area available for heat conduction through the water and slow grain growth.

Table 3.4 ICSI classification system for water content of snow

Term	Remarks	Water Content (% by volume)	Graphic Symbol
Dry	Usually T is below 0°C, but dry snow can occur at any temperature up to 0°C. Disaggregated snow grains have little tendency to adhere to each other when pressed together, as in making a snowball.	0%	
Moist	T = 0°C. The water is not visible even at 10 x magnification. When lightly crushed, the snow has a distinct tendency to stick together.	< 3%	
Wet	T = 0°C. The water can be recognized at 10 x magnification by its meniscus between adjacent snow grains, but water cannot be pressed out by moderately squeezing the snow in the hands. (Pendular regime)	3-8%	
Very Wet	T = 0°C. The water can be pressed out by moderately squeezing the snow in the hands, but there is an appreciable amount of air confined within the pores. (Funicular regime)	8-15%	
Slush	T = 0°C. The snow is flooded with water and contains a relatively small amount of air.	> 15%	

SNOW WITH LOW WATER CONTENT

When the water content drops below about 8%, grain growth occurs by vapor flux through the air in the pores. For this case, the air in the pore space is completely interconnected. The vapor flux responsible for metamorphism is caused by the vapor pressure excess over the convex portion of the grain due to curvature: The vapor pressure increases as the radius of curvature decreases just as in dry snow. The resulting grain growth is very slow. For water contents between 3% and 8% by volume, snow is termed *wet* although water cannot be pressed by squeezing gently by hand. However, a meniscus of water may be seen between grains with a hand lens. The border between wet and moist snow (less than 3% water content) can be difficult to recognize in the field.

As the water content in wet snow decreases, a capillary pressure develops and the pressure increases in the pore water between the grains (Figure 3.21). This pressure is the difference between the air and water pressures, and it forces water out of the pore space between the grains. When the water content becomes low enough (usually less than about 7% by volume), the grains form ice-to-ice bonds and they readily form clusters. (Since

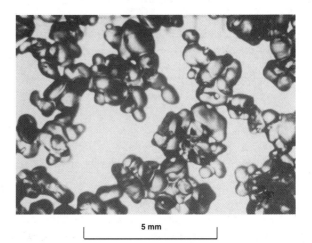

Figure 3.22. Clusters of wet snow (frozen). (Photo by R. Perla)

alpine snow is highly porous and therefore permeable to water flow, water usually drains freely through it unless an impermeable layer is present nearby.) Low water content snow is a common occurrence and the ice bonds between the grains can give the snow some strength. The distinguishing feature is that the grains cluster together and this is easily recognized in the field. Snow that clusters is called *moist*—water is not visible even with a hand lens (water content of less than 3%), but the snow should stick together when gently pressed to form a snowball (Figures 3.22 and 3.23). If there is any doubt about whether snow is wet at low water contents the snow temperature should be measured. If the temperature is 0°C, the snow has some degree of wetness. The easiest and best method of directly measuring snow water content is by measuring the dielectric constant of

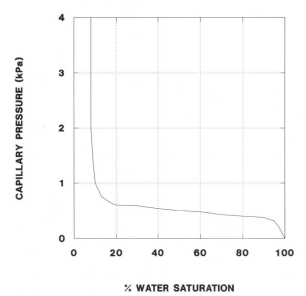

Figure 3.21. Capillary pressure in wet snow as a function of water content (% saturation).

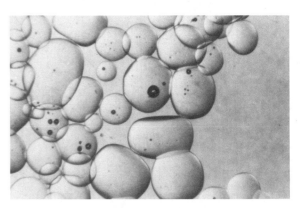

Figure 3.23. Slush. (Photo by S. Colbeck)

snow (a function of density and water content) using a portable instrument. The disadvantage is the expense of the instrument.

In general, growth in wet snow speeds up with increasing water content, while the strength of wet snow decreases with increasing water content. The transition point where grain growth occurs mostly by vapor flux occurs when 8% or less of the pore volume is filled by water. The term *pendular regime* has been applied for this low water content snow, but descriptive terms based on an approximate measure of the actual water content are used by avalanche field workers. Table 3.4 lists the descriptive terms from the ICSI classification system.

CLASSIFICATION OF WET SNOW

In Appendix C, Table C.3 gives the ICSI classification for wet snow. The basic scheme has only one class and three subclasses are listed. In avalanche work, the basic class and the subclasses are sometimes used. The classes in Table C.3 refer only to snow that has been wetted long enough to produce rounded forms. For example, if faceted snow suddenly becomes wet, it is still classed as faceted according to its morphology.

BOND FORMATION IN DRY ALPINE SNOW

Formation of bonds (also called *sintering*) between snow crystals is a crucial element in avalanche formation since bond formation is closely related to snow strength. Formation of bonds occurs by diffusion of water vapor through the pore space between grains as well as by molecular motion on the surfaces when crystals touch. Therefore, like metamorphism, bond formation is strongly affected by conditions at and near crystal and grain surfaces (Figure 3.24).

Although curvature effects are *not* generally the primary driving force to move the water vapor through the pore space in an alpine snowpack, they can play a role in determining where water vapor molecules condense on a crystal to form a bond. In general, the vapor pressure is higher over convex surfaces than flat surfaces or concave surfaces. Thus, there is a greater tendency for water vapor to condense at concave surfaces (low-pressure areas) where grains touch to form necks. Laboratory experiments performed at constant temperature (a virtual impossibility in a dry snowpack) showed that about 90% of the mass deposition at necks

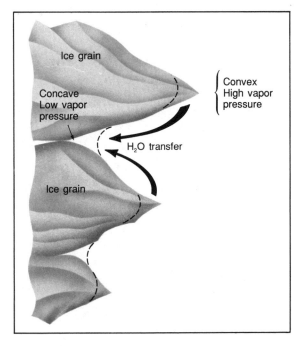

Figure 3.24. Vapor pressure is higher over a convex ice surface than over a concave ice surface. This aids mass transfer to concave surfaces.

between spherical particles occurs by vapor transport through the air from convex regions to the (concave) neck and about 10% occurs by motion of molecules over the surface toward the neck (Figures 3.25 and 3.26).

As in metamorphism, the temperature gradient and pore space geometry in a snowpack strongly affect the character of bond formation. Since thermodynamic processes occur faster at warmer temperatures, bond formation increases rapidly with increasing snow temperature. This concept is very important in avalanche stability evaluation. The temperature also affects the conditions of the surface of the crystals. There is a highly mobile "liquidlike layer" at the surface of crystals that thickens with increasing temperature. One idea proposed is that this layer can partially obscure the potential landing sites on the surface (ice lattice features) at high temperatures so that the landing sites for molecules are controlled more by curvature effects as long as the overall growth rate is not too high. This combination produces rounded crystals with strong bonds at the necks.

When the temperature gradient is high, mass transport is rapid and the vapor pressure gradient that provides the driving force is apparently high enough such

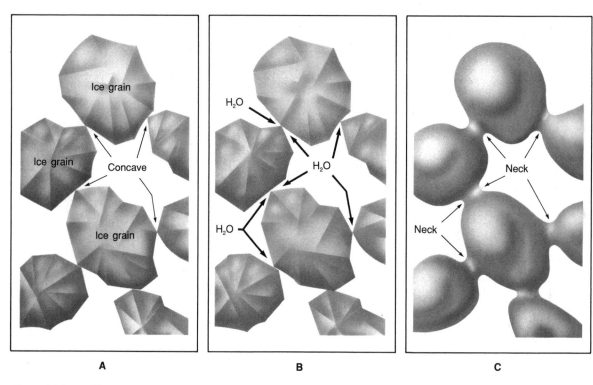

Figure 3.25. Bond formation in dry snow. Water molecules move through the air and along the grain surfaces to concave regions (low vapor pressure) to form bonds (necks) in a process called sintering.

that curvature effects do not have much influence on the landing sites for water vapor molecules. In this case, observations show that water vapor molecules are no longer deposited preferentially at necks, and growth occurs on the faces and edges of crystals as well. The result is weak snow with faceted grains and anisotropic character. For example, depth hoar develops in this manner and it is relatively weaker in shear than in compression (see Chapter 4). Depth hoar can be associated with big avalanches with initial snowpack failure at or near the ground.

The bond formation rate increases rapidly as the snow temperature increases. Field observations clearly show this effect on avalanche formation. For example, dry snow that falls at warm temperatures commonly stabilizes in place without avalanches developing due to rapid bond formation in new snow. However, this is only one aspect of temperature dependence that is of interest to avalanche forecasters. In general, rounded forms that grow at slow rates are small and tend to pack closer together; therefore, they have more bonds per unit volume and greater strength. Faceting in the presence of high temperature gradients can produce larger grains

with fewer bonds per unit volume. In addition, these angular grains do not pack as closely as rounded grains. The overall effect of this is to produce weaker snow.

In addition to the shape and size of individual grains,

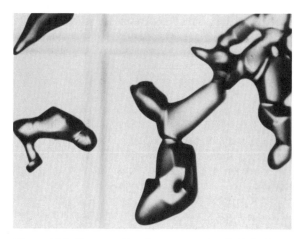

Figure 3.26. Close-up of bonds among grains. Grid size 2 mm. (Photo by R. Perla)

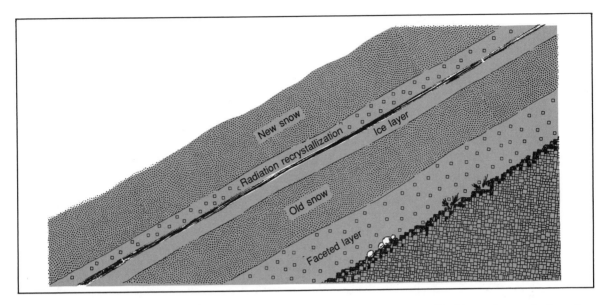

Figure 3.27. Snowpack stratigraphy from a continental climate with the radiation recrystallized layer above an ice layer (see Chapter 2) and the weak faceted layer above the ground.

bond formation between layers of snow also depends on the geometry of adjacent grains between the layers. For example, in general, new snow crystals do not bond well to an ice layer. Also, when the degree of riming changes during a storm, unrimed crystals can experience difficulty bonding to their more heavily rimed neighbors or to each other. Crystals broken by wind packing are usually small and they pack well into a cohesive strong slab. If they bond poorly to the surface below, a condition promoting avalanche formation may be imminent.

The temperature, temperature gradient, grain geometry, and pore space configuration all combine to produce the complicated patterns of bond formation and layer strength observed in dry snow. Avalanche forecasters should be aware of the general concepts with respect to bond formation. However, since it is virtually impossible to understand precisely what is happening at a given instant in time, it is better to use direct methods of assessing snow stability (see Chapter 6) conditioned by a knowledge of the physics of bond formation.

GROWTH OF CRYSTALS AROUND CRUSTS IN DRY SNOW

The influence of a crust can significantly alter the conditions for transport and deposition of water vapor in a dry snowpack. Faceted crystals sometimes form above

crusts to produce a future, serious avalanche situation when buried by subsequent snowfall. In fact, weak bonding of snow above crusts is the most important feature of crusts with respect to avalanche formation. Radiation recrystallization (Figure 3.27) provides an example. However, the presence of crusts, since they are relatively impermeable to vapor transport, can also allow faceted snow to grow immediately *below* a hard layer even when the surrounding crystals are well rounded. Below a crust, it is believed that the extra water vapor present due to blockage causes the excess vapor density (supersaturation) near crystal surfaces to increase, allowing facets to form when they might otherwise not form (see the right side of Figure 3.5).

BOND MELTING AND FORMATION IN WET SNOW

The heat flow between particles of different sizes (radius) causes metamorphism and bond melting or formation in wet snow. Efficient heat transfer through the water is the principal element that produces the observed rapid growth (large particles) and decay (small particles and bonds) of ice grains in saturated snow.

When grains touch in saturated snow, the equilibrium *melting* temperature at contact points decreases as the *pressure* between grains increases. (The pressure that forces the grains together is due to the weight of the snow above.) The melting temperature also decreases as the *area* of contact decreases. These effects combine to promote melting at grain contacts and densification (since the distance between particle centers decreases). When melting takes place at grain contact points, the contact area increases. The loss of bond strength at high saturations due to melting of contact points (a result of combined pressure and curvature effects) can be an important element in avalanches that initiate over impermeable layers such as ice layers or the ground where the water saturation is high.

When the water content is very low, surface processes are thought to play a very important role in the mass transfer. In this case, minute temperature differences (caused by curvature) between the region of water tension (bond) and the grain surface determine whether heat flow is toward the area affected by surface tension (in which case melting takes place) or away from the bond (resulting in freezing and true bond formation). If bonds form in this way, they are, of course, much stronger than "bonds" produced by the surface tension of water.

At low water contents, clusters of grains form near the snowpack surface where melting and freezing cycles can occur due to day warming and night cooling, particularly in late winter or early spring. After night cooling this combination produces very strong crusts composed of frozen grain clusters that lose almost all their strength after midday heating. The mass transfer over the crystal surfaces during melt causes the average grain size to increase, and the small grains and bonds disappear. The end result after a number of day–night cycles is clusters of large grains. This process is called *melt–freeze metamorphism*. Melt–freeze metamorphism builds crusts that (if buried) can serve as future sliding layers for avalanches. During the melt phase, wet loose snow may be formed at the surface to initiate wet surface avalanches (see Chapter 4).

References

Bader, H., et al. 1939. Snow and its metamorphism (Der Schnee und seine Metamorphose). Translated January 1954. Snow, Ice and Permafrost Research Establishment, U.S. Army, 313 pp.

Breyfogle, Steven R. 1986. Growth characteristics of hoar frost with respect to avalanche occurrence. *International Snow Science Workshop Proceedings*, Lake Tahoe, California, October 22–25, 1986. Homewood, CA: ISSW Committee, pp. 216–222.

Colbeck, S. C. 1975. Grain and bond growth in wet snow. IAHS Publication No. 114, pp. 51–61.

Colbeck, S. C. 1980. Thermodynamics of snow metamorphism due to variations in curvature. *Journal of Glaciology* 26(94): 291–301.

Colbeck, S. C. 1983. Theory of metamorphism of dry snow. *Journal of Geophysical Research* 88(19): 5475–5482.

Colbeck, S. C. 1983. Ice crystal morphology and growth rates at low supersaturation and high temperature. *Journal of Applied Physics* 54(5): 2677–2682.

Colbeck, S. C. 1985. Temperature dependence of the equilibrium form of ice. *Journal of Crystal Growth* 72: 726–732.

Colbeck, S. C., E. Akitaya, R. Armstrong, H. Gubler, J. Lafeuille, K. Lied, D. McClung, and E. Morris. 1990. The international classification for seasonal snow on the ground. International Commission on Snow and Ice, 23 pp. (Available from World Data Center on Glaciology, University of Colorado, Boulder, CO.)

Fletcher, N. H. 1970. *The Chemical Physics of Ice*. Cambridge, UK: Cambridge University Press, 271 pp.

Hobbs, P. V. 1974. *Ice Physics*. Oxford: Clarendon Press, 837 pp.

Knight, Charles, and Nancy Knight. 1973. Snow crystals. *Scientific American* 228(1): 100–107.

LaChapelle, E. R. 1969. *Field Guide to Snow Crystals*. Seattle, WA: University of Washington Press, 101 pp.

Lang, R. M., B. R. Lee, and R. L. Brown. 1984. Observations on the growth process and strength characteristics of depth hoar. *International Snow Science Workshop Proceedings,* Aspen, Colorado, October 24–27, 1984, pp.188–195.

Magono, Choji, and Chung Woo Lee. November 1966. Meteorological classification of natural snow crystals. *Journal of the Faculty of Science,* Hokkaido University, Sapporo, Japan, Series VII (Geophysics), II(4): 321–335.

CHAPTER 4
AVALANCHE FORMATION

The problem of primary shear fracture or primary tensile fracture of an avalanche is not just an academic question. Very often it is observed that slab avalanches are released by skiers traversing a neutral zone with a tensile fracture occurring high above them. Thus, the crack travels upward.

—Marcel de Quervain

TYPES OF AVALANCHES

The two general types of snow avalanches are called *loose snow avalanches* and *slab avalanches* (Figure 4.1). Loose snow avalanches start at or near the surface and they usually involve only surface or near-surface snow. Loose snow avalanches start at a single area or point and spread out as they move down the slope in a triangular pattern as more snow is pushed down the slope and entrained into the slide (Figure 4.2). The other type, the slab avalanche, is usually more dangerous. It initiates by a failure at depth in the snow cover, ultimately resulting in a block of snow, usually approximating a rectangular shape, that is entirely cut out by propagating fractures in the snow (Figures 4.3 and 4.4).

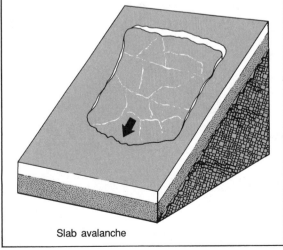

Figure 4.1. Illustration of loose (left) and slab (right) avalanche failure types.

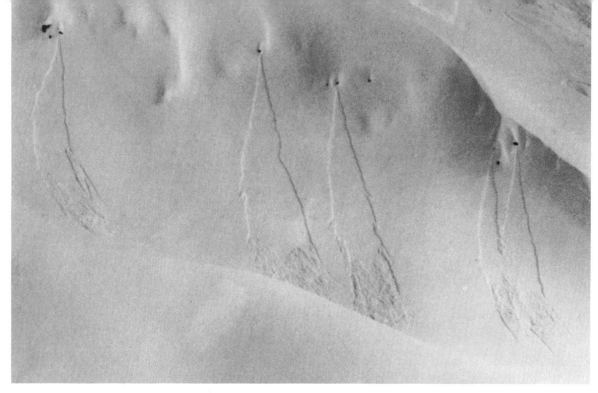

Figure 4.2. Above and below, left: Photos of loose snow avalanches. (Photos by A. Roch and C. O'Leary)

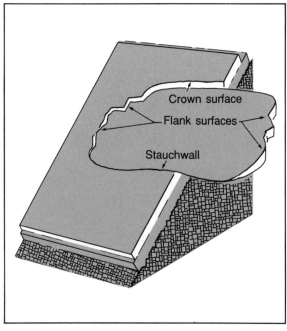

Figure 4.3. Terms to describe slab fracture surfaces.

Figure 4.4. A classic example of a soft slab avalanche.

DEFORMATION IN THE ALPINE SNOWPACK

On a snow slope, deformation occurs in three patterns (usually combined): (1) In tension the grains are pulled apart, (2) during compression the grains are forced together, and (3) in shear the grains are forced past each other. Figure 4.5 illustrates these modes. For either loose or slab avalanches, the initial failure is in shear. That is, loose or slab avalanche formation requires that the applied shear stress in snow approach, equal, or exceed the shear strength. Therefore, the shear strength of snow deserves special attention if avalanche formation is to be understood. However, in order to fail in shear, the state of deformation must be chiefly in shear and the snow must be deformed at a fast enough rate to provoke fractures.

Snowpack Creep

Alpine snow is always creeping because metamorphism is always occurring and the porosity is high. Porosity is the percent of the material that is air between individual snow grains. Creep rates in alpine snow are extremely high in comparison with other materials because of this high porosity and the fact that temperatures are normally within 95% of the melting point on the Kelvin scale. Creep rates in snow, like other materials, increase exponentially with the reciprocal of the temperature. Under the action of gravity and metamor-

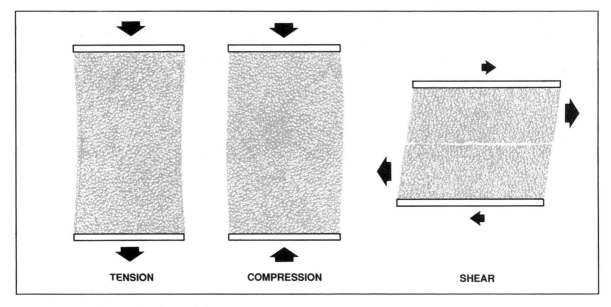

Figure 4.5. The three modes of snow deformation.

phism, it is estimated that about 90% of the slow motion (creep) of high-porosity seasonal snow responsible for density increases is due to the rearrangement of grains and 10% or less is attributed to mechanical effects such as deformation of the ice grains.

The long-term effect of compressive snowpack deformation is to increase the density and hardness with depth in the alpine snowpack. Density is defined as the amount of mass per unit volume with units of kilograms per cubic meter (kg/m^3). It is determined by weighing a sample of snow with a known volume. Typically, densities of snow vary from about 30 to 600 kg/m^3 in seasonal snow. The density of alpine snow can easily be related to its porosity (it is the most porous natural material).

The ratio of the density of dry snow to the density of ice (917 kg/m^3) gives the fraction of the volume of a snow sample that is composed of ice. When this fraction is subtracted from 1, the fraction composed of air is obtained (called the *average porosity*). Density near 30 kg/m^3 is a very low value for newly fallen snow; it implies a porosity of 97% (3% ice, 97% air). At the other limit, 600 kg/m^3 might be measured for wet snow from the bottom of a spring snowpack; it corresponds to a sample that is about one-third air (porosity 35%). The upper limit for dry snow is usually about 550 kg/m^3, which is close to that expected for a collection of ice

spheres packed as close together as possible in a random fashion.

During densification, snow hardness increases. Hardness is actually a measure of strength in compression. It has units of force (Newtons) per unit area (N/m^2; 1 N/m^2 equals one Pascal, abbreviated "Pa"). Because hardness is more closely related to strength, it is more useful than density in avalanche work. Hardness usually increases with depth in a uniform layer of an alpine snowpack. Hardness is normally measured by a hand test in avalanche work. A hand test involves pressing objects of various size into the snow to break it in compression. The hand test has been calibrated using snow hardness gauges. A hardness gauge consists of a series of circular metal plates of known area which are pushed into the snow. The force recorded when the snow breaks is a measure of the hardness. The hand test and its calibration are listed in Table 4.1. By international standards, hardness changes in the hand test are sensed by applying about 5 kg-force (50 N) to the snowpack. However, it is common in North America for avalanche workers to use only about 1.5 kg-force (15 N) to test layer hardness in the hand test. Experience has shown that important variations in softer layers will be missed using 5 kg-force.

The simplest snowpack is a horizontal one of constant depth. In this case, deformation is virtually all in

Table 4.1 ICSI Hardness Classification for Snow

Term	Swiss Rammsonde (N)	Order of magnitude strength (Pa)	Hand test	Graphic symbol
Very low	0-20	$0\text{-}10^3$	fist	
Low	20-150	$10^3\text{-}10^4$	4 fingers	/
Medium	150-500	$10^4\text{-}10^5$	1 finger	✕
High	500-1000	$10^5\text{-}10^6$	pencil	//
Very high	> 1000	$> 10^6$	knife blade	✻
Ice				▬

the vertical direction (called *settlement*). Under the action of gravity, the weight of the snow presses on the individual grains below causing settlement and generally resulting in densification and strengthening (Figure 4.6). Rates of settlement vary widely in alpine snow, ranging from 10 cm per day or more in low-density

newly fallen snow to perhaps 1/100 mm per day in dense snow at the end of the winter under a deep snow cover. The rate of creep generally decreases with depth in the snowpack because density increases with depth (i.e., there is less room for grain rearrangement).

Less settlement is exhibited in well-developed faceted snow (e.g., depth hoar) than in other types of snow with comparable density. Field studies show that the density of snow may *decrease* or not change much with depth in layers of depth hoar or coarse-grained faceted snow. This is likely because even though compressive forces cause densification, metamorphism results in a flux of material upward in the snowpack.

When the snowpack is on an incline, the total displacement of snow grains (deformation) is in the downslope direction (Figure 4.7). This deformation is easier to understand if it is resolved into vector components parallel and perpendicular to the snow surface. The perpendicular component is defined as settlement and the slope parallel component is shear deformation. Shear deformation and the shear stresses causing it are

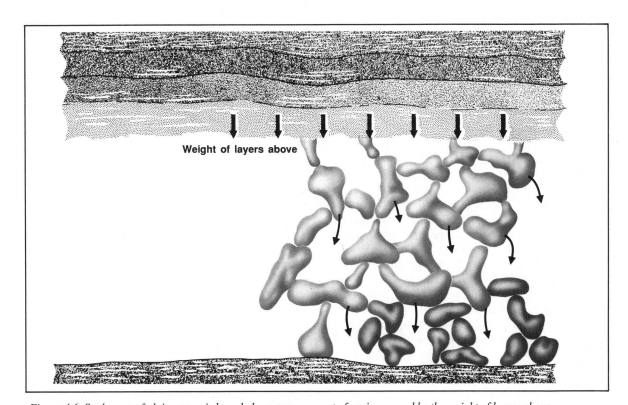

Weight of layers above

Figure 4.6. Settlement of alpine snow is largely by rearrangement of grains caused by the weight of layers above.

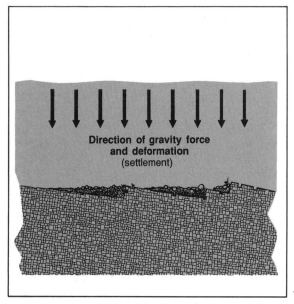 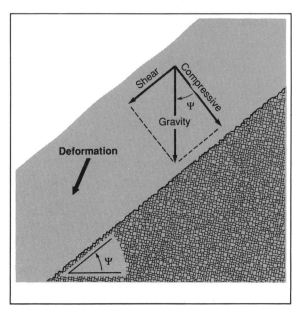

Horizontal snowpack   **Inclined snowpack**

Figure 4.7. Deformation components of the snowpack. Settlement (compressive deformation) produces densification. Shear deformation promotes failure.

ultimately responsible for avalanche formation. There-fore, generally speaking, shear stresses (and shear de-formation) promote instability and compressive stresses (and settlement) promote stability.

The relative magnitude of the shear displacement in comparison to the settlement component depends on the type of snow and the slope angle (both components are the same order of magnitude on slopes prone to ava-lanches). Figure 4.8 illustrates approximate estimates of shear creep deformation as a percentage of total defor-mation (shear and settlement displacement) for *low-density* homogeneous snow. This figure shows that more than two-thirds of the total deformation is in shear by slope angles of 25° and nearly 90% of the total deformation is in shear when the slope angle reaches 45°. When the density increases above that in Figure 4.8, as would be expected for most slab avalanches, shear deformation will become even more dominant. The slope dependence of the deformation components is one explanation of the slope angle dependence of slab avalanche formation: Slab avalanches become rare for slope angles near 25° and they increase in frequency as slope angle increases due to higher shear stresses and a greater percentage of shear deformation. For some types of nonhomogeneous snow (such as buried surface hoar),

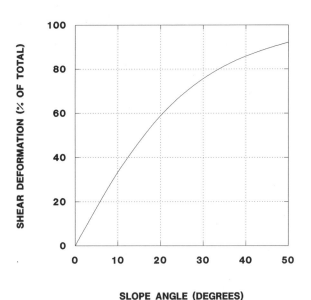

Figure 4.8. Fraction of shear deformation as a percentage of total creep (combined shear and compressive) deformation versus slope angle. The calculations are made for low-density snow.

settlement is expected to be very low and shear deformation may dominate almost completely.

Snow Gliding

Snow glide is the third component of snowpack deformation (Figure 4.9). It occurs on slopes when the snowpack slips at an interface (such as an ice layer) or over the ground. In conventional usage, the term usually refers to slip of the entire snowpack over the ground. When snow is dry, glide is very small or negligible because dry snow has high interface friction; it would fracture in shear before it could sustain large slip deformation. Snow gliding is important in the formation of slab avalanches that involve the full depth of the snowpack, and gliding can be responsible for high forces on structures such as ski lift and power line towers erected in deep snow covers. Typical glide speeds are in the range of 1 to 100 mm/d.

Field measurements have shown that a number of

Figure 4.10. Viscous deformation of snow. (Photo by L. Vuilloud)

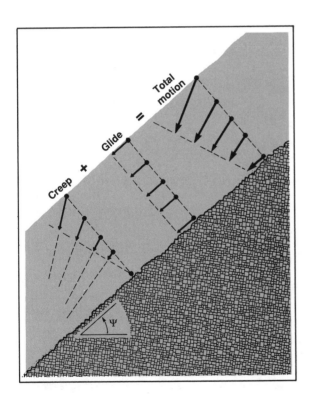

Figure 4.9. Creep and glide deformation components. Glide (slip of the entire snowpack over sloping ground) occurs with wet, smooth interfaces.

conditions must be met before gliding takes place. These include the following: (1) The interface must be fairly smooth. (2) The temperature at the interface or bottom of the snowpack must be at 0°C; this guarantees free water will exist at the interface. (3) The slope angle must be at least 15° for roughness typical of alpine ground cover.

Snow gliding at the ground is thought to be the result of creep of snow over the roughness features there. It is also known that the rate of gliding is very sensitive to the amount of water present at and near the ground. Increasing amounts of water, usually caused by rainfall or heavy snow melt during warm weather, cause reduced friction at the snow/ground interface by drowning small roughness features, hence, increasing the glide rate. In addition, snow stiffness (viscosity) (Figure 4.10) decreases with increasing water content, making creep over the ground roughness features easier. Once excess water drains away, the glide rate slows.

The fastest glide rates occur on smooth grassy slopes (Figure 4.11) or smooth rock slabs. These are the most important prototypes for full-depth avalanches caused by gliding. However, any smooth steep surface that has wet snow at the bottom can produce this type of avalanche, including water ice faces and glacier ice surfaces in the high mountains.

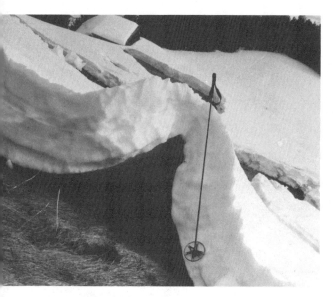

Figure 4.11. Formation of folds in the snow cover by glide over a grass-covered slope. (Photo by H. Frutiger)

Shear Failure of Alpine Snow

Under normal circumstances, snow on a slope deforms in shear and settlement almost like a viscous fluid.

During this slow motion, a tiny elastic portion of deformation also occurs (Figure 4.12). The viscous portion of the motion is called unrecoverable or permanent deformation, while the elastic component (like a spring) is recoverable. In general, the proportion of stored elastic energy increases as the deformation rate increases (simultaneously, the viscous portion decreases). During creep, the elastic portion is nearly negligible, but at very high deformation rates, catastrophic brittle fracture becomes possible. There is also a temperature dependence associated with this effect. As the temperature increases, viscous effects become more important. When snow becomes wet, the energy required to propagate brittle shear fractures is extremely high. In fact, the mechanism initiating slab avalanche release changes from brittle shear propagation (dry snow) to glide-induced tensile fracture (wet snow) when slush is found in the failure layer.

In general, dry snow cannot fracture unless a critical deformation rate is exceeded that is about 100 or more times the rate of deformation during ordinary creep. Such a high deformation rate is easy to achieve by application of explosives or perhaps when a skier crosses a slope.

To generate high enough rates to cause propagating fractures under conditions not introduced by human or

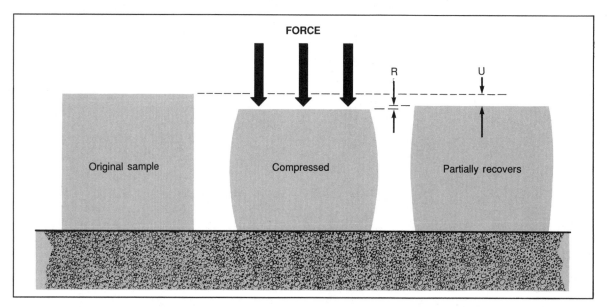

Figure 4.12. Illustration of the components of viscous (U = unrecoverable) and elastic (R = recoverable) deformation of a snow sample.

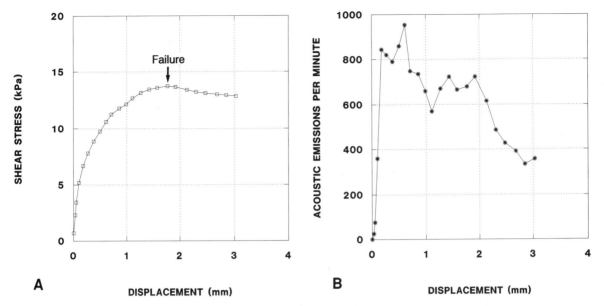

Figure 4.13. A: Shear failure (strain-softening) of alpine snow deformed at 0.1 mm/min. Failure is attained when a peak on the curve is reached. B: Pattern of acoustic emissions during shear failure. Breakdown of the structure is progressive with the greatest rate of emissions before peak. Test temperature is–2°C.

natural disturbances such as falling cornices, it appears that stress or strain concentrations introduced by *imperfections* in snow structure are necessary to achieve the critical rates. If a flaw or crack is present, theoretical estimates from fracture mechanics show that, locally, deformation and stresses boosted by a factor of 100 or more are easily possible. In practice, it is virtually impossible to locate a critical flaw or imperfection visually while examining a snowpack.

Snow, like other granular materials, displays a property called *strain-softening* when it is failed slowly in shear (Figure 4.13). Strain-softening means that resistance to deformation decreases after a peak is reached during deformation. In general, strain-softening materials form shear bands or slip surfaces during deformation. Thus, such a band of highly localized deformation can be formed by the snow itself as it shears without requiring prior existence of an imperfection. This effect, in combination with naturally occurring flaws, can nucleate concentrated shearing deformation. The combination is a powerful mechanism for generating the critical rates and stresses necessary to produce rapidly propagating shear disturbances in a weak layer, causing snow slab release.

COMPONENTS OF SHEAR STRENGTH OF ALPINE SNOW

The formation of snow avalanches is first and foremost determined by the mechanical properties of snow and its failure as a result of applied stresses. Under a given applied stress, whether or not snow fails depends on a number of physical properties that include, among others, density, hardness, temperature, rate of deformation, and quality of bonding to adjacent layers.

The slow shear failure of dry snow consists of a complicated progressive breakdown of the bonds within to result in strain-softening and formation of slip surfaces and shear bands, which ultimately allow shear fracture. However, the shear strength of snow may be idealized as having two basic components: cohesion and friction. Both of these components play a role in avalanche formation.

Cohesion

The strength property that determines the *type* of avalanche that will occur once a failure has taken place is called *cohesion*. Loose snow avalanches are caused by a *lack* of snow cohesion, while slab avalanches *require* a snow texture cohesive enough to form a block of snow. Cohesion in snow is directly related to how well snow grains and crystals are bonded to their neighbors (bond strength). Cohesion also depends on the shape of the snow grains and crystals and the density of bonds (number of bonds per unit volume), which is related to snow density.

Three optimum conditions produce low cohesion in dry snow: (1) cold temperatures (slow bond formation), (2) snow falling under relatively windless conditions so that it is not fragmented and packed (low number of bonds per unit volume), and (3) low density (low number of bonds per unit volume). These three conditions are often found together when new unrimed, dendritic snow falls during cold, windless conditions to produce dry loose snow avalanches. However, other combinations produce low cohesion. For example, rounded graupel crystals do not bond easily to their neighbors and they form layers of low cohesion snow, which results in loose snow avalanches (sluffs).

When snow becomes wet, the cohesion drops drastically as the water content increases and bonds are melted. For completely saturated snow, the cohesion is virtually zero. Low cohesion is the cause of wet loose snow avalanches.

Friction

Friction is the other component of snow strength that plays a role in avalanche formation. However, friction is important primarily in the formation of slab avalanches. In general, the strength of snow at a given depth in the snow cover is the sum of cohesion and friction. Friction refers to the resistance to motion of the snow grains in one layer relative to grains in another (similar to other types of friction). Friction in snow depends primarily on the texture (type, size, and shape of grains), water content, and the weight of the snow layers above (which forces the grains together to resist motion).

The friction component of snow strength is zero at the snowpack surface, but it increases with depth in a complicated fashion. Thus, the *usual* state of affairs is that both components of snow strength increase with depth in an alpine snowpack: The cohesion increases primarily when bond strength and number of bonds per unit volume increase; friction increases primarily because the weight of the snowpack over layers increases with their depth below the surface. The situations of most interest to avalanche workers are when the cohe-

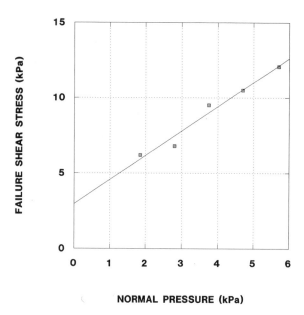

Figure 4.14. Results of shear failure for five similar samples sheared under different normal pressure. The cohesion (strength at zero normal pressure) is about 3 kPa; friction increases roughly linearly with normal pressure from zero (at zero normal pressure) to 10 kPa (at 6 kPa normal pressure).

sion is close to zero in near-surface layers (loose snow avalanche threat) and when snow strength (cohesion plus friction) is low in a layer below the surface (slab avalanche formation) compared to neighboring layers between which it is sandwiched (Figure 4.14).

SHEAR FAILURE PROPERTIES OF SNOW

For release of the snow slab, the strength in shear is the most important property. Some important variables determining shear strength are discussed in this section.

Density

The best estimates of shear strength are from avalanche fracture line studies. Figure 4.15 shows the variation of shear strength as a function of density. Most values are in the range of 100 to 1,000 N/m^2; strength clearly increases markedly with density. For comparison, strength values of surface hoar layers (not in avalanche failure layers) have been reported in the range of 25 to 400 N/m^2.

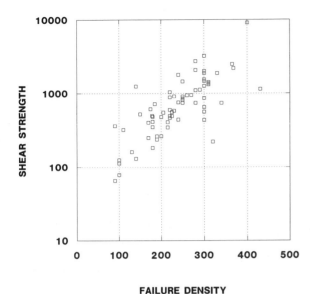

Figure 4.15. Shear strength (Pa) as a function of failure density (kg/m³) from slab fracture line studies. The strength is calculated from the downslope component of weight above the failure layer. The strength can also be related to the ICSI hardness scale calibrated at 5 kg-force (refer to Table 4.1).

Grain Size and Shape

Strength is usually highest in fine-grained snow with rounded forms. Snow tends to be weaker for larger coarse-grained snow with the same density. Snow with facets tends to be weaker than that with rounded forms. The geometrical combination that gives the closest packing and highest number of bonds per unit volume gives the highest strength (Figure 4.16).

Temperature

Snow becomes stiffer and stronger as it gets colder. It also takes on a much more brittle character with respect to fracture characteristics as the snow temperature decreases. Estimates from laboratory studies show that the *stiffness* (initial resistance to deformation) increases by a factor of 3 as the snow temperature decreases from $-2°$ to $-15°$C during slow shearing. By contrast, failure *strength* increases due to temperature decrease are only a second-order effect when snow is failed slowly (refer to Figures 4.13 and 4.16).

Overburden

The compressive load due to the perpendicular component of weight of the snowpack on a weak layer increases the friction component of strength, causing

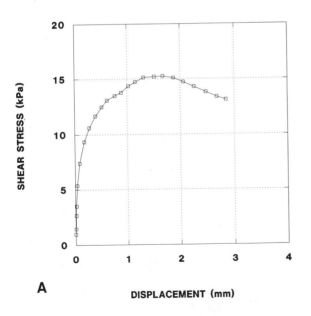

A

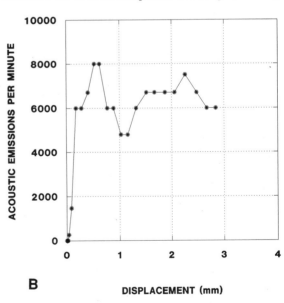

B

Figure 4.16. Slow shearing failure of a sample at $-15°$C for snow similar to that in Figure 4.13. The failure stress (A) is similar, but the sample stiffness is three times as great as for Figure 4.13A and acoustic emissions (B) are at a 10 times higher rate than Figure 4.13B.

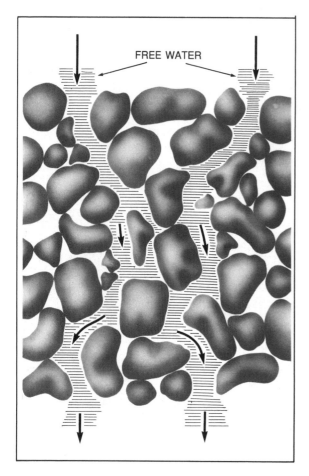

Figure 4.17. Illustration of free water flow through snow. In general, air, ice (snow grains), and free water may be present.

the overall strength to increase. Once densification occurs, the cohesion component of strength may also increase.

LOOSE SNOW AVALANCHE FORMATION

Loose snow has little or no cohesion. Loose snow avalanches form near the surface and they involve near-surface snow on initiation. Once the descent starts, subsurface snow beneath the surface may be swept along, particularly if the snow is wet (Figure 4.17). Snow of low cohesion may be either dry or wet, but the important point with respect to water content is that wet loose snow avalanches can be much more massive than

dry ones. For either dry or wet loose avalanches, the basic mechanism is the same: The slope angle exceeds the critical angle (called the *angle of repose* or *static friction angle*) necessary to cause motion. A static friction angle may be defined for each type of snow to initiate downslope motion depending on grain geometry, temperature, cohesiveness, and water content.

Loose snow avalanches are easily recognizable because they start from a point and the mass of snow displaced forms a triangular pattern on descent. They involve a small initial volume of surface snow, which slips out (usually less than 10^{-4} m^3). Natural loose snow avalanches are triggered by a local loss of cohesion due to metamorphism or the effects of sun or rain (Figure 4.18). Often the initiation is near rock outcrops, which cause locally high snow temperatures. Of course, natural or artificial disturbances to surface snow are also important triggers of loose snow avalanches (e.g., skiers, falling rocks, or snow).

Wet loose avalanches are usually triggered by heavy melt due to warming by the sun or rainfall on the

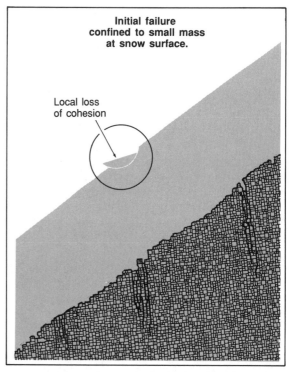

Figure 4.18. Mechanism of loose snow avalanche failure.

Figure 4.19. Moist snow has a small amount of strength and can cling to very steep slopes. (Photo by R. Emetaz)

snowpack. The cohesion of wet snow decreases with water content to provide the basic cause of wet loose avalanches. Wet loose avalanche activity is highest when the water content of the near-surface snow is increasing, and activity slows down when the water content is decreasing. Wet loose avalanches can occur at any time during the snow season and they can involve snow of quite high density. The strength of wet snow depends not only on water content, but also on the grain forms and bonding characteristics (Figure 4.19). New snow can, for example, fail at a lower water content than older snow if its initial strength is less. If snow has a small enough water content to be classified as moist (see Table 3.4), surface tension and bond formation between grains may develop to give the snow modest cohesion, which allows it to cling to very deep slopes and surfaces. Loose snow avalanches often present the greatest problems when midwinter rainstorms strike a mountain range (frequently in maritime climates).

Dry loose snow avalanches commonly form under cold, relatively windless conditions. Cold temperatures retard bond formation so that the snow remains cohesionless. Also, snow falling through a cold atmosphere tends to be unrimed. It has been suggested that the conditions for multiple-bond formation for stellar or dendritic crystals are less favorable for unrimed crystals, thus limiting increased cohesion (bond formation). If the wind is not blowing, the snow will tend to be less cohesive due to absence of windpacking and breakage effects. Dry loose avalanches tend to involve snow of very low density when they form in snow composed of dendritic or stellar crystals (unrimed). Dry loose avalanches can also involve heavily rimed crystals such as graupel with fairly high initial density. In fact, it has been suggested that these two extremes—unrimed dendritic and stellar crystals and fully rimed crystals (graupel)—form the two main prototypes for loose snow avalanche formation. A further—and persistent—observation is that dry loose avalanches can release a day or two after a storm stops in cold weather. Possibly, initial metamorphism by decomposition (disappearance of crystal branches) can decrease cohesion. Laboratory tests show that the critical angle of repose decreases as the initial stage of metamorphism (destructive) takes place.

With respect to crystal forms, general guidelines are available from laboratory studies of the angle of repose for dry disaggregated snow. Dendritic or stellar crystals have the highest angle of repose (up to 80°), decreasing to 35° for rounded forms. For wet snow, more emphasis is placed on the water content: The angle of repose decreases rapidly as water content approaches saturation. However, it is known that slush can avalanche off of slopes of 15° or less. Slush avalanches usually involve snow much deeper than surface snow and they are generally classified as slab avalanches (discussed later). Alpine snow is so porous it is difficult to maintain fully saturated (slush) conditions in near-surface snow unless some impermeable layer (such as an ice crust) lies below (Figure 4.20).

When snow moves, motion is resisted by kinetic friction, which may be expressed as an angle depending on the same variables as the static friction angle. If the slope angle exceeds the kinetic friction angle, loose snow in motion will continue in motion. However, once the slope angle is less than the kinetic friction angle, deceleration will begin to slow and eventually stop the mass—provided it is moving slowly. Laboratory studies show that the kinetic friction angle is about 10° less than

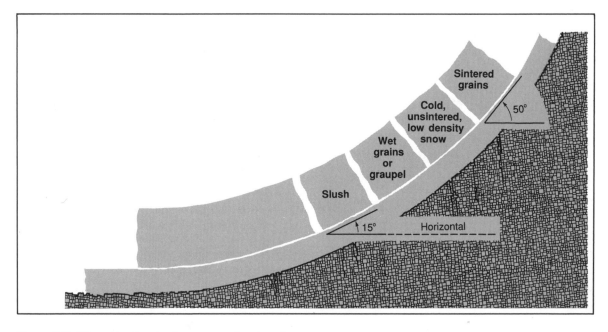

Figure 4.20. Schematic of angle of repose as a function of snow type.

Figure 4.21. The steep faces preferred by ice climbers are swept frequently by dry loose avalanches. (Photo by D. McClung)

the static friction angle (angle of repose) for most crystal forms. If the mass is moving rapidly (more than a few meters per second), other mechanisms dominate the braking action due to kinetic friction.

Dry loose avalanches are usually not massive or dense but they can be hazardous to people in precarious situations such as mountaineers climbing steep ice faces. However, wet loose avalanches are potentially more threatening to mountaineers on steep faces or gullies during warm weather or rain since they can be more massive with much higher snow density than dry loose avalanches. When noncohesive snow is present or expected, it appears that these two extremes in weather (cold or very warm) form the prototypes for loose snow avalanche formation (Figure 4.21).

Large wet loose avalanches can and do affect highways with adjacent steep slopes and they can be large enough to damage vehicles and structures. Loose snow avalanches have two other important effects: (1) They tend to prevent slab avalanche formation on steep slopes by sluffing activity and (2) they may serve as a trigger for slab avalanches on slopes below.

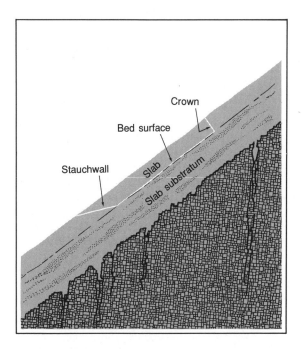

Figure 4.22. Cross section of a typical snow slab.

SNOW SLAB NOMENCLATURE AND FRACTURE GEOMETRY

A snow slab is a cohesive layer of snow with a thinner, weaker failure layer beneath it. A snow slab becomes a slab avalanche once it is cut out around all boundaries by fractures (refer to Figures 4.3 and 4.4).

A standard nomenclature has been developed with respect to the prominent features of a fallen snow slab. These terms are discussed here (Figure 4.22).

Bed Surface

This is the surface over which the slab slides. It may or may not be close to the initial shear failure surface under the slab because a shallow slab can sweep out a deeper slab during downhill motion (a common occurrence above depth hoar). The bed surface can be the ground.

Crown

This is the breakaway wall of the top periphery of the slab. It is usually at a right angle to the bed surface. It is formed by tension fracture through the depth of the slab from bottom to top.

Flanks

These are the left and right sides of the slab. Downslope motion of the slab causes the fractures at the flanks. All fractures associated with dry slab release propagate rapidly once they initiate. The flanks are usually smooth surfaces formed by shear fractures, tension fractures (indicated by a sawtooth pattern), or a combination of shear and tension fractures.

Stauchwall

This is the lowest downslope fracture surface. It is usually overridden by the slab material and it consists of a diagonal shear fracture of wedgelike shape. The stauchwall appears to form at about the same time as the flanks, just before the slab moves downhill.

CHARACTERISTICS OF DRY SLAB AVALANCHES

The characteristics of slab features measured at fracture lines in the field provide important information that can affect decisions about travel in avalanche terrain. They also provide important information about how snow slabs fail.

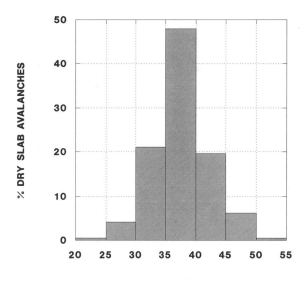

Figure 4.23. Slope angle dependence from fracture line studies.

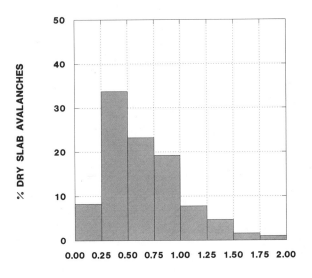

Figure 4.24. Distribution of slab thickness from fracture line studies.

Slope Angle

The normal range of slope angles for slab avalanche release is about 25° to 55°. For slopes with inclinations of less than 25°, the shear stress and shear deformation are apparently not large enough to cause failure and fracture (Figure 4.23). For steeper slopes (>55°), sluffing (loose snow avalanching) routinely prevents slabs from forming. It is worth mentioning that it is possible for a traveler to trigger slabs on slopes above while skiing on a horizontal or low angle surface under highly unstable conditions (fatalities have occurred by this mechanism). In this case, it is observed that a shear fracture may be produced that runs upslope underneath a slab to cut it free, with the fracture line occurring above on a slope of 25° or more. Secondly, even though sluffing (not slab formation) is usually expected on slopes in excess of 55°, there is no *guarantee* that a slab cannot be produced on such steeps slopes as well.

Figure 4.23 illustrates a distribution of dry slab avalanches as a function of slope angle measured at the crown. The distribution shows that about two-thirds of avalanches in the sample (about 200 slabs) occur for slopes with inclines between 30° to 45°, with the peak in frequency near 40°. This distribution is expected to change only slightly for different snow climates. Field observations show that instability (and the chance of avalanching) increases with increasing slope angle. For this reason, terrain features such as convex rolls must be dealt with carefully (see Chapter 5).

Crown Thickness

Figure 4.24 shows a frequency distribution taken from 200 dry slabs. The average value is about two-thirds of a meter, with a range from about 0.1 to 2 m. Field data show that slabs thicker than 2 m can release, particularly when large explosives are used. In practice, crown thickness is found to vary greatly around the perimeter depending on the deposition characteristics of the starting zone. A slab of any thickness greater than about 10 cm can be dangerous enough to bury skiers depending on terrain features and slab mechanical properties.

Average Slab Density

Figure 4.25 shows a distribution of average slab density measured at the crown for 70 dry slabs. The average value is about 200 kg/m³ with a range of 50 to 450 kg/m³. Figure 4.25 shows that the prevalent range of densities is between 100 to 350 kg/m³ with densities above and below this range being rare. Generally speaking, most slabs consist of cohesive wind-deposited or

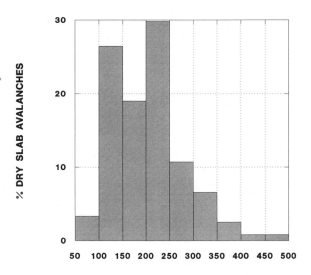

Figure 4.25. Slab densities(kg/m³) from fracture line studies.

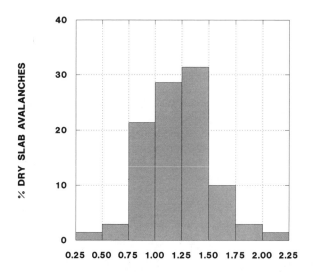

Figure 4.26. Ratio of bed surface and slab density from fracture line studies.

well-bonded old snow and the density data demonstrate this well.

Failure Layer Density

In general, measurements show that the density at the failure plane is higher than the average slab density. Since the failure layer is always beneath the slab, this is expected because density generally increases with depth in alpine snowpacks. These data show why density is not a very reliable indicator of strength in snow stability work: Density may increase with depth, but strength may or may not do so. This is because strength is so importantly linked to flaws and imperfections found in a snow cover. Analysis of 70 slabs (Figure 4.26) showed that the failure layer density was on average about 20% higher than the average slab density. The ratio of bed surface density to average slab density has a range from about 0.5 to 2 for the data in Figure 4.26. In this sample, about 75% of the slabs had a higher failure layer density than average slab density.

Slab and Bed Surface Hardness

The hardness of slabs may range from very low (a fist on the hand test) to high (pencil) or even harder (see Table 4.1). As a rough guide, slabs with a hardness rating that is low or very low are usually called *soft slabs* and those of medium hardness or harder are called *hard slabs*. The material in hard slabs often does not break up readily during descent, whereas soft slab material may be deposited as a nearly powderlike material resembling a slurry. Hard slab material appears more brittle during failure and it propagates fractures over long distances very efficiently.

The hardness of the weak layer is nearly always found to be low or very low (see Figure 4.15) using the ICSI hardness calibration scale (5 kg-force). Failure surfaces of medium hardness or harder are very rare and therefore potentially very dangerous because they can be exceptional cases that may be overlooked. The contrast between slab hardness and failure layer hardness is an important indicator of potentially unstable conditions. Unfortunately, the thickness of a weak layer may be only about 1 mm or less in some cases so that standard hardness tests in a snow profile may not easily detect the differences in hardness. In such cases, a mechanical stability test is necessary to locate a potentially weak failure plane (see Chapter 6).

Slab and Bed Surface Temperature

Figure 4.27 gives a distribution of temperature data from 100 dry slabs. More than 90% had a bed surface

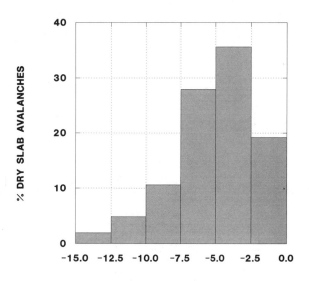

Figure 4.27. Distribution of slab failure layer temperature.

Figure 4.28. Examples of fracture lines and layering in slab fractures (Top photo by E. Wengi, Swiss Federal Institute for Snow and Avalanche Research; bottom photo by T. Auger)

temperature greater than –10°C. Thin slabs tend to have colder bed surface temperatures than thick slabs since temperature usually increases with depth in the snowpack. In Figure 4.27, the frequency distribution of temperatures decreases as the slab failure temperature approaches 0°C. The frequency must approach zero as the temperature approaches 0°C (otherwise the snow would be wet). For a full-depth avalanche it is possible to have a dry slab with wet snow at the bed (glide) surface due to geothermal warming. Examples of this kind of failure are not included in the data for Figure 4.27.

In agreement with the temperature data, field observations persistently show that natural dry slab failures usually become less frequent as the air temperature decreases. Often cold temperatures occur during clear relatively windless weather when there is no new loading to trigger a slab. Also, field-measured creep measurements show that deformation rates slow markedly as snow temperatures become colder (i.e., the snow becomes stiffer). These two effects work together to produce the observed result (Figure 4.27).

Slab Stratigraphy and Failure Layer Forms

Slab stratigraphy and bed surface forms come in such a variety of combinations that it is virtually fruitless to classify them (Figure 4.28). It has been suggested that in continental climates, slab failures tend to initiate more on the actual discontinuity between snow types or layers rather than within a failure layer, but no general proof of this supposition is available. Studies show that in continental climates there is a greater tendency for slabs to fail on weak layers present in old snow (usually faceted snow) than in maritime climates. Depth hoar is but one example of this and it can be associated with large avalanches. It has also been suggested that depth hoar failures most often initiate above (rather than in) the depth hoar. The possibility exists that when a slab releases from failure above the depth hoar, it provides a jolt to sweep out material beneath all the way to the ground. Few data are available to verify how general this hypothesis is.

Slab Geometry

The width of slabs is extremely dependent on terrain (Figure 4.29). For slabs on unconfined, open terrain without curvature, theoretical estimates and field data indicate that the width of slabs generally exceeds the downslope length. Figure 4.30 illustrates field measurements from 26 slabs. For this limited sample, the mini-

Figure 4.29. Illustrations of slab width. Top: Width is usually much larger than length. (Photo by Gabriel) Bottom left: Wet slab confined to a gully. Length exceeds width. (Photo by A. Judson) Bottom right: Fracture width can be unlimited in some instances. (Photo by N. Wilson)

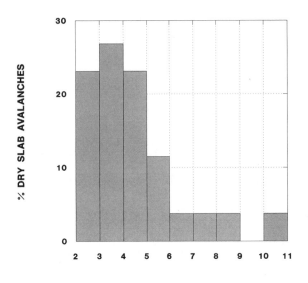

Figure 4.30. Distribution of slab width to length from 26 slabs.

mum ratio of width to length is about 2, and 85% of the values are between 2 and 6. There is no known upper limit to the ratio since it is known that shear fractures can propagate more than 1 km. Typical flank-to-flank dimensions are 10 to 1,000 times the slab thickness. In a confined region, such as a gully (see Figure 4.29b), the length may exceed the width. Field data show that there is a general increase in slab width with slab stiffness. However, this can be misleading because fracture propagation can occur over long distances, even with soft slab material.

Measurements show that the crown surface makes an angle close to 90° to the bed surface. It has been suggested from mechanics that this observation means the bed surface is nearly friction free in order for the 90° angle to appear. This would be expected if a shear fracture had propagated underneath the slab first to precipitate tension failure at the crown/bed surface interface.

Field observations show that most dry slabs occur on a planar slope (rather than convex or concave). Experience shows, however, that slab initiation (by skiing, for example) is much easier at the top of convex rolls. This is probably due to an increase in the ease of shear fracture propagation as the slope angle increases in the downslope direction.

DRY SLAB AVALANCHE FORMATION

Dry slabs are responsible for most of the damage and fatalities from avalanches. They constitute the single most important class of natural hazard in winter alpine terrain. Their release is characterized by rapid propagation of fractures underneath and at all boundaries of the slab. The vast majority of dry slabs release due to loading by new snowfall.

Studies at the crowns of fallen avalanches show that the stratigraphy consists of a relatively thick cohesive slab over a weaker, much thinner layer at the bed surface. In fact, a fallen slab usually has a structure rather like a sandwich: a weak layer in between thicker cohesive layers. A slab avalanche may be defined in simplest terms as a block of snow cut out by fractures. Whereas loosely bonded snow is a prerequisite for loose snow avalanche formation, a certain degree of cohesion is necessary to form a block of snow. From the sample in Figure 4.25, nearly 90% of the avalanches have average densities between 100 to 300 kg/m³. In general, these densities are higher than that of newly fallen snow without wind packing (usually less than 100 kg/m³) or snow that has not undergone bond formation. Experienced field observers are usually able to judge when snow has the proper consistency to form a slab as opposed to snow that is noncohesive.

To understand how a slab avalanche develops, in general, it is necessary to distinguish between failure and fracture. *Failure* in a dry slab avalanche occurs when the downslope component of the weight of the slab approaches the shear strength in the weak layer (peak value of stress on a stress-strain curve). It is possible, however, to have failure in a material such as snow (called strain-softening) without fracture. At failure, a sample of snow has absorbed the maximum load that it can bear (see Figure 4.13). If snow has been deformed slowly in shear, it can fail without fracturing. Fracture means catastrophic failure of the material and this is a prerequisite for slab avalanche release. Controlled laboratory studies show that fracture takes place only if snow is sheared at a critical rate, which is about 1 mm/min for layer thicknesses typical of avalanche weak layers (e.g., 10 mm). Therefore, two requirements must be met before a propagating shear fracture takes place: (1) The shear stress must approach the shear strength in the weak layer and (2) the rate of deformation in the weak layer must be fast enough to provoke fracture. Instability develops when the first condition is met, but dry slab

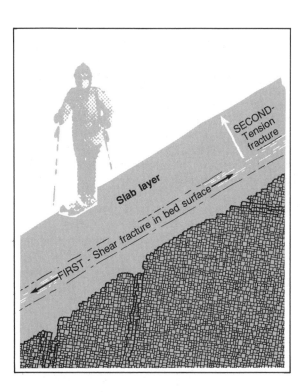

Figure 4.31. Possible fracture sequences for dry slab initiation.

avalanches can start only when both requirements are fulfilled. The intermediate condition (in which failure is approached, but fractures have not yet occurred) provides a serious threat to travelers in snow-covered alpine terrain (Figures 4.31, 4.32, and 4.33).

Although the fracture sequence is believed to be the same, it is convenient to distinguish between *natural* slab avalanches (not caused by humans) and *artificial* releases (caused by humans), including releases by explosives, skiing, or other influences. The principal difference is usually the rate of application of the energy that starts the failure process. It is easy to see how the critical rate of deformation may be applied to the failure process when energy is supplied rapidly, for example, by explosives, skiers, sonic booms, or earthquakes. However, it is more difficult to understand how the critical rate is achieved in the weak layer by much slower loading from new snowfall or by natural straining in the snowpack. These failures may result from a combination of natural imperfections and shear band

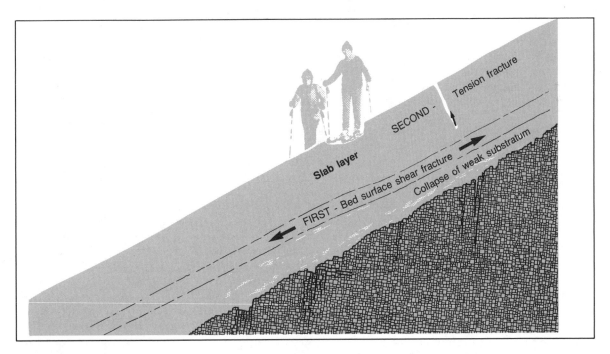

Figure 4.32. Initial failure accompanied by collapse of a substratum. Shear fracture produces a tension fracture at the crown.

Figure 4.33. Initial shear fracture produces a crown tension fracture near a skier.

formation (see the preceding section "Shear Failure Properties of Snow") to produce the necessary high deformation rates.

After a shear failure, a fracture develops that spreads upslope and across the slope. As it does so, it reduces the attachment of the slab to the bed surface and rapid tensile fracture occurs from the bottom to the top of the slab to form the crown. As the crown fracture propagates across the slope, it also allows the slab to displace downslope, providing further driving stresses to propagate shear fractures across and downslope over the bed. The flanks (and stauchwall) form rapidly once the crown fractures to allow downslope displacement of the slab.

A situation of interest is the failure of a thick layer of depth hoar or highly faceted snow near the bottom of the snowpack. This is often referred to as a collapse of the layer since it is sometimes possible to sense a drop or falling sensation during the failure process. Properly speaking, however, the release mechanism is classified as a shear fracture, and a disturbance can be sensed to propagate away (up or downslope). The collapsing sensation is due to compression failure, but the actual fracture (and propagating disturbance) is a shear frac-

ture. Snow, like all other materials, allows fracture *propagation* in shear and tension. (See Chapter 6 for further discussion.)

Tensile fractures have sometimes been observed to occur just upslope from a skier crossing a slope, particularly (but not exclusively) when traversing a convex roll. In general, it is possible for shear fractures to propagate upslope as well as downslope and across the slope. In this case, shear fracture propagation (across and downslope propagation) is responsible for generating the tensile fracture that forms the crown. As in other cases, the elastic energy necessary to produce tensile fracture is produced by rapid deformation generated by shear fractures.

The most common trigger for natural dry slab avalanches is addition of weight by new snowfall, blowing snow, or rain. Other natural triggers include impact by pieces of falling cornices and vibrations by earthquakes.

Natural dry slab releases are also possible as a result of temperature influences at and near the surface of the snowpack because of warming effects during which the snow surface may or may not reach 0°C. Temperature releases are observed for thin slabs, usually less than 0.5 m, over very unstable weak layers such as weak surface hoar. Since incident solar radiation cannot penetrate the snow cover more than a few centimeters and since low-density alpine snow conducts heat very slowly, surface warming cannot quickly penetrate very far (see Chapter 2). Field observations suggest the effect is confined to thin slabs in which warming can affect a significant fraction of the slab depth. Under unstable conditions, it is not necessary to have warming penetrate to the weak layer; reduction in slab stiffness by warming can provide the trigger. Since temperature effects are enough to release thin slabs naturally, they clearly can have a strong influence on snow slab stability when combined with other effects.

Temperature increases are sometimes cited as the cause of slab release when avalanches release (minutes or hours) after application of explosives (called *post-control releases*). However, most case histories are inconclusive because explosive control is often applied in the morning and release is observed later when the temperature is rising. The far more likely explanation of these delayed events is that, rarely, explosive control causes failure initiation without immediate fracture, placing the slope in a highly unstable condition. The great majority of documented cases of post-control release have involved triggering by skiers and it is likely that the prime cause is because the slope was left in a weakened state by explosives. It is possible to start a slowly propagating failure that does not immediately reach a fracture condition due to delayed effects since snow is a strain-softening material with both elastic and viscous properties. It may also be that areas of accelerated deformation are created by an explosion that results in a growing failure region, which eventually attains a critical size. Achievement of just the right balance at which failure is approached accompanied by delayed fracture is expected to be rare, in agreement with observations.

WET SLAB AVALANCHE FORMATION

Wet slab avalanches occur by means of three principal mechanisms: (1) loading by new precipitation (rain), (2) changes in strength of a buried weak layer due to water, or (3) by water lubrication of a sliding surface, which may be partially or totally impermeable to water. In cases 2 and 3, water may be added to the sliding surface by melt or rainfall. If the sliding surface is at the ground, stored or geothermal heat can also help to maintain water production there. Whether one, two, or all of these mechanisms operate at any given time

depends on the snowpack structure and details of supply and storage of water.

When rainfall occurs on dry snow, the most common cause of avalanche release is probably just due to the added load from the rainfall. In this situation, field observations show that controlled release by explosives is crucially dependent on timing. If the wetted front reaches and substantially wets the weak layer, it becomes very difficult or impossible to release an avalanche using explosives because shear fracture propagation in wet snow requires so much more energy than in dry snow.

When water reaches a weak layer, the strength of the layer will be reduced. The strength of wet snow depends not only on the same variables as dry snow but it also decreases with increasing water content. Cases of avalanche release have been documented in which the water content at the failure layer was *less* than that of other layers in the snowpack above. These observations show that the strength of wet snow depends on structure as well as water content (Figure 4.34).

When water reaches an impermeable boundary in the snowpack (or the ground), slip of the slab over the boundary may be initiated over a region and friction there will be reduced. If the sliding surface is within the

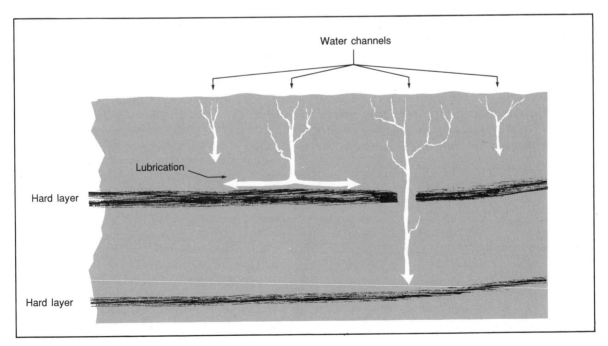

Figure 4.34. Schematic showing complexity of water flow in wet snow.

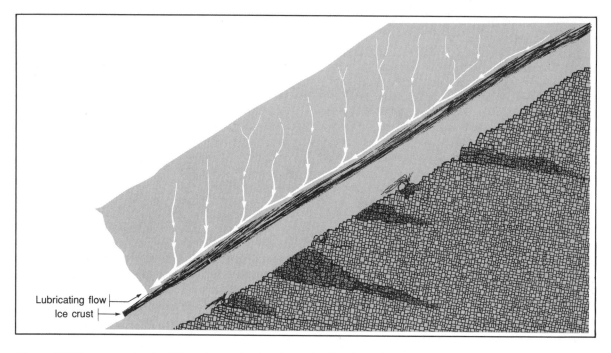

Figure 4.35. Schematic showing lubrication mechanism for avalanches that release by gliding on an ice layer.

snowpack (such as a buried ice layer), this can result in wet slab avalanche release by formation of a tensile fracture due to the friction reduction (Figure 4.35).

When water is present at a smooth ground surface such as rock or long grass, the friction is reduced and the rate at which the snow glides increases. Two important mechanisms may promote faster gliding in this case: (1) The snow viscosity near the boundary decreases due to increased water content, thereby allowing easier deformation of the snowpack over the ground roughness obstacles, and (2) water reaching the interface may drown out the small roughness features there so that the snow can move over them virtually unimpeded.

The two mechanisms of promoting fast gliding sometimes combine to reduce friction over a region of the slab that is probably at least 10 slab thicknesses long and just as wide or wider. When the downslope friction is reduced, the slab is forced to absorb the extra load above (upslope) the region of reduced friction. The result is often the formation of a tensile crack (called a *glide crack*) that starts at the ground and propagates upward at an angle of roughly 90° to the bed surface. Once the tensile crack opens, slab release often occurs quickly, but it is also very common for slab release to occur after the crack has been in place for days or even months. This is in contrast to dry slab avalanches, most of which

release quickly once a shear fracture starts. Since these full-depth avalanches are caused by the interaction of water and the ground roughness features, they can be very unpredictable. There are documented examples of unexpected releases when the air temperature was below −10°C (Figures 4.36 and 4.37).

Glide crack formation is a prerequisite to full-depth avalanches that release by gliding. Crack formation requires a *decrease* in friction conditions (increase in glide velocity) in the downslope and cross-slope directions; the crack will form preferentially in the region where the friction change is greatest. Fast gliding by itself is not a sufficient condition for glide crack formation; there must be an increase in glide speed in the downslope direction. Glide cracks form readily on convex rolls, on slopes where the ground bed surface roughness changes, and below steps in rock. Measurements of gliding on a convex roll have confirmed that gliding increases in the downslope direction.

There are scattered but persistent reports of thin wet slab avalanches releasing after slopes become covered by shadows as the sun sets in the evening. One explanation is that surface cooling causes the release of a slab that is already in tension due to water lubrication of an interface below the surface. Snow with low water content (as would be expected near the surface) is known to

Figure 4.36. Slab avalanche released by gliding snow cover. (Photo by D. McClung)

contract as it freezes. This effect can increase the tensile stresses rapidly to cause crown fracture and avalanche release. The special conditions required (a thin, wet slab under tension) combine to make this a relatively rare occurrence.

ICE AVALANCHES

The effects of ice avalanches are frequently observed by travelers in glaciated mountain ranges and have been responsible for large avalanche disasters. The two classes of ice avalanches discussed here are based on size. The failure mechanisms for both classes may be the same.

The first class is a result of *calving* (falling) of ice masses or séracs at positions where glacier ice flows over a steep slope or cliff band. The result is a tensile failure of the ice caused by the combination of internal flow (creep) and sliding of the glacier over its bed (cold or polar glaciers usually have a very small or negligible sliding component). These events are encountered frequently by mountaineers. When in motion, the debris consists of ice chunks that roll and bounce along the surface and a powder or "dust" cloud that envelops the chunks. The motion of the ice chunks is analogous to rockfall (glacier ice is a metamorphic rock). The powder component runs much further than the ice debris with less destructive power (see Chapter 5).

Collapse of glacier séracs in icefalls has caused many fatalities in the high mountains (the Khumbu icefall on Mount Everest has provided many examples). Since the failures are usually caused by glacier motion (or, less commonly, earthquakes), there is very little relation of time of occurrence to the weather or time of day even though melt water often plays a role in the release. Since glacier sliding is known to be faster in spring or summer when more basal water is available (analogous to snow gliding), more events may occur during these seasons. However, any information about timing of these events (either by time of day or season) is useless to a mountain traveler: Hanging ice should not be crossed (or camped beneath) if possible. If such an area must be crossed, it should be traversed as quickly as possible (Figure 4.38).

A second class of ice avalanche occurs when a large piece of glacier ice breaks off to form a massive ice avalanche analogous to a landslide. This size class is much rarer than the simple calving of smaller pieces or séracs from an icefall (typically 10^6 m^3 or more of ice can be involved). The Huascaràn avalanches of 1962 and 1970 in Peru accounted for approximately 25,000 lives lost and the destruction of a number of villages and tens of thousands of livestock. The 1970 event was triggered by an earthquake, but for both events, the initial ice mass

Figure 4.37. Wet loose avalanche that has swept out snow to the ground. (Photo by P. Schaerer)

had combined with unstable soil and rock below to cause the destructive effects. The Allalin disaster on August 30, 1965, in Switzerland occurred when a relatively large piece of ice (10^6 m^3) broke off the snout of the glacier to invade the Mattmark construction site below (88 lives lost). The cause was fast sliding of the glacier in connection with an oversupply of basal melt water resulting in surgelike behavior (Figure 4.39).

SLUSH AVALANCHES

Slush avalanches constitute another class of wet slab avalanche, but they occur under rather unusual conditions. In fact, they are almost always found at high latitudes such as northern Norway or the Brooks Range

Figure 4.38. Powder avalanche formed by small ice avalanche off glacier ice cliff. (Photo by A. Roch)

Figure 4.39. Ice avalanche debris formed by a slab of ice from the Allalin glacier in Switzerland. The avalanche resulted in 88 fatalities. (Photo by A. Roch)

of Alaska, but they can occur (rarely) at mid-latitudes as well. The prevalence for formation at high latitudes is partially due to the rapid onset of snowmelt in spring as the sun returns to provide direct, intense radiation input to snowpacks that have been previously subjected to strong temperature gradients and a lack of solar radiation input. Five other characteristics distinguish most slush avalanches:

- Starting zone slope angles are in the range of 5° to 40° but they rarely exceed 25° to 30°.
- The snowpack is usually partially or totally saturated with water.
- The release is associated with a bed surface that is nearly impermeable to water.
- In most cases depth hoar is present at the base of the snow cover.
- Release is usually associated with sudden intense snowmelt or heavy rainfall.

Documented measurements at the time of slush flow release give clues about the mechanism of release. The most likely cause of slush flows is the reduction of snow cohesion due to the presence of water and substantial reduction of the friction component of snow strength by the hydrostatic pressure resulting from standing water in the snowpack. The standing water is possible due to the low slope angles involved such that drainage is slowed. The combination of these factors can reduce the shear strength at the interface to a very low value. Since it is doubtful that shear fractures can propagate in slush, the bed surface failure is probably progressive with formation of a slurry after local failure.

Densities of saturated snow in slush flow deposits have been measured that exceeded 1,000 kg/m^3 due to the combination of water, ice, snow, and entrained earth or rock material. Such high densities imply that impact forces on objects struck by slush avalanches can rival those of the most destructive avalanches known (Figure 4.40).

Figure 4.40. Slush avalanche debris in northern Norway. (Photo by E. Hestnes)

ROOF AVALANCHES

Slab avalanches off roofs can injure or bury people. They have been known to cause damage to parked cars and other objects below. Obstructions in the path of moving snow including chimneys and plumbing vents are also commonly damaged. The avalanche deposits also make extra snow removal necessary (Figure 4.41).

No international standards have been agreed on, but most countries recommend that snow can be expected to slide off roofs steeper than about 20° to 30°. However, recommendations in the United States allow for sliding off of smooth roofs when the slope angle exceeds 15°. There is at least one documented case of avalanching off of a roof covered by a smooth plastic membrane at a slope angle of 10°.

Roof (slab) avalanches are caused by a mechanism similar to full-depth avalanches, which release by gliding over the ground. However, they may also occur with dry snow sliding on a cold (below 0°C) roof as well as for the case of wet snow gliding on a wet roof. Formation of glide cracks can (sometimes) be observed in either case. Since roofs do not usually contain the small roughness features of the ground surface of alpine terrain, snow (including dry snow) can slide over them easier than it can over the ground. Once the adhesion of snow to the roof is overcome, slip can take place at the snow/roof interface and tensile stresses will develop in the snow cover, which may ultimately fracture and release as a slab. Roof avalanches have been observed to occur

Figure 4.41. Large roof avalanche caused by gliding. (Photo by C. Stethem)

because of cooling on the shady side of a roof as the sun sets, similar to wet avalanches, which release due to surface contraction following the onset of evening shadows.

References

Bader, H. P., and B. Salm. 1990. On the mechanics of snow slab release. *Cold Regions Science and Technology* 17:287–300.

Brown, C. B., R. J. Evans, and E. R. LaChapelle. 1972. Slab avalanching and the state of stress in fallen snow. *Journal of Geophysical Research* 78:4950–58.

Conway, H., S. Breyfogle, and C. R. Wilbour. 1989. Observations relating to wet snow stability. *Proceedings of the International Snow Science Workshop, Whistler, British Columbia, October 12–15, 1988.* Vancouver, BC: Canadian Avalanche Association, pp. 211–222.

Hestnes, E. 1985. A contribution to the prediction of slush avalanches. *Annals of Glaciology* 6: 1–4.

McClung, D. M. 1987. Mechanics of snow slab failure from a geotechnical perspective. IAHS Publication No. 162, pp. 475–508.

Perla, R. I. 1976. Slab avalanche measurements. *Proceedings of the 29th Annual Canadian Geotechnical Conference, Vancouver, British Columbia, October 13–16, 1976.* Canadian Geotechnical Society, Part VII, pp. 1–15.

Perla, R. I. 1980. Avalanche release motion and impact. *Dynamics of Snow and Ice Masses.* S. C. Colbeck, Ed., New York: Academic Press, pp. 397–462.

Roethlisberger, Hans. 1977. Ice avalanches. *Journal of Glaciology* 19(81): 669–671.

Taylor, D. A. 1985. Snow loads on sloping roofs: two pilot studies in the Ottawa area. *Canadian Geotechnical Journal* 12(2):334–343.

CHAPTER 5

AVALANCHE TERRAIN, MOTION, AND EFFECTS

In questions of science, the authority of a thousand is not worth the humble reasoning of a single individual.

—Galileo Galilei

DEFINITIONS

The following terms are essential to an understanding of the concepts discussed in this chapter.

An *avalanche area* is a location with one or more avalanche paths (Figure 5.1). An *avalanche path* is a fixed locality within which avalanches move (Figure 5.2). Avalanche paths may cover a vertical distance of only 50 m or may fall the full length of a mountainside with a vertical drop of 2,000 m or more. Within an avalanche path, smaller avalanches may start and stop at various places, each avalanche having its own *starting zone, track,* and *runout zone* (Figures 5.3 and 5.4).

The *starting zone* (or zone of origin) is the location where the unstable snow failed and began to move. The crown (or fracture line) of a slab avalanche and the initiation point of a loose snow avalanche define the upper limit of the starting zone for each avalanche. While the lower limit of avalanche origin is usually ill defined, it is sometimes quite obvious. For example, it is often possible to see the stauchwall. Sometimes a guess has to be made when trying to define the length of the starting zone for avalanches with ill-defined upper or lower limits (stauchwall).

The *track* (or zone of transition) is the slope below the starting zone that connects the starting zone with the zone where debris collects (runout zone). While the track is the major terrain feature for large avalanches, it

is often ill defined in avalanches with a short running distance (see Figure 4.4 in Chapter 4 and Figure 5.2). Avalanche speed attains its maximum value in the track, but speed variations are smallest there. Snow may col-

Figure 5.1. Avalanche area with several paths through the forest. (Photo by H. Frutiger)

larger avalanches. Similarly, small avalanches often run out in the track of larger avalanches. While the terms *starting zone, track,* and *runout zone* are specific for every avalanche, the terrain descriptions in an avalanche atlas or avalanche mapping refer to the largest avalanche expected in a specific path and by convention the three terms are defined for a path as a whole (Figure 5.4). For example, small avalanches often end up being deposited in the track, so they are not used to define the track.

The term *multiple starting zones* applies when several starting zones, well separated by ridges or forests, connect to a single track (Figure 5.5). With unstable snow conditions, several starting zones could release at once, combining into a very large avalanche in the track or runout zone (Figure 5.6).

Figure 5.3. Avalanche path. The avalanches can start at several locations where the slope is most favorable. Runout zones vary with avalanche size. Ross Peak, Rogers Pass, British Columbia. (Photo by B. Engler)

Figure 5.2. Short avalanche path with starting zone, track, and runout zone not well defined. (Photo by A. Roch)

lect behind trees, rocks, or in narrow gullies but usually deposition in the track is insignificant for maximum events.

The *runout zone* (or zone of deposition) is the area where deceleration is rapid, debris is deposited, and the avalanche stops. An abrupt change in slope angle can mark the transition between track and runout zone but this is often not the case.

The three zones can vary for individual avalanches within an avalanche path. Some avalanches may start low on a mountain with their starting zone in the track of

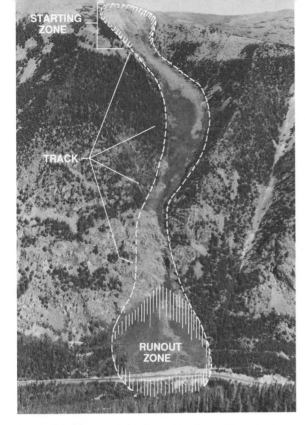

Figure 5.4. Three sections of an avalanche path: starting zone, track, and runout zone.

Figure 5.6. Major avalanche path winding from the back of the mountain and down the slope, resulting in starting zones on all steep slopes below terrain rolls. Large avalanches starting on the slope below the rocky peak could run into the valley. Smaller avalanches would run out on the benches and the cirque with the lower incline. (Photo from CMH Heliski)

STARTING ZONE CHARACTERISTICS

SLOPE INCLINE

The primary terrain requirement for avalanche initiation is a slope incline that will allow an avalanche to start and accelerate. Other terrain features are secondary and

Figure 5.5. Avalanche tracks with multiple starting zones. Small, single avalanches will stop in the common track, while combined flows will advance further down the track.

Figure 5.7. While insufficient snow for avalanches can accumulate on the steep rock slope, sluffs onto the 40° slope below can create additional loading to produce slab avalanches. Monashee Mountains, British Columbia. (Photo by P. Schaerer)

simply modifiers of the incline. There is no precise lower limit for inclines below which slopes are safe; the minimum slope angle depends on snow conditions (Figure 5.7). Guidelines for starting zone inclines developed from experience (detailed studies are rare) are given in Table 5.1. Dry snow avalanches initiate where a portion of the slope has an incline ≥25° (lower limit); lower inclines can produce wet avalanches (see Chapter 4 for details).

Table 5.1 Guidelines for Starting Zone Inclines

60°–90°	Avalanches are rare; snow sluffs frequently in small amounts
30°–60°	Dry loose snow avalanches
45°–55°	Frequent small slab avalanches
35°–45°	Slab avalanches of all sizes
25°–35°	Infrequent (often large) slab avalanches; wet, loose snow avalanches
10°–25°	Infrequent wet snow avalanches and slush flows

ORIENTATION TO THE WIND

Wind exposure is the second most important consideration when analyzing terrain. Given an adequate incline, slopes that collect drifting snow are most likely to produce avalanches. Slopes with wind-deposited snow can be found on the lee side of high ridges, as shown in Figure 5.8, behind ridges that run with the fall line of major slopes (cross-loading), behind any high and convex parts of slopes, and behind rows of trees (see Chapter 2 for details).

When evaluating wind action, it is important to remember that the wind direction and speed vary with elevation and terrain features as well as storm features (again, refer to Chapter 2).

Wind-exposed slopes are not necessarily safe from avalanches. During calm or periods of light winds enough snow can accumulate to overload weak layers; even partially wind-eroded snowpacks can fail.

ORIENTATION TO THE SUN

The exposure of slopes with respect to the sun influences incoming radiation, which determines snowpack temperatures and strength (see Chapters 2, 3, and 4). Shady slopes, on the north sides of ridges and in valley bottoms, receive little direct heat from the sun and lose heat by long-wave radiation. The snowpack remains cold in midwinter, stabilizes slowly, and tends to develop weak layers of faceted crystals, depth hoar, and surface hoar. The stability of snowpacks on shady slopes increases slowly as the temperatures rise in the spring.

Sunny slopes tend to have warmer snow temperatures and better stability than shady slopes in midwinter. However, in late winter and spring, sunny slopes can rapidly become unstable. Exposure to the sun has a strong influence on the day-to-day stability of the snowpack. However, on the average over several years, given equal topography, sunny slopes can generate as many avalanches as shady slopes. In the mountain ranges of western Canada and the United States, the shady side is often the lee side for prevailing storm wind direction. As a result, the influences of sun and wind are often difficult to separate. It would appear that the shady, north- and east-facing slopes have more frequent avalanches as a result of wind rather than sun. Note, however, that stability evaluation (see Chapter 6) must be based on physical evidence, not the general rules discussed here.

FOREST COVER

A forest on steep slopes inhibits large avalanche formation because it influences the character of the snow cover. Forests interrupt and prevent snow transport by wind (Figure 5.9).

Figure 5.8. Ridge with cornice. (Photo by P. Schaerer)

Figure 5.9. Effects of forest on the snowpack.

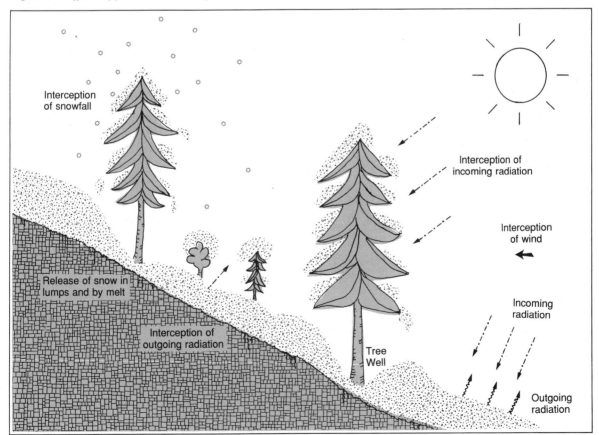

Figure 5.10. Scattered trees are not protection against avalanches. Floral Park, Berthoud Pass, Colorado.

Tree crowns intercept the snowfall, allowing only 50% to 90% of the falling snow to reach the ground. Snow is released gradually as lumps and melt water to produce an irregular snowpack structure. Tree crowns also control the incoming/outgoing radiation, moderating the snow surface temperature; this can limit the formation of faceted crystals and surface hoar.

Tree trunks may support the snowpack, inhibiting slab avalanches if the density of the trees is great enough. A density of about 500 conifers per hectare is considered best for gentle slopes, and 1,000 conifers per hectare on steep slopes. A mix with species of variable height and age is preferable; deciduous trees alone and open-spaced forests have a limited effect. Scattered trees on open slopes are not protection against avalanches (Figures 5.10 and 5.11).

While forests can assist in avalanche prevention on slopes, moving avalanches may be almost unaffected by trees. Small avalanches flow between the trees without damaging them. Large avalanches often break trees, developing into a mixed flow of snow and trees, which results in greater mass and damage potential.

The effect of shrubs (willows, slide alders, berry bushes) on avalanche formation is complex. Shrubs penetrating the surface of a shallow snowpack can prevent avalanches, but they also inhibit snow settlement, creating a loose, weak base for future snowfalls.

GROUND SURFACE

Rough ground will anchor the snowpack until it is deep enough to form a relatively smooth surface. Bedrock, boulders (about 2 or 3 m apart), stumps, logs, short stiff shrubs, and benches are all surface features that provide good anchors to hold the snowpack. Approximate guidelines for maximum snow depths that prevent slab avalanches are given in Table 5.2.

Table 5.2 Approximate Snow Depths for Avalanche Prevention

0.3 m	Relatively smooth ground cover: fine scree, bedrock, grass
0.6 m	Average terrain: boulders, small trees, shrubs, irregular surfaces
1.0 m	Rough terrain: large boulders, stumps, logging debris

The stabilizing effect of boulders may reverse after they are covered by the snowpack. Boulders (as with other fixed objects such as trees and structures) can act as stress concentrators to increase the chance of fractures taking place. Also, snow near covered or partially

Figure 5.11. Dense forest lost in fire 100 years ago has been unable to renew beyond sparse growth because of continuous avalanche activity. (Photo by P. Schaerer)

covered boulders can be weaker than the surrounding snowpack due to influences of snow metamorphism. Since snow temperature extremes tend to take place near rocks (sideways temperature gradient), large, weak crystals with increased porosity tend to form near irregularities.

Glide-initiated avalanches are more likely to occur on smooth bedrock or long grass than on rubble or short, brushlike grass. Observations in the Alps showed that avalanches occurred more frequently after the farmers stopped cutting the grass on steep open slopes. In Japan, bamboo shoots on slopes have been used to inhibit avalanches caused by gliding. Variations in ground temperatures across an area resulting from geothermal heat, or input of surface or groundwater, can also lead to full-depth avalanches initiated by glide (see also Chapter 4).

SLOPE DIMENSIONS

Slab avalanches require a minimum width and length of failure on the bed surface in order to overcome the support at the flanks and the stauchwall. These minimums tend to increase with slab strength and depth and they may also vary with slope incline, but no general guidelines can be set (see Chapter 4 for slab dimensions).

ALTITUDE

Altitude influences avalanche initiation because snowfall, wind, and temperatures vary with elevation (see Chapter 2). Upper slopes can have different snowpack conditions, exposure to wind and sun, and ground cover than the lower slopes. This can therefore produce avalanches on upper slopes when conditions on lower slopes are stable and vice versa.

CROWN AND FLANK LOCATIONS

Knowledge of probable starting locations is very important for route selection and planning avalanche control (Figure 5.12). Crown and flank positions (fracture lines) of slab avalanches are often dictated by

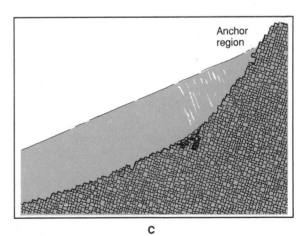

Figure 5.12. Possible sources of tensile stresses. A: Slope curvature; B: uneven depth, such as a snow cushion; and C: anchoring at the top boundary.

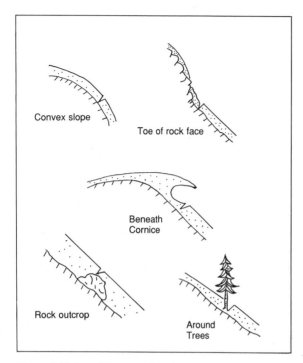

Figure 5.13. Possible crown locations.

Figure 5.14. Avalanche on an open slope. (Photo by A. Roch)

terrain features (Figure 5.13). For example, crowns caused by explosive control are often found at the top of slopes or under cornices where the slab may change thickness (taper). Likely crown and flank locations occur when shear fractures propagating up or across a slope reach the influence of terrain features, which forces tensile fractures. These features include convex rolls and anchor points (stress concentrators) such as rocks and trees. The majority of natural dry slab fracture lines occur on terrain without significant curvature (neither concave nor convex); avalanches caused by gliding have a bias to form on convex terrain. Experience shows that dry slab instability is higher for travelers on convex slopes and where the snowpack tapers on concave slopes.

TRACK CHARACTERISTICS

Avalanche tracks have a variety of configurations but two main categories are recognized: *open slope* and *channel* (International Commission on Snow and Ice, 1981). Open slopes have no lateral boundaries (Figure 5.14). Channels are gullies and other depressions (Fig-

ure 5.15). Long tracks often have mixed terrain; for example, a gully may widen into an open slope.

Avalanches usually follow the fall line, but they are not always confined by lateral boundaries and can take unexpected paths and also meander from side to side in a gully (Figure 5.16).

Because kinetic (motion) friction is lower than static (stopping) friction beneath an avalanche, relatively shallow slope angles can allow an avalanche to keep moving. The required angle for continuing motion depends on mechanical properties of the flowing snow and the size of the avalanche as well as the surface hardness of the path. Maximum avalanches in long paths decelerate significantly when the slope angle decreases to 10° or less. Typical track slope angles are 30° to 15°.

Avalanche tracks often contain flat sections or cliffs. Observations have shown that variations in slope angle over small sections of the track have little influence on avalanche speed. However, very high speeds are possible when avalanches become airborne over long sections (friction with the ground is very low).

RUNOUT ZONE CHARACTERISTICS

Debris eventually comes to rest when the slope angle equals the static friction angle (which, as mentioned, depends on the mechanical properties of the flowing snow and the character of the sliding surface; details are given in a later section). The runout zone can be a wide

Figure 5.15. Avalanche paths with (top) channeled and (bottom) unconfined tracks.

Figure 5.16. Trimlines in the forest show how avalanches ricochet in the track. Future avalanches may not follow the same line. (Photo by P. Schaerer)

bench, a talus slope, a valley bottom, the opposite side of a valley, or anywhere that an avalanche stops running.

Due to the slow speeds (and high friction) in the runout zone, avalanches are sensitive to terrain variations there. This allows deflection by small obstacles. Avalanches may take unexpected turns or stop in a very short distance when the slope angle decreases. Typical slope angles for the runout zone are 15° or less. Some avalanches can run long distances over essentially flat terrain.

A forest in the runout zone can retard avalanche flow depending on the tree spacing, height, and elasticity and the type of avalanche. Forest cover cannot be relied on to stop all avalanches because, as mentioned earlier, avalanches may either move through the trees or break them. This can make avalanche paths difficult to recognize.

GULLIES

Steep gullies, filled with ice and snow, are a frequent source of avalanches because they combine several hazardous features:

- Often slope angles exceed 40° so that slab and loose snow avalanches are frequent.
- Several independent starting zones can occur on the sides and at different elevations.
- The snow condition/stability can vary widely over the length of the gully, making evaluation difficult.
- Snow deposition and characteristics are radically affected by the weather in a gully. For instance, a wind shift can load them with drifting snow, or direct sunlight and radiation from the sides can cause rapid heating of the snowpack.
- The difficulty of escaping to the side and the probability of hitting rocks magnify the danger for persons caught. Numerous climbers have been caught in gully avalanches in both summer and winter, resulting in injuries and deaths.

TERRAIN ANALYSIS

A cardinal rule for mountain travel is to choose routes and stopping places that have as few hazards as possible.

BASIC RULE

The basic rule for route selection is: *Avoid steep slopes when the snow is unstable; do not enter them and do not cross below them.* "Steep" is generally considered to be a slope angle of greater than 25°, the minimum angle required for dry snow avalanches. It could be less under conditions of very wet snow. The critical incline refers to the steepest part of a slope (not the average incline).

Travelers should develop a feel for terrain steepness by estimating slope angles (for example, with a clinometer). Simple guides include: 26.6°, two horizontal units to one vertical; 45°, one horizontal unit to one vertical. When stability is assessed on gentle slopes, it can be assumed that, as the slope angle becomes greater, stability will become poorer. This effect results because the percentage of slope-parallel slab weight for driving shear fracture propagation increases with slope angle (see Figures 4.7 and 4.8 in Chapter 4).

GENERALLY SAFE TERRAIN

The following are preferred travel routes that avoid steep slopes and are generally safe:

- High points of the terrain: ridge tops, knolls, hills, backs, ribs (Figure 5.17)
- Wide valleys and wide benches some distance away from steep slopes. It is useful to develop a feel for runout distances and frequency of avalanching based on terrain variables and vegetative clues, as discussed in later sections (Figure 5.17). An extra-wide detour should be made around the runout zone of long, channeled avalanche tracks if poor stability is expected.
- Gentle slopes without steep terrain above
- Dense forests

POTENTIALLY UNSAFE TERRAIN

Choice of terrain that is absolutely safe is not always possible or desirable. Often steep slopes are used because they offer the only route uphill and downhill, where pleasurable skiing can be found. Guidelines for

recognition of potentially hazardous locations when the snow is unstable are discussed in this section.

The wind is a very important modifier of snow conditions. Areas with deposition of drifted snow should be assessed very carefully: the downwind sides of ridges, hills, and ribs, and local depressions on a steep slope, "caps" of gullies, and notches. Bowls, cirques, and wide depressions have complex wind action patterns that increase the uncertainty when predicting snow stability.

Consider the exposure to sun and the influence of incoming and outgoing radiation on snow stability, as discussed in Chapters 3 and 7. Also consider the hazard from slopes above—snow stability might be lower than on the travel route—and be aware of short steep slopes (for example, at moraines, mine dumps, and road cuts) where stability may be lower than on adjacent terrain.

Finally, do not assume that the old tracks of skiers, hikers, and snowmobilers lead through safe terrain—use your own judgment.

TERRAIN AROUND UNSTABLE SNOW

Terrain where small avalanches could be hazardous when the snow is unstable includes rock, snow, or ice

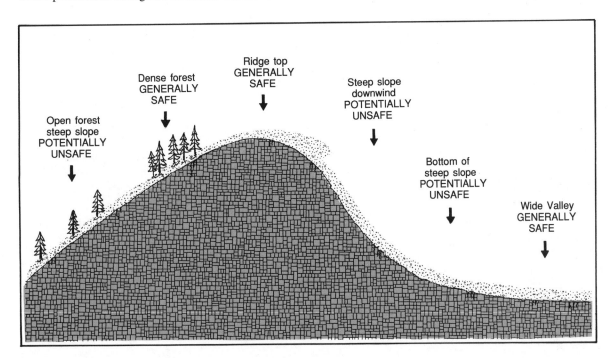

Figure 5.17. Schematic of terrain, forest cover, and general safety levels.

Figure 5.18. Gully where frequent unexpected avalanches run. Start positions can include the open slope above, the sides, or the center of the track. Avalanches can be triggered by blowing snow or the sun. (Photo by B. Engler)

Slopes above a steep drop-off or cliff can also be hazardous. Even very small avalanches can become serious when people are in precarious postions; be aware of the distance to drop-offs and evaluate the seriousness if an avalanche initiates.

TERRAIN AT ROADS

Consideration of terrain at a road is important because potentially unsafe areas should be crossed without stopping. Safe areas must be located at which vehicles can wait when avalanches are on the road, and maintenance work should not be carried out in unsafe areas when moderate or high hazard exists (see Appendix F for a rating scale) (Figure 5.20).

Generally safe areas exist below rock spurs, slopes with a low incline, and dense forest. Moderately safe areas that could be exposed to small avalanches or large avalanches under unusual snow conditions are below

gullies (Figure 5.18). Narrow valleys and depressions (terrain traps) also need to be evaluated because a small avalanche could deposit deep snow and dramatically increase the chance of burial (Figure 5.19).

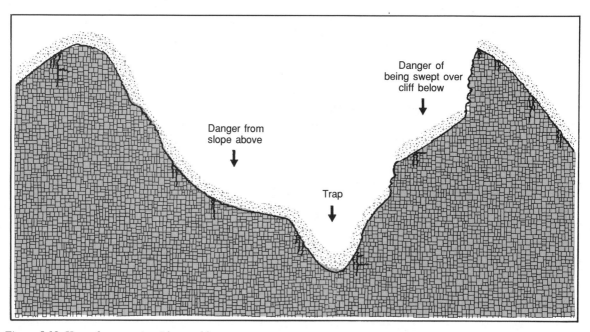

Figure 5.19. Hazardous terrain with unstable snow.

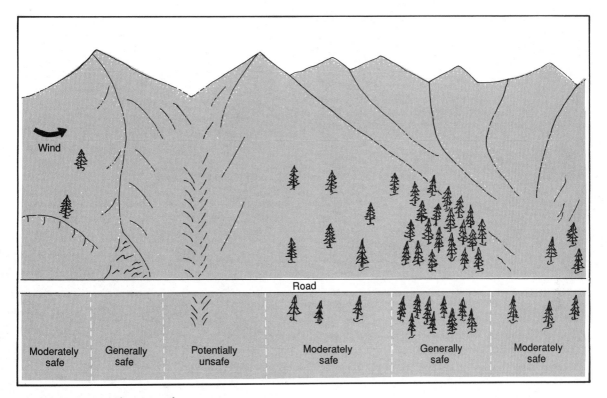

Figure 5.20. Terrain above a road.

short steep slopes, including cut slopes; below slopes exposed to wind; and below a thin forest on a steep slope. Other moderately safe areas are at avalanche paths on the other valley side and at through-cuts and at the bottoms of narrow valleys.

Unsafe areas when snow is unstable are below gullies; below long steep slopes that are open or covered with small, scattered trees (Figure 5.21); and below cornices and snow pillows.

Many potential avalanche paths can be recognized by an open slope bordered with dense forest (Figure 5.22). Sometimes when the frequency of major avalanches is low, forests can be dense with old growth and a path is virtually unrecognizable. In the high mountains, vegetation will not be present. In this case, experience and an appreciation for the expected scale of avalanche runout based on terrain variables may be the only available aids.

BACKCOUNTRY ANALYSIS

One of the important steps in backcountry avalanche hazard evaluation (see Chapter 7) is to *analyze* the terrain. One must ask the question: Can avalanches occur on the terrain in question? A checklist of some, but not all, of the important factors to watch for is given here. The reasoning was explained in the preceding sections.

Slope Angle

- Slope angles between 25° and 60°; 35° to 40° are most common for skier-triggered slabs (see Table 5.1 and also Chapter 4).
- For high or extreme instability, it is possible to generate propagating shear fractures while moving on gentle or flat terrain to produce an avalanche on a slope above.
- Degree of instability usually increases as the slope angle increases.
- Increased instability appears on *convex* slopes.

Slope Orientation (Aspect)

- Lee, wind-loaded slopes
- Lee slopes under cornice roofs

Figure 5.21. Weak snow and a fracture line formed near small trees. (Photo by Swiss Federal Institute for Snow and Avalanche Research)

- North-facing slopes (persistence of instability)
- South-facing slopes (direct exposure to sunlight)

Terrain Roughness and Vegetation

- Open slopes or thinly forested areas
- Deep snowpacks (bury anchors)
- Smooth slopes (without anchors)

Terrain Traps

- Drop-offs
- V-shaped valleys and gullies

IDENTIFICATION OF AVALANCHE PATHS

Avalanche paths need to be recognized when housing, industrial developments, ski areas, roads, railway lines, transmission lines, and other facilities are planned in mountainous terrain. The following procedures have been found useful:

1. Determine from contour maps, aerial photos, and ground observations whether the slopes meet the conditions for avalanche formation—incline, exposure, orientation.

2. Using the same sources, estimate the location of tracks and runout zones below previously identified starting zones.

3. Using aerial photos or visual confirmation, look for signs of past avalanche activity such as sharp trimlines in treed areas, new tree growth, different species (Figure 5.22). A comparison of earlier aerial photos is useful, particularly for areas disturbed by logging or fires.

4. Evaluate the climate to determine whether maxi-

Figure 5.22. The trimline in the forest indicates the width of a track and the maximum runout distance. (Photo by P. Schaerer)

mum snowfalls, including drifting snow, could cover surface roughness.

5. Investigate clues to earlier avalanche activity using a ground vegetation survey (discussed later in this chapter). Look for younger, different species of trees and broken trunks, limbs, and scars on the uphill side of trees. Other clues are broken wood, needles, and twigs outside the forest area; leaning trees; and fallen trees aligned with the expected direction of avalanche flow.

   Clues applicable to open areas include rock debris perched on boulders and scattered on roads; gullies and creeks filled with avalanche snow; "brushed" shrubs; and rock cones, mounds, and pseudo-moraines deposited by avalanches.

6. Observe avalanches during the winter and spring. It might be sufficient to make an inspection in the spring when half the snow has melted and avalanche debris is visible on the surface. Avalanche snow is harder and coarser than fallen snow; it is usually contaminated with debris. Other signs of activity are fracture lines, flow marks in gullies, and snow plastered on the uphill sides of trees.

7. Collect information on historical avalanche events from local residents, road maintenance crews, and newspapers.

8. Calculate runout distances for maximum avalanches (see section later in this chapter).

9. Compare inclines, slope lengths, exposures, and runout distances with known avalanche terrain in the area.

10. Report conclusions about the width and runout distances of expected average and maximum avalanches *using all of the collected information*.

CATALOGING AVALANCHE PATHS

Operators of permanent facilities identify the avalanche paths in their areas by name, number, or aspect and elevation. On roads, railways, and transmission lines the identifier is usually the running kilometer. Lists, maps, and aerial photos may refer to avalanche path locations using these identifiers. Avalanche paths may also be described in an avalanche atlas.

AVALANCHE ATLAS

An avalanche atlas is a catalog with descriptions of the avalanche paths in an area. It is compiled from aerial photos, ground observations, surveys, and on-site ob-

servations. The atlas may contain the following information.

Introduction

- Area referred to by the atlas
- Area climate including snowfall and snow on ground
- Volume of winter road traffic
- Topographical map showing avalanche paths with their identifiers (name, number)
- Definition of terms
- Method of compilation and time span of observations

Avalanche Paths

- Identifier
- Photo of entire path (preferably in winter)
- Description of starting zone(s) (elevation, incline, aspect, and general topography)
- Description and incline of track for significant avalanches
- Description of runout zone(s) for significant avalanches, including incline, ground cover, and stopping location for small, medium, and large avalanches
- Catchment area (maximum area that can contribute avalanching snow)
- Effect on roadway where applicable
- History; observed past avalanches classified according to size, stopping location, frequency, and whether wet or dry
- Measurements of terrain variables needed for calculation of runout distances (see later section in this chapter for details)

AVALANCHE MOTION AND EFFECTS

Knowledge of avalanche motion (avalanche dynamics) is important when estimating avalanche speeds because the speed has an effect on the design and placement of structures that may be in the path of flowing snow. The principles of avalanche dynamics are also useful when considering route selection in mountain travel, camp placement in mountaineering ventures, and survival when one is caught in an avalanche.

The mathematical problem of describing the interaction of flowing snow over complex mountain terrain to predict avalanche speeds along the incline has not been solved. However, some descriptive features of the problem are available from field observations and measurements.

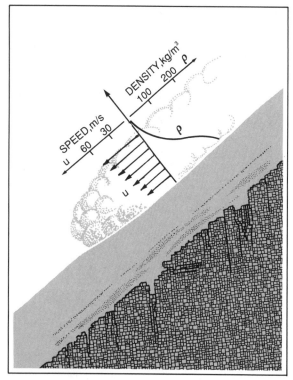

Figure 5.23. Possible speed and density variations in a large flowing avalanche.

DESCRIPTIVE FEATURES OF AVALANCHE MOTION

Dry Snow Avalanches

Avalanches can begin their descent either as loose snow or as a slab. In the latter case, due to interaction with the roughness features of the terrain, the slab breaks into blocks or particles. As the descent continues, the particles become smaller due to the grinding action as they continually collide with each other and the sliding surface (snow or ground). What normally evolves is a region of relatively high-density material of snow particles and air (called a *core*) at the bottom of the avalanche. An avalanche with a high-density core at the bottom is called a *flowing avalanche* (also termed a *mixed-motion avalanche*) (Figure 5.23). If the snow is dry, a snow "dust" cloud of low density covers the exterior of the core when avalanche speed is greater than about 10 m/s (Figure 5.24). This material is suspended

by turbulent eddies of air generated by the friction of the flowing snow interacting with the air.

The two important differences between the core and dust cloud are as follows: (1) It is estimated that about one-third of the space in the core is filled with snow particles and about two-thirds is air. In the dust cloud,

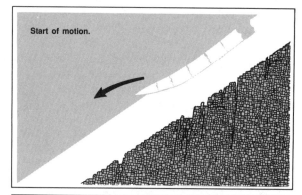

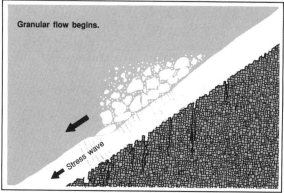

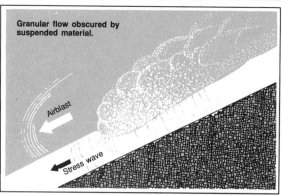

Figure 5.24. Stages of motion of a dry flowing avalanche. Stress waves propagate in the snow beyond the snow front. An air blast sometimes precedes the avalanche.

only about 1% of the space is filled with snow particles and 99% is air; therefore, the density is about a factor of 10 higher in the core than in the dust cloud. (2) Usually the depth of flow of the core is less than 5 m, but the depth of the dust cloud can be tens of meters. Therefore, the resistive forces that govern the speed of the avalanche depend on the interaction of the dense (granular) core of snow with the sliding surface (bottom) and the snow dust with the ambient air at the top (exterior). It is expected that resistive forces at the bottom will account for most (perhaps 90% in some cases) of the total friction for a dry flowing avalanche.

At the sliding surface (and in the core), the friction is determined by particles (snowballs and crystals) interacting by collisions with each other and the sliding surface. This interaction takes the form of collisions and frictional rubbing between snow particles. The collision and rubbing friction causes heat to be generated on the exterior of particles, which produces small amounts of water on their surfaces. Once the deposit comes to rest, the water on particle surfaces can freeze to fuse the particles together, producing a very hard deposit. This explains why strong shovels and steel probes are required when persons or equipment must be dug out of large avalanche deposits and why burial is so serious.

Figure 5.25 shows accurate frontal speed data for a large dry avalanche measured using radar in Switzerland. Important characteristics of the motion are evident: (1) Acceleration is very rapid in the early stages of motion due to high downslope driving force (motion over steep terrain); it is also possible that bottom friction is fairly low after the early stage of motion. Field data show that relatively high speeds (>25 m/s) can be attained by avalanches falling less than 200 m in height. (2) Deceleration is very rapid at the end of motion, which implies high friction in the runout zone. Field observations show that during this phase of motion, particles lock together in the upper portion of the flow as the speed decreases. Friction at the base of the flow is expected to be high because particles will be forced to rub together. Finally, friction will approach a high (static) value corresponding to a mass of particles locked together.

Powder Avalanches

Powder avalanches are those in which a dense core at the bottom is absent. A source of confusion comes with respect to the name powder avalanche. Any high-speed dry avalanche will have a powder or dust cloud

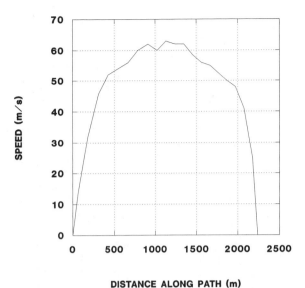

Figure 5.25. *Precision measurements of avalanche speed for a large dry avalanche (Aulta avalanche, Switzerland). Note rapid acceleration and deceleration at the beginning and end of motion. (Data supplied by Hans Gubler, Swiss Federal Institute for Snow and Avalanche Research)*

associated with it and this tends to make powder avalanches and dry flowing avalanches *look* similar. To distinguish between powder and dry flowing avalanches, one must make an observation of the deposit, destructive effects, or flowing snow properties to determine the presence of a core (Figures 5.26 and 5.27).

In a true powder avalanche, almost all of the material is suspended by turbulent eddies. They often form by falling ice from steep icefalls (see Chapter 4). Usually, the ice chunks drop out as the slope angle decreases at the bottom of the slope, and the powder cloud continues for a long distance without much destructive power. They are also habitually formed by sluffs off of steep terrain. Powder avalanches are sometimes thought to attain higher speeds than flowing avalanches, but since powder avalanches have flow densities of only about 10% of flowing avalanches, their overall destructive power is less. From an engineering point of view, the powder component of an avalanche is important for two reasons: (1) It can run farther than the main deposit and (2) impact forces will extend over a much greater height on a structure than the dense core at the bottom. If the material in a powder avalanche is truly suspended by

Figure 5.26. Release and motion of a powder avalanche. (Photo by G. Buscaini)

turbulence, then the air/snow dust cloud may be "mixed," resulting in smaller-density increases from top to bottom than in a flowing avalanche. In flowing avalanches, a significant increase in density is expected with depth from top to bottom (Figure 5.28).

Air Blast

Another phenomenon that is occasionally associated with avalanche motion is air blast. Air blast is an air pressure wave that runs beyond the visible avalanche front or deposited snow. The concentration of snow particles in an air blast pressure wave is small or negligible so that the density of the moving fluid is simply

Figure 5.27. Airborne flowing avalanche descending a cliff in Colorado. It has been hypothesized that airborne avalanches are responsible for air blast. (Photos by S. Standley)

Figure 5.28. Motion sequence of a dry flowing avalanche in Colorado. The dust cloud is about 40 m high, but the dense flowing core would probably be less than 5 m. (Photos by Cleveland)

that of air at the appropriate pressure and temperature. The density of air is only about 10% of that in the snow/dust mixture in the dust cloud so that the destructive potential from air blast is expected to be less than from a powder avalanche. Air blast is relatively rare overall, but it is known to be associated with some regularity on certain avalanche paths. One theory proposed is that air blast occurs as a pressure wave generated when free-falling (airborne) avalanche debris strikes the ground to compress air underneath, which then moves ahead of the debris. This hypothesis has not been verified with any measurements, however. Another idea is that some

Figure 5.29. Release of dry slab avalanche by explosive and subsequent motion in Whistler, British Columbia. The dust cloud is very small in this case, showing the character of granular flow. (Photos by T. Salway)

avalanches behave like oceanic "turbidity currents"—pressure falls off in a logarithmic manner with distance in advance of the head. Since the concentration of snow particles in a powder cloud is only about 1%, any deposit from a powder avalanche may not be obvious at first glance since it will settle out as "dust." Therefore, it is possible that damage due to powder avalanches has been mistaken for air blast damage in some cases.

Wet Snow in Motion

The descriptive features for the beginning of wet snow motion are similar to that for dry snow. However, no dust cloud of suspended material forms (Figure 5.29).

Wet snow in motion can result from either wet slab or wet loose avalanche release. The important characteristic of wet snow motion, which distinguishes it from dry snow, is much higher friction at the sliding surface. This causes the speed of wet snow avalanches to be less than that of dry snow for equivalent mass and fall height. Usually, the sliding surface is also wet during wet avalanche release. Evidence of the higher motion friction is that wet flowing material often plows into the soft sliding surface, causing scoring or the formation of grooves and entrainment of rocks, dirt, and other material (Figure 5.30).

The high friction during wet snow motion is often enough to significantly alter the path the debris follows down the mountainside. Wet snow will follow terrain features much more readily than dry snow. Therefore, it it is easier to divert wet flowing snow and stop it using defenses.

SCALE AND SIZE

The size (mass) of snow avalanches depends on the amount of snow that releases initially in the starting zone, plus the amount entrained (picked up) or deposited during downslope motion. The initial release volume depends on the size and steepness of the starting zone, the thickness of the slab, and the mechanical properties of the snow there. Usually, initial snow volume decreases as steepness increases and starting zone

Figure 5.30. Wet flowing snow off Avalanche Crest, Rogers Pass, British Columbia. (Photo by B. Engler)

size decreases. Studies from long-term records show that the maximum mass measured in runout zone deposits at the end of the winter is about 30% of the maximum possible amount of snow that *could* collect in the starting zone given the snowfall for that winter.

The mechanical properties of snow also affect the size of an avalanche. As snow hardness increases, the chances of larger widespread fractures increase. However, with harder snow the chance of entrainment of snow during downhill motion decreases because the snow tends to remain in blocks rather than in a loose, granular form. Moisture content also plays a role: Loose, dry snow is picked up easier than wet snow. However, wet snow has higher friction with the ground than dry snow. Therefore, it has a tendency to scour the surface of the snow as it passes to entrain snow.

The mass of snow avalanches varies from small amounts occurring as a result of sluffs to deep slabs with

long continuous fracture lines up to about one million tonnes (order of magnitude). Figure 5.31 shows a mass-frequency distribution for more than 6,000 large avalanches measured at Rogers Pass, British Columbia (sluffs were excluded). Many of the avalanches were initiated by artillery so that the frequency of very large avalanches is small. The mass is one element of classifying sizes of avalanches. There is, however, no accepted international system for classifying avalanche sizes. The systems used in several countries are discussed in Appendix D.

Avalanche speed is another variable that varies with the scale of avalanches; it varies with both mass and distance traveled down a mountainside. In a first approximation, the *maximum* speed reached by avalanches depends on (1) initial mass of snow and the amount entrained or deposited along the incline, (2) the external friction at the top and bottom of the avalanche, and (3) the scale (length, vertical drop) and possibly steepness of the path.

An example of the effect of scale of the path is shown in Figure 5.32, in which measurements of maximum speed of flowing avalanches (both wet and dry) are scaled with the square root of the total vertical drop, H.

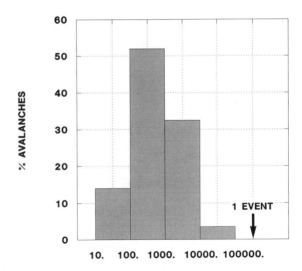

Figure 5.31. Mass distribution for 6,000 avalanches measured at Rogers Pass, British Columbia. Most of the events were controlled by gunfire, which eliminated very large avalanches and reduced the mean size.

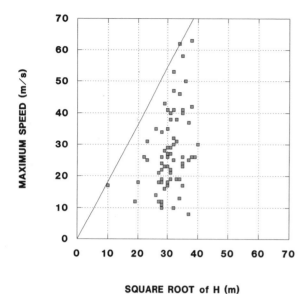

Figure 5.32. Maximum speed in the middle (track) of avalanche paths scaled with the square root of total vertical drop H. Measurements from Rogers Pass, British Columbia.

The figure shows that an *upper limit envelope* is given by approximately $v_m = 1.8\sqrt{H}$, with H given in meters. For example, if H = 1,000 m, maximum speed is predicted to be about 60 m/s, whereas if H = 500 m, the upper envelope touches 40 m/s.

It is also expected that avalanche speeds are higher when the flow is confined to gullies than for open slope flows. Since the same amount of material per second is forced through a confined space when an avalanche is in a gully, the speed must increase. Also, speeds are higher at the center of a gully than at the sides (due to side friction).

IMPACT FORCES

Buildings and other structures in mountainous terrain are occasionally hit by avalanches and it is routine for engineers to consider potential impact forces in design (see Figures 5.33 through 5.36). Impact forces range from relatively harmless blasts from powder clouds to the high destructive forces of a full-scale dry flowing avalanche capable of destroying reinforced concrete structures. Generally, dry flowing avalanches with their combination of high flow density and speed are considered the most destructive. However, any avalanche that produces a combination of high density and speed will

have great destructive potential. There are no impact measurements of slush avalanches, but they are known to have debris densities in excess of 900 kg/m³. Slush avalanches have been clocked at speeds of 30 m/s so that the destructive potential rivals that expected for the largest dry snow avalanches (Figure 5.37).

Impact forces due to moving snow are proportional to the avalanche speed squared, v^2, and the flow density of the moving material, ρ. Flowing snow is a mixture of snowballs (ice and air), snow crystals, and air. The

Figure 5.33. Highway guardrail destroyed by powder component of flow. Note the avalanche deposit in the background. (Photo by A. Dennis)

Figure 5.34. Wood-frame structure destroyed by impact force. (Photo by T. Auger)

Figure 5.35. Steel beams on a bridge bent by impact from an avalanche. (Photo by M. Martinelli)

Figure 5.36. Train derailed by avalanche. (Photo by D. Fesler)

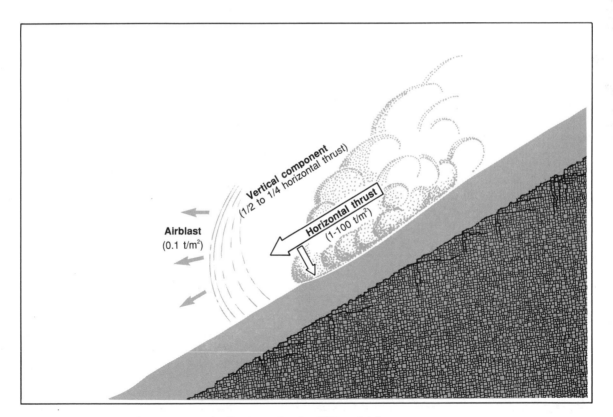

Figure 5.37. Schematic of pressures in a dry flowing avalanche, 10kPa ≈ 1t/m².

density of the mixture depends on the concentration of solid material, C: percent of the volume filled by snow and ice particles, the density of the snowballs and particles, ρ_S, and the density of the air between the snowballs, ρ_A:

$$\rho = \rho_S C + \rho_A (1 - C)$$

where $\rho_A \approx 1$ kg/m^3 and ρ_S is typically from 200 to 917 kg/m^3 (snow crystals). For the powder component $C \approx 0.01$ (1%), $\rho_S = 917$ kg/m^3 so that $\rho \approx 10$ kg/m^3. For flowing snow (wet or dry) it is estimated that $C \approx 0.30$ to 0.50 (30% to 50%) and ρ_S (measured from deposits) ranges from 200 kg/m^3 (dry) to 550 kg/m^3 (wet or dry). (See Table 5.5 later in this chapter.) With the expression above for the density, the impact pressure due to flowing snow may be estimated by dimensional analysis:

$$I \approx \rho v^2$$

Table 5.3 gives typical impact pressures expected for avalanches in relation to destructive effects. Figure 5.38 shows typical impact pressures measured in dry and wet flowing avalanches and a powder avalanche. Note that for the latter, the speed is highest but the impact pressures are, on average, lower than the more massive flowing avalanches. Usually, dry flowing avalanches have the highest product of speed squared and flow density so their destructive potential is highest. From data, peak pressures are found to be two to five times higher than average pressures in avalanche impact.

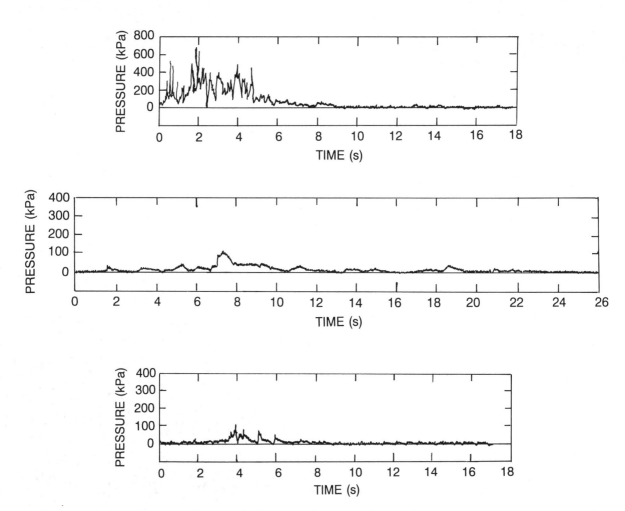

Figure 5.38. Impact pressure records. Top: A dry flowing avalanche; middle: a wet flowing avalanche; and bottom: a powder avalanche. Measurements from Rogers Pass, British Columbia.

Table 5.3 Correlation Between Impact Pressure and Potential Damage

Impact Pressure (kPa)	Potential Damage
1	Break windows
5	Push in doors
30	Destroy wood-frame structures
100	Uproot mature spruce
1000	Move reinforced-concrete structures

Impact data show that the highest forces come near the avalanche front, usually within the first one or two seconds of impact. In engineering design problems, this implies that peak pressure avalanche loads must be treated as a rather sharp impulse load. In some avalanches there are several distinct waves that contain high-pressure impulses.

Approximate impact pressures can sometimes be estimated from studies of objects that have been broken or moved by avalanches. The most common case is analysis of trees broken or damaged by avalanches. The lower limit of impact force is provided by evidence of study of trees that have failed by high bending stresses, and the upper limit is given by evidence of trees that have resisted the forces. Laboratory tests of the strengths of objects similar to those broken on structures are also performed by duplicating the expected loading conditions as closely as possible to estimate impact forces (Figure 5.39).

In addition to direct impact, when they fall into fjords or open lakes, avalanches have been known to cause disruptive wave action and kill fish. Engineers in Norway and Switzerland have developed methods to calculate wave height for expected avalanche volume and speed (Figure 5.40). It is estimated that 50% of the kinetic energy of an avalanche can be converted into wave energy.

DEBRIS RECOGNITION AND DESCRIPTION

The characteristics of debris in avalanche deposits depend on the hardness and moisture content (dry, moist, or wet) of the snow that originally released, the hardness of snow in the track, and the total distance the avalanche traveled. A hard slab usually has large chunks of debris in the deposit (Figures 5.41a and b), whereas a soft slab (Figure 5.41c) breaks up into smaller pieces

Figure 5.39. Extensive damage to a forest by an avalanche. (Photo by H. Frutiger)

Figure 5.40. Avalanche debris that has struck a lake. Dangerous waves are possible in such cases. (Photo by P. Anhorn)

Figure 5.41. Debris from top left: hard slab (Photo by P. Schaerer); top right: hard slab (Photo by D. Fesler); bottom left: soft slab (Photo by P. Schaerer); and bottom right: wet avalanches. (Photo by A. Roch)

114

Table 5.4 Typical Deposit Densities

Small dry avalanche	200 kg/m³
Medium to large dry avalanche	300–400 kg/m³
Wet avalanche	500–600 kg/m³
High-speed dry avalanche	500 kg/m³
Slush flow	Up to 1,000 kg/m³

Table 5.5 Typical Flow Densities and Percent Solid Concentration*

	Flow Density	Concentration of Solid Material
Air blast	1 kg/m³	0%
Powder	10 kg/m³	1%
Dry flowing	100–150 kg/m³	30–50%
Wet flowing	150–200 kg/m³	30–50%

*Derived from impact pressure measurements (McClung and Schaerer, 1985).

or balls. In general, the further the avalanche travels, the smaller the particles in the deposit. Snow from dry avalanches is often mistaken for that from moist or wet snow avalanches because it can become moist or wet due to frictional rubbing of particles during descent in the runout zone. In general, the friction at the bottom of a dry avalanche is low so that during motion it may be difficult to hear an avalanche coming. Also, dry avalanches tend to travel in straight lines rather than being deflected by terrain features such as gullies (as wet avalanches are) (Figure 5.41d). Another persistent feature of debris in dry snow deposits is that the average size of the particles decreases with depth into the deposit. This observation indicates that the grinding action that breaks up the particles becomes more intense closer to the (sliding) surface over which the avalanche runs. Also, smaller particles will tend to "percolate" to the bottom by gravitational forces by falling through the air spaces between particles during the motion. In large dry avalanches, the particles are nearly all small for more than half the deposit depth above the bottom.

Debris from wet snow avalanches may generally be characterized as hard and it may become icelike if the water on the surface freezes. Usually the individual particles are large in wet debris with snow "boulders" up to 0.5 m in diameter or larger present in some cases. Since the bottom friction is high, it is often possible to hear wet avalanches during descent. They frequently create grooves or score the surface while passing the lower portion of the track or runout zone.

The snow density in avalanche deposits is usually higher than that in the starting zone (Tables 5.4 and 5.5).

Deposit snow may be up to twice as dense as starting zone snow in the case of a high-speed dry snow avalanche. Sometimes, however, the density of debris particles does not differ from that in the initial slab (for example, in the case of a small dry hard slab that has not run far). Field measurements show that the density of avalanche deposits increases with depth. This is due to the fact that the particles get smaller with depth: They are more efficiently packed and therefore less air is available between particles. This may be a major factor in determining the survival rate of deeply buried victims in avalanche deposits (see Chapter 8). Not only does the overburden increase with depth due to the weight of snow above, but the air available per unit volume decreases with depth.

RUNOUT DISTANCES

The runout distance of an avalanche is defined by the point of furthest reach of the debris. Specification of runout distances is a key parameter for land-use planning in avalanche-threatened areas. The best policy, overall, is to avoid areas with avalanche hazards, but when structures or highways must be built in these areas, it is of vital interest to know the potential stopping distance of avalanches.

The best methods of determining runout distances are (1) long-term observations of avalanche deposits; (2) observations of damage to vegetation, ground, or structures; or (3) searches of the historical record as preserved in newspapers, old aerial photos, or other written material. Such information allows one to avoid using models of avalanche flows, which contain risky assumptions.

Unfortunately, in many areas of the world, particularly North America, the historical record of avalanche runout is not long enough. It may be completely absent or invisible when areas of interest are disturbed by human activity such as logging. In such cases, models must be used if an answer is required.

Modern runout prediction can be divided into two approaches—the conventional method or statistical prediction. The conventional method involves selecting friction coefficients as input to a speed model to calculate the speed of the avalanche all along the incline. When the speed reaches zero, the runout position is defined. Statistical prediction of extreme runout is based on terrain variables for a given path. A collection of runout distances for the mountain range in question is required to fit the measurements to a probability distribution or to formulate a regression equation to predict the runout position as a function of terrain variables.

Both of those methods are currently used by consultants to estimate runout distances. However, both methods have disadvantages. The principal disadvantage of using a conventional dynamics model to predict runout is that the mechanical properties of flowing snow (which the models are supposed to simulate) are largely unknown. Therefore, this method involves some speculation (called engineering judgment by some). Dynamics modeling has always been a very active research area. The recognition that flowing avalanche description requires application of the mechanics of dense granular flows provides great prospects for future prediction of speeds and runout.

The statistical approach provides direct quantitative interpretation of runout distances based on the historical record of avalanche runout in a given mountain range and therefore it is on a much better practical foundation. However, its application requires a data set of runout distances for each mountain range of interest (at least 30 data points are recommended). The precision of the method is not as good as is required in many applications, but the uncertainty can be specified in standard statistical terms.

When using terrain variables it is now common to quantify extreme runout distances using an angle α, which is defined by sighting from the extreme runout position to the top of the starting zone using a clinometer or map (Figure 5.42). Values of α for extreme runout vary from about 15° to 50° in most avalanche terrain. However, the mean value and standard deviation of α is

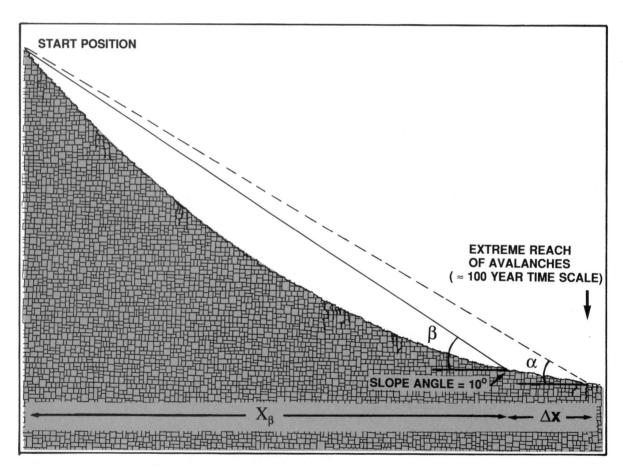

Figure 5.42. Definition of terrain variables for calculation of avalanche runout. Distance measures Δx and X_β are defined.

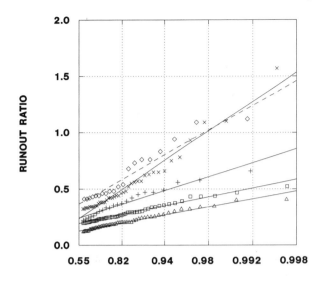

Figure 5.43. Runout ratio fitted to extreme value probability distribution for 500 avalanche paths from five different mountain ranges. The probability is the fraction of runout distances that will not exceed the given value of runout ratio for the mountain range in question. (◊) Sierra Nevada, (x) Colorado Rockies, (+) coastal Alaska, (▢) western Norway, (Δ) Canadian Rockies. (U.S. and Norwegian data courtesy of A. Mears and K. Lied)

proportional to β. Since the reference point β can be found on any avalanche path, it then becomes possible to define a regression equation to calculate α and, hence, the runout position is defined.

It has also been found that extreme runout fits an extreme value probability distribution similar to water discharge from floods. This is shown in Figure 5.43 by plotting a nondimensional runout ratio versus probability of avalanches not exceeding a given point on a path (nonexceedance probability). [The runout ratio is the horizontal runout distance marked from β divided by the horizontal reach from the start position to β ($\Delta x/X_\beta$) Figure 5.42 gives definitions of Δx and X_β.] Such studies are useful in practice for estimating the probability of a given position being overrun and for comparing data from different ranges.

When determining runout distances, it is important to use clues from all the various methods available when making a decision. In almost all cases, various methods are combined before a final decision is made. Any observable clues at the site are almost always given priority over theoretical models due to the complexity of the problem and implied uncertainty in statistical models. Important clues include those from damaged vegetation or analysis of aerial photos (best) or satellite imagery (usually inferior to aerial photos). Precision topographic (large-scale) maps are also highly prized for avalanche runout mapping. When using maps to determine or map avalanche runout, map accuracy must

different for each range of mountains due to variations in terrain. Therefore, individual ranges have runout distances that differ greatly.

The most common method of calculating α for a path on which it is unknown is to relate it statistically to the steepness of the path from a data set of terrain parameters collected from other avalanche paths in the mountain range. A companion angle β is usually defined from the position at which the slope angle first reaches 10° when proceeding downslope from the starting zone. The parameter β is then a measure of path steepness. From this position, β may be determined using a high-quality map or by sighting with a clinometer to the start position of the avalanche path. The reference slope angle of 10° comes from mathematical analysis and worldwide experience that large avalanches in typical mountain terrain generally stop at slope angles near or below 10° when avalanches are dated back about 100 years. In a number of ranges it has been found that α is directly

Figure 5.44. Steep avalanche paths showing evidence of high frequency of avalanching. (Photo by P. Anhorn)

be carefully judged against the accuracy with which the parameters are known. Normally, maps of scale 1:50,000 or smaller are not accurate enough to determine slope angles, for example.

One method for dealing with the complex problem of determining both runout distances and speed prediction is to solve the problem in two parts. First the runout distance is determined by field evidence or a statistical method. Once the runout distance is specified, the entire path geometry is defined so that the dynamics problem is more manageable. This method is gaining popularity.

RETURN PERIOD OF AVALANCHES

Another parameter of high interest in avalanche land-use planning is the return period for which avalanches will reach selected locations. It is essential to know the return period (or frequency) in order to be able to estimate the chance that avalanches will strike a position in a specified period of time (called the *encounter probability*). It is common in engineering practice to relate the acceptable risk for facilities to the avalanche return period (see Chapter 9 for details).

The frequency can vary from several times per year to as low as once per 300 years or even lower (Figure 5.44). Also, the frequency of avalanching may be high in the upper portion of the path, but it generally decreases lower down in the runout zone. In avalanche work, the return period is the average interval of time within which the runout distance is reached at a given location. The frequency is the reciprocal of the return period. Therefore, it is possible, in principle, to produce a mapping of return periods in the runout zone corresponding to different locations proceeding downslope; for example, 1 year, 10 years, 100 years corresponding to average yearly probabilities of 1, 0.1, 0.01. These locations increase with distance into the runout zone as the return period increases.

The encounter probability E is the probability that avalanches return to a given location at least once during a period of observation. It can be calculated from the return period T in years and the length L of time of interest in years (length of exposure to risk or of observation time). Since avalanche events in each year are statistically independent of those in previous years, E is given by (LaChapelle, 1966; Mears, 1992):

$$E = 1 - [1 - (1/T)]^L$$

From this equation, if $L = T$ (observation period = return period), the probability of encountering an ava-

lanche at the location is about 0.65. If $L = 2T$, the encounter probability is near 0.90. For example, if the expected return period is 100 years, then 200 years of careful observations would be required to be 90% confident that the 100-year avalanche has been recorded (100 years for 65% confidence). This simple analysis shows why long-term observations cannot yet be used with high confidence to specify long return period events in North America.

In general, frequency depends on (1) starting zone characteristics (slope angle, aspect, elevation, ground roughness, size, and shape); (2) climate characteristics (maritime, continental, or transitional); (3) latitude; and (4) state of vegetation patterns, ground roughness, and path confinement characteristics in the track and runout zone.

The determination of return periods may be made by three methods in order of accuracy: (1) by direct, long-term observations of avalanche runout; (2) by examination of vegetation or other datable destructive effects in the runout zone; or (3) by examination of climate records and then comparison of these records with frequencies from known avalanche paths in other areas with similar terrain, aspect, and climate. Methods 2 and 3 are discussed below.

AVALANCHE FREQUENCY FROM VEGETATIVE CLUES

If direct observations of avalanche frequency are not available, the next best method of determining frequency is by examination of vegetation in the runout zone (preferably during the snow-free period). By counting annual tree rings from cores, the ages of trees may be determined. In this way it is possible to produce a map of avalanche return periods for a given path in the runout zone (Figure 5.45).

When avalanches occur more frequently than once in 10 years the coring method is not considered as easy to interpret and the heights of the vegetation (shrubs, willows, and small trees) may provide the simplest clues about frequency. At sites where the avalanche frequency is high, the trees are destroyed whenever they reach a critical age and height. This results in growth of small trees with varying age. However, the heights are also related to the length of the growing season (altitude, latitude, and snow cover depth) so the accuracy may not be good enough for practical applications when height is used as a sole indicator.

In general, determination of frequencies is no simple

Figure 5.45. Trimlines of forest showing different frequency of avalanching as a function of runout distance and width. The forest was also damaged by fire. (Photo by H. Frutiger)

Figure 5.46. Scar on tree trunk in avalanche path. (Photo by D. McClung)

matter. A number of methods (used in combination) may be needed to obtain estimates. The following criteria can be used to infer magnitude, frequency, and extent of avalanches on selected tracks from examination of vegetation:

Time of Appearance of Reaction Wood

If a tree growing vertically is pushed over by an avalanche, but not killed, a specialized type of wood called *reaction wood* is produced abruptly in the following growing season. Sawed cross sections from trees are the best source of this information because reaction wood can be examined in combination with growth ring widths on all sides of the tree. In conifers, reaction wood is formed on the lower side of leaning trunks and is called *compression wood*. In deciduous trees, it is formed on the upper side and is called *tension wood*. Trees can also be tilted by snow creep and other forces of nature, but by taking several samples, these other possibilities can often be eliminated.

Datable Scars on Trees

Cross sections of trees can be used to determine the year in which a tree was scarred. If a scar is visible externally, a slice of wood may be cut such that it includes the scar and the wood produced since scarring. Since falling rocks and fires can also produce scarring, the cause of scarring must be investigated (Figure 5.46).

Datable Breakage

Avalanches are often responsible for breaking the main stems of trees. On conifers, a lateral branch may begin to grow vertically and become the new leader, so that the number of growth rings in the new leader will give a rough indication of the minimum number of years since the break.

Figure 5.47. Sawed cross section showing datable scar and reaction wood on a tree struck by avalanches. (Photo by O. Niemann)

Abrupt Changes in Growth Patterns

Avalanche activity can directly or indirectly account for differences in growth patterns between trees growing on avalanche tracks and trees growing outside trimlines. Sawed cross sections are the most reliable source of growth rate information (Figure 5.47).

Age of Debris

The growth ring pattern of dead trees may be compared with the growth ring pattern of live trees of the same species growing nearby. The additional rings in live trees indicate the number of years since the tree was killed.

Reforested Areas of an Avalanche Track

Vegetation characteristics such as species composition, community structure, age distribution, and damage patterns can provide information on avalanche frequency (Figures 5.48 and 5.49).

Of these six methods, the first two are the most reliable. The other four involve more variables and assumptions. When possible, several methods should be used as a cross-check to get as consistent a picture as possible. In general, proper use of vegetation clues for determining avalanche frequency is complex, time con-

Figure 5.48. Trees of pioneer species indicating possible high frequency of avalanching. Broken trees are aligned in the direction of flow.

suming, and not very precise. However, it may be the only method available in many instances. Table 5.6 provides some examples. Remember also that not all avalanches damage vegetation. Sometimes the snowpack covers small shrubs and trees to prevent damage. Avalanche paths at high latitudes or altitudes may not have vegetation.

Table 5.6 Examples of Vegetation as an Indicator of Avalanche Frequency

Frequency—At Least One Large Avalanche in an Interval of:	Vegetation Clues
1–2 years	Alder and willow, bare patches, and shrubs No trees higher than about 1 to 2 m
3–10 years	No large trees and no dead wood from large trees Presence of trees higher than 1 to 2 m
10–30 years	Dense growth of small trees; Young trees of climax species (e.g., conifers) Increment core data useful
25–100 years	Mature trees of pioneer species (e.g., nonconiferous) Young trees of climax species. Increment core data useful
More than 100 years	Mature trees of climax species Increment core data useful

Figure 5.49. Branches stripped from uphill side of tree. (Photo by David McClung)

INFLUENCE OF CLIMATE AND TERRAIN

Avalanche frequency is determined by both climate and terrain. The major influences from climate are magnitude, frequency, and rate of snowfalls; air temperature; and wind speed and direction (see Chapter 7). Terrain can also influence avalanche frequency, but climate must always be considered for a complete picture of avalanche frequency with terrain features a secondary effect.

Prediction of major avalanches is not entirely related to the probability of major storms. Major avalanches occur only during the coincidence of the correct combination of weather and snowpack conditions for release of large slabs that have the flow characteristics to run long distances (Mears, 1992). This coincidence of conditions may only be met locally on a small percentage of paths in an area even during an extremely large snowstorm. Field observations show that mechanical properties of flowing snow and the sliding surface can be more important than the mass of avalanches for producing long runout distances for rare events.

In general, the historical record is more reliable for determining the frequency of avalanches in high snow-

fall areas than in low snowfall areas. If an area is subject to frequent large snowstorms, large avalanches will occur more frequently giving greater confidence in the observations. In low snowfall areas, a short observation period may not include major avalanches and the difference between the 10-year and the 100-year avalanche may be great. For low snowfall areas, other methods (such as vegetative clues) must be used more often to estimate major avalanche potential.

The principal terrain factors contributing to avalanche frequency include slope incline of the track, shape of the track, ruggedness of the track, vegetative cover, exposure to the wind and sun, and starting zone size and steepness. Evidence appears to show that the frequency of occurrence of large avalanches increases with the average slope angle of the track. Figure 5.50 illustrates a study which showed that frequency is higher for avalanches with channeled tracks than for open slope tracks for a given average track incline (in the area of Rogers Pass, British Columbia). The other terrain factors influencing avalanche frequency are important, but they have not yet been quantified.

An often used, important method for estimating the return period of avalanches is that of examining climate records and then using avalanche frequencies determined on paths with similar terrain, aspect, and climate

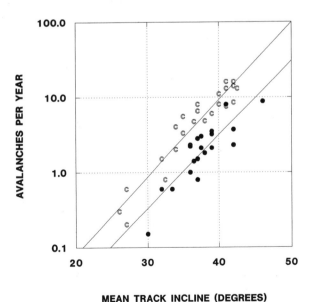

Figure 5.50. Avalanche frequency for channeled (C) and open slope (•) paths as a function of average track incline in degrees.

from another area. This method is important in areas where long-term avalanche runout data are nonexistent or where clues from vegetation cannot be used (disturbed areas or those above the timber line). However, the method has a high uncertainty because of the problem of extrapolating data from one area to another.

HYDROLOGICAL ASPECTS OF SNOW AVALANCHES

Snow avalanches can affect the hydrology of glacierized basins and mountainous basins in general. Avalanches add mass to glaciers (significantly in some cases) and their effect on damming rivers can be significant. When avalanches transport snow from the tops of mountains to the valleys below, the timing of snowmelt can be affected. The net effect can be either acceleration of snowmelt or a retardation (depending on the circumstances), and the peak discharge can be altered.

The maximum annual yield M_0 (mass in kilograms) of an avalanche path that collects in the runout zone may be calculated from

$$M_0 = fAS$$

Here f is a fraction between 0 and 1 (determined by mathematical analysis) of the total that could potentially collect (0.10 as a rule of thumb). The total area of the starting zone (in square meters) is given by A, and S is the maximum water equivalent of snow statistically determined (in millimeters) for an entire winter appropriate to the average time period in question, for example, 10, 50, 100, or 300 years. When f is determined for avalanche paths in a basin, the total mass of snow moved by avalanches in the basin is estimated as the product of f, the basin area affected by the avalanche activity, and the total water equivalent of the snow. Estimates of snowmelt runoff from avalanching range from 2% to 34% of total snowmelt in mountainous basins and from 3% to 11% of total runoff in actual field examples. Examples have been recorded with great variability in these figures during severe winters. Percentages can increase by a factor of three in a severe winter over normal or minimum estimates.

When snow is transported to the valley bottoms from near the tops of mountains, it lands in a generally warmer environment than that from which it came, due to the effect of the atmospheric temperature lapse rate. This causes faster melt than would have occurred if avalanching had not taken place. Another factor that can

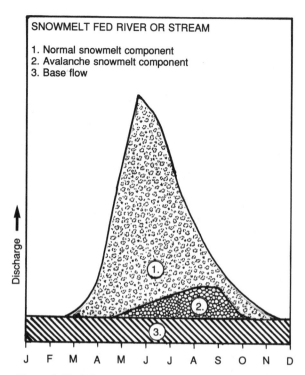

Figure 5.51. Schematic of stream flow influenced by avalanche debris. Both the timing and value of peak discharge are influenced.

accelerate or delay melt is color on the surface of an avalanche deposit. Avalanches sometimes entrain dirt or rocks during descent; also snowmelt causes dirt to collect at the snow surface as the snow in the deposit melts. Because a dark surface absorbs a greater percentage of incoming solar radiation, melt may be accelerated in a deposit. If the foreign material on the surface is thick enough (about 20 mm), it can provide shading to retard melt.

Two effects that can retard melt in avalanche deposits compared to melt from an undisturbed snowpack are caused by the transport of the snow: (1) Because snow in avalanche deposits is more dense than nonavalanche snow (typically one-third more), melt can be slow. (2) The effective surface area in an avalanche deposit is generally much less than it was in the initial undisturbed slab. Avalanche deposits are generally much deeper on average than the initial slab. Since snowmelt takes place mostly by surface processes, snow in an avalanche deposit melts much more slowly than undisturbed snow. Field observations show that thin arms of avalanche deposits melt quickly. Deep deposits melt slower since most snow underneath is shielded from the sun. Both increased density and depth in a deposit combine to slow snowmelt in avalanche-fed basins (Figure 5.51). Snowmelt from avalanching can affect both the timing and overall magnitude of runoff in a very significant manner in basins for which the density of avalanche paths is high during severe winters. Hydrologists seeking precision in runoff forecasts will have to consider avalanche snow in some instances to predict the timing and magnitude of runoff.

References

Burrows, C. J., and V. L. Burrows. 1976. Procedures for the study of snow avalanche chronology using growth layers of woody plants. Boulder, CO: Institute of Arctic and Alpine Research, University of Colorado, Occasional Paper no. 23, 54 pp.

International Commission on Snow and Ice. 1981. *Avalanche Atlas. Illustrated Avalanche Classification.* Paris: UNESCO, 265 pp.

International Union of Forestry Research Organizations. 1979. *Mountain Forests and Avalanches: Proceedings of the Davos Seminar*, September 1978. Davos, Switzerland: Swiss Federal Institute for Snow and Avalanche Research, 358 pp.

LaChapelle, E. R. 1966. Encounter probabilities for avalanche damage. USDA Forest Service Miscellaneous Report 10. Alta, UT: Alta Avalanche Study Center, Wasatch National Forest, 10 pp.

Martinelli, M. 1974. Snow avalanche sites—their identification, and evaluation. Agriculture Information Bulletin 360. Washington, DC: U.S. Department of Agriculture Forest Service, 26 pp.

McClung, D. M. 1990. A model for scaling avalanche speeds. *Journal of Glaciology* 36(123): 188–198.

McClung, D. M. 1990. Hydrologic effects of avalanches. *Cold Regions Hydrology and Hydraulics*, Technical Council on Cold Regions Engineering Monograph. New York: American Society of Civil Engineers, pp. 164–176.

McClung, D. M., and A. Mears. 1991. Extreme value prediction of snow avalanche runout. *Cold Regions Science and Technology* 19: 163–175.

McClung, D. M., and P. A. Schaerer. 1981. Snow avalanche size classification. *Proceedings of Avalanche Workshop,* Vancouver, British Columbia, November 3–5, 1980. Associate Committee on Geotechnical Research Technical Memo 133. Ottawa: National Research Council of Canada, pp. 12–27.

McClung, D. M., and P. A. Schaerer. 1985. Characteristics of flowing snow and avalanche impact pressures. *Annals of Glaciology* 6: 9–14.

Mears, A. I. 1992. Snow-avalanche hazard analysis for land-use planning and engineering. Bulletin 40. Denver: Colorado Geological Survey, Department of Natural Resources, 54 pp.

National Research Council Canada. 1989. Hydrology of floods in Canada: A guide to planning and design. Ottawa, Canada: Associate Committee on Hydrology, 245 pp.

Perla, R., T. T. Cheng, and D. M. McClung. 1980. A two parameter model of snow avalanche motion. *Journal of Glaciology* 26(94): 197–207.

Salm, B., and H. Gubler. 1985. Measurement and analysis of the motion of dense flow avalanches. *Annals of Glaciology* 6: 26–34.

Schaerer, P. A. 1972. Terrain and vegetation of snow avalanche sites at Rogers Pass, British Columbia. *Mountain Geomorphology: Geographical Processes in the Canadian Cordillera.*, B.C. Geographical Series No. 14, pp. 215–222.

Schaerer, P. A. 1988. The yield of avalanche snow at Rogers Pass, British Columbia, Canada. *Journal of Glaciology* 34(117): 188–193.

Smith, Laura. 1973. Identification of snow avalanche periodicity through interpretation of vegetative patterns in the North Cascades, Washington. *Methods of avalanche control on Washington mountain highways—Third Annual Report*, Seattle, WA: Washington State Department of Highways, pp. 55–99.

CHAPTER 6

AVALANCHE PREDICTION I:
ELEMENTS OF STABILITY EVALUATION
AND SNOWPACK OBSERVATIONS

Most adventures are a sign of incompetence.

—Vilhjalmur Stefansson

METHOD OF STABILITY EVALUATION

Stability evaluation is the process of determining whether avalanches can start given the current snow conditions. It is an essential element of avalanche prediction. Snow with good stability can support additional load without failing. Snow with poor stability has little reserve; avalanche initiation can occur with a small additional load. Avalanche hazards do not exist when the snow is stable; therefore, snow stability is a key to avalanche hazard evaluation.

Snow stability evaluation involves the collection and analysis of a combination of factors. In this chapter, directly relevant factors are described along with snowpack measurements that are important for snow stability work. This chapter provides the necessary background information for Chapter 7, which describes avalanche forecasting. Stability *evaluation* largely refers to assessment of present conditions, whereas *forecasting* refers to both current and future prediction. In practice, stability evaluation and forecasting are not usually separated.

Stability is defined as the ratio of the resistance to failure versus the forces acting toward a failure. Failure occurs and avalanche initiation is possible when the combined forces from the downslope (slope parallel) weight of snow (shear force) and triggers equal or

exceed the shear strength of snow. Snow stability has two aspects:

- *Loose snow avalanche formation:* Gravity forces on the snow grains and the friction between grains determine the stability of snow with low cohesion.
- *Slab avalanche formation:* This is found from the relationship between shear strength in a weak layer (or the bond between layers) and the shear stresses on that weakness. The discussion below is targeted for snow slab stability unless otherwise stated.

The best method of stability evaluation is to load the snow in an avalanche starting zone until the snow fails, for example, by test skiing or application of explosive charges. Unfortunately, difficult and hazardous access to most starting zones and limited time restrict this type of destructive testing to relatively short and accessible slopes. Strong variations in snow properties (and stability) across slopes are an additional difficulty. It is impossible to test all starting zones or to find the most critical spots for testing. Because stability usually needs to be evaluated for a variety of slopes, there is always residual uncertainty.

Since direct slope testing is normally limited, more indirect factors must usually be relied on to assess stability. These factors include snowpack and weather elements. Knowledge of snowpack physics, terrain, and empirical relationships is used to analyze the factors and correlate them with snow stability. The quality of the snow stability evaluation depends on the quality of data used and the reliability of correlations between the factors.

In conclusion, stability is evaluated by collecting information about relevant factors and by analyzing the information with respect to stability.

NATURE OF FACTORS

All data about snow stablity are potentially useful, but some are more relevant than others. The usefulness is related to the data's relevance to slab failure and ease of interpretation. Ease of interpretation depends on the number of alternatives a given datum has associated with it. A yes/no report of avalanche occurrence has two alternatives; it is easy to interpret and directly relevant. On the other hand, a wind velocity report has many possible values and is more difficult to interpret.

The factors used to interpret snow stability may be roughly stratified into three classes based on their ease of interpretation and relevance for assessing snow stability. The higher the class number, the more uncertain the interpretation and the less direct the evidence. The following fairly general chain of causes exists:

Class III: Meteorological Factors
(precipitation, wind, temperature, radiation by sun)
↓
Class II: Snowpack Factors
(snowpack weaknesses and loads on them)
↓
Class I: Stability Factors
(relationship between downslope load on
a weakness and strength)
↓
Avalanches

Class I: Stability Factors

This class deals with the direct relationship between loads on weak layers. The snowpack has been deformed (by nature, humans, or explosives). Information on how the loads and weak layer are related (interact) and the potential for fracture propagation is sought. The data are relevant to current stability.

Examples of Class I data are current avalanches,

Figure 6.1. Slab release by skier. The fracture line at the upper right indicates high instability—an extremely important indicator. (Photo by R. Ludwig)

loading tests (by skiing, explosives, slope stability tests), and fracture propagation and cracking of the snow cover (Figures 6.1 and 6.2).

Class II: Snowpack Factors

This class provides evidence about presence, strength, and loading of weak layers. Information is sought from within the snow cover. The information is fairly relevant but it is less directly related to snow stability than are Class I factors.

Because the snowpack and weak layer have not been deformed together or directly related, the stability is usually not directly tested. The data allow analysis of snowpack structure and its influence on stability. Examples of Class II data are snowpack depth; previous slope use; past avalanches; and snowpack structure, such as hardness, texture, layering, crystal forms (size and shape), and free water content. Also included in Class II are depth and hardness of snow above weak layers; snow temperature; penetrability; and the snowpack deformation indexes of acoustic signals and glide speed.

Figure 6.2. Slab release by explosives indicates obvious instability. (Photo by A. Dennis)

Class III: Meteorological Factors

This class provides indirect evidence about current or future snow stability or weaknesses. The data are usually collected at or above the snow surface. They can be used to develop conclusions about the presence, strength, and loading of weak layers and are often correlated directly with snow stability through empirically developed relationships. The data are used for predicting both current and future stability. Discussion of Class III factors is reserved for Chapter 7.

Examples of Class III factors include amount of new snow, wind speed, wind direction, air temperature, solar radiation, humidity, and the condition of the snow surface. Weather forecasts (including freezing levels and precipitation amounts and type) are included in Class III, as are blowing snow activity, precipitation intensity, and snow settlement.

The nature of the factors is diverse. Information about some of them is collected with instruments and rulers (for example, wind speed, depth of snowfall, snow temperature, and shear strength of weak layers). Subjective classifications are applied to numerous oth-ers (for example, quality of bonding and fracture propagation potential in weak layers, results of ski testing). Most factors are not directly observed in starting zones; instead they are determined at safe, convenient locations that yield relevant index information.

DATA COLLECTION

How Much Information Is Needed?

An abundance of information is needed to compensate for uncertainties. Uncertainties exist for the following reasons: (1) Many observations are not collected in avalanche starting zones, (2) snow conditions vary with terrain and time, (3) no single factor may give a full answer, and (4) the knowledge about how individual factors relate to stability is incomplete. The following general rule of decision-making is applicable to decisions about snow stability: "The greater the uncertainty, the more relevant information is needed." Conscientious analysts never have enough relevant information and they spend considerable time moving around the area collecting clues. They test the snow, make visual observations on the terrain, and screen and evaluate every piece of information for its significance. Of course, there is a limit, and a balance must be found between the time and effort spent on collecting data and their usefulness.

The need to screen the data is particularly important with respect to Class III information. Automated weather stations usually supply too much data during periods when the stability is not rapidly changing.

Which Observations Have Priority?

Factors that give direct evidence of snow stability (Class I) should have the greatest priority and weight, followed by those that reveal the structure (including clues about strength) of the snowpack (Class II). In practice, however, the local weather, extent of the area, access to observation sites, type of activity, and avalanche control measures determine the type and number of observations.

For example, patrollers in ski areas have many opportunities to gather high-quality information by testing slopes with skis and explosives and observing avalanche occurrences. Conversely, avalanche occurrences may be the only Class I observations available to road maintenance personnel. Observers on roads usually have few opportunities to test the snow in the avalanche starting zones before applying avalanche control, and therefore weather observations (Class III) are often relied on heavily.

Should Observations Be Recorded?

Travelers in the backcountry usually make mental notes of the observed factors and draw immediate conclusions about snow stability. Snow safety operations, however, usually retain written records of the observations. The records are needed for future analysis, for application in forecasting models, and for communication with other operations and agencies. In operations, good notes should be kept, but even in a well-organized operation, it is impossible to write down every piece of information.

The following guidelines are useful for data collection:

- Observations should be carried out accurately, reliably, and according to standards (when standards for data collection exist). For example, weather observations should be made according to meteorological and industrial guidelines, and snowpack observations should be made according to the International Snow Classification.
- Every observation should be relevant to snow stability. For example, the observation of the water equivalent of the entire snowpack may not always be relevant to the snow stability, therefore, it might be omitted from analysis in some instances.
- Observations should be carried out in places where weather and snow conditions simulate avalanche starting zones as closely as possible.
- For a comprehensive evaluation, numerous Class I and Class II observations should be made at a variety of locations. For example, as many slopes as possible should be ski tested and test profiles should be taken at various exposures and elevations.
- Operations at permanent locations such as highways and ski areas should maintain records of weather observations and snow profiles at study sites, avalanche occurrences, and other snowpack observations (such as fracture time profiles) depending on the time and personnel available.

ANALYSIS

Even though stability evaluation is a geophysical problem, at present, it involves aspects of both science and art. In reality, an evaluation consists of analyzing numerous factors acting together in a complicated fashion, recognizing which factors are relevant, and determining their relative weights. The analysis involves skills and judgment in applying snowpack physics, empirical relations, experience, and the feel of the snow's texture.

Because no well-defined recipes or equations are available, part of snow stability evaluation must be learned through experience. However, a few of the skills can be learned formally. Examples include recognition of weak layers in the snowpack, measurement of the shear strength of weak layers, and performance of appropriate slope stability tests. Other skills must be acquired through practice. Examples include selection of test profile locations; judgment of snow strength from the texture, type, and size of snow grains; and conclusions from the results of explosives.

Often only the feel and consistency of the snow give the final answer. Analysts are usually uncomfortable when they have not felt the snow under their skis, made their own avalanche occurrence observations, or have not personally examined snowpack weak layers. Albert Einstein's remark applies: "All knowledge about reality begins with experience and terminates in it."

Conventional (non-numerical) snow stability evaluation is a cumulative integration of information. The analyst forms an opinion from readily available observations, then tests his or her prediction against additional observations and field experiments. The prediction is continuously reevaluated and improved as additional information becomes available. The key is to identify the regions of greatest data uncertainty and actively seek critical, *relevant* pieces of data to reduce that uncertainty.

Helpful Techniques

A few techniques can help remove some of the intuition in stability evaluation. Their success is limited because, in reality, there are complex interactions among factors. There is always a need to consider a mixture of quantitative and qualitative information in any analysis (see Chapter 7 for more information).

Rules of Thumb

Rules of thumb are sometimes applied with the description of the *individual* factors on the basis of people's experience. Rules of thumb should not be used operationally in avalanche work: "The only rule of thumb in avalanche work is that there is no rule of thumb" (Perla's rule of thumb). Rules of thumb are useless in a given situation. However, some are given in this book along with descriptions of some of the individual factors for *rough* guidelines about the numerical values of factors.

Models

Predictive models have been developed by correlating snow stabilities with observations of individual factors separately or in combination. They are most successful for instability that is a direct result of weather changes (for example, snowfall, wind, temperatures) (see Chapter 7 for more information).

Point Systems

Methods utilizing assigned points for the significance of each factor (and a summary) are generally unsuccessful because the combined effect of the factors is not considered adequately.

Checklists

A simple way of analyzing snow stability is to list all the factors and give a "yes" or "no" (or "maybe") answer for criticality of each. Afterward, all the "yes" answers are reviewed in combination. This method allows screening of the factors; only the significant ones are retained for further consideration.

Need for Thoroughness

The number and variation of factors that influence snow stability is overwhelming; this is a reflection of the complex nature of the snowpack in mountainous terrain. Experience has shown the need to screen all factors. Shortcuts, such as considering only a few of the most obvious and common factors, could lead to surprises and dangerous conclusions.

A complete analysis of all the factors is needed when a new area is visited and after major changes of the weather (for example, arrival of a snow storm or high temperatures). Usually personnel in operations analyze snow stability daily. However, not all factors are studied thoroughly every day. In practice, people simply check the list of factors for changes that have occurred since the day before; then, only those factors that have changed may need evaluation.

A few common mistakes of analysis are as follows:

* *Neglecting the influence of solar radiation:* In early winter (say, December or January) warming from solar radiation is usually not significant at high latitudes and therefore it might be neglected. It could become critical in early February, but by that time the analyst may have forgotten to include it.
* *Neglecting thin weak layers deep in the snowpack:* These layers are often the cause of snow failure when surface snow is very stiff. Good surface stability can lead to false conclusions if potential weak layers deep in the snowpack are not considered.
* *Neglecting earlier avalanches:* Earlier avalanches may have removed snow from an avalanche path. This can lead to wrong conclusions about the condition of the snowpack in avalanche paths.
* *Underestimating the influence of wind:* Underestimating the influence of the wind above the tree line by observers working in a valley can result in errors regarding the effects of loading by blowing snow.

Accuracy

Snow stability evaluation is probabilistic. It is not possible to make a precise analytical assessment because of inaccuracies in data gathering, incomplete knowledge of the relationships between observations and stability, and the variations of snowpack properties across the terrain. This uncertainty is usually compensated for by a generous safety margin when decisions are made. The variation of snowpack properties across the terrain accounts for a share of the uncertainty; each slope contains weak and strong spots that cannot be precisely located. Predicting very poor stability (when natural avalanches run) is not difficult. It is more difficult to evaluate fair (conditional) stability: One must estimate how much additional load the snowpack could support and which slopes have the weakest snow.

CLASS I: STABILITY FACTORS

Current Avalanches

Significance

Avalanches that are running are strong and reliable evidence of unstable snow. They indicate that the snow is unstable on the respective slope and it is most likely unstable on other avalanche paths (similar exposure and elevation) (Figure 6.3).

In some areas, avalanches tend to run first on certain steep slopes when periods of unstable snow develop, such as during a snowstorm. For this reason, avalanche

Figure 6.3. Slab avalanches that have released naturally, indicating high instability. (Photo by A. Roch)

observers attempt to identify such indicator slopes from experience and keep them under close observation. Avalanche activity on indicator slopes is a signal that poor snow stability is developing. Avalanche occurrences on indicator slopes are very important for stability evaluation at roads. Indicator slopes cannot always be found and are not always reliable.

Data Collection

Collection of occurrence data is simple: Move around and be observant (binoculars are a help); note and record the location of the avalanche paths, exposure and elevation of the starting zones, and the character of terrain features and avalanches. Limited visibility during snowfalls and at night presents difficulties.

Detection devices such as seismometers, radar, light beams, and trip wires (slide fences) have been placed in avalanche paths to record avalanche occurrences and transmit the information automatically. They have the advantage of reporting the avalanche events immediately, but only the occurrence is registered; the type, size, and runout distance of the avalanche cannot be determined by this method. Radar and light beams have proven to be unreliable, because they tend to record anything that moves across the beam: falling snow, drifting snow, birds, persons. Trip wires are sometimes applied for the detection of avalanches on roads and railways combined with activation of traffic signals.

Record Keeping

The amount and character of records kept depend on the activity pursued. Casual ski tourers, mountaineers, and snowmobilers mentally note avalanche occurrences and integrate the information with other observations. People in avalanche safety operations at permanent locations find it valuable to keep records of avalanche activity. On a short-term basis, these records are useful for identifying the slopes where avalanches have released, therefore providing information about where the snow stability might be different later in the winter. On a long-term basis, the data are valuable when protective works are planned, when the effectiveness of control measures is assessed, and when avalanche hazard forecasting models are developed.

The format of records depends on the type of operation and the extent of the area. Field books, forms, computer data bases, and oblique aerial photos are used for recording avalanche occurrences.

Occurrences are commonly recorded in detail for cataloged avalanche paths that affect roads, developed ski runs, and other permanent facilities. In ski guiding, the effort and time spent recording every observed avalanche in detail is unreasonable, therefore avalanches are usually recorded in summary form. For example, the summary for a day may read: Three avalanches of moderate and large size (usually a size system is used; see Appendix D for details and examples) on NE slopes elevation 2,000 m; one day old. More details including the exact location would usually be recorded for avalanches on slopes that are frequently skied. (Fairly general rules about recording avalanche events are given in Appendix E.)

Stability Tests

Stability tests are used to apply stresses to the snow cover and to observe whether or not it fails. When a failure occurs, information may be provided about the depth and areal extent of unstable snow.

Stability tests can yield high-quality, direct information about the snow sampled but one should evaluate them in association with other factors. Caution must be used when making conclusions if no failure resulted: A poor test procedure, poor site selection, or insufficient force application may have prevented a failure.

Stability tests are best if carried out on slopes steep enough to allow avalanches to start (usually an incline of at least 30°). Extrapolation of test results to different inclines is part of the interpretation. In general, steeper slopes or convex rolls are expected to allow easier avalanche initiation.

In some operations, suitable slopes are fenced off and reserved for testing. For all stability tests, selection of relevant sites is crucial for obtaining useful information. The area tested (sample size) varies with the type of test. Usually, the larger the area (sample size) tested, the more reliable the data from a stability test. Explosives test the largest areas and shear frames test the smallest. *The disadvantage of all the stability tests is that only a small area of the snowpack is tested. The spot sampled might happen to be a strong or a weak spot on a slope with great variability. For this reason, it is best to repeat the tests elsewhere on the same slope. More tests with less detail are favored over detailed observations at one spot.*

Each kind of stability test has a unique interpretation with respect to snowpack stresses and the rate at which they are applied. All the tests are indexes to be interpreted mainly by experience. Each test involves application of stresses much too fast to be *directly* applicable to failures during natural avalanche release.

TEST SKIING

Test skiing is a stability test whereby a skier adds stress to the snow through his or her weight and by jumping, kicking, and turning. By being present, the tester can immediately observe the depth and type of the weak layer that fails.

In general, test skiing is limited to short slopes where no serious consequences would result if an avalanche or fall by the skier takes place. It is applied principally for testing the stability of the most recently deposited snow. Test skiing is normally avoided when a weakness is suspected deep in the snowpack or when the snow at the surface is hard. Under these snow conditions, either the skier would not be able to add enough stress to initiate failure in deep weak layers or the resulting avalanche could be dangerously large.

Safety measures must always be observed because the results are not always predictable (Figure 6.4). The following guidelines generally apply for test skiing:

- Assign a watcher who observes the skier from a safe place with good access to the path.

Figure 6.4. Test skiing. (Photo by A. Roch)

- Approach the slope cautiously from the top.
- Stand at the transition to the steep slope and attempt to start an avalanche by kicking and bouncing.
- Ski diagonally along the top of the slope by making side kicks, bounces, and jumps.
- Stop at the side of the slope in a safe place and observe the results.
- Traverse the slope again and ski the lower part without stopping.
- Secure roped belays are required for testing long slopes and snow with deep unstable layers (only with a good understanding of the consequences if an avalanche takes place).

In ski areas, test skiing is often carried out in association with *ski stabilization* (also called *ski cutting*). Ski stabilization involves the release of small avalanches and the breaking up of weak layers by tracking the snow.

In backcountry skiing, usually numerous short, steep slopes and bumps can be found for testing the snow during downhill skiing or climbing. Avalanche analysts always look for these opportunities to test the snow and update their analyses.

EXPLOSIVES

Explosives are primarily used for avalanche control in snow safety work (see Chapter 9 for techniques, effects, and discussion). However, explosives may also be used to test snow stability. Some advantages of explosive testing are that long slopes with unsafe access, deep weak layers, and hard snow can be tested and explosives apply greater stresses at a more rapid rate over a wider area than a skier.

Avalanche release with explosives indicates fair to poor stability on the test slope and probably on other slopes with similar wind loading, aspect, elevation, and snow conditions. An explosive crater with cracks around but no avalanche release also indicates some weakness in the snowpack. A crater without an avalanche or cracking tends to indicate stable snow. In the latter case, placement of the explosive in an area with good stability could be another reason, but this area may be surrounded by areas of poorer stability. Tests are sometimes repeated at different locations.

RUTSCHBLOCK TEST

The *Rutschblock test* (or *glide block test* as translated from German) involves loading a block of snow by a person in several stages (Figure 6.5). On a slope (an incline of at least 30° is preferred), a rectangular block of snow is exposed by shoveling a vertical (plumb) trench in front and two narrow trenches at the sides. The block should be about 1.5 m wide in the downslope direction (i.e., the approximate length of a pair of ski poles) and 2 m wide across the slope (i.e., the approximate length of a pair of skis). After shoveling, the back is cut with a rope or ski. The trenches and backcut must be at least deep enough to reach the point at which weak layers and weak bonds are suspected. The area of the block (3 m²) is a significant fraction of the area of a deep snow layer loaded by a skier. After the block is cut, it is loaded to produce weak layer failure in stages that give a rough numerical rating as an index of stability, as shown in Table 6.1. After failure, the snowpack is examined to determine the location and conditions of the failure plane including the type and size of snow grains.

Figure 6.5. Illustration of Rutschblock test. (Photo by M. Shubin)

In Switzerland, where the test was developed, the reaction of the block is interpreted as follows:

- Failure with load levels 1, 2, and 3: stability poor
- Failure with load levels 4 and 5: stability fair
- Failure with load level 6 or no failure: stability good

For a discussion of stability rating scales, see Appendix F.

The Rutschblock test yields high-quality information for a large sample of snow at the test site. The principal difficulty is finding a slope that is steep enough, safe, and representative of starting zones. Testing time is usually 10 to 20 minutes, depending on the number of persons assisting and the depth of the weak layer. Two further caveats apply: it is not reliable for weak layers deeper than 1 m; and load level 6 may not yield informa-

Table 6.1 Load Levels for Rutschblock Failures

Load	Description of Load at Failure
1	Failure under the weight of the block alone
2	One person on skis steps carefully on the block from above
3	The person weights the skis by making a rapid knee bend
4	The person on skis jumps
5	The person on skis jumps a second time
6	A person jumps onto the block without skis
7	No failure observed

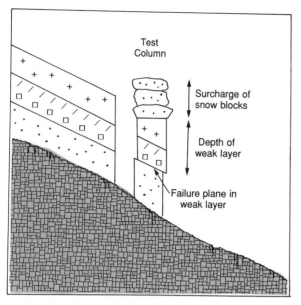

Figure 6.6. Schematic showing the collapse test: Snow blocks are added until failure occurs.

tion on soft slabs because boots may penetrate too deeply.

COLLAPSE TEST

The collapse test (or loaded column test) involves cutting of a column of snow (a cross-sectional area about 0.3 m x 0.3 m), and loading it with blocks of snow or pressing down with a shovel until a failure occurs (Figure 6.6).

The test is most useful for finding the weakest layer, but it also enables estimation of the loading required for layer failure. The load to failure can be estimated from the depth and density (measured or estimated) of snow added. Pressing with a shovel gives a more subjective rating of the failure load.

TILT BOARD TEST

The tilt board is used to locate weak layers in soft and very soft snow close to the surface. The observation is cumbersome for testing snow layers deeper than about 0.4 m from the surface. The test is best applied at a weather observation site with a horizontal snowpack.

A rectangular block of snow (with sides about 0.3 m long and a depth of 0.3 to 0.4 m) is cut from the undisturbed snowpack and lifted on a metal plate to a horizontal board. The board, which is mounted on a frame with a swivel joint, is tilted to an angle of about 15°; the board is then gently tapped from underneath until a failure occurs in the snow block. The 15° angle allows the snow to fail in shear, but not to slide off (Figure 6.7). The observer then returns the board to a horizontal position and the location of the failure plane from the surface is measured. With a sampling tube, a vertical sample of the snow above the failure plane is taken and weighed for measurement of the load above the weak layer; this weighing procedure can be applied to any stability test.

A rough tilt board test can be done with a test profile observation (discussed in a later section): A block of soft snow is held on a slightly inclined shovel, the shovel is tapped, and the snow block observed for shear failure.

SHEAR FRAME TEST

The shear frame test is used to measure the shear strength of weak snow layers that have been identified

Figure 6.7. Tilt board test. (Photo by M. Shubin)

Figure 6.8. Shear frame test. (Photo by M. Shubin)

either by eye or finger touch or with the shovel shear test, the tilt board, or the Rutschblock test.

The equipment required is a shear frame and a pull gauge. A shear frame is a rectangular metal frame with thin cutting edges and crossbars. Frames of cross-sectional area either 0.01, 0.025, or 0.05 m² have proven most convenient.

After the weak layer is marked at a fresh pit wall, the snow is removed above the weak layer (about 5 cm for the 0.01-m² frame). The shear frame is then pressed gently into the snow with the edge parallel to and a few millimeters above the weak layer. With the gauge attached to the frame, a pull is applied rapidly until shear failure occurs. The shear frame index is the force at failure (read on a maximum pointer of the gauge) divided by the cross-sectional area of the frame (Figure 6.8).

Operation of the shear frame requires practice for consistent results. For the larger frame sizes, it is more difficult to align the frame parallel to the weak layer. Therefore, even though a larger frame tests a larger snow sample, this benefit can be negated if the frame cannot be aligned properly. Working on inclines presents a further difficulty in using the frame.

The shear frame index and the normal pressure (weight of snow per unit area) above and perpendicular to the weak layer allow the calculation of an effective friction coefficient called (improperly) the stability factor:

Stability factor = Shear frame index/Weight per unit area

In practice, shear frame stability factors are usually measured on the flat. Since the stability factor is only an index, correlation of the factor with avalanche occurrences extends the index to slopes by empirical guidelines. In some operations, a stability factor of approximately 1.5 is considered to be the border between fair and poor stability; however, this is only a rule of thumb (Figure 6.9).

For a level study site and new snow, the mean of three tests is required for reliable results. Observations in old snow and on slopes require the mean of five to eight tests, with a time commitment of 20 to 30 minutes. The test cannot be performed if hard snow exists above the weak layer because the frame cannot be inserted.

SHOVEL SHEAR TEST

The principal objective of the shovel shear test is to locate weak layers and interfaces. The shovel shear test

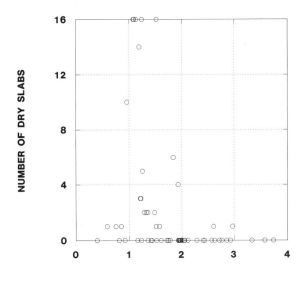

Figure 6.9. Data showing avalanche occurrences in an area versus the stability factor measured in a study plot using shear frames. The data show that the stability factor can have a complex and imprecise relationship to avalanching. (Data supplied by B. Jamieson)

Figure 6.10. Shovel shear test. (Photo by M. Shubin)

is prepared by cutting a vertical column of snow to a depth below suspected weak layers. The shear force is applied by inserting the shovel blade behind the column and pulling in a downslope direction until a failure occurs (Figure 6.10).

A snow shovel with a blade at least 250 mm wide (not curved) is the principal tool. A saw with a blade length of at least 300 mm is a useful addition, but may be substituted for by the tail of a ski, a section of a collapsible probe, or a string. The test procedure includes:

1. *Cutting the column:* A fresh vertical wall is exposed in a snow profile observation pit and soft snow at the surface is removed. The cross section of the column—0.3 to 0.4 m in the downslope direction and about 0.25 m across the slope—is marked on the new surface. The cross section is slightly trapezoidal, with the front wider than the back.

    A trench, wide enough to allow the insertion of the saw for cutting the back side, is dug at the side of the column. A narrow cut (usually conveniently triangular in shape) is made at the other side of the column. The backside of the column is cut vertically and the cutting tool (saw) left at the bottom for depth identification. The backcut should not be deeper than about 0.7 m and it should end in me-

dium hard or hard snow if possible. (*Note:* A longer column could fail in bending at its base, causing weak layers near the surface to be overlooked.)

2. *Application of force:* The shovel is inserted into the backcut. A pull force is applied in the downslope direction by holding the shovel handle with both hands.

3. *Locating a weak layer:* The column shears in a smooth plane when a weakness exists. When no weak layers are present, the column usually breaks obliquely at the lower end of the backcut. The observer marks the location of the weak layer at the rear wall, then measures the distance from the snow surface or from the ground. After the test, the type and size of snow grains in the shear plane can be determined. Because grains responsible for weaknesses (for example, surface hoar) often stick to the underside of the sheared-off column, it is advantageous to turn the column upside down to inspect the grains.

4. *Repetition:* A second, lower column is tested by repeating steps 1 to 3 when weak layers are suspected below the first column.

5. *Recording shear strength:* The magnitude of the force required to cause a failure is estimated and recorded using the descriptions given in Table 6.2. The strength may be estimated when the column is tested for the presence of weak layers. However, a separate test on a previously identified weak layer (the column should not be longer than the shovel blade) is more reliable.

Table 6.2 Failure Description for Shovel Shear Test

Very easy	The column fails during cutting or insertion of the shovel (shear frame index < 100 N/m²)
Easy	The column fails with a very low shovel pressure (shear frame index 100–1,000 N/m²)
Moderate	The column fails under a moderate shovel pressure (shear frame index 1,000–2,500 N/m²)
Hard	The column fails after a firm, sustained pressure (shear frame index 2,500–4,000 N/m²)

The shovel shear test is best applied for finding weak layers, but it is not a reliable measuring method for shear strength unless numerous tests are carried out. It has the advantage of being quick (one observation requires about 4 minutes) and only a shovel is required (standard

Figure 6.11. Fracture propagation indicates high instability. Normally, fracture propagation can only be sensed by hearing shear fracture propagation under the slab (a "whumpf" sound) or by feeling a drop of the snowpack. (Photo by E. LaChapelle)

equipment carried in avalanche terrain).

The shovel shear test has some restrictions. It cannot be applied in very soft and soft snow that would fail in compression under the downslope shovel pressure. For this reason, the test is restricted to harder layers. Also note that two tests should be made for finding weak layers in order to compensate for errors. At least six columns (not longer than the blade of the shovel) should be tested in order to determine a fairly reliable shear strength index of a weak layer.

Fracture Propagation

Fracture propagation (sometimes incorrectly called rapid settlement, collapse, or compression failure) is the sudden subsidence of the snowpack due to shear fracture propagation when weight or other forces are added, often by persons or machines. (For snow, like all other materials, fractures propagate only in tension and shear, not in compression.) Fracture propagation results in a structural collapse of a snow layer as a shear fracture propagates through it; the layer usually contains depth hoar or surface hoar. Often the subsidence is accompanied by a "whumpf" sound as air in the snowpack is compressed by the propagating shear disturbance. On flat terrain, the surface might drop suddenly between 1 and 5 cm, and on slopes, the propagating disturbance may travel upslope to initiate a slab avalanche. Often, fracture propagation takes place without any noticeable subsidence of the snowpack when thin layers fail; the seriousness of the potential for avalanche release is just as great in this case (Figure 6.11).

Fracture propagation is an extremely sensitive indicator of high instability and the presence of weak layers that have low strength and exactly the right characteristics to produce slab avalanches. It is a warning signal that should *never* be ignored. Since fracture propagation is often observed in connection with layers containing large grains in cold snow, instability can persist for long periods of time.

CLASS II: SNOWPACK FACTORS

Past Avalanches

When avalanches have run earlier and removed snow, the snowpacks on avalanche paths are different from those on undisturbed slopes. The consequence on snow stability may be one of the following:

- Avalanches have removed weak snow layers and unstable snow, therefore the remaining snowpack is stable. This is the most frequent case.
- The snowpack that remains in the starting zone is shallower than at undisturbed sites, therefore it is subject to a stronger temperature gradient. Weaker snow would develop in cold climates.
- Small avalanches can deposit snow on weak snow lower down the slope and change the snow stability there.
- Snow removed is not available for avalanches when an instability develops later, in particular, when the snow becomes weak due to melting. The avalanches later in the winter and in the spring would be smaller.
- When a slab releases, a polished, hard bed surface can remain. This can result in a poor surface for bonding the next snowfall or drifting snow. In addition, the entire track may be polished so that subsequent avalanches can run further with more destructive power than normally expected.

Because of the significance past avalanches have on future snow stability, operational personnel keep records of slopes that have produced avalanches and their character.

Snowpack Depth

Snow depth observations have several purposes: to determine whether or not there is enough snow to cover terrain and vegetation anchors so that avalanches can start easily, to monitor snowpack settlement, and to observe snow distribution across the terrain.

A basic requirement for avalanches is enough snow in the avalanche starting zones and tracks to reduce surface roughness features. The snow must cover the irregularities of the ground, shrubs, and boulders, which could anchor the snow and cause friction when the snow moves. A frequent situation on long avalanche paths at roads is enough snow for avalanches to start, but not enough in the track for them to move very far. In this case, the avalanches run a short distance and stop high on the path, but they can reach the road later in the winter when fallen snow and avalanches have smoothed the track.

Observation Techniques

Snow depth data are normally taken from a graduated, permanent stake at a level, wind-sheltered study plot. According to meteorological standards, snow depths are measured to the nearest centimeter. Snow cones around the measuring stake must be leveled with a stick before the reading is made, and hollows must be bridged with the stick (Figure 6.12). Probing with a ruler (low snow depth) or a metal probe (deep snow) is adequate

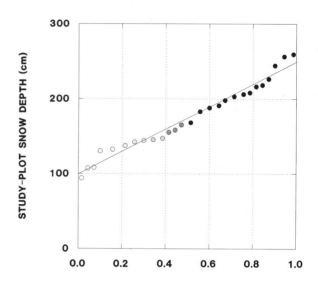

Figure 6.13. Probability plot for thirty-five years of records for depth of snow recorded at a study plot for the earliest avalanche reaching Little Cottonwood Canyon Road, Utah.

for observations of snow depth variations across the terrain. Care should be taken that the probe penetrates ice layers.

Snow depth can also be measured by ultrasound or radar. Ultrasound snow depth gauges time the flight of an ultrasonic signal from a transmitter to the snow surface and back. Knowing the speed of sound allows the calculation of the distance between the snow surface and the fixed transmitter-receiver above. Sophisticated instruments make corrections for variations of the speed of sound due to variations of temperature, moisture, and air pressure. The measuring accuracy is within about 3 cm; the largest errors are observed with blowing snow and loose snow at the surface.

Frequency-modulated continuous-wave radar allows the measurement of both the height of the snow surface and snow layer boundaries. Radar systems are complex and costly, therefore their use has been limited.

Interpretation for Avalanche Initiation

The threshold snow depth for avalanches to start and reach the usual runout zone depends on the ground surface roughness and incline. Critical depths may be determined by correlating snow depth observations at a study plot with observations of avalanche occurrences

Figure 6.12. Observation of snowpack depth with leveling stick. (Photo by D. McClung)

Figure 6.14. Left: Illustration of slope use. Heavy skier use results in fewer and smaller avalanches; right: prior to the development of the ski area, the slope yielded large avalanches. Blackcomb Mountain, Whistler, British Columbia. (Photos by W. Flann)

over several years (Figure 6.13). Statistical values obtained this way are usually meaningful for steep starting zones that produce frequent avalanches. Rough guidelines are available as threshold snow depths for avalanche initiation with terrain roughness features (see Chapter 5).

Avalanche hazard forecasters and backcountry travelers usually determine from visual observations whether or not the terrain is covered with enough snow. As a general rule, avalanches probably would not be significant when numerous boulders and shrubs are showing at the snow surface in potential starting zones. Keep in mind that shrubs might appear on one slope, but may not be present on an adjacent one.

Areas with low average snowfall—for example, dry belts on the east side of the Sierra Nevada, the Cascades, the Coast Range in British Columbia—may receive insufficient snow to reach the threshold depth for avalanches in most years; therefore, observers could be led to believe that the slopes are avalanche free. In an unusually snowy winter, however, heavy snow deposition could overcome the ground roughnesses and unexpected avalanches may result.

Slope Use

Slopes previously disturbed (skied, walked on, machine packed, disturbed by explosive charges, or over-

run by avalanches) contain snow that is different from the snow on unused slopes. These treatments usually result in compaction and strengthening of the snow near the surface, with less effect on deep, weak layers (Figure 6.14).

Avalanche deaths have occurred on tracked ski runs by failure of deep, weak layers formed early in a season before skiing started. Footprints penetrate deeper than ski tracks and, therefore, they are more effective in compacting weak layers than ski tracks in early winter (see Chapter 9 for a discussion of compaction techniques).

Previously used slopes tend to have greater stability. In evaluating the effect of slope use, one must consider when the slope was used and which snow layers were affected (Figure 6.15).

Surface Penetrability

A measure of the vertical depth of penetration by foot, the ramsonde, or ski into the snow surface is not an index of stability. Surface penetration is only useful for studying soft snow for potential soft slab formation. It may not yield reliable conclusions when the surface is hard. Penetration has the following applications:

- It may give a rough indication about the availability of soft snow for avalanche formation and wind trans-

Compaction needed

Figure 6.15. Example of avalanche paths needing compaction from the beginning of the season.

port. Very deep penetrations indicate adequate snow is available for large avalanches.
- Measurement at regular intervals allows monitoring of the strength gain of near-surface snow. For example, after a snowstorm, penetration decreases as strength increases.
- Measurements across the terrain show variations in snow deposition and hardness and texture.

Foot Penetration

To measure foot penetration, a person steps into undistrubed snow, puts his or her full body weight on one foot, and steps out. Penetration is measured with a ruler as the average depth of the footprint. On inclined terrain it is best to line up the foot across the slope and average the measured depths at the upper and lower edge of the footprint. Foot penetration depends on the weight of the observer and the size of boots, but the boot size usually compensates for the weight; heavy persons have large boots and light persons small boots. Variations among observers usually differ by less than 5 to 10 cm.

Ram Penetration

Ram penetration is measured with the first section of a standard ram penetrometer, which has approximately a 1-kg mass and a cone diameter of 40 mm. The ram penetrometer is placed on the snow surface (plumb) and allowed to penetrate the snow under its own weight (Figure 6.16). The depth of penetration is read from the scale on the rod. Ram penetration furnishes more reproducible results than foot penetration.

Ski Penetration

Ski penetration is the depth of a ski track with the full weight of a person on one ski. Ski penetration is not as deep as foot and ram penetration. Deep ski penetration indicates locations of deep, potentially unstable snow. Lower-than-average penetration points to exposed wind or sun crusts. Skiers, hikers, and snowmobilers should continuously note the depths of their tracks and evaluate

Figure 6.16. Use of the penetrometer for studying surface snow. (Photo by A. Judson)

Figure 6.17. Ski penetration.

the significance when the depth changes (Figure 6.17). A key aspect of ski penetration is its importance in assessing snow texture (slab potential) and potential for fracture propagation due to the shear stresses imparted over a large area by a person on skis.

Snow Temperature

Snow temperature affects stability in two ways: (1) Snow stiffness increases rapidly with decreasing temperature and at the same time brittleness increases, causing increased potential for rapid fracture propagation. Strength decreases significantly when the temperature approaches 0°C. The effects take place immediately (see Chapter 4). (2) The temperature and its gradient control the metamorphism of the snow, which, in turn, influences its strength. Strength changes under strong temperature gradients are slow (the time scale is days to weeks except for radiation recrystallization) (see details in Chapters 3 and 4).

Snow temperatures are part of standard snowpack observations, but during periods of warm weather it may be desirable to measure them separately without detailed examination of snow layers. In some countries, measurement of the snow temperature 10 cm below the surface is part of the daily, routine weather observations. Temperatures are usually measured at regular depth intervals (usually 10 cm; 20 cm in lower portions of deep snowpacks).

Observation Technique

Temperatures are measured by pushing a thermometer or thermistor probe horizontally into a vertical, shaded face of a snowpit. An accuracy of 0.5°C has been found adequate for snow temperature observations, although when the temperature is between 0° and –1°C, an accuracy of 0.1°C could be useful.

Glass thermometers (filled with mercury or alcohol) usually adjust to the ambient temperature slowly; therefore, many observers prefer thermistor probes. Metallic, dial stem thermometers are also preferred because they do not break easily in hard snow; however, they do develop errors more readily. All thermometers require frequent calibration by inserting them into a snow-water mixture at 0°C. High-quality thermistor probes are recommended for accuracy and ease of use but they are expensive (Figure 6.18).

Interpretation

Examples of snow temperature influence in a rough, general sense are described here. Variations will occur depending on density and structure (see Chapter 3).

- The snow temperature is low (< –5°C). Bond formation is slow; existing weaknesses persist for a long time.

Figure 6.18. Measurement of snow surface temperature in the shade of the shovel and the snow temperature with thermometers at the side of the ruler. (Photo by M. Shubin)

- The temperature is between about –1° and –5°C and the temperature gradient is less than 10°C/m. Rounding and sintering of the grains occurs rapidly; strength gain is rapid.
- The temperature is between 0° and –1°C. The snow is in a delicate balance: Rapid rounding, settling, and sintering promotes a strength increase, but the absolute value of strength may be low if the temperature is close to the melting point.
- The snowpack is isothermal. This condition is usually a requirement before deep avalanches can occur with snowmelt. If the snowpack has temperatures below 0°C, then small amounts of melt water from the surface would freeze before reaching deep, weak layers. (See Chapter 3 for more information on wet snow.)

The major difficulty in evaluating wet snow stability is that water penetrates seasonal snow in an irregular manner. It moves downward in channels and fingers and may pond on layers with a low permeability, or flow in the direction of the slope, or suddenly break through dense layers. Flooded snow at some spots and dry, stronger snow a short distance away would be the result. The surface of crusts, fine-grained snow above coarse-grained snow, and the ground surface are favorable locations for water-soaked, weak snow. Failure at a water-saturated spot could either spread across the weak dry adjacent snow or stop at dry islands between wet spots.

- A strong temperature gradient (>10°C/m) is present. The snow loses strength with facet formation (see Chapter 3).
- A weak temperature gradient (<10°C/m) is present. The strength increases at a rate that increases with the temperature and depends on the shape and size of snow grains. The rounding, sintering, and settling is slow at low temperatures and for large crystals, faceted grains, surface hoar, and depth hoar.

Acoustic Emissions

When the snowpack deforms rapidly, bonds between grains break to produce stress waves, which can be picked up by sensors. When the signals are amplified and displayed, the rate of emissions increases prior to the release of natural avalanches. This has led to the hope that acoustic emissions might be applied as an index of snow stability.

The acoustic method has not yet been developed for

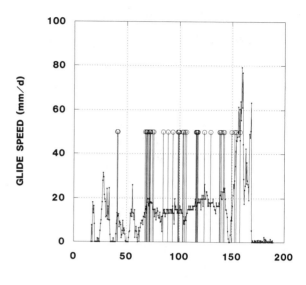

Figure 6.19. Snow gliding measurements and full-depth avalanche occurrences recorded at Coquihalla, B.C. Days with avalnche occurences are denoted by ○ in the middle of the figure.

practical application. Problems that still need to be solved are the choice of the best frequency, the filtering of background noise (ski lifts, skiers, and machines), and the optimum location in the snowpack for the sensors. With further research, this method could produce direct (that is, Class I) information. Field measurements have shown that the signals are very strong prior to release of full-depth avalanches that release by gliding.

Snow Gliding

It has been confirmed that an increasing rate of snow gliding occurs prior to full-depth avalanches which release by gliding. Therefore, gliding measurements represent an index of stability for this special class of avalanches. Study has shown that full-depth avalanches can release unexpectedly under cold, stable weather conditions. In this case, gliding activity increases due to the interaction of water and the ground topography, which may be largely unaffected by the current weather. It appears that air temperatures, gliding measurements, and snowpack water content and distributions are required for predicting these full-depth events. Further research is needed to utilize this information effectively in avalanche prediction (Figure 6.19).

Snowpack Structure

Snowpack structure investigations are used to find the ingredients that determine stability. Observations are analyzed for answers to these questions:

- Do weak layers and weak bonds exist in the snowpack?
- What is the strength of the weak layers and bonds?
- What is the depth of weaknesses below the surface and what is the snow load on them?
- How strong are the snow layers above the weaknesses?
- How are the layers and weaknesses distributed across the terrain?

A variety of observations is applied, but no single one provides all the answers. Usually several kinds of observations need to be considered in combination. In what follows, the individual observations are described and we illustrate how the questions above are answered.

FORMAL (FULL) SNOW PROFILE

A snow profile (snowpit study) is a record of the layer sequence and of the individual layers' properties. It is obtained by digging a pit and observing the snow layers. Snow profiles have several applications: identification of weaknesses where the snowpack could fail; estimation of the load above a weak layer and the stiffness of a potential snow slab; monitoring of the changes of layering, snowpack strength, and temperatures during the winter as a result of regular observations at the same location; and predictions about stability development under given weather conditions. Snow profiles provide winter climate records by revealing the individual snowfalls, the amount of snow contained in them, the effect of temperatures, and the water equivalent of the snowpack. They also provide educational demonstrations of the nature of mountain snowpacks, forcing observers to be accurate and inquisitive. In addition to stability evaluations, snow profiles have been applied to predictions of snowmelt runoff, studies of vehicle traction in snow, wildlife mobility, and snow–vegetation interaction.

One disadvantage of snow profile observations is that the procedure requires between 30 minutes and 2 hours' time—a long time commitment when decisions about the snow stability must be made. Another disadvantage is that a profile is site-specific with no account of snow variations with terrain. Because of these disadvantages, full snow profiles are mainly a baseline record of the nature and development of the snowpack in an area.

Location

Snow profile observations are often carried out in a snow study plot, which is an area selected and marked for that purpose. A study plot may be adjacent to a weather observation site or at another relevant spot. Guidelines for plot selection include the following:

- The location should provide snow conditions relevant to avalanche starting zones; study plots are usually located at high elevations, not at valley weather stations.
- A plot should not be exposed to strong wind or drifting. Wide openings in forests are preferred, but often locations above the tree line must be chosen to represent starting zone conditions.
- The ground may be level or sloped. Level plots represent average snow conditions better when nearby avalanche paths have a variety of exposures. Sloped study plots have better correlation with the snow conditions in avalanche starting zones of similar exposure.
- The ground should be fairly smooth and dry. It should not contain trees, large shrubs, or large rocks.
- A study plot location should not be affected by skiers, traffic, and avalanches.
- Preferably, the distance of the snow pits from trees and buildings should be at least equal to the heights of these obstacles.

It is best to select study plots in the summer in areas known to have reasonably uniform snow deposition. The area for snow profile observations should be marked and the ground prepared. The area should be roped off to prevent trespassing in the winter.

Frequency of Observations

The time interval between the snow profile observations depends on the climate and the type of operation. In many operations, snow profiles are done every two weeks or twice monthly. Observations at fixed dates, for example, at the end of each month, may be advantageous for climate records. In addition, it is useful to observe snow profiles whenever changes in snow conditions are suspected, for example, after a major snowstorm.

Observation Technique

Snow profiles consist of snow layer examination and measurement with classification of layer properties according to the International Snow Classification.

As a general rule, snow profile observations cover the full snowpack depth. However, in avalanche work it is often not necessary to dig to the ground when the snowpack is deep and previous observations at the same spot have shown dense, strong snow near the ground. In this case, the profile may include only the upper part of the pack; layering and hardnesses near the bottom may be confirmed by probing or by use of a ram profile.

Observations are carried out on smooth, vertical snow pit faces in the shade (refer to Figure 6.18). For snow profiles on a slope, it is advantageous to make the observations on a face parallel to the fall line. The work is carried out in the following sequence:

1. Recording of the date, time, location, elevation, slope incline, name of observer, and the weather (including the measured air temperature).
2. Excavation of the pit. The pit should be large enough to allow shoveling at the bottom (about 2 m x 1.5 m). Two observation faces in the shade are cut smooth and vertical.
3. Observation of the snow temperatures.
4. Definition of the snow layers by observing variations in snow hardness. The changes of hardness and layer boundaries may be detected by the touch of the finger, by sliding the edge of a crystal screen or ruler (knives or credit cards are usually too thin) through the snow, by brushing the surface gently, or by scraping the surface with a crystal plate (Figure 6.20). It is important to find weak layers and weak interfaces between layers. The shovel shear test can be used to help find the weakest layers.
5. Identification of layer boundaries. The boundaries of important layers are marked and their distance from the ground is measured.
6. Classification of the hand hardness of each layer (see Table 4.1 in Chapter 4).
7. Classification of the snow grain form and size in each layer using a crystal screen and magnifying glass.
8. Classification of the free water content of each layer that has a snow temperature of 0°C.
9. Observation of the density of the snow layers that are thick enough to allow the insertion of a sampler. The density (mass per unit volume) is deter-

Figure 6.20. Snow profile observation face depicting layers by brushing. (Photo by M. Shubin)

mined by taking a sample of snow of known volume and weighing it. Snow density samplers usually have volumes between 100 ml (cm^3) and 500 ml; 1,000-ml samplers have been used for measurements in coarse-grained depth hoar.
10. The pit face is marked with a pole for later location.

When working with wet snow, extra care must be taken with respect to the hardness and water content of layers in both cold (below freezing) and warm conditions. Samples should be taken quickly from snow within the pack rather than directly from a pit wall that has been exposed to the air for more than a minute or so because properties will change very quickly.

Records

Snow profile observations should be recorded in a field book. Data about the properties of the snow layers are usually noted with standard symbols. Observers are encouraged to add as many comments as necessary because snowpacks are often complex and not all the information can be described in symbols.

The observed snow profiles are commonly plotted in graphical form by using symbols and the format recommended by the International Snow Classification. (See Figures 6.26 through 6.30 in the section "Examples of Snow Structure Interpretation" later in this chapter.)

TEST PROFILE

A test profile is an abbreviated form of snow profile with concentration on the few essential observations that are indicative of snow stability. Because a test profile requires relatively little time, numerous profiles can be observed at various exposures and elevations. Whereas formal snow profiles allow for monitoring of the development of the snowpack over time, test profiles are used principally to examine variations in snow conditions from one slope to another.

In choosing test profile sites and the amount and type of data to be collected, the observer must make decisions based on the objectives and type of snowpack. Objectives include finding weak layers in a shallow snowpack; determining the strength of weak layers and loading on them for a slope with deep wind-transported snow; and determining the strength of layers at a sun-exposed or a shady site. Other objectives may be finding the condition and strength of a known weak layer, for example, buried surface hoar; observing the bonding of the snowpack on glacier ice; and studying the snow structure on a slope where avalanches have removed part of the snow.

Most test profile observations concentrate on the location of weaknesses, strength of weak layers and bonds, grain type and size in the weak layers, strength of layers above weaknesses, and snow temperatures (usually only when snow is close to its melting point). Rather than collect numerous detailed data at one site, it is better to observe several test profiles at a variety of sites.

Location

Site selection for an informative test profile requires experience, intuition, and skill in terrain evaluation. The exact test profile location is determined by probing the slope for the site that meets the purpose of the profile. Guidelines for site selection include:

- Spots found weak by probing are favored.
- The snow depth should be near an average value in the vicinity (determined by probing).
- The area should be at least 5 m from branches of trees.
- The location should be safe from avalanches but relevant to slopes in question (e.g., potential starting areas, if safe).
- No tracks from skiers, snowmobiles, or wildlife should be present.
- Slopes with an incline of at least 30° are preferred.

Observation Techniques

The techniques for observing and recording snow profiles essentially apply to test profile observations. A graphical representation of the profile may be useful for quick analysis and record keeping.

When the information is brief and simple, the profile may be recorded as a note easily understood by others. For example, a note might read: "Weak interface with faceted crystals of size 1 to 2 mm, 45 cm below surface. Snow above this layer has hardness Four Fingers. Snow temperature –5° to –8°C."

RAM PROFILE

The ram profile is a record of a hardness index through a vertical section of the snowpack. It supplements other information in a snow profile by showing variations of the hardness of snow layers quantitatively. The ram profile may also be observed without a snow profile to study hardness variations.

Ram profiles are commonly applied for soil investigations. They became a formal part of snowpack observations when snow and avalanche studies began in Switzerland during the 1930s.

Observation Technique

The ram hardness is measured by driving a ram penetrometer (also called a ram or ramsonde) vertically (line of plumb) into the snow. The ram is a tube or rod with a centimeter scale for depth and a standard cone-shaped tip (diameter of 40 mm, apex angle of 60°). A hammer dropped by an observer applies the driving force (Figures 6.21 and 6.22).

If n hammer blows from a drop height f (in cm) give a penetration p, then the ram hardness R (in newtons) over the distance p is:

$$R = \frac{nfH}{p} + T + H$$

where T is the total weight of the ram penetrometer tubes applied (a 100-cm-long section weighs either 10 or 5 N). Tube sections are added when the penetration approaches 100 cm since addition of the last section. Parameter H is the weight of the hammer (usually 5 or 10 N or greater). The distance p between two readings is usually chosen to be between 3 and 8 cm. After calculating the ram hardness R over the full depth of the snowpack, R is plotted against depth.

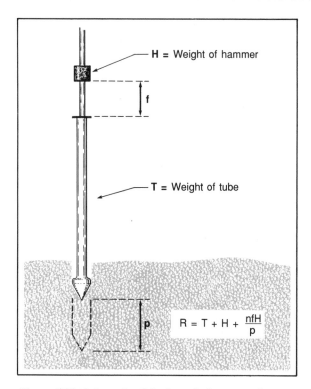

Figure 6.21. Schematic of the formula for converting ram penetrometer data to ram hardness (in newtons) with depth.

Figure 6.22. The ram penetrometer can be used for studying variations in snow hardness with depth. See the text for limitations of its applicability.

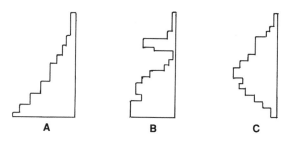

Figure 6.23. Typical shapes of ram profiles illustrating hardness variations with depth.

Application

Ram profiles have many applications. Ram hardness has better resolution as an index of snow hardness than the hand test; it can be used to illustrate hardness variations within a layer. The graphical representation clearly illustrates (Figure 6.23) the sequence of layers and their relative hardness. It allows the explanation of snowpack conditions to a layperson.

The ram profile also allows for monitoring of the strength of deep snow layers without digging a pit to the ground. In areas with deep snow, it may be sufficient to observe snow profiles regularly in the upper part of the pack and verify the condition of the lower part with a ram profile. The ram profile can also be used to monitor the weakening of the snowpack during snowmelt periods.

The ram profile has three major disadvantages in avalanche stability work: (1) It cannot be used to locate very thin, weak layers, which are often prime locations for failure (the penetrometer will pass through unnoticed). The ram is therefore most useful for studying the structure of strong layers, whereas stability work is primarily concerned with finding and evaluating weak layers. (2) The standard ram does not have good resolution in soft and very soft snow (most avalanche failure layers are soft or very soft). (3) A standard ram is expensive and heavy; this largely excludes its use in backcountry analysis.

PROBING

Probing is used to check the structure of the snowpack at numerous locations. It can be done quickly and frequently during travel, climbing, and skiing with readily available tools: ski poles, avalanche probes, and ice axes.

Probing is used to check the relative hardness of the snow layers, to detect weaknesses, and to determine

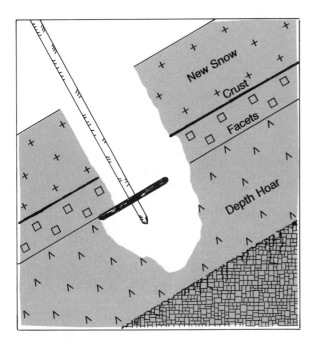

Figure 6.24. Technique for ski pole probing.

the depth of weak layers from the surface. Probing to the ground also allows depth determination for studying snow distribution. A test profile on the same slope is useful for interpreting probe results.

Ski Pole Test

Ski pole probing, as shown in Figure 6.24, is used to study surface hardness variations. Application steps include:

1. Push the ski pole with the basket end into the snow at a right angle to the snow surface as deep as possible.
2. Determine variations in snow hardness by applying just enough pressure to overcome the resistance.
3. After reaching maximum penetration, withdraw the pole by scraping the side of the hole with the basket. Thin, weak layers can often be felt this way.
4. Examine the layers close to the surface by putting a hand into the hole.

The ski pole method is limited to the investigation of surface and relatively soft layers. Deep weak layers and weaknesses under hard layers that cannot be penetrated remain undetected. Pushing the ski pole down with the handle first allows better penetration of hard layers, but this method gives unreliable observations of thin weak layers. The ski pole method does not provide much information on the amount of force needed for failure.

Probe Test

The collapsible avalanche probe can be pushed down gently in a vertical direction (line of plumb) for observations of the layering, strength, and depth of the snowpack. The vertical direction allows the best comparison of snow depths on terrain with variable incline.

RADAR

Remote sensing of snow layers and their strength is an attractive alternative to the time-consuming digging of snow profiles and test profiles, but the instruments available are cumbersome and expensive.

Frequency-modulated continuous-wave radar, operating in several frequency bands together with a powerful logger system has been applied for observations of the snow structure. Radar, buried in the ground at a study plot and looking upward, allows continuous monitoring of snowpack depth and layer settlement. Mobile instruments look downward and are pulled on a sleigh behind an oversnow vehicle. This allows continuous profiling across an area to examine variations in snow depth and layering in an area.

The logger system supplies a continuous printout of layer locations, but does not provide information about strength. However, it helps in detecting accumulations of water, which permits some conclusions about snow strength.

Interpretation of Snowpack Structure

Snowpack observations are taken to determine the properties responsible for avalanche initiation. The principal properties for starting avalanches are discussed in this section (Figure 6.25).

Presence of Weaknesses

The most important snowpack observation is the discovery of potential failure planes (weak layers). Weaknesses may be within layers that are typically 1 to 100 mm thick, poor bonds between layers, or cohesionless snow on the surface. Thick weak layers can be identified readily in profiles and by probing, but finding thin layers and weak bonds sometimes requires detec-

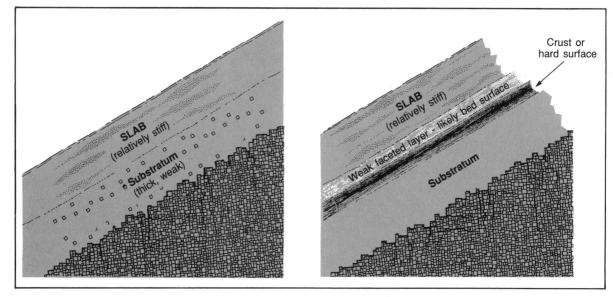

Figure 6.25. Illustrations of snowpack structure that can indicate instability.

tive work. Likely locations include places where differences in hardness emerge during ski pole probing or when a snow profile face is brushed and scraped, positions of softer touch by finger or an instrument on the pit observation face, and old snow surfaces formerly exposed to low temperatures. Other locations are at the surface and bottom of crusts, old bed surfaces of avalanches, layers that break with the shovel shear test, and failures found by ski testing and the Rutschblock test.

Strength of Weak Layers and Bonds

Shear frame measurements are the best quantitative strength observations of layers and weak bonds, but the method requires special equipment, time, and skill. In other tests, the shear strength is not measured directly but its magnitude is estimated from a combination of the following clues.

- *Hardness:* As a general rule, shear strength increases with hardness. Though the important layers are often too thin for application of the hand hardness test, experienced observers have developed a feel for strength with the touch of the finger and by scraping the snow across a bonding surface.
- *Size and shape of grains:* Snow tends to have high strength when the grains are small and round. Snow with large grains tends to have a lower strength than that with the same shape but smaller size. Grains with

angled surfaces and an elongated shape—surface hoar, faceted grains, depth hoar, needles, plates, and columns—often indicate weak snow. Graupel usually consists of large spherical grains, which often form weak snow.
- *Bonds of grains:* Bonding between grains (sintering) is more significant than grain size and shape. It can be estimated roughly by examination with a magnifying glass and by noting the effort required to disaggregate the sample.
- *Free water content:* Wet snow tends to be weak, and strength decreases with the amount of free water in the snow. Wet snow is often found on top of crusts. Wet snow strength is complex (see Chapter 4). The decrease in fracture propagation potential as snow becomes wet is an important factor.
- *Density:* Strength increases with density but hardness is a more sensitive indicator in stability work. Densities are useful to calculate the load on a weak layer. In avalanche work, it is recommended that density not be used as the only strength indicator for weak layers.

Loading of Weak Layers and Bonds

The ratio of strength to load on a weak layer determines the stability. The load is calculated as the sum of the product of density and depth of snow (perpendicular to the layer) for layers above the weak layer. However,

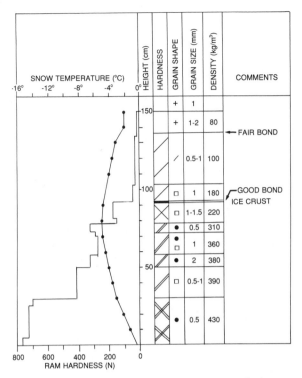

Figure 6.26. Snow structure interpretation, example A.

ported by test profiles, helps form conclusions about variations in weaknesses and loads with exposure and elevation. Skiers should use ski pole probing at every opportunity. The correlation of variations in snow distribution and strength and their influence on slab formation cannot be emphasized enough with respect to test site selection. Tests at poor sites are worthless.

Examples of Snow Structure Interpretation

In this section, snow profiles are used to demonstrate how snowpack observations are interpreted by combining visual observations, hand hardness finger tests, measurements, and experience. The conclusions refer to the site where the profiles were observed. Test profiles, probing, slope testing, weather observations, and terrain analysis are also required for determining variations in snowpack properties and stability in relation to the terrain.

SNOW PROFILE A

For profile A (Figure 6.26), the snowpack is the result of heavy snowfalls and moderate temperatures. The strength increases with depth from the surface. The

few observers have the time, opportunity, and dedication to do the calculations. In practice, the depth of the weak layer (measured from the surface) is often used as a rough loading index. This depth may be used in conjunction with feel, grain size, and potential for fracture propagation in the weak layer to give a rough intuitive estimate of stability.

It is common to distinguish between stabilities of new snow or old snow. New snow contains all the snow that was deposited during the most recent storm. Old snow is that below the most recent storm; weaknesses in old snow are referred to as *deep instabilities*.

Hardness of Snow Above Weakness

Usually, but not always, the width of slab avalanches increases with slab strength and hardness (see Chapter 4). The hand test, ram profile, and probing give information about the slab hardness, and their graphical representations illustrate the hardness variations.

Distribution of Layering Across the Terrain

Frequent probing (across and down slopes), sup-

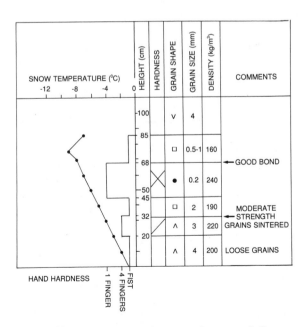

Figure 6.27. Snow structure interpretation, example B.

high strength in the lower part of the snowpack is evident from the high ram hardness, high hand hardness, round grains, small grain size, and high densities.

In this profile, two layers needed closer investigation: the crust 92 cm from the ground and the new snow. Faceted grains above and below the crust could form a weak bond, but the observer has determined by the touch of a hand that the bond with the crust is good.

The new snow at the top of the snowpack contains needle crystals 136 cm from the ground. Needles usually form weaker layers than dendrites. The observer concluded from testing with the hand, visual appearance, and the type of crystals that the strength was fair. For both of these layers, the ram penetrometer was not sensitive enough to pick up the strength *distribution* surrounding the weak layers.

The load on the weakness at the 136-cm level is very small (14-cm-deep new snow, density of 80 kg/m³), and together with the fair strength of the bond an instability is not evident. In conclusion, the snow stability is good; it could be fair at locations with deeper, wind-deposited new snow.

SNOW PROFILE B

The snowpack for profile B (Figure 6.27) is typical for areas that receive low snowfall, cold temperatures, and considerable windpacking (for example, a continental snow climate).

The snowpack contains two weaknesses. The first is a layer between the ground level and 20 cm above. The layer has low strength because it has fist hand hardness, the grains are depth hoar of large size with very few bonds, and the density is relatively low for a layer close to the ground. The load on the layer is 65-cm-deep snow with a pressure of 1310 N/m², which is considered moderate (see Table 6.2, for example).

The second weakness is a layer 32 to 45 cm from the ground. Though the hardness is very soft, the crystal shape and size indicate moderate strength. A shovel shear test revealed that the layer is weakest at its bottom where it is loaded with 53-cm-deep snow and a pressure of 1050 N/m².

The layer closest to the surface (68 to 85 cm) contains fine grains, has high density for surface snow, and a good bond with the snow below.

The medium-hard layer at height 45 to 68 cm and supported by the two weak layers is important. The layer was deposited by wind, therefore, it contains small grains and is denser and harder than the layers below.

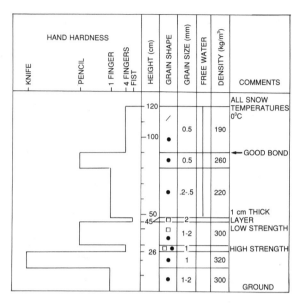

Figure 6.28. Snow structure interpretation, example C.

The combination of a strong layer above weak ones is part of a recipe for a slab avalanche. The bar diagram of hardness in Figure 6.27 depicts the slab well.

In conclusion, the snow stability is poor due to weak layers, their low strength, and the relatively large load on them. A failure could occur at the 32-cm height. During downslope motion, the avalanche might break into the lower layer and sweep out snow to the ground. The avalanche could be wide because of the medium-hard layer above the weak ones.

SNOW PROFILE C

This kind of snowpack, profile C (Figure 6.28), with snow (temperature 0°C) over the full depth, is often observed near the end of winter before the snow melts.

A weakness exists in a thin layer 45 cm from the ground. The strength of this layer is low to moderate because it felt very soft to the touch of the finger and pencil and the snow dislodged easily when the observation face was brushed. Also, the grains are faceted and of medium size, the layer failed easily with the shovel shear test, and the snow temperature is 0°C.

The weak layer supports medium-hard to hard snow with a depth of 74 cm and a pressure of 1550 N/m². The combination of low strength, moderate normal load, and hard snow above the weakness results in poor stability.

The isothermal condition of 0°C and the free water in

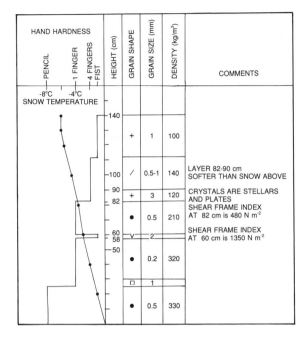

Figure 6.29. Snow structure interpretation, example D.

the upper snowpack are also important considerations. With additional surface melting, water will percolate through the snowpack, wet the weak layer, and further decrease its strength. However, once the weak layer becomes wetter, it will become more difficult for fractures to propagate there. This can cause the stability to increase.

Another suspicious layer is the one at 26 to 30 cm. A close examination by touch and visual inspection of the small faceted, partially rounded grains suggests high strength.

SNOW PROFILE D

For profile D (Figure 6.29), the snowpack contains two weak layers: one at 82 to 90 cm and one at 58 to 60 cm. The first, at 82 to 90 cm, has low strength because the grains are stellars with plates at their branches and crystals of this shape become rounded and form bonds slowly. Also the grains are large, the density is low for a layer 50 cm below the surface, and the shear frame index is 480 N/m², which is a fairly low value for new snow (see, for example, Table 6.2).

The lower boundary of the layer is loaded with 58-cm-deep snow exerting a normal pressure of 670 N/m².

The stability factor, $480/670 = 0.7$, means poor stability. Though the snow above the weak layer is soft, it has enough cohesion for slab avalanche formation.

The layer strength of the second weak layer, at 58 to 60 cm, is low because it is easily visible due to its coarse-grained structure, and it felt much softer than the layers above and below when touched with a finger and pencil. In addition, the grains are surface hoar with sharp edges and few bonds, and the strength measured with the shear frame is 1350 N/m², which is a low value for old snow.

The layer is loaded with 80-cm-deep new and old snow having a pressure of 1120 N/m². The stability factor, $1350/1120 = 1.2$, indicates *potentially* unstable snow at the snow profile site. Experience has shown that the stability tends to be poor to fair over the whole area when the stability factor is 1.0 to 1.5.

In summary, the new snow at the 82-cm height is weaker and has a lower stability index than the surface hoar layer at 58 cm. Avalanches could start in the new snow and, when in motion, step down to a bed surface at 58 cm of height. The medium-hard snow layer between 60 and 82 cm above the ground indicates conditions favorable for a wide slab avalanche.

SNOW PROFILE E

Test profile E (Figure 6.30) displays a snowpack with a strong base and weaker layers above. A layer of

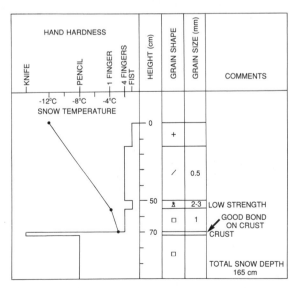

Figure 6.30. Snow structure interpretation, example E.

graupel, 50 to 55 cm from the surface, is the primary weakness and it had poor cohesion. The weak layer was readily visible at the observation face; it was found with the shovel shear test.

The graupel layer is loaded with 50-cm-deep new snow. Experience has shown that more than 30 cm of new snow on a weak layer could cause failures with additional loading; therefore, the stabiliy is fair. The stability may be poor at locations where the wind has deposited deeper new snow.

The crust surface 70 cm from the surface is another suspected weakness, but a close examination indicated a good bond between it and the snow above.

References

Avalanche Research Centre, NRCC, and Canadian Avalanche Association. 1989. Guidelines for weather, snowpack, and avalanche observations. Associate Committee on Geotechnical Research Technical Memorandum No. 132. Ottawa: National Research Council of Canada, 49 pp.

Föhn, Paul M. B. 1987. The stability index and various triggering mechanisms. IAHS Publication No. 162, pp. 195–207.

Föhn, Paul M. B. 1987. The "Rutschblock" as a practical tool for slope stability evaluation. IAHS Publication No. 162, pp. 223–228.

LaChapelle, E. R. 1980. The fundamental processes in conventional avalanche forecasting. *Journal of Glaciology* 26(94): 75–84.

Perla, R., and T. M. H. Beck. 1983. Experience with shear frames. *Journal of Glaciology* 29(103): 485–491.

Perla, R., T. M. H. Beck, and T. T. Cheng. 1982. The shear strength index of alpine snow. *Cold Regions Science and Technology* 6(1): 11–20.

Schaerer, P. A. 1989. Evaluation of the shovel shear test. *Proceedings of the International Snow Science Workshop*, Whistler, British Columbia, October 12–15, 1988. Vancouver, BC: Canadian Avalanche Associates, pp. 274–276.

Sommerfeld, R. A., and H. Gubler. 1983. Snow avalanches and acoustic emissions. *Annals of Glaciology* 4: 271–276.

Wilson, N. 1977. Everything you wanted to know about snow. *Mariah Magazine* II(4): pp. 26–28, 82, 84, 104–108.

CHAPTER 7

AVALANCHE PREDICTION II:
AVALANCHE FORECASTING

The object of all science, whether natural science or psychology, is to coordinate our experiences and to bring them into a logical system.

—Albert Einstein

Snow avalanche forecasting is defined as supplying estimates of both current and future snow stability. When estimates of the destructive potential or effects of avalanches on people and facilities are integrated with snow stability assessments, the term avalanche *hazard* forecasting is applied. Thus, it is possible for highly unstable snow to exist with no hazard if people or facilities are not threatened. Avalanche hazard rating scales are related to the type of hazard described; a rating scale for backcountry skiing differs from one applicable to highway protection.

Avalanche forecasting involves the integration of all available information into a prediction. The first two classes of data (Class I, stability factors; Class II, snowpack factors) were discussed in Chapter 6. In this chapter, Class III type factors, or meteorological factors, are introduced along with methods of avalanche forecasting and an example of the analysis for backcountry avalanche forecasting. Appendix B gives examples of basic snow and weather observation techniques.

CONTRIBUTORY FACTORS IN AVALANCHE FORMATION

The term *contributory factors* originated with Mont-gomery Atwater in the United States in the early 1950s. It refers to the variables (mostly Class III factors) used in predicting avalanches; sometimes *threshold* values of parameters favorable for producing significant avalanches are provided. These factors depend on local conditions such as altitude, latitude, orientation of the mountain range (aspect), and snow climate. Threshold values are useful only as rough rules of thumb; they are not applicable to individual situations in forecasting.

The early attempts to define contributory factors were based largely on field observations and experience. The current trend is to determine forecasting variables using mathematical analysis systematically for use later in numerical forecasting models. In some numerical models, variables are sometimes chosen because they are conveniently measured or easily determined rather than for their physical significance to avalanche formation. There is no universally applied set of contributory factors and it is clear that the importance (weighting factors) of the individual contributory factors will change with the climate and time of year. The discussion below gives examples of the most universally recognized factors. The ease of interpretation of these factors is not straightforward. Some are retained because they have appeared as significant in statistical analyses of snow, avalanche, and weather data bases.

Figure 7.1. Rough snow surface. (Photo by A. Kelner)

CLASS III: METEOROLOGICAL FACTORS

Surface Condition

The surface condition has a strong influence on whether new snowfall or drifting snow will bond well. The surface condition has two elements: roughness and physical character (temperature, hardness, crystal form). If the surface is rough, such as when rough features (sastrugi) form by wind sculpturing or sun (suncups), new snow might bond well to the surface (Figure 7.1). A smooth crust (some ice or wind crusts, for example) can make it unlikely that dry new snow will adhere to the surface, increasing the subsequent avalanche risk. In general, the concepts of bond formation apply: Snow at warm temperatures (near 0°C) can bond well to a warm surface. When a temperature mismatch occurs between the surface and new snowfall (one warm and the other cold), chances of failure increase. The same concepts apply to crystal form mismatches. (See the discussion of bonding in Chapter 3.) Normally, surfaces that are either warm, soft, or rough (or combinations of these) produce

better bonding than those with cold, hard, or smooth conditions (or combinations of these). Examples of surface snow that could produce weak bonding later include faceted grains, surface hoar, graupel, needles, plate crystals, crusts, and machine- and ski-packed snow.

Observations of surface conditions are a part of snow profile, test profile, and regular weather observations. Symbols for recording surface roughness are given by the International Snow Classification (see Table 7.1 and Figure 7.2).

Depth and Water Equivalent of New Snow

Snowfall is the most frequent cause and trigger of avalanches. Therefore, snowfall observations are an important element of avalanche prediction. As the depth of new snow increases, the load on any weak layer below increases. Because slab avalanches are possible when the load (shear stress) applied to a weak layer approaches the layer strength, the depth of new snow is an important, easily measured index for predicting subsequent avalanching. The hazard usually increases rapidly as the snow depth increases. The wind is an additional factor because strong winds assist loading of the slopes even without much new snowfall. Snowpack structure is also a consideration because buried weak layers may result in formation of large avalanches after only a small amount of new snowfall.

The total precipitation (in millimeters of water equivalent) is more fundamental than new snow depth for

Table 7.1. ICSI Surface Roughness Classes

Term	Graphic symbol
Smooth	————
Wavy	∿∿∿
Concave furrows	⋏⌣⋏⌣
Convex furrows	⋎⋎⋎
Random furrows	∧∨∧∨

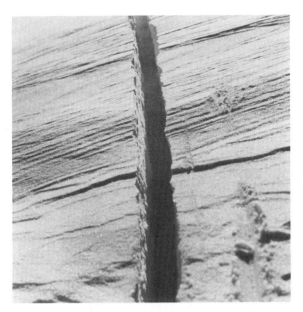

Figure 7.2. A hard snow surface does not mean stable snow; cracks may form and avalanches could start. (Photo by D. Fesler)

avalanche prediction. It is calculated as the product of new snow depth (in millimeters) and the specific gravity of new snow:

$$\text{Water equivalent (mm)} = \frac{\text{Snow depth (mm) x Snow density (kg/m}^3\text{)}}{\text{Density of water (1,000 kg/m}^3\text{)}}$$

Data Collection

Snowfall is best observed manually on boards of about 400 mm x 400 mm that were placed on the surface prior to snowfall. At least two boards—a new snow board and a storm board—are required for settlement observations. Calculations require measurements of snow depths on the boards using a ruler. Determining the water equivalent also requires sampling of the snow and weighing of the accumulated snow. The recording process is demonstrated in Table 7.2.

Data collection of snowfall at remote weather stations is obtained by recording precipitation gauges. These gauges measure the water equivalent and the intensity of precipitation, but give no information about the depth and settlement of the new snow. Ultrasound depth gauges, radar, and television cameras aimed at a measuring stake are automatic measuring devices estimating total, new snow depth, and storm snow.

Table 7.2 Example of Snowfall Observations

Day	1	1	2	2
Time	0800	1800	0800	1100
Depth on New Snow Board (cm)	10	12	20	8
Depth on Storm Board (cm)	10	21	37	43
Weight (g)	19	32	57	22
Water equivalent (mm)	6	10	18	7
Density of new snow (kg/m³)	60	83	90	88

Comments: The snow on the new snow board was removed after each observation. The depth of snow on the storm board is the total snow accumulation since the snowfall began. A core sample of snow was weighed from the new snow board with a sampling tube 63.5 mm (2.5 in) in diameter (cross-sectional area of 31.7 cm²).

Interpretation

The water equivalent of the new snow represents the weight added directly to the snowpack. In practice, however, the depth of new snow is more easily measured than the water equivalent.

As a rough rule of thumb, an accumulation of 30 cm of new snow (water equivalent about 30 mm) has been quoted as a critical value to produce widespread avalanching in new snow at Alta, Utah, when associated with wind. When actual data are used, a study of 20 years of storm records from Alta showed close to a 50% chance of a large avalanche for 50 mm water equivalent and about 80% for 100 mm. A similar example, using records of water equivalent during three days of continuous snowfall, is given in Figure 7.3 for an avalanche path in Norway. The total precipitation (in millimeters) during the previous three days (measured in a study plot) is plotted versus the probability (in percent) of avalanche occurrence. The data indicate a 50% probability of a large avalanche with 48 mm of precipitation and 90% probability with 79 mm of precipitation. With a density of 150 kg/m³, these figures correspond to 31 and 53 cm of snow, respectively (Figure 7.4). This kind of analysis is always site specific and it must be integrated with other information such as wind records. When taken together, these examples show how imprecise a rule of thumb (30 mm) is.

Data from Table 7.2 suggest that the snowfall may have approached a critical amount on day 2 at 0800 hours (storm depth 37 cm and water equivalent 34 mm) but clearly wind, temperature, and other effects would have to be factored in to make any useful conclusion.

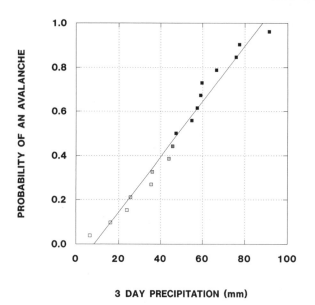

Figure 7.3. Probability of avalanching versus three-day precipitation (water equivalent) for an avalanche path in Norway. (Data supplied by S. Bakkehöi)

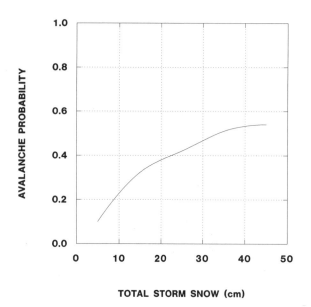

Figure 7.4. Avalanche probability versus storm snow totals for a road. Based on 11 years of storm records for Kootenay Pass, British Columbia.

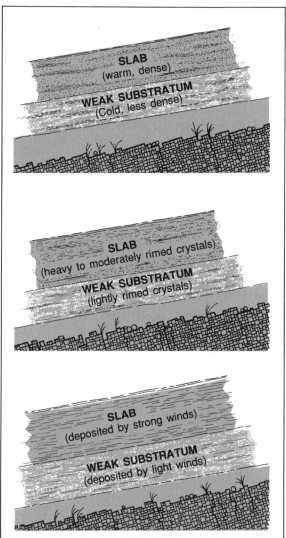

Figure 7.5. Patterns of new snow instability.

Type of New Snow

The crystal type of the new snow can determine the form of instability that will follow. When stellar crystals or spatial dendrites are deposited under cold, calm conditions, they tend to produce loose snow avalanches immediately or with a delay as metamorphism destroys branches and reduces cohesion. Crystals of simpler form (e.g., needles, columns) or wind-broken fragmented crystals tend to pack closely, promoting bond formation and a slablike texture.

Crystal riming is also thought to influence the type of instability: rime-free crystals tend to produce loose snow avalanches. Partially rimed crystals tend to form a slablike texture and graupel can provide a future sliding layer and occasionally it might form an unstable slab.

Density of New Snow

The density of newly fallen snow can be a factor in predicting snow stability because it is an indicator of strength and whether a slablike texture will develop (Figures 7.5, 7.6, and 7.7). Data from slab fracture lines (see Chapter 4, Figure 4.25) indicate that optimal density ranges for slab avalanche formation are in the range of 100 to 250 kg/m^3. Field data show that slabs also occur outside this density range. Low-density (low-strength or low-cohesion) dry snow can be responsible for loose snow avalanches. Typical new snow densities range from about 30 kg/m^3 (dry snow in calm weather) to 300 kg/m^3 (wind-packed snow). Average values for dry snow are typically in the range of 50 to 100 kg/m^3 depending on the location. Higher values predominate in maritime snow climates; lower values are prevalent in colder continental climates. Wet snow or graupel can easily have initial densities exceeding 200 kg/m^3. Some rough guidelines are given in Table 7.3.

Snowfall Intensity

The snowfall intensity (rate of increase of snow depth per unit time) is regarded as an easily measured

Table 7.3 Rough Guidelines for Ranges of Dry New Snow Density

Very low	10–30 kg/m^3	Loose snow avalanches expected
Low	30–60 kg/m^3	Loose snow; slab formation possible
Medium	60–250 kg/m^3	Optimal for slab formation
Dense	Greater than 250 kg/m^3	Slab formation possible

factor affecting snow stability. Since the load (shear stress) on a snowpack is proportional to the product of density times depth, clearly, snowfall intensity is not as fundamental as precipitation intensity (water equivalent per unit time) in determining whether avalanches will occur. Snowfall intensity as an indicator has an advantage because no special equipment is needed to estimate it. Therefore, estimations of snowfall intensity are often used by skiers in the backcountry.

Figure 7.7. Graupel. (Photo by B. Jamieson)

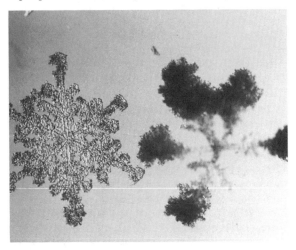

Figure 7.6. Rimed crystals. (Photo by E. LaChapelle)

Interpretation

The intensity of snowfall (the depth of snow that falls per hour) and the precipitation intensity (the water equivalent of the snowfall per hour) govern the outcome of the race between the shear stress and the increase of strength. Rough rules of thumb have been quoted as a result of experience: Instability can appear when the intensity is greater than 2.5 cm/h. A rate of 3 cm/h represents intense snowfall; therefore, the rule of thumb is roughly equivalent to stating that avalanches are likely when it snows hard—which is expected. Temperature, wind, and other factors would have to be considered to make a final conclusion.

In Table 7.2 snowfall in the 10-hour period between 0800 hours and 1800 hours on day 1 was 12 cm with 10 mm of water equivalent. This corresponds to an average snowfall intensity of 1.2 cm/h and 1.0 mm/h precipitation intensity. On day 2, over the 3-hour period between 0800 hours and 1100 hours, the snowfall intensity increased to an average of 2.7 cm/h (2.3 mm/h precipitation intensity).

Precipitation Intensity

The precipitation intensity refers to the millimeters of water equivalent delivered to the snowpack per hour. It is a direct measure of the load applied to the snowpack. It can be calculated as the product of snowfall intensity and the specific gravity of snow deposited (defined as the density divided by the density of water) or it can be measured directly using a precipitation gauge. Estimates of average precipitation intensity (water equivalent) in the range of 0.5 to 2.5 mm/h (during storms) have been quoted by forecasters in different mountain ranges as typical (threshold) values. Sometimes the duration of the storm and wind speed are mentioned in combination with critical values to produce a rule of thumb suitable for prescribing a high probability of avalanching, but these are much too imprecise to be used operationally.

The reason precipitation intensity (rate of loading) is considered important is because failure (and fracture) of alpine snow is produced only when a critical rate of loading is applied (see Chapter 4). However, if the load is applied at a slower rate than critical value, the snow may densify (settle) to gain strength because enough time is allowed to adjust to the new load. In one study with data from Alta, Utah (20 years of storm records), the *maximum* precipitation intensity was found to be

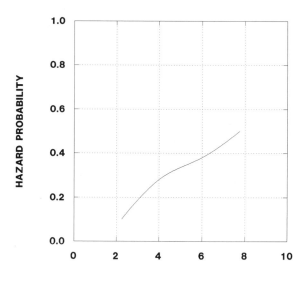

Figure 7.8. Maximum precipitation intensity (in millimeters per hour) recorded during storm periods versus hazard probability (probability of at least one large avalanche occurring). Compiled from 20 years of storm records for Alta, Utah. (Data supplied by R. Perla)

more meaningful than *average* precipitation intensity; this result appears to be in agreement with the measured shear strength and rate properties of alpine snow (Figure 7.8).

Settlement of New Snow

Settlement is the percentage decrease in the height of new snow as densification proceeds (see Figure 4.7 in Chapter 4). Settlement provides an index of how much densification is taking place and, therefore, it is related to gain in strength as time proceeds. Settlement depends on the temperature and initial density of the new snow as well as grain size and shape: Low-density snow at warm temperatures settles the most rapidly. The two aspects to settlement are as follows: (1) Slow settlement rates may imply the persistence of instability for a long period (such as under cold conditions). Settlement of 15% or less of total new snow depth in a 24-hour period has been suggested as a rough rule of thumb for a slow increase in strength. (2) Very high settlement (>30% per 24 hours) appears to be associated with avalanche activity. A study using 20 years of storm records for Alta,

Figure 7.9. Settlement cones around objects provide a rough index of settlement for the backcountry traveler. (Photo by P. Schaerer)

Utah, showed that settlement did not correlate well with avalanche hazard probability except for rates in excess of 30% during storms. This is probably redundant information because such high settlement rates imply lots of new snow, which usually implies high avalanche risk.

Snow cones around trees and poles provide a rough index of snowpack settlement and strength increase of the snow. The cones develop because friction on the obstacle causes the snow to resist the settlement there in comparison to the surrounding snowpack (Figure 7.9). This evidence must be used cautiously because obstacles affect drifting and also snow temperatures in their vicinity, which may lead to false conclusions.

Settlement within a snowpack during snowmelt indicates densification. However, during melt, the snowpack depth also decreases by loss of snow. Thus, the change in snowpack depth is the result of both densification and loss of snow. Furthermore, these effects can produce a complicated pattern of snow strength: Densification generally produces an increase in strength, but local concentrations of water content can produce important decreases in strength. Such decreases raise the chances of slip or glide, which adversely affect stability.

New snow settlement is measured by comparing the sum of snow depths measured on the new snow board with the depth measured on the storm board:

$$\% \text{ Settlement rate} =$$

$$\frac{\text{Sum of new snow depths} - \text{Storm snow depth}}{\text{Sum of new snow depths}} \times 100$$

For the snowfall observations of Table 7.2, the settlement at 0800 on day 2 is:

$$\% \text{ Settlement rate} =$$

$$\frac{10 + 12 + 20 - 37 \text{ (cm)}}{10 + 12 + 20 \text{ (cm)}} \times 100\% = 12\%$$

A rate of 12% in 24 hours may indicate a fairly slow strength increase if the rule of thumb is followed. However, other variables affecting strength gain would have to be checked.

Wind Speed

The wind speed controls the type and location of instability and the timing of avalanche release. Dry snow falling under calm conditions often produces loose snow avalanches. When the wind speed exceeds a threshold value (varies with each surface snow type; see Chapter 2), blowing snow becomes a factor and slabs form. When the wind speed exceeds 7 m/s wind transport and wind packing usually begin. For speeds in the range of about 10 to 25 m/s, drifting is strongly developed and snow is transported most efficiently into avalanche starting zones. When the wind speed is greater than 25 m/s snow can be transported in plumes high above mountain ridges, resulting in loss due to evaporation, and a deposit may take place beyond starting zones, resulting in less effective slab formation. In this case, isolated deep pockets lower on the slope are the preferred locations for slab formation.

Wind packing can produce dense, cohesive snow, which aids in slab formation. Also, wind usually scours large windward areas to produce deeper snow upon deposition in a smaller lee (avalanche starting) zone. During scouring, weak surface snow such as surface hoar may be destroyed to rid the snowpack of future weak layers in exposed areas.

Wind Direction

Wind direction determines lee zones and favorable exposures for producing avalanches. The prevailing wind (or storm) direction has a strong effect on the frequency of avalanches expected from individual avalanche paths. Localized variations in wind direction and speed must also be kept in mind. Local winds depend principally on prevailing winds, terrain features, and temperature (see Chapter 2). When assessing risk in backcountry travel, the local character of winds should be given careful attention. Usually, direct relevant observations of current or recent wind direction are possible on the microscale in the backcountry, which may not be accessible to people forecasting on a larger scale, for example, for protection of highways and villages.

Data Collection

Information about the direction and speed of wind is obtained from local, visual observations; measurements with anemometers and wind vanes; and upper atmosphere observations from weather offices.

The current wind direction and range of speed can easily be estimated from *visual observations* of moving flags, smoke, swaying trees, snow drifting along the surface, and other signs. For snow stability evaluation it is important to observe the wind at the avalanche starting zones and to consider not only the direction and speed of wind at present, but the wind on previous days. The continuous visual observation of the wind is important for all operations and in particular for backcountry travelers, because the wind can change significantly with the exposure of the slopes. Good snow stability analysts continuously watch for signs and clues of snow drifting, even when they ride a chairlift, fly in a helicopter, and drive on a road.

The following clues assist in making conclusions about the present and past wind direction and snow transport:

- Ripples on the snow surface. The ripples run perpen-

Figure 7.10. Drifts indicate the direction of wind. (Photo by T. Auger)

dicular to the direction of the wind and their sharp edge faces the wind.

- Sastrugi (elongated erosional ridges on the snow surface) point in the direction of the wind.
- Cornices face downwind. They indicate deep wind-transported snow below them (distance depends on wind speed).
- Small drifts at terrain breaks. These drifts occur on the downwind side and they indicate deep snow in the vicinity (Figure 7.10).
- Drifts and scour holes around rocks, trees, and posts. Scours appear on the windward side and elongated drifts form on the downwind side.
- Deep loose snow (called snow pillows) on the downwind side of ridges, behind hills, mounds, and in gullies.
- Rime accumulations occur on the windward side of trees, lift towers, and poles (see Chapter 2, Figure 2.26).
- Snow blown off wind-exposed trees and plumes of blowing snow off of ridges and peaks indicate the present wind direction at those locations.

Wind vanes and anemometers supply continuous data about the wind direction and speed from remote locations (Figure 7.11). Wind observations at snow study plots are usually not indicative of the wind in avalanche starting zones, therefore remote anemometers may be essential for an operation. Good correlations between anemometer readings and wind at specific locations can usually be obtained with several years of data.

Figure 7.11. Wind vane and anemometer measuring wind direction and speed. Radiant heaters keep the anemometer cups free of rime.

Finding a site for an anemometer that gives good index observations relevant to avalanche starting zones requires skill as well as trial and error. Mountain peaks and ridges are not always the best locations because their positions may be too exposed.

Weather offices supply data on the observed and predicted wind direction and speed in the free atmosphere near the mountain ridges. This information allows conclusions about the wind, but local topography must be taken into account (see Chapter 2).

Blowing Snow Activity

The concepts that govern the effect of precipitation intensity also govern blowing snow activity. (See Chapter 2 for a discussion of the effects of blowing snow on avalanche and cornice formation.) One reason the effects of blowing snow on avalanche formation are hard to quantify is because measurements are difficult. Snowdrift gauges that measure the amount of snow moved by the wind can supply better index observations than wind speed. Instruments that either trap samples of drifting snow, count the number and size of particles that cross a light beam, or measure the extinction of a light beam in blowing snow are research tools. This equipment has not proven to be applicable for snow stability evaluation yet because of difficulties in finding relevant locations

for drifting in an area and in maintaining equipment. Therefore, most blowing snow observations are still made visually and correlation is made with wind speed based on experience.

Air Temperature

Dry Snow

In addition to temperature effects within the snowpack (see Chapter 6), the air temperature can influence the type and likelihood of instability. Both the trend in air temperature and the mean value of air temperature during storms are important to avalanche forecasting.

The air temperature determines the temperature of the snow that is deposited. Cold temperatures slow the formation of bonds, allowing weakness to persist. Warm temperatures during storms produce snow that often stabilizes in place. Field observations show that this is a very important effect. There is sometimes an association with density: Cold snow tends to be deposited at lower density than warm snow, but the effects of wind can alter this.

It is useful to observe the *trend* in air temperatures during a storm. Rising air temperatures indicate that warm snow (which usually settles and gains strength rapidly) will be deposited over cold snow (which can remain weak). This can set up a condition for slab avalanche formation: a strong slab over a weaker layer. Increasing avalanche hazard in storms during which the temperature rises has long been observed by forecasters. Data from Alta, Utah (Figure 7.12) have shown that hazard probability increases with *maximum* temperature change during a storm.

Wet Snow

The air temperature is critical for forecasting wet snow avalanches. In maritime and transitional snow climates, avalanche forecasters keep a close watch on prediction of freezing levels and mountain-top air temperatures. It has been observed that avalanching can sometimes begin immediately when the air temperature reaches 0°C in starting zones. This is thought to be related to warm air, which causes snow to sluff off trees or cliffs. Once rain begins, avalanches can release (on any aspect) within minutes, but delays of up to half a day or more are possible. The most useful indicators appear to be temperature measurements at starting zone elevations in upwind locations that can intercept warm fronts or warm storms before they reach starting zones.

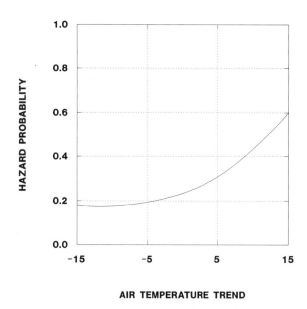

HAZARD PROBABILITY

AIR TEMPERATURE TREND

Figure 7.12. Avalanche hazard probability (the probability of several large avalanches) for a road as a function of total (maximum) air temperature trend (in degrees Celsius). Compiled from 20 years of storm data for Alta, Utah. (Data supplied by R. Perla)

Chapter 4); they are observed to occur at any time of the day or night.

Observation Techniques

Instruments for air temperature observations include thermographs, maximum and minimum thermometers, thermistors at remote weather stations, and pocket thermometers and thermistor probes.

Thermographs are preferred at manually operated, permanent study sites, because the temperature trend can be recognized readily on the graph. It is difficult to see the trend of temperature with maximum and minimum thermometers (standard equipment for meteorological and climate stations), unless the thermometers are read frequently.

Glass, metal, or thermistor pocket thermometers (with accuracies of 0.5°C) are standard for both air and snow

Prolonged periods of warming can produce deep wet slabs, which are difficult to forecast because release often depends on the complex interaction of water and the topography and character of the sliding layer (see

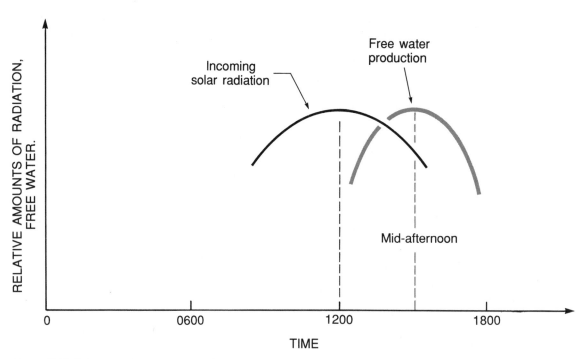

Figure 7.13. Schematic showing timing of free water production and solar radiation input.

temperatures. Three rules for measuring air temperatures follow:

1. The thermometer should be about 1.5 m above the snow surface. If locations are closer to the ground, the temperature can be influenced by the snow surface temperature.
2. The measuring device should be in the shade. At weather stations the thermometers are housed in screened boxes (Stevenson screens) with the door facing the shady side. At remote stations, thermistors are contained in small, sun-protected enclosures.
3. The thermometer should be at least 0.3 m from the body of the observer. The observer should stand back as far as possible when reading the thermometers in a Stevenson screen.

Relative Humidity

High humidity (about 85% to 100%), in association with deposition of wind-transported snow, is thought to be favorable for formation of cohesive snow to form slabs. High humidity is usually measured during storms when warm, moist air is present so that humidity may, in some instances, provide redundant information. High humidity also slows sublimation of particles in blowing snow, allowing it to be transported greater distances before it is lost. High humidity is also essential for surface hoar formation (see Chapter 3). Relative humidity is easily measured at weather stations so many operations include it with other observations. It is measured either by hair hygrometers or psychrometers.

Solar Radiation

Solar radiation changes snow properties and therefore it can affect snow stability. At high latitudes, incoming radiation increases considerably as the winter progresses. During the spring, solar radiation becomes the dominant influence on snow temperatures and it controls snowmelt rates. The principal effects of radiation are discussed in Chapter 2 (Figure 7.13).

Observation Techniques

Visual observations of the local sky condition and cloud cover are useful in avalanche prediction. (See Appendix B for examples of snow and weather observations.) Radiometers for recording the incoming, outgo-

Figure 7.14. Sluffing activity initiated by radiation input. (Photo by A. Kelner)

ing, and net radiation are available but they are rarely applied—the high price, maintenance difficulties, and reliability are the obstacles.

Interpretation

Even though the heat exchange at the snow surface is complex, a few guidelines can be given for frequently observed situations. In midwinter, north-facing, shady slopes receive little incoming radiation, but they lose heat from outgoing radiation. On shady slopes, the snow tends to be cold and strength gains are slow. Slopes with a north-facing aspect are more likely to contain faceted crystals, depth hoar, and surface hoar than other aspects. In the spring, south-facing sunny slopes receive intense solar radiation, which can weaken snow (Figure 7.14). During spring, north-facing slopes have small gains from radiation. They tend to warm slowly and the snowpack is slow to stabilize. Changes on shady slopes are also slow; instability may persist for a long time.

Because rocks absorb radiation readily, sideways temperature gradients can produce weak snow nearby. Solar radiation can also soften new snow rapidly.

Radiation is not a significant factor when the sky is covered with dense clouds. Thin clouds allow incoming short-wave radiation to reach the snow, but inhibit the outgoing long-wave radiation (greenhouse effect). In this case, surface snow gains heat rapidly and it may weaken significantly in a short time.

Due to the reflection from surrounding slopes, snow in cirques and gullies receives more heat than open slopes. Conversely, the snow in such places loses heat at a slower rate; therefore it can remain unstable for a longer time. On a clear night, the snow surface cools and surface hoar can form when humid air is present. Surface hoar often melts during the day on sunny slopes, but it remains on shady slopes (see Chapter 3).

Note also that contraction of wet surface snow after it becomes shaded can cause avalanches (see Chapter 4).

CHARACTER OF DATA TYPES

The character of data types in relation to forecasting models and procedures is discussed in this section. The three types of data available to a forecaster are measured at different time intervals and they differ in character (numerical or non-numerical). A general description of each class follows.

Class III (meteorological) factors are mostly real-time observations and the data flow is continuous. With the coming of data loggers connected to computers, it is possible to measure some data at intervals of 10 minutes (or less) for 24 hours per day. These data are largely numerical and they can therefore be adapted into numerical analysis software prediction schemes. The data can be applicable throughout an entire forecasting area (or even an entire mountain range). Regional (office-based) forecasters rely most heavily on this data group. Numerical techniques are most readily applied to this data group but usually on a local scale rather than for a region.

Class II (snowpack) factors are usually measured twice a day at most and sometimes weekly or less often. Some of the data are numerical and some are not. Therefore, not all of the information is easily included in traditional numerical schemes: symbolic and numerical techniques would be required to include all the information for computer forecasting. The data are of much more local areal applicability than Class III factors due to changes in aspect, elevation, and terrain. Local (field-based) forecasters make good use of these data.

Class I (stability) factors are highly specific data, which are generally not in numerical form and they are usually observed at irregular times, often only when avalanche danger is perceived to be increasing or high. Generally symbolic techniques would be required to include this information in a computerized scheme. Often the data are easy enough to interpret that no computer analysis is necessary or desirable. Backcountry travelers *must* pay close attention to data from this group because the data relate directly to current stability. Fredston and Fesler (1985) refer to this type of information as *bulls-eye information*.

REGIONAL AND LOCAL FORECASTING

Avalanche forecasting in the broadest sense is practiced on different scales, which can vary from stability evaluation for a given slope (micro) to forecasting future avalanching for an entire mountain range (synoptic) (Figure 7.15). The resolution and accuracy generally decrease as the area for which the forecasting is done increases. Forecasters try to use as much information as possible from all three classes of data. However, accessibility and practical considerations including regional variability exclude comprehensive data sets at each scale.

Regional forecasting, which ranges from the meso-scale to the synoptic scale, refers to avalanche prediction on the scale of a mountain range or a significant fraction thereof. Regional forecasting is principally office-based with heavy reliance on meteorological data to forecast mountain weather and its influence on producing avalanches. The principal products used can include quantitative precipitation forecasts (QPF) in millimeters of water equivalent, precipitation rates, and prediction of freezing or snow levels, and surface (e.g., at the level of mountain passes), ridge-top, and free-air winds. In addition, snow, avalanche, and weather reports from stations in the mountains can contribute data that are integrated along with mountain weather (current and expected) to produce an avalanche forecast. The method of producing such an avalanche forecast is usually conventional (largely nonquantitative; see a discussion in the next section), being based primarily on the judgment of the forecaster. The first system of regional forecasting was developed in Switzerland. Regional forecasting is also employed extensively in the United States (several centers), France, and Austria.

Local forecasting (meso- to microscale) is, as the

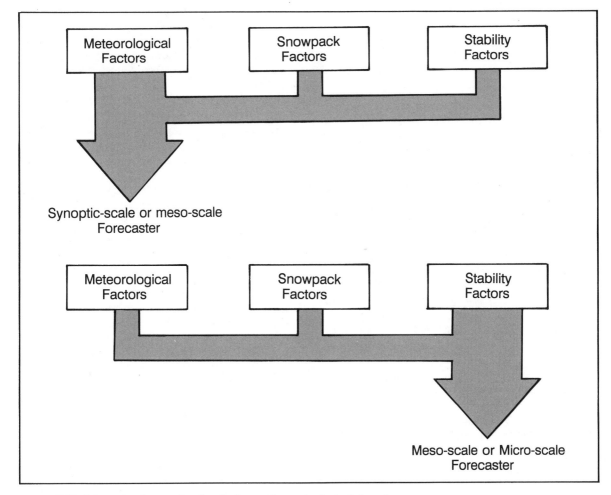

Figure 7.15. Schematic of types of avalanche forecasting and principal data classes.

name implies, avalanche prediction on a small scale, usually for an area less of than 100 km². Local forecasting is applicable to ski areas, sections of mountain highways, helicopter ski operations, and villages. Usually more precision is required than is available from regional forecasts; sometimes local forecasting stations provide data to regional forecasting centers to provide "ground truth" to forecasts largely based on weather. In Canada, the mountain ranges and snow climates are so diverse that local forecasting is the preferred method: Forecasts with greater precision are needed where people and facilities are located rather than regional forecasts with less detail covering vast unpopulated areas. Local forecasting is usually more heavily based on snowpack

data and stability observations than regional forecasting. Also, local forecasting is the domain in which some success in application of numerical avalanche prediction methods has been achieved.

A third level of forecasting is that concerned with individual slopes in backcountry travel, which can be termed *microscale forecasting*. The procedures involve using directly relevant data (stability observations) along with a careful analysis of terrain and current weather data. Snowpack data, primarily weak layer locations and stability, are used. Meteorological data are also useful. However, since the majority of avalanches in backcountry accidents are triggered by the victims themselves, data directly relevant to current stability are the most necessary to obtain. Backcountry forecasting analysis is described later in this chapter.

CONVENTIONAL AVALANCHE FORECASTING

Conventional avalanche forecasting refers to prediction of current and future snow stability by means of information and data from diverse sources largely without the aid of analytical techniques (formal numerical procedures) or encoded symbolic logic (e.g., expert systems). In practice, conventional forecasting consists of assimilating the relevant information (measurements, observations, weather forecast) and using it to formulate a forecast based on experience, intuition, and local knowledge of the mountain range.

Conventional forecasting is the most widely used method for snow avalanche stability prediction and it is regarded as the most successful. It has the advantage of using the human mind as a computer to assimilate data from all sources—numerical data, the forecasters' experience, knowledge, and personal observations—to produce a forecast. In contrast, completely computer-based forecasting systems usually are forced to leave out important sources of data. The disadvantage of conventional forecasting is the lack of objectivity and the length of time it takes people to learn techniques that are based largely on experience. In addition, there is an uneven quality and uncertainty about results that are based largely on human intelligence, intuition, experience, and local knowledge. Modern forecasting is moving away from conventional methods toward partially computerized systems.

There is no written prescription about how to forecast avalanches given a set of data and observations if formal mathematical procedures are not used: The weighting factors given to the various pieces of information are at the discretion of the forecaster. The techniques are best learned by working with an experienced forecaster. This type of forecasting combines practical experience and science.

NUMERICAL AVALANCHE PREDICTION

In modern avalanche forecasting, there are too many variables and too many situations that produce avalanching for the human mind to assimilate systematically. There is a need for mathematical analysis to help provide objective guidance for use in operational forecasting. Numerical avalanche prediction refers to organization of a data base of previously measured parameters, including avalanche occurrences, for use with a computer to help compare current conditions with past ones. It is necessary to have a high-quality data base before any numerical methods are attempted; good records of avalanche occurrences are essential. Several techniques have been employed with some success for local forecasting. The data can come from any of the three data types, but the primary emphasis is on meteorological data since these are usually measured by instruments at regular intervals. Snowpack data and stability observations must be included in any successful forecasting procedure and this is the primary limitation on the amount of data used: To be usable, each set of variables must be available every time measurements are input. Therefore, if meteorological data are measured hourly, all of these data cannot be easily used in combination with avalanche occurrence data (usually measured, at most, several times per day), for example. The frequency of avalanche occurrence observations often controls the number of times per day that numerical forecasting procedures can be applied.

Numerous attempts at numerical avalanche prediction have been made, but two methods have emerged as the most popular: *discriminant analysis* and *nearest neighbors*, as described in the following two sections.

Discriminant Analysis

The basic concept in discriminant analysis (Figure 7.16) is to relate avalanche occurrence data to combinations of the measured variables. Avalanche occurrence data are stratified into distinct groups, and combinations of variables are used to describe the occurrence groups. Each set of variables at a given instance of time defines a case that can then be classified into two to four classes (or groups) of avalanche occurrences. Thus far, most attempts have chosen the groups to be days with dry avalanches, days with wet or moist avalanches, and days without avalanches. Some models have also included the magnitude of avalanching to define the groups of occurrences.

Once distinct groups of occurrences have been formed, based on a previously compiled data base, it is possible to classify today's collection of measurements into one of the groups. The mathematical procedures of discriminant analyses provide classification rules that minimize the probability of misclassification of cases into one of the groups.

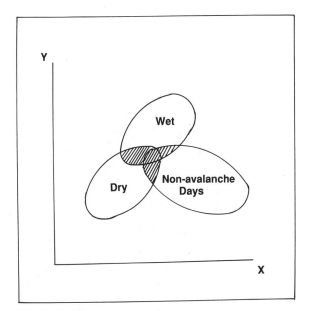

Figure 7.16. Schematic showing days with groups of avalanche occurrences (wet, dry) and nonavalanche days for classifying cases in a discriminant analysis.

Discriminant analysis is also used as a tool to define which variables are important for other types of forecasting models, such as nearest neighbors, as discussed next. However, discriminant analysis is also used as a forecasting tool by itself.

Discriminant analysis works best when the groups used to classify cases do not overlap much and when the variables used represent data that have a completely random character. Usually, it is difficult to completely satisfy these mathematical constraints.

Nearest Neighbors

Each set of measured parameters at a given time (including avalanche occurrences) constitutes a case within a data set. The nearest neighbor method (Figure 7.17) is concerned with finding cases in a data base of past measurements that are most similar to the current set of measurements. The problem is to define a cluster of cases in which the distance (numerically) is smallest between the present situation (case) and all the other cases in the data base. The distances are defined by considering each case as a vector with the number of dimensions equal to the number of variables; the distance between vector tips is then defined by the choice of a suitable distance measure (metric). Once distances

are calculated between the present case and all the previous ones, the nearest cases (neighbors) are retained (usually 30 or less) by the forecaster. The forecaster must analyze the information from the nearest neighbors along with other observable parameters to develop a forecast.

The principal advantage of the nearest neighbor method over a discriminant analysis is that the mathematical constraints necessary to perform a discriminant analysis are avoided. The disadvantage of the nearest neighbor method is that it is not as physically or mathematically rigorous as a discriminant analysis. For example, by itself there is no formal way to test whether a variable is really contributing to a proper result or whether it is redundant. Basically nearest neighbors and discriminant analysis can be contrasted by the following descriptions: (1) Based on the data, a discriminant analysis classifies avalanche and non-avalanche situations into groups and asks the question: In which group do today's data fall? (2) The nearest neighbor method takes today's data (a case) and asks the question: Which of the sets of data (cases) in the past form a group (cluster) around today's data? As with a discriminant analysis, the nearest neighbor method can be formulated to include a memory effect by utilizing data from previous days in with the analysis.

EXPERT SYSTEMS

The true character of avalanche prediction using computers is one that will ultimately encompass both

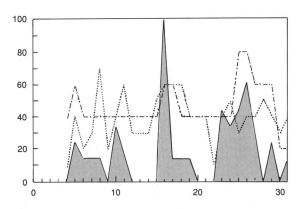

Figure 7.17. One month of nearest neighbors forecasting compared with avalanche occurrences: (———) observed avalanches; (··········) model forecast; (—·—·—) conventional forecast. (Results supplied by O. Buser)

numerical and symbolic computing. Numerical computing involves using data including snow and meteorological data, avalanche occurrences, and perhaps some data from snow profiles. Well-defined procedures are used to produce a numerical description of the hazard. There is, however, information available to avalanche forecasters that cannot be included in numerical algorithms. This latter information involves the logic and reasoning that come from the forecaster. If a prediction scheme is to incorporate such information, symbolic capabilities must be included. Since humans can successfully forecast avalanches by conventional techniques, it follows that in order for a computerized system to match human capability, all of the data sources must be used.

Symbolic computing involves incorporating the reasoning of an expert with rules or pattern recognition given by the expert to encode information that cannot be easily included in mathematical terms. To be useful, symbolic computing must be applied to a well-defined problem, and the rules incorporated must generally be agreed on by experts in the field. The application of expert systems to avalanche forecasting is in a very primitive state, but true promise seems possible in the future if numerical and symbolic computing can be combined. Since numerical procedures have already proven to be partially successful, and since there is definitely important information experts use that cannot be described in purely numerical terms, a system that allows the use of both numerical data and non-numerical information will ultimately be required.

EXAMPLE OF AVALANCHE FORECASTING

On a worldwide basis, more than 80% of fatal avalanche accidents now occur during backcountry travel. Furthermore, in the majority of cases, the victims themselves trigger the avalanches that capture them. For this reason, backcountry hazard evaluation is chosen as an example of avalanche forecasting in this section; it is the most important type of forecasting from the view of saving lives. It must be stressed that backcountry travelers need a *survival strategy;* avalanche forecasting and hazard evaluation are only part of that strategy. Chapter 8 provides a description of the other safety measures necessary for survival.

The *principles* of backcountry hazard forecasting are the same as for other types of avalanche forecasting, but

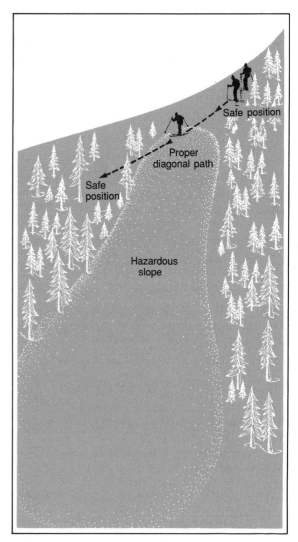

Figure 7.18. *Safe travel may involve microscale route selection during backcountry travel. Skiers move across from one safe position to the next, one at a time, observed by companions.*

the *details* are very different. A major difference between backcountry avalanche forecasting and other types of avalanche forecasting is that an intimate connection of terrain data must be combined with other data in backcountry hazard evaluation. Backcountry forecasting is relevant on the microscale and on this scale, terrain is extremely important (Figure 7.18).

Hazard ratings are appropriate for roads, railways, and ski areas where public access may be regulated and avalanche control is an option. However, in the backcountry, the hazard can change on a microscale and decision-making is the key element for determining whether a hazard exists. In some areas general snow stability forecasts are provided and these are very useful guides. However, safe backcountry travel requires a continuous evaluation of snow stability integrated with terrain and meterological parameters and an awareness of what might happen if the slope avalanches. Application of these principles involves both education about avalanche hazards and practical experience. In most cases, the problem must be attacked using a minimum of equipment with reasoning and common sense being the primary survival tools. Even if the instability is extreme, it may still be possible to travel safely in the backcountry.

In general, backcountry hazard evaluation, like all proper forecasting, involves an analysis. In this case, three groups of factors are used: terrain, snow stability, and weather, and they are combined to predict the most likely scenario. After this step, a decision-making process must be used prior to implementing the results. An evaluation that leaves out consideration of any of these steps is incomplete and increases the uncertainty and potential risk to the traveler.

The first step in a hazard evaluation consists of forming an opinion about the current snow stability. All relevant data should be used to form the opinion. These data may include direct observations of local conditions (new snowfall, avalanche occurrences, etc.), general backcountry forecasts, past knowledge of stability in the mountain range, news items on radio stations or in papers, and questioning of other travelers. Once an opinion is formed, one must be ready to revise it continually as more data become available. One *must* always have an opinion about snow stability *before* venturing into avalanche terrain.

Terrain Analysis

The next step in backcountry hazard evaluation is to analyze the terrain. The following question must be answered: Can avalanches occur on the terrain in question and how likely is such an occurrence? This portion of the analysis is given in the section "Backcountry Analysis" in Chapter 5 (Figure 7.19).

Stability Analysis

A stability analysis attempts to answer the question: Can avalanches initiate with the current snow condi-

Figure 7.19. Illustration of a V-shaped valley that served as a terrain trap. A skier was buried under 5 m of snow in this instance. (Photo by D. Gallagher)

tions? Important factors include (but are not limited to) the following:

Layering

- A relatively thick, cohesive layer (slab) over a weak layer constitutes a potential avalanche.
- Depth (and hence size) and distribution of potential slabs are estimated by studying layering and ski penetration.

Stability Observations

- All of the data entries under stability observations (Class I) may be used as directly relevant to current stability; usually explosives and shear frame tests are not used in backcountry analysis. The tests and data can give an indication of how much force is required to make a slab fail. The force to trigger a slab will vary considerably even on an individual slope. Be prepared to extrapolate your findings to a worst-case scenario.

Weather Analysis

Analysis of weather and meteorological data attempts to answer the question: Is instability increasing due to weather factors? Important factors include (but are not limited to) the following:

- Precipitation type (rain or snow) as a function of elevation
- Precipitation amount
- Precipitation rate
- Blowing snow as a function of elevation
- Temperature effects (both air and snow)
- Solar radiation
- Sky cover

See discussion earlier in this chapter of Class III factors for further details.

Decision-Making Analysis

Decision-making is concerned with using the data collected about terrain, snow stability, and weather to formulate a safe plan of action. This plan must be based on facts and tests that are as directly relevant to the problem as possible. The words of the great Swiss avalanche expert and mountaineer André Roch, are still relevant today: "Our best way of judging consists of knowing the influences provoking an avalanche and observing nature which usually shows its tricks in a generous fashion." Once a goal has been established, decision-making attempts to answer the question: Should safer alternatives be chosen? Important elements include (but are not limited to) the following:

- *Problem identification:* This may involve definition of the aspect, elevation, and terrain to be negotiated as well as the human and weather factors such as group strength and will, approaching darkness, and peer pressure (including client pressure in guided groups).
- *Data collection:* Relevant, objective data have been collected and analyzed about stability, terrain, and weather. In making a decision, stability and terrain data usually take precedence.
- *Evaluation of the consequences of the alternatives:* A key question to ask is: What will happen if the slope avalanches? This should include an analysis of potential terrain traps and exposure time in crossing avalanche paths. In almost all cases, if a slope can avalanche one *cannot* assume that survival is very likely (see Chapter 8).
- *Hazard evaluation:* Make an objective estimate of the hazard and examine your assumptions. Exchange information and suggestions freely with your fellow travelers. Evaluate the assumptions made by yourself and others. Ask the four key questions:
  1. Can avalanches occur on the terrain in question? (terrain analysis)
  2. Can avalanches initiate with the current snow conditions? (stability analysis)
  3. Is instability increasing due to weather factors? (weather analysis)
  4. Should safer alternatives be chosen? Evaluate the consequences if you are wrong. (decision-making)

The answer to question 4 depends on the answers to questions 1, 2, and 3. The degree of uncertainty and risk increases when the analysis is not done in an objective manner. Data used must be as relevant to the problem as possible. If a moderate or high degree of uncertainty is felt, the answer to question 4 will be *maybe*. In that case, either more direct information of the kind that will reduce the uncertainty must be sought or alternatives *must* be chosen. (The only thing that can change the avalanche hazard probability for a human being is more relevant information.) With *experience,* which cannot be learned from a book such as this, and objective analysis, the number of times the answer to question 4 is *maybe* can be reduced. A phrase from the video "Avalanche Awareness: A Question of Balance" seems appropriate: "Education teaches the rules, experience teaches the exceptions." Both elements are necessary prior to safe backcountry travel. Proper data collection and analysis combined with good decision-making then follow logically.

GENERAL STABILITY AND HAZARD RATINGS

After analyzing the contributory factors and considering them in combination, the avalanche forecaster rates the stability. The rating is used to communicate the forecaster's assessment to coworkers and the public.

A *stability rating* describes the probability of avalanches starting and it should not be confused with the term *hazard rating,* which describes the consequences to people or facilities if avalanches start. Both stability and hazard rating scales can take terrain into account but a hazard scale also considers the location of persons and objects and is, therefore, much more complicated than a stability rating. In backcountry travel, a stability rating is useful but since the hazard changes on the microscale, a hazard rating scale would be virtually useless.

In addition to the degree of stability, a stability rating may contain two additional elements. The first is the probability of avalanche release. This may be phrased by describing the magnitude of the trigger required (e.g., natural, skier, explosive charges). The second element is the location for probable avalanche release. It can be described in general terms or specifically by aspect, incline, elevation, or valley. Often the spatial extent (e.g., local or widespread) is referred to. The rating may also include comments about the depth of the instability and the expected size or type of avalanches to indicate consequences as input for hazard assessment.

At this time there is no international system for rating snow stability or hazards. The rating systems vary according to the needs and tastes of various countries. Examples of both stability and hazard scales are given in Appendix F.

References

The Avalanche Review. 1988. 6(4): 6–9.

Bakkehøi, S. 1987. Snow avalanche prediction using a probability method. IAHS Publication No. 162, pp. 549–555.

Buser, O., P. Föhn, W. Good, H. Gubler, and B. Salm. 1985. Different methods for assessment of avalanche danger. *Cold Regions Science and Technology* 10(3): 199–218.

Buser, O., M. Bütler, and W. Good. 1987. Avalanche forecast by the nearest neighbor method. IAHS Publication No. 162, pp. 557–569.

Ferguson, S. A., M. B. Moore, R. T. Marriott, and P. Speers-Hayes. 1990. Avalanche weather forecasting at the Northwest Avalanche Center, Seattle, Washington, U.S.A. *Journal of Glaciology* 36(122): 57–66.

Föhn, P., W. Good, P. Bois, and C. Obled. 1977. Evaluation and comparison of statistical and conventional methods of forecasting avalanche hazard. *Journal of Glaciology* 19(81): 375–387.

Fredston, Jill A., and Doug Fesler. 1988. Snow sense—a guide to evaluating snow avalanche hazard, 3rd ed. Anchorage, AK: Alaska Mountain Safety Center, Inc., 48 pp.

LaChapelle, E. R. 1967. The relation of crystal riming to avalanche formation in new snow. *Physics of Snow and Ice, Part 2, International Conference on Low Temperature Science,* Hokkaido University, Sapporo, Japan, August 14–19, 1966, pp. 1169–1175.

LaChapelle, E. R. 1980. The fundamental processes in conventional avalanche forecasting. *Journal of Glaciology* 26(94): 75–84.

LaFeuille, J., and E. Pahaut. 1989. Avalanche forecasting and communication: experiences in avalanche hazard scales. *Proceedings of the International Snow Science Workshop,* Whistler, British Columbia, October 12–15, 1988. Vancouver, BC: Canadian Avalanche Association, pp. 251–258.

Perla, R. I. 1970. On the contributory factors in avalanche hazard evaluation. *Canadian Geotechnical Journal* 7(9): 414–419.

Figure 8.1. Rescue of skier caught in avalanche. (Photo by A. Roch)

CHAPTER 8

SAFETY MEASURES AND RESCUE

You better start swimmin'
or you'll sink like a stone.

—Bob Dylan

Due to the uncertainty associated with stability evaluation and because avalanche terrain cannot always be avoided during periods of instability, learning proper safety measures and rescue techniques is essential to minimize risk of death and injury as a result of an avalanche (Figures 8.1 and 8.2).

The keys to personal safety and survival in avalanche terrain are:

1. *Be prepared*
   • Be educated about the nature of avalanche hazards.
   • Have a safety and rescue plan (informal for backcountry travel; written for ski areas, road maintenance, and other operations).
   • Maintain and carry safety equipment and practice how to use it.
   • Form an opinion about snow stability *prior* to traveling or working in avalanche terrain.
   • Be alert and mentally prepared for an avalanche encounter.
   • Know how to react in an emergency; act calmly and efficiently.

Emergency preparation includes appointing a leader when traveling or working. The leader checks group equipment at the departure point, briefs members on emergency procedures, and organizes party decision-making.

2. *Evaluate hazards* (see Chapter 7)
   • Analyze the terrain; select routes and work sites to minimize the hazard.
   • Make and evaluate snow stability and weather observations.
   • Use rational decision-making.
3. *Observe safety measures when traveling and/or working*
   • Take precautions by organizing the party, safety equipment, and the travel and/or work plans.
4. *React defensively when caught in an avalanche*
5. *Carry out a quick search and rescue when a party member is buried*

Only avalanche safety measures are described in this book. Additional safety considerations, such as weather forecasting, trip timing, adequate and complete equipment for travel and emergencies, clothing, food, and physical fitness of the party members are covered elsewhere in winter outdoor recreation books (Figure 8.3).

EDUCATION METHODS

Accident prevention begins with education about hazards and avoidance. Ignorance, stupidity, and egocentricity continue to cause numerous accidents and needless deaths year after year.

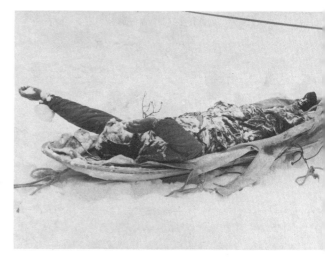

Figure 8.2. Body recovery of mountaineer killed by an avalanche. (Photos by Warren)

Publications

Various publications are available for avalanche education. Their objective is to promote rational decision-making rather than to frighten mountain travelers. The amount and detail of information in publications varies but most cover the basic elements:

• The nature of avalanches and their dangers
• Recognition of safe terrain
• Safety measures for travel and work
• Snow and weather conditions that frequently cause avalanches
• Rescue procedures

Numerous avalanche safety publications are available (Figure 8.3). Brief, usually free, pamphlets describe the basic elements. They are sponsored by groups wishing to promote public avalanche safety. Usually, technical language is avoided and safety measures are stressed. Pamphlets should not contain rules of thumb but many do.

Outdoor publications, club publications, and newspapers often feature articles on avalanches that reach a wide readership. The quality and educational value is enhanced when experienced avalanche workers supply as much rational and factual information as possible.

Books are aimed at the recreational mountain user who wants in-depth knowledge about avalanches. They contain photographs, drawings, and accident case histories. Books form the backbone of avalanche education programs.

Exhibitions of photos, drawings, text, and slide shows at park information centers and ski lodges are effective methods of informing backcountry users about avalanche hazards and safety measures.

Publications are a useful supplement for field experience, but they cannot replace it.

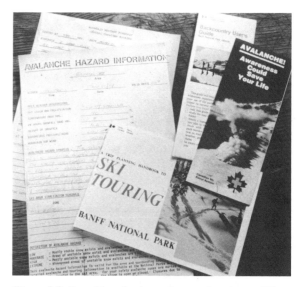

Figure 8.3. Pamphlets, books, and course brochures. (Photo by T. Auger)

Training Programs

Training programs are a vital, vibrant part of modern avalanche safety. They include a wide range of coverage: one-hour evening presentations, one-day seminars, weekend information courses, week-long courses, and university-credit courses. Numerous clubs, schools, private training institutions, recreational organizations, individuals, and companies offer a variety of programs to the general public and to their own members. Organizers and instructors have made the following generalizations about training programs:

Sessions are best held for groups of people who share a common interest; for example, a course should contain only snowmobilers, ski mountaineers, or highway maintenance staff. Such groups usually have similar experience, operate in the same type of terrain, and feel more comfortable among themselves.

Instructors should know and share the interests of the group. Instructors *must* have personal experience with mountain travel and avalanche hazard evaluation and know how to tailor the appropriate information to fit a given audience. For example, different information is required for skiers than for highway maintenance personnel.

Introductory material should stress avalanche terrain recognition and route-finding rather than snow science. Field sessions are extremely beneficial. Two-day courses with one day in a classroom and one day in the field provide a useful introduction.

Films, videos, and slides illustrate the message and assist in reviewing the topics but they cannot replace an experienced, credible speaker.

AVALANCHE SAFETY PROGRAMS

Ski area, highway maintenance, mining, and forest operations and other industries in avalanche areas usually have a *snow safety plan* with the following content: hazard description; an outline of appropriate protective and safety measures; assignment of responsibilities for hazard evaluation, ordering area closures, and enforcing safety measures; and a rescue plan.

Supervisors and managers may be trained in programs ranging from half-day sessions to week-long field courses (depending on the size of the operation, the magnitude of the avalanche hazard, and the level of decision-making). The objective of the training is to create an understanding of the purposes and procedures for protective measures.

Operational staff should become familiar with the safety plan through realistic field training sessions. Operational and field personnel should have regular in-house training. Standard training sessions at the beginnning of the winter cover the following topics:

- Familiarization with the safety plan, rescue plan, rescue equipment, and personnel
- Familiarization with potential avalanche paths
- Practice of personal safety measures; for example, rescue practices and the use of rescue transceivers
- Review of weather factors producing avalanches

Local police, helicopter pilots, dog handlers, ski instructors, and office support staff should join training sessions if possible. Guidelines for training rescue personnel are given in the section "Organized Rescue."

EQUIPMENT

Each person traveling in avalanche terrain should carry a rescue transceiver and appropriate protective clothing. In addition, a party should be equipped with shovels, probes, and first-aid kits (numbers depend on the size of the party and the availability of backup equipment). When small groups travel in the backcountry, each person should carry a shovel and probe. Large groups (for example, helicopter skiers or

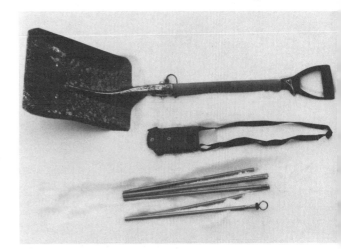

Figure 8.4. Collapsible shovel, transceiver, and collapsible probe. (Photo by B. Jamieson)

snowmobilers) might need fewer shovels and probes distributed among the group (Figure 8.4).

Persons who work with mechanical equipment in avalanche areas should wear transceivers and protective clothing. Vehicles should be furnished with a shovel, probe, and communication equipment.

Transceivers

Transceivers (also called *rescue beacons*) are electronic devices that emit a beeping signal when transmitting. Each transceiver must be checked out for its transmitting and receiving capabilities and verified in the transmitting mode before leaving the trailhead. When a person is buried in an avalanche, the survivors switch their units to receive and locate the victim. Transceiver use is described in the section "Transceiver Search."

Shovel

A shovel is essential for digging out a buried person within a reasonable time period. To be effective, an avalanche shovel must be strong and have a large scoop and a sturdy handle. Portable shovels should be as large and sturdy as is practical to carry.

Probe

Collapsible (or sectional) probes are preferred over ski pole probes. Ski pole probes may be lost in the avalanche (even if the survivor comes to rest on the surface), often they are hard to assemble, and their large diameter and conical shape make probing more difficult.

PRECAUTIONS WHEN TRAVELING

Backcountry Travel

The following precautions are recommended for travel on foot, ski, and snowmobile in avalanche terrain.

1. Do not travel alone. A person buried in an avalanche must rely on survivors for live rescue.
2. Maintain a distance between persons and machines. This will minimize exposure to avalanche danger, distribute the load on the snowpack, and distribute the equipment to ensure it is available for use if needed (Figure 8.5). There is no fixed rule for spacing. Ideally, one person at most should be

Figure 8.5. Party crossing a potential avalanche slope. Only one skier is exposed while others wait at a safe spot. (Photo by A. Kelner)

exposed to the hazard at a time; any exposed person must be kept in sight. Sometimes, the ideal distance cannot be maintained in wide avalanche paths without causing long delays. Therefore, on occasion, shorter distances may have to be chosen. The proper spacing should be maintained until the last person has left the avalanche path safely.

3. Make rest stops and set up camps only at safe

locations. When skiing steep slopes, stop only at the side or beyond the potential runout.

4. Do not wear ski safety straps and ski pole wrist loops; skis and poles attached to a person hold the body down in an avalanche. In addition, attached skis and poles can cause injury by snagging trees and rocks or hitting their owner during descent in an avalanche. All skis used in potential avalanche terrain (*including* telemark and cross-country skis) should have release bindings (Figure 8.6).

5. During backcountry travel by ski tourers, the group should actively discuss emergency procedures and decision-making (for the benefit of the newer participants). This is a good practice. The key points for rescue are:
   - How to "spot" the last seen point in an actual emergency situation
   - The importance of staying and searching rather than going for help
   - The basics of search
   - How to be prepared if an avalanche does occur by taking additional precautions as outlined here

Additional measures recommended for times when a marginally safe area must be traversed are as follows:

6. Wear jackets, mitts, and hats. Warm clothing helps prevent hypothermia following burial.

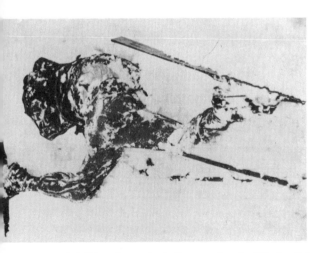

Figure 8.6. Skier who was buried in an avalanche. Skis that did not release assisted in twisting his legs. (Photo by Swiss Federal Institute for Snow and Avalanche Research)

7. Select routes carefully. Avoid likely trigger spots, use microscale route finding, move from one relatively safe spot to another (thick trees, closely spaced trees or rocks, large rocks, high spots) (Figure 8.7). If skiing an open glade surrounded by trees, stay close to the trees.

8. Plan the reaction and escape route if an avalanche should start: ski to the side (best choice) or down, accelerate the snowmobile. Being prepared for an emergency can save valuable seconds that might be vital to an escape. In addition, the group will know which way you were trying to escape.

9. Assign a spotter who watches the slope and gives an agreed warning signal (for example, the call "avalanche").

10. In mountaineering, it is often better not to rope up in avalanche paths. If one person is caught, the others may be pulled along and maneuverabilty is limited on a rope. Avalanche forces are usually greater than the strength of a belay in snow (except when the rope is tied to a rock or a tree). On glaciers, it must be determined whether the hazard from avalanches is greater than that from crevasses.

Travel on Roads

Public and industrial roads are closed when the avalanche hazard to traffic is high, but are usually open during low and moderate hazard (see the hazard scale in Appendix F). Safety measures recommended for road users include:

1. Do not stop in avalanche paths. Stopping increases exposure time (refer to Figure 5.20). On public roads warning signs AVALANCHE AREA, DO NOT STOP and END AVALANCHE AREA should mark entrances and exits to avalanche paths (Figure 8.8).

2. Carry warm clothing for protection.

3. Keep windows tightly closed to prevent snow from entering the vehicle.

4. When an avalanche has blocked the road:
   - Turn around or back up and wait in a safe area (beyond AVALANCHE AREA signs).
   - Do not attempt to drive through a small deposit of avalanche snow. The snow is usually deeper than it looks.
   - Do not attempt to dig out a vehicle stuck in avalanche snow. Carefully assess whether it would be safer to leave a vehicle and walk to safety or to remain in the vehicle.

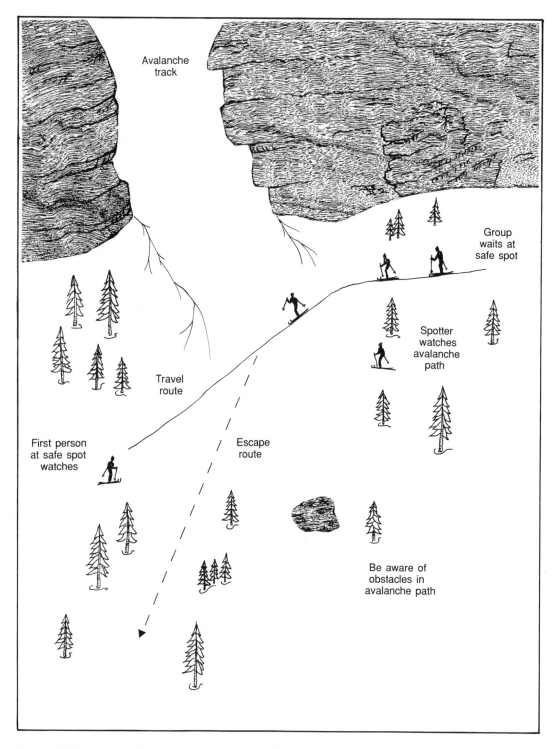

Figure 8.7. Precautions when crossing a suspicious slope.

Figure 8.8. Avalanche warning signs on road. (Photos by D. McClung)

- When avalanches block the road in both directions, remain in the vehicle and wear seatbelts.
- If a radio is available, call for help and wait inside the vehicle for instructions.

At Work

Occasionally, maintenance crews must repair utilities or remove snow when the hazard is moderate or greater. The following safety measures apply while working in avalanche paths during moderate hazard:

1. Work in tandem with machines properly spaced, or if one machine is working, include a spotter in a truck.
2. Bulldozers and loaders should have closed roll-over cabs.
3. Wear transceivers on your person (around the neck); people may be separated from machines and vehicles.
4. Carry probes and shovels in machines and vehicles.
5. Equip vehicles and persons working outside with two-way radios.
6. Have a reaction plan if an avalanche should strike.

SURVIVAL CHANCE IN AN AVALANCHE

Several countries (the United States, Canada, Switzerland, France, Austria) maintain statistics on the number of people caught in avalanches and the number and causes of death. Tables 8.1 and 8.2 summarize the approximate statistics.

Table 8.1 Percent Survival of People Caught in Avalanches

80%	Survive if they remain on the surface
40–45%	Survive if partially or completely buried
55–60%	Survive if protected by buildings or vehicles

Table 8.2 Causes of Death in Avalanches

65%	Suffocation
25%	Collisions with trees, rocks, and other obstacles
10%	Hypothermia and shock

Remember that the *only* known cause of death for humans is inadequate transport of oxygen to the cells. Collision can cause death instantly but suffocation does not take much longer. Once oxygen is cut off, people can suffer irreversible brain damage within minutes. However, there are examples in which burial by snow lowered body metabolism enough to prolong survival for hours. Chance of suffocation depends on the duration and depth of burial, the character of the avalanche snow, and the character of the victim's entrapment. The probability of finding persons alive decreases rapidly with time. Of those completely buried and unprotected by buildings or vehicles, only about 40% of the total survive. As time marches on, the following percentages of the total apply (based on U.S. statistics):

- 20% live longer than 30 minutes (50% of survivors)
- 13% live longer than 1 hour
- 7% live longer than 2 hours
- 4% live longer than 3 hours

Avalanche snow is less dense close to the surface, therefore persons with a shallow burial may live longer. Live rescues of victims buried deeper than 2 m are rare (about 4% of all live recoveries); usually deep burial survivals occur because the victim had an air space near trees, in buildings, or in vehicles. As depth of burial increases, pressure from snow above increases on a victim to further inhibit breathing. Formation of an "ice mask" around the face by freezing of wet snow produced by warm breathing is a further limitation on burial survivals. The deeper the burial, the smaller are the snow particles in avalanche deposits, making this effect more likely.

Survival Strategy when Caught Unprotected

Survival strategies differ based on whether you are caught in a vehicle or caught unprotected in an avalanche on foot, skis, or snowmobile. This section discusses a survival strategy when caught unprotected.

The statistics about survival and burial and the principles of avalanche motion (see Chapter 5) yield safety measures that can be summarized based on four priorities: (1) avoid being caught or buried, (2) avoid suffocation, (3) avoid collision, and (4) try to attract the attention of people nearby.

Usually, poles and skis are ejected by snow forces immediately when one is caught in an avalanche; if not they should be discarded if possible. Snowmobilers should jump off the machine if it cannot be steered to the side. It is easier to fight when not attached to equipment.

Whether or not a pack should be discarded is an open question. A backpack limits maneuverability in flowing snow (particularly if heavy), but it prevents back injuries if obstacles are hit. Dropping a pack results in loss of rescue and first-aid equipment and clothing that might be needed later.

During initial avalanche motion:

- Try to escape to the side before being hit; a few seconds can be enough time to escape.

- Call out for attention when caught; then try to keep flowing snow from entering the mouth and nose.
- Try to grab trees or other anchors.
- Try to remain upright and near the surface: swim, kick, and fight.
- Steer to the side.
- Watch out for collisions with trees and rocks.

During deceleration:

- Make a strong thrust and kick to the surface just before the snow stops (once snow stops, motion may be impossible).
- If possible, make an air space in front of the face and push one arm to the surface; this alerts searchers and makes a possible air vent when the avalanche stops.

After motion has stopped:

- Try to dig yourself out.
- Call when rescuers are near. Snow attenuates sound, but a person's voice can be heard if the burial is shallow (however, depth of burial may not be known by a buried person).
- Conserve oxygen; do not fight the sensation of blacking out.

Defense against powder avalanches:

- Seek shelter behind obstacles, for example, rocks, trees, and buildings.
- Turn away and cover nose and mouth to prevent snow dust from entering.

Survival Strategy when Caught in a Vehicle

The occupants of vehicles have a better chance of survival than unprotected persons because the vehicle affords protection from avalanche forces and provides an air space. Carbon monoxide poisoning is a principal hazard when a vehicle is buried in the snow, because the exhaust gas of a running engine may escape into the vehicle instead of the snow.

Recommended action for persons buried in a vehicle include:

- Shut off the engine and lights.
- Conserve the oxygen in the vehicle by not smoking or using matches.
- When equipped with a radio, call for assistance; leave the radio in the receiving mode.

Figure 8.9. Rapid action is required for an organized rescue party to move to an accident site near a ski area.

- When the vehicle is equipped with a flasher, turn on the flasher.
- Push a probe, rod, or other object toward the surface as a check for the depth of burial and as a clue for rescuers.
- Try to dig out.
- When digging out is possible, leave the vehicle only when safe to do so.

REACTION BY SURVIVORS

A buried victim's life depends crucially on the action of survivors in the few minutes following an avalanche. Organized rescues are often much too slow to rescue people alive (Figure 8.9). Avalanche rescue is very similar to dealing with a drowning victim—self-help is the key. All people traveling in avalanche terrain *should* know search and rescue techniques. When persons are caught in an avalanche, the survivors should react *calmly and methodically* (Figure 8.10). The action sequence as one witnesses an avalanche is as follows:

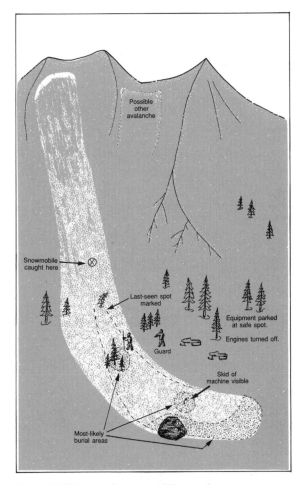

Figure 8.10. Rescue by snowmobile travel party.

1. Quickly look to be sure you are in a safe spot; you may have to move to a safe location.
2. Immediately, note the *last-seen point* of people caught in the avalanche. To properly "note the last-seen point" takes some skill and composure. If party members are caught, you must be prepared to *concentrate* on the job of spotting them. (It is worthwhile to stress the importance of this with your party before it happens.) If the victim disappears, attempt to locate the last-seen point by marking its position relative to another object. For instance, take note of a tree in line with the spot and your location—this gives a straight line reference. Mark the spot with a ski pole, ski, branch, or other visible object as accurately as possible (Figure 8.11).

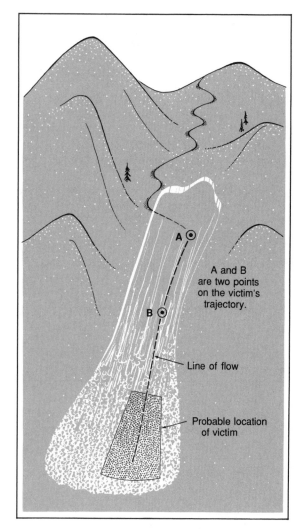

Figure 8.11. If two points along the victim's trajectory can be established, the location of the victim will most likely be near the line joining the points.

3. Count the survivors to determine who is lost. Try to determine the location of lost persons when the avalanche occurred.
4. Quickly assess the hazard from other avalanches. Post a guard at a safe spot if avalanches from adjacent slopes could threaten the search area. Make sure any escape route and warning signal is understood by all.
5. Make a visual search of the deposit surface with concentration on the most likely burial areas. Look for parts of the victims and their equipment on the surface; equipment indicates the approximate movement of victims and allows a more accurate identification of most likely burial areas. Leave the clues in place and mark them. Use your eyes and ears.
6. Alert the base station of accident and details if a radio is available.
7. Switch transceivers to receive. The leader checks that none of the survivors' transceivers is transmitting. Rescuers have sometimes wasted valuable time by homing in on each other. Sometimes rescues have been hampered by people listening to their own transmitting signal or their own quartz watch. Virtually all transceivers have instructions that, when practiced, make finding the victim an easy task.
8. Determine the most likely burial areas (see the section "Most Likely Burial Areas"). Allow for the fact that victims may have been moving when the avalanche struck.
9. Make a search by transceiver first at the most likely burial areas, then on other parts of the avalanche. Simultaneously keep looking for signs of the victims and equipment.
10. Stop from time to time, call to the victims, and listen for voices of buried persons.
11. Consider keeping backpacks on during search so that shovels, probes, and first-aid equipment are readily available. Whether or not skis should be worn during the search depends on snow conditions and slope incline.
12. Keep everyone involved in the search by searching with transceivers or probing and investigating most likely burial areas.
13. When the victims are located, quickly dig them out (see the following section for victim care).
14. When equipped with a radio, keep the base station informed about search progress.

If a transceiver search is unsuccessful and eye and ear searches do not give clues, then:

15. Call for an organized rescue by radio if available.
16. Mark the locations of clues (equipment and clothing) found on the surface. Spot-probe around the clues.
17. Continue to spot-probe most likely burial areas in front and behind trees and rocks, in depressions, and at the tip of the avalanche and near clues from the victims.

18. Decide whether or not to go for help if help was not already summoned by radio. A messenger should be dispatched only if the party is large. Other survivors continue the search even when assistance is very close and quick response time is assured. The victims' best chances of survival rest with the abilities of the survivors at the accident site. Before leaving the scene of the accident, the messenger-witness must know the exact location of the avalanche and be able to direct a rescue party to the scene, and the messenger-witness should return his or her transceiver to the transmitting mode. It is useful to write down the location (on a map or sketch), time of accident, number of persons buried, and number of persons on the scene.

19. Organize a probe line at most likely burial areas and mark areas already probed with ski poles, skis, branches, or packs.

20. Keep the surface of the avalanche clean of food, garbage, and urine (for possible dog search later).

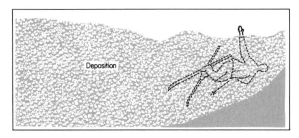

Figure 8.12. Live rescue of a skier. (Photo by Whitmire Photography)

21. Keep searching and probing until all reasonable hope for a live recovery has passed or until help arrives and takes over (Figure 8.12).

Care of the Victim

Once found, the primary consideration is fast restoration of breathing. An outline of avalanche victim care is given in the following list. First-aid courses *must* be taken to learn correct application of first-aid measures; the procedures can only be learned through supervised practice.

After checking for further avalanche danger and after finding the victim, quickly free the head, chest, and stomach, then follow these steps:

1. Clear the patient's airway, check for breathing, then use normal first-aid procedures.
2. If the victim is not breathing, check for a pulse.
3. If no pulse is found, begin cardiopulmonary resuscitation (CPR) to restore pulse and breathing.
4. If a pulse is present but breathing is not, begin artificial respiration. Resuscitation should be continued until breathing and/or pulse is restored *or* until unmistakable signs of death are obvious.
5. Check for deadly bleeding; control by applying pressure immediately.
6. Examine for and treat fractures.
7. Treat for shock: Elevate legs and lower body, control pain, administer plasma or plasma substitutes if possible.
8. Treat for hypothermia.
9. Examine for internal injuries.

The victim must be stabilized before attempting evacuation.

Hypothermia is a major consideration for avalanche victims due to contact with snow and exposure to cold and wind. Treatment involves insulation from the environment and snow beneath, exchanging wet for warm dry clothes, application of external heat, and providing nutrients (including hot drinks). External heat is best applied by placing a warm healthy person next to the victim inside a warm sleeping bag, or by placing hot water bottles, chemical hot pads, or whatever is available next to the thorax area. Handle victim gently to minimize further trauma and limit the triggering of irregular heart rhythms.

Some surviving avalanche victims may have only minor injuries that permit them to move to the trailhead under their own power. During travel, victims should be checked continuously because the effects of shock, hypothermia, and injury might be slow to develop.

Evacuation

To prepare for evacuation, if the victim is unconscious, keep the airway open, keep the head level with body or slightly lower, and continue treatment for shock and hypothermia.

If the party is not equipped to transport the victim, help may have to be summoned for unconscious victims or conscious victims unable to travel. While waiting for help, an injured person should be constantly monitored. Vital signs and times should be written down. The victims should be protected with all available clothing and sleeping bags, made as comfortable as possible, and continuously treated for shock and exposure. The shelter should be clearly marked with probe poles, skis, or branches. The bodies of dead victims may be moved, but the location should be clearly marked for subsequent investigation by local authorities.

Evacuation of victims with major injuries will require the help of trained emergency personnel. Immediate transport to a hospital may be necessary for survival of some victims.

It is common to have a medical doctor as one team member of mountaineering expeditions. Almost all workers who deal with avalanche safety are now required to have up-to-date mountain first-aid training. These include ski patrol, highway personnel, mountain guides, park wardens, and snow rangers. It is highly recommended that all winter mountain users obtain relevant mountain first-aid training and be current in that training. It is not appropriate to discuss mountain first aid in detail here, but it is an essential component of avalanche safety work.

ORGANIZED RESCUE

Rescue Plan

An organized rescue is conducted by a trained and equipped organization (ski area, heli-ski operation, highway maintenance, backcountry lodge) according to a prepared *rescue plan*. The avalanche rescue plan is a set of written instructions containing:

• Generic rescue instructions and communications
• Area-specific procedures

• Organization chart
• Instructions for the key positions of the organization
• Equipment and resource lists
• Forms for notes and reports

The plan identifies the key functions and gives clear instructions for delegation of support functions. It is important that organization leaders at each level delegate the work.

Often the rescue plan is part of an area or operational safety plan. Figure 8.13 shows a typical organization chart. The rescue plan contains the names of the persons who would occupy the various positions.

Base Rescue Leader

The base rescue leader, must be familiar with the area and the rescue plan. The base rescue leader is the coordinator of personnel, equipment, transportation, and supplies. The base rescue leader may be located at the office of the ski area, the lodge, or the highway administration office. The base rescue leader must be in telephone and radio contact with support agencies and the accident site commander (the field rescue leader). He or she dispatches personnel and equipment, briefs the media, and maintains communications with other local agencies. The base rescue leader must keep a journal, including a time log, of the events surrounding all parts of the rescue.

Written instructions for the base rescue leader typically contain the following (priorities will vary according to local operation):

1. You are base rescue leader until you are relieved by a superior authority.
2. Question the witness (messenger of the accident) using the accident reporting form (enclosed); keep the witness where he or she can be questioned for further information (Figure 8.14).
3. Appoint first party leader immediately.
4. Notify headquarters: (names and telephone numbers supplied here).
5. Close area or road if necessary.
6. Arrange for transportation:
   • Helicopter: (names and telephone numbers supplied here)
   • Snowmobile: (location and contact names and telephone numbers supplied here)
   • Road vehicles
7. Dispatch first party. Record names of party members.

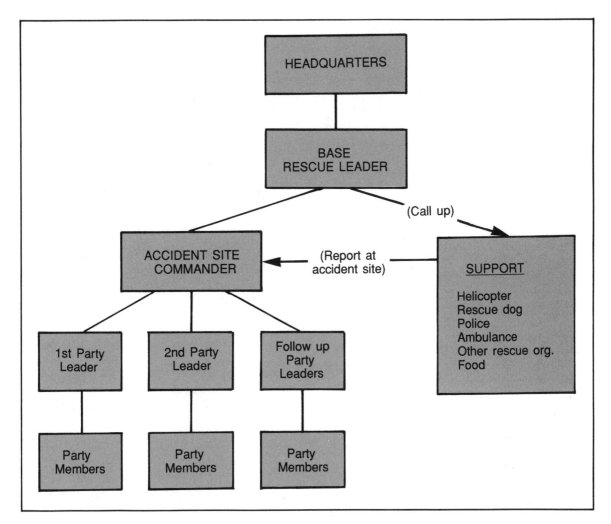

Figure 8.13. Schematic of organized rescue.

8. Request a rescue dog: (names and telephone numbers of dog handlers supplied here).

9. Notify authorities: (location and names and telephone numbers supplied here).

10. Appoint a second party leader. Dispatch second party. Record the names of party members.

11. Maintain communications with the accident site commander and the party leaders.

12. Arrange transportation of the victims: toboggan, helicopter, ambulance, doctor: (names and telephone numbers of hospitals supplied here).

13. When the rescue is prolonged, arrange for:

• supply of food and hot drinks
• shelter
• replacement of rescuers from: (names and telephone numbers of support personnel and agencies supplied here)
• dispatch third party with additional support equipment

14. Upon completion of the rescue:
• account for all personnel
• notify the completion of rescue operation to headquarters and support agencies
• check and store the equipment

15. Keep records of the times and events.

Witness Report of an Accident

Location of Avalanche_____

Number of Persons Buried_____ Rescue Beacons_____

Number and Conditions of Others at the Site
_____
_____
_____
_____

Size of Avalanche_____

Survival Equipment at Accident Site
_____
_____

Date and Time of Accident_____

Time Now_____

Describe Access/Route
_____
_____
_____

Briefly Describe Accident and Action of Survivors
_____
_____
_____
_____
_____

Reporting Person's Name and Location
_____

Signature_____ Date_____

Figure 8.14. Accident report form.

Accident Site Commander

The accident site commander is in charge of the search and rescue at the accident location (Figure 8.15). He or she keeps the operation moving by assigning probe leaders, searchers, shovelers, first-aid attendents, etc.; the primary consideration is the safety of the rescue personnel team. The accident site commander assesses the avalanche hazard at the accident, determines which areas will be searched, and oversees the care of survivors and victims. The site commander requests assistance and equipment as needed from the base rescue leader.

The accident site commander should be well trained in avalanche hazard evaluation and search and rescue, be physically fit, and have leadership and management skills. The first-party leader is the accident site commander when he or she arrives at the accident site and may be replaced later if a more experienced person arrives.

First Party

The first-party leader assembles a small group of readily available persons who can travel fast. All members should use the same means of travel (for example, all on snowmobiles or all on skis). Since the equipment in a first-party pack is light, the first party can move to the accident site quickly.

The instructions *in writing* for the first-party leader may include:

1. Organize a party of three to five fast-moving persons.
2. Take the first-party pack and radio.
3. Check personal equipment of each party member:
   - transceiver
   - portable shovel
   - probe
   - clothing: jackets, hats, mitts, ski gear
4. Move quickly but safely to the accident site as directed by the base rescue leader. Take the messenger-witness with you, if possible.
5. Mark route for following rescuers if necessary.
6. Maintain communication with the base rescue leader.
7. At the accident site:
   - evaluate the hazard
   - post an avalanche guard, if necessary, and arrange for a warning signal
   - designate escape routes
   - question witnesses and survivors at the scene about how the accident happened, persons buried, locations of the party members when the avalanche occurred, last-seen point, and search carried out so far
   - mark the last-seen point if known
8. Take care of the survivors.
9. Report to the base rescue leader.
10. Determine most likely burial areas.
11. Organize and delegate authority for a visual search, transceiver search, spot-probing at most likely burial areas, and shoveling; mark with wands locations of clothing, equipment, and persons found.
12. Keep notes of actions and sketch a map of the avalanche site with locations of clues.
13. When the second party arrives:
    - inform new rescuers about safety measures, the accident, and actions taken
    - store equipment at safe area downwind from the avalanche
    - assign tasks for new rescuers

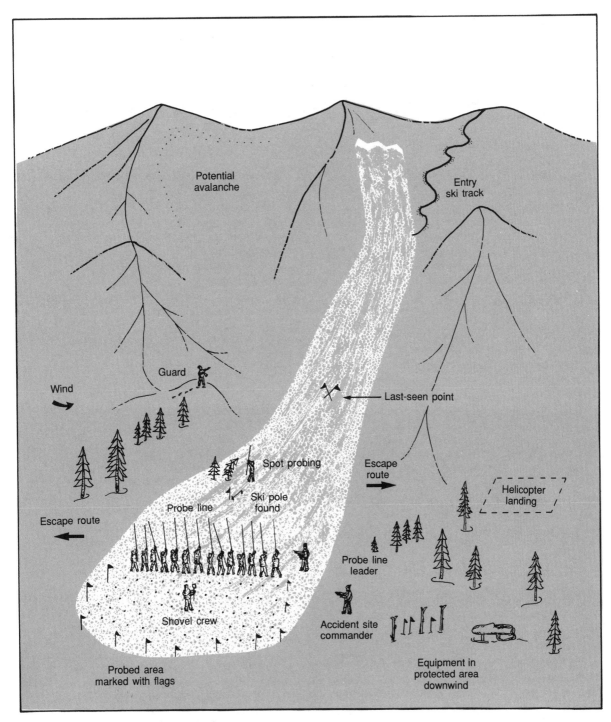

Figure 8.15. Accident site with organized rescue.

- organize a probe line for coarse probing of most likely burial area

14. Consider equipment, food, and support needed for a prolonged rescue and communicate needs to the base rescue leader.

15. Arrange rest for tired searchers. Tired searchers leaving the accident site must move in groups under a leader; keep records.

16. Keep the search moving.

17. Act as accident site commander until relieved. Brief the new accident site commander about all actions prior to his or her arrival.

18. Upon conclusion of the operation, account for all personnel and equipment.

19. If time and the terrain allow:
    - sketch the avalanche paths with the locations at which the parties entered, where persons were caught, and where persons were found
    - observe a fracture line profile
    - estimate terrain slope angles
    - record the characteristics and dimensions of the avalanche (see Appendix E)

Second Party

The second party leaves for the accident site as quickly as possible after the first party. The second party's task is to supply additional personnel and probes and to bring the heavier and bulkier equipment needed for resuscitation, first aid, transport, and protection of the victims.

The second-party leader checks the equipment, clothing, and physical condition of his or her team before leaving. At the accident site, the leader reports to the accident site commander.

Follow-up Parties

Follow-up parties bring equipment needed for a prolonged rescue: food, drinks, tents, clothing, bivouac gear, and additional personnel. The party leader has the same responsibilities as the second-party leader.

Equipment

Equipment is stored at the base station in a marked, easily accessible rescue room and in lift houses and other safe locations near known avalanche paths.

Contents of First-Party Pack

1 rescue plan; pencil and small notebook
10 sectional probes, lightweight
2 shovels, aluminum and collapsible
2 last-seen point markers
25 wands, color A
50 wands, color B
2 rolls flagging tape, color C

Contents of Second-Party Pack

2 shovels, aluminum and collapsible
2 last-seen point markers
100 wands, color B
2 rolls flagging tape
1 rescue plan; pencils and small notebook
10 sectional probes
5 chemical heat packs
2 wool blankets (or sleeping bags)
1 ground sheet, space blanket, or bivouac sack
1 set of airways

Other Avalanche Rescue Equipment

Oxygen/resuscitation kit, complete with airways, bag/valve masks
Light sticks for route markers at night
Headlamps
Spare radio batteries
Steel shovels for dense, hard, or wet snow
Additional probes
Spare rescue transceivers
Camp kits, complete for overnight requirements
Camera, flash, and film
Climbing rope
Sectional toboggan
Air warning horn and/or megaphone
Tents
Bulletin boards with paper and marking pens

TRAINING RESCUE PERSONNEL

Training personnel is the key to a successful organized search and rescue. The Canadian Parks Service makes the following recommendations with respect to training:

1. A major component of rescue training should focus on winter travel skills in bad weather. All aspects of backcountry travel skills, including

skiing upslope and downslope, route selection, snow stability evaluation, and group management, must be in place before specialized rescue training is effective. These skills must be practiced periodically or they will decline over time.

2. Conduct training sessions periodically throughout the winter, not just during the preseason.

3. Rescue practices should be as realistic as possible. They should be held in avalanche terrain, use real avalanche deposition, have realistic scenarios, and have entry tracks, lost articles, etc., at the appropriate locations. Scenarios should vary, so they don't become routine.

4. Organizational authority and reporting structure should be integrated into training exercises. Regular supervisory personnel should be trained to fill various leadership roles to develop the skills and abilities necessary to fill actual rescue positions.

5. Role playing should stress positive reinforcement by practicing only correct systems and techniques. Mistakes should be corrected immediately so that the role players do not undergo an overly critical debriefing. Practice leaders should be capable and comfortable with their roles, so that effective and positive images are delivered to all participants. These leaders should conduct debriefings containing descriptions of decision-making processes to all participants. Observers/trainers should limit their input to technical comments concerning the simulation.

6. Recorded video coverage is an excellent way to document practices and illustrate methods and systems employed.

7. In training sessions, stress self-preservation, caution, and safety. The potential for further avalanches must always be respected.

8. Practice should be done in good weather. This allows productive on-site group discussions and avoids complications such as frostbite and hypothermia. However, controlled real-weather scenarios can be extremely valuable.

9. The appropriate rescue plan should always be used. Training sessions should be structured to test the plan and the plan should be updated immediately if flaws are found.

10. When using radios during practices, periodically broadcast "This is a practice" to prevent false alarms to those who scan radio frequencies.

11. Some practices should be conducted without relying on helicopters, snowmobiles, and other forms of mechanized transportation.

12. Rescue personnel should not have unrealistic expectations. They should be mentally prepared for fatalities and frustrations.

13. Use winter travel and avalanche rescue training as opportunities to develop trust and teamwork within the group.

MOST LIKELY BURIAL AREAS

Most likely burial areas are the locations for initial search where the probability of finding a buried person is greatest. Initially, it is extremely important to determine the locations of all people involved and how they might have reacted at the time of the avalanche. Most likely burial areas (Figure 8.16) will often be:

- Below entry tracks
- On or below the road (accidents on roads)
- Along the general flow-line of the avalanche below the last-seen point. Identify the last-seen point accurately; victims have been found above an *assumed* last-seen point (see Figure 8.11)
- Above and below trees, rocks, or other obstacles in the path
- Near the toe of the deposited avalanche snow
- In depressions, such as creeks, road grades, crevasses, and other places deep snow can collect
- At the lateral edges of the avalanche

Areas outside the most likely burial areas should not be neglected. People could be thrown out or near the edge of the deposit. Lost persons might have been able to ski or drive out. In a few instances, avalanching snow has pushed victims a short distance under undisturbed snow adjacent to the toe of the avalanche.

TRANSCEIVER SEARCH

Transceivers (rescue beacons) are electronic devices that can transmit and receive radio signals. The 457-kHz radio frequency is now standard but numerous old units with a 2.275-kHz frequency and dual-frequency units that operate on both 457 and 2.275 kHz are in use. Party leaders must ensure that all the party members carry instruments that are compatible with respect to frequency: 457-kHz or dual-frequency models.

A buried, transmitting transceiver is located because the signal is stronger closer to the transmitting instru-

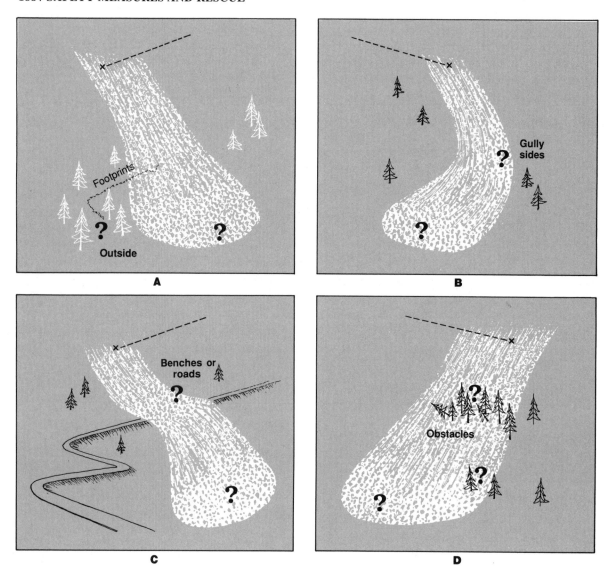

Figure 8.16. Most likely burial areas.

ment. A strict search procedure must be followed in order to home on the victim effectively. Most instruments have a volume control to allow volume to be reduced as the transmitting transceiver is approached. Differentiation of signal strength is easier when the ear is not saturated with sound. This helps to pinpoint the location of the transmitter. Instruments with visual read-out meters are available for people with hearing difficulties. Visual read-out meters also are very useful when training rescuers in transceiver use.

The guidelines for use and maintenance of transceivers follow:

- When in the field, wear the transceiver attached to the body near the head (around the neck), not in the pocket of an article of clothing. Do not keep it in the rucksack, on the snowmobile, or in the cab of a vehicle or machine.
- The instrument should be in the transmitting mode from the beginning until the end of the trip.

- Check the battery before leaving the base. Some instruments have a battery condition indicator; the transmitting and receiving strength of all transceivers should be checked against all other transceivers.
- At the start of a trip, the group leader should check that all transceivers can receive and transmit. Additional checks during the day should be made.
- Practice searching at the beginning and throughout the winter. Search speed increases considerably with practice. As a guideline, a searcher should be able to locate a transceiver within 0.5 m in not more than 3 minutes after picking up the first signal.
- Keep the transceiver dry to prevent contact and switch corrosion. (Do not wear the instrument on the bare skin.) After use, store the instrument in a dry environment and charge the batteries.
- Remove nonchargeable batteries and clean the terminals for summer storage. If rechargeable, completely discharge and recharge the batteries to cycle the batteries before the next season begins.

To conduct a search, each rescuer switches the transceiver to the receiving mode (they can be switched to transmit if another avalanche occurs or if any person leaves the accident scene). Searchers begin by moving across the most likely burial areas in a pattern designed to acquire a signal from a buried transceiver if one exists in the avalanche debris. The most effective patterns are usually described in the instructions that come with new transceivers. The search parameters include the number of searchers, the width of the area, the locations of the survivors when the avalanche occurred, and the effective range of the weakest transceiver used by the group (Figure 8.17). Some searches may proceed from the top down and work downhill; others begin at the bottom to cover the lowest part of the avalanche first.

When a searcher hears a signal he or she calls out "signal" and marks the location. When only one victim is sought, two searchers should carry out the final transceiver search pattern, while the others assemble probes and shovels. When more than one victim is buried, two persons concentrate on locating the first victim and the remainder continue searching.

After hearing a signal, the searcher orients the transceiver by rotating it through three axes for optimum signal strength. The optimum transceiver position should be maintained throughout the search because a change will cause a variation in signal volume; this could prolong the search. The searcher continues to move in a straight line, listens for the signal becoming stronger then weaker. When the signal begins to fade, the searcher immediately returns to the midpoint of the strongest signal bracket, makes a 90° turn, reduces the volume until the signal can just be heard, maintaining the orien-

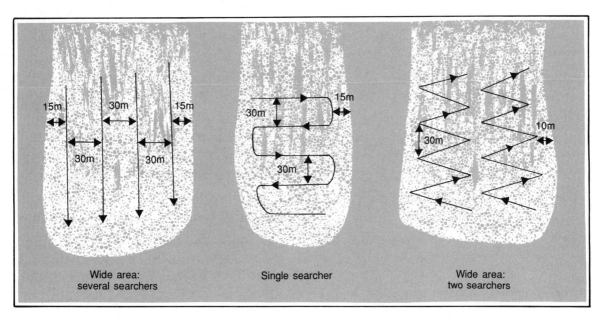

Figure 8.17. Patterns of transceiver search.

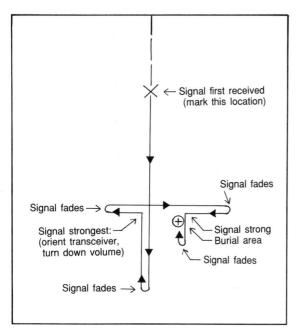

Figure 8.18. Terminal phase of transceiver search.

A *probe line* is a coordinated and systematic three-dimensional group search for a victim of an avalanche. The patterns differ for coarse probing, fine probing, and vehicle probing. Working a probe line is slow and tedious: It is close to the last resort when a visual search of the surface, a transceiver search, spot-probing, and dog searches have been unsuccessful (Figure 8.20).

Equipment

Probes are thin metal rods or tubing with lengths between 3 and 4 m. Probes for backcountry travel are collapsible into sections of about 0.5 m. Probes in rescue packs or on snowmobiles may have section lengths up to 1 m, and those that can be moved by truck to an accident site may be in one piece. For very deep burials it is possible to combine numerous sections of collapsible probes into very long probes. The depth of probing is limited by the lesser of the length of probes or the deposition of avalanched snow.

tation for optimum signal strength, then walks in a straight line at a right angle to the original direction (Figure 8.18).

By now the buried transceiver should be within an area of about 2 m². The exact location of the buried person inside this area is then determined with a probe (Figure 8.19). After making contact, a probe is left in place and a hole is dug along the probe. In digging, the depth of the burial should be considered: Deep holes need to be wide. Remember the victim's head, chest, and stomach should be excavated before the rest of the body is freed. The victim's transceiver is switched off, first aid is rendered to the victim, and the search continues for other victims.

PROBING

Probing involves finding a victim by contact with a rod (probe) that is pushed into the snow. In *spot-probing* the probe is repeatedly pushed into the snow at a strongly suspected burial location, for example, at the final, 2-m x 2-m area of a transceiver search, at a location indicated by a dog, around a snowmobile or other equipment or clues at the surface, or around trees.

Figure 8.19. Terminal phase of transceiver search: Begin probing within 2 m of recovery. (Photo by P. Anhorn)

Figure 8.20. Probe line. (Photo by P. Anhorn)

Normally, maximum probing depth is about 3 m. Insertion of probes should be incremental, tapping downward and rebounding to prevent possible freezing of super-cooled probes into mud at the bottom of the snowpack and for the best indication of a living target.

Collapsible probes must be strong and lightweight, and have a secure locking system between sections. Commercial probes for backcountry travel are usually made of tubing about 15 mm in diameter and are adequate for most avalanches. Thin steel rods may be essential to penetrate hard avalanche snow. Special ski poles are made to be assembled into a probe (after the baskets and handles are removed). Because of their greater diameter, conical shape, and shorter length, ski

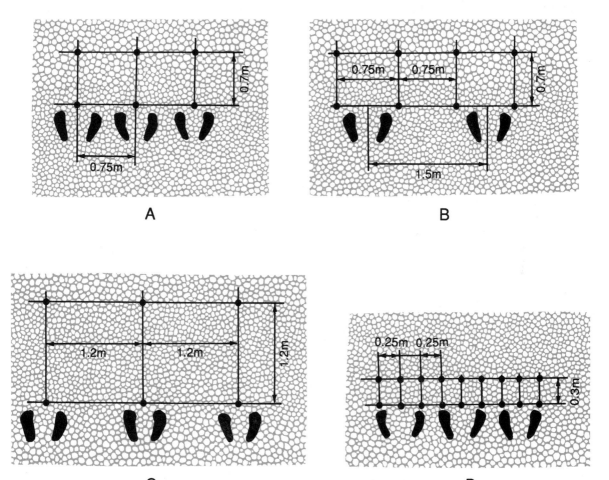

Figure 8.21. Probing patterns. A: coarse probing; B: open-space coarse probing; C: probing for a vehicle; and D: fine probing for body recovery.

191

pole probes are more difficult to use, but they can be valuable tools in emergencies. Ski pole probe users are advised to practice removal of handles and baskets and assembly prior to use. In an emergency, ordinary ski poles (basket removed), skis, saplings, branches, thin poles, and stakes may be used if necessary.

Coarse Probing

Coarse probing is tedious, but the implication is that hope for live recovery remains. The searchers line up about one elbow width (approximately 25 cm) apart (Figure 8.21A). Practice using a guidon cord (line or tape with markings every 0.75 m). A mark centering each rescuer will quickly acquaint probers with how to estimate probe spacing; use of such guidon cords in the field is advised when enough personnel are available. Each searcher inserts the probe once as deeply as possible on the centerline in front of him- or herself on the line joining the prober's boot tips; this gives a distance about 0.75 m between probe thrusts. On command, the line advances one step (approximately 0.7 m of distance) and probe insertion is repeated. The pattern of 0.75 m x 0.7 m was determined by combining fast search speed with a high probability of finding the buried victim.

Note that multiple coarse probing of the most likely burial area may be done to increase the chances of locating a live victim. A number of live recoveries have been made on the follow-up coarse probing of the same area.

Open-Space Coarse Probing

The spacing between persons may be increased when there are few searchers, a rugged avalanche surface, or steep terrain. For open-space coarse probing, the searchers line up about fingertip to fingertip (Figure 8.21B). On command, they insert the probe first at the side of the left foot, then at the side of the right foot, then advance one step (0.7 m). Open-space coarse probing gives the same density of probe insertions as the standard coarse probing.

Probing for a Vehicle

The distance between probe thrusts is increased when a buried car is sought. Searchers line up fingertip to shoulder and each one pushes the probe down in center, which yields a distance about 1.2 m between probes (Figure 8.21C). The line of probers advances two steps before the next probe insertion.

Fine Probing

Fine probing is high-density probing. Fine probing is time consuming (about five times longer than coarse probing); therefore, it is carried out *rarely* and only after likely burial areas have been coarse-probed unsuccessfully several times and *live rescue is not normally expected.* Searchers line up in the same order as for coarse probing. Each person first inserts his or her probe in front of the left foot, then in the center between both feet and finally in front of the right foot (Figure 8.21D). When the three probe insertions are made, the line advances a distance of 0.3 m (1 foot).

Organization of a Probe Line

The accident site commander determines the most likely burial areas and their priorities for probing. The commander assigns probe leaders and informs them of the emergency warning signal (whistle, call) and the emergency escape route if the signal is given. A probe line should not include more than 20 people; wide lines are difficult to control. More than one probe line at different locations may be organized when the number of rescuers is large. The probe line may move upslope or downslope; upslope motion is preferred because it is easier for probers to probe upslope and the distance between steps is easier to manage.

Probers should have their transceivers in the transmitting mode, and have gloves or mitts and footwear that allows them to stand in the snow for prolonged times. Gloves prevent probe warming and ice formation. Probers must be alert and maintain alignment. The probe leader checks the equiment and briefs probers about the possible hazard from other avalanches, the emergency warning signal and escape route, the expected feel with the probe (body, vehicle), and probe commands. The probe leader should be the only person talking so that briefings and probing commands are easily heard and so that audible signals from the victim could be heard.

Probing is carried out in unison (Figure 8.15). The probe leader, standing at the end of the line gives commands such as "down," "up," "step," and checks the alignment, spacing, and penetration of the probes. Remember, probes are inserted into the snow in short increments as deep as the probe length will allow or as deep as is necessary to search the avalanche deposition (usually 2.5 to 3 m). "Probe unto others as you would like to be probed upon." The persons at the ends of the line use colored wands, flags, branches, ski poles, or skis to delineate the boundaries of probed areas. Probing is interrupted only briefly for straightening the line and checking connections of probe sections.

When a strike is made, the prober calls out, leaves the probe in place, and takes a spare probe from a shoveler waiting behind or he or she forms part of a small shoveling crew that drops out. Probing continues while the shovelers confirm the strike by probing with additional probes and by shoveling along the probe to the buried object.

Probability of Finding a Victim

A probe contact is usually recognized by a soft, spongy feeling. The theoretical probability of contacting a buried person is about 70% for coarse probing on the first pass; with fine probing, the probability is close to 100%.

In practice, the probability of finding a victim is lower. For example, probes are often deflected in the snow, altering the effectiveness of the search grid. In addition, probers sometimes fail to notice when the probe has hit a body. A prober might not be alert at a crucial moment—due to monotony and fatigue—or might mistake the body for wood, shrubs, or the ground. False strikes also are common, but the best rule is "when in doubt, check it out." Deposits heavily contaminated with rock, wood, and ice make probing particularly difficult.

Note that location of the avalanche victim is only the precursor to extrication and admininstration of first aid in a successful rescue. Time will be consumed while shoveling out a correctly located victim. Digging down to a buried victim buried at 1.5 m (about average burial depth) in snow with the consistency of avalanche-deposited snow requires about 20 minutes. The rescue is operating on a decreasing time budget before first aid can even be attempted.

AVALANCHE RESCUE DOGS

The sensitive nose of a trained avalanche rescue dog is very efficient for locating buried persons and articles. Dogs search large areas rapidly and usually find victims within 10 minutes when the scent reaches the surface readily (for example, in low-density snow or for shallow

Figure 8.22. Avalanche rescue dog with handler at work. (Photo by T. Auger)

burials, i.e., not deeper than 2 m). Greater difficulties are encountered in dense snow, during windy conditions, or if the avalanche deposition surface is contaminated (broken trees, tree branches and needles, food, cigarette butts, clothing, urine, oil and gasoline, etc.).

The dog is usually part of a formal rescue organization and often it may take time for a trained avalanche rescue dog and master to reach the accident site. A dog and his handler work as a team. They must practice frequently in order to perform successfully. Dogs for avalanche work must be hardy and intelligent, have a good nose, and be able work in adverse weather. The handler must be able to direct the dog, to travel on skis, to evaluate avalanche accident situations, and to be familiar with search and rescue procedures. Rescue dog associations and the police have set skill standards for both dogs and handlers, with certifications for three levels of competence (Figure 8.22).

Guidelines to assist an accident site commander with the dog search include:

- Apply other appropriate methods of search prior to the arrival of the dog.
- Use wands to mark the articles (skis, poles, clothing) found on the surface.
- Do not allow helicopters or snowmobiles on the deposit.
- Avoid other surface contamination by placing packs, skis, and other equipment outside the avalanche

Figure 8.23. Even a family dog can be useful for finding a buried party member.

deposition, downwind if possible.
- When the dog arrives, brief the dog handler about the accident, action taken, most likely burial areas, and last-seen point. Keep the probe line going unless the dog handler requests otherwise.
- Assign the dog handler a searcher who carries a probe and shovel.
- Remember a dog is not a machine; rest is required periodically.

Even an untrained family dog can be useful in some cases (Figure 8.23). Cases have occurred in which a dog has sat directly over the buried master beneath. This possibility should not be overlooked.

OTHER SEARCH METHODS

Numerous other methods for finding avalanche victims have been investigated, but most are either partially successful or not applicable. Most alternatives are applicable to organized rescues only and they require sophisticated equipment, such as radar and magnetometers. They are not available for rescue of backcountry travelers by party members. Instrumented detection of persons from emissions of heat, scent, carbon dioxide, and dielectric effects have proven unreliable.

Radar

Radar signals penetrate the snow and are reflected by the ground and objects in the snow. Continuous read-out of the radar allows one to determine the presence of an object between the snow surface and the ground, but signal interpretation is complex.

Radar is very effective when the victim carries a special reflector to return the radar signal. Small reflectors that can be attached to clothing and gear are available commercially. The method has two disadvantages: (1) skiers, snowmobilers, climbers, and workers must wear the reflectors and (2) searchers must use expensive and bulky electronic detectors that may require mechanized transport and an organized rescue party.

Magnetometer

Magnetometers, either simple ones used for locating buried pipes or sophisticated models for exploration work, have been used successfully to find large metallic objects such as vehicles and snowmobiles. Individuals normally do not carry enough metal to be detected by magnetometers.

Search of Buildings and Industrial Sites

Probing is often useless for persons buried in collapsed buildings. In such cases, a search is carried out by front-end loaders and bulldozers that carefully remove snow and building materials under the watchful eye of a spotter. At roads, trenches may need to be excavated by machines and by hand after everything else has failed and the area has been probed several times. After excavation, probing can be continued downward and sideways in the trenches. When the avalanche deposit is very deep, and prolonged searching is unsuccessful, it may be necessary to suspend searching with victim recovery later when the snow has melted.

**Table 8.3 Typical Search Times to Cover 10,000 m²
(from experience, mainly in Western Europe)**

Transceiver	1 experienced searcher	5 minutes
	1 inexperienced searcher	15 minutes
Coarse probing	20 searchers	4 hours
Fine probing	20 searchers	20 hours
Dog	Favorable conditions	5–10 minutes
	Coarse search with unfavorable conditions	30 minutes
	Fine search	2 hours

Table 8.3 shows approximate average search times to search 10,000 m² (1 hectare) using various techniques. Rescue by survivors at an avalanche accident requires time to assemble, to decide on a plan of action, and to move to the most likely burial area. Additional time is consumed in locating and digging out the victims. If the rescue must be mounted from a rescue headquarters at

some distance from the accident, additional time is lost in travel time to the accident site. Comparing the time consumed by mounting a rescue operation by survivors at the accident site to the percent survival of people caught in avalanches (Table 8.1), it is obvious that speed, brought about by careful practice, is the key to successful avalanche rescue.

References

Aerztekammer Salzburg. 1982. Aerztliches Lawinensymposium, Fusch (Austria) 16 October 1982 (Medical Symposium on Avalanche-Caused Accidents). Salzburg, Austria: Aerztekammer Salzburg.

ANENA. 1988. *Ski et securite* (Ski and safety). Grenoble, France: Association Nationale pour l'Etude de la Neige et des Avalanches, 8 pp.

Armstrong, B. R., and Knox Williams. 1992. *The Avalanche Book.* Denver: Colorado Geological Survey, 240 pp.

Canadian Ski Patrol System. 1985. *Avalanche! Awareness could save your life.* Calgary, Alberta: Canadian Ski Patrol System, 8 pp.

Foundation Internationale "Vanni Eigenmann." 1975. Avalanches—protection, location, rescue. Foundation "Vanni Eigenmann," Casella Postale 1693, 20100 Milano, Italy.

Province of British Columbia. 1990. Snow avalanche safety information. Information handout. Victoria, BC: Ministry of Transportation and Highways, 3 pp.

Schaerer, P. A. 1987. Avalanche accidents in Canada III. A selection of case histories 1978–1984. Publication NRCC 27950. Ottawa: National Research Council of Canada, 138 pp.

Schneider, W. 1988. CARDA, and the avalanche rescue dog. Proceedings of the International Snow Science Workshop, Whistler, British Columbia, October 12–15, 1988. Vancouver, BC: Canadian Avalanche Association, pp. 162–165.

Williams, K. 1975. The snowy torrents: avalanche accidents in the United States, 1967–1971. General Technical Report RM-8. Fort Collins, CO: USDA Forest Service.

Figure 9.1.Trans-Canada Highway through avalanche area at Rogers Pass, B. C. (Photo by Canadian Parks Service)

CHAPTER 9

AVALANCHE PROTECTION

There was a time in this fair land
When the railroad did not run;
When the wild majestic mountains
Stood alone against the sun.

—Gordon Lightfoot

DEFINITIONS

Accidents and damage from interaction of avalanches with human activities can be prevented either by controlling the avalanches, by regulating the presence of persons, or by placing structures out of avalanche paths. *Avalanche control* interferes with the natural occurrence of avalanches. Methods include preventing avalanche initiation, avalanche release under controlled conditions, or deflection and deceleration of avalanches in motion. *Regulating the presence of persons and planning structures* includes locating facilities in safe areas, designing structures against avalanche forces, restricting the access to hazardous areas, and choosing safe locations for travel, work, and recreation (see Chapter 8).

Avalanche protection may be divided into temporary and permanent measures. *Temporary measures* (or *active measures*) are applied for short periods when avalanches are expected to occur. Their advantages are flexibility and low cost, but they require a continuous evaluation of avalanche hazards and the application of safety measures. *Permanent measures* (or *passive measures*) usually require expenses for engineering works, which perform without the need for a daily hazard evaluation.

The following groupings of protective measures are in use:

Temporary Control of Presence

- Choosing safe travel routes
- Temporary closures of roads and ski runs
- Evacuation of buildings during hazardous times

Permanent Control of Presence

- Location of buildings, roads, lifts, ski runs, power lines, and other facilities in safe areas
- Design of structures for avalanche forces
- Permanent closure of ski terrain

Temporary Control of Avalanches

- Compaction of snow in avalanche starting zones
- Release of avalanches by explosives

Permanent Control of Avalanches

- Engineering works that retain the snow in the starting zone or deflect and retard the avalanches in the track and runout zone
- Forests

Frequently, different methods are applied in combination. For example, a deflector at a road might be designed to control small and medium-sized avalanches, with large avalanches prevented by timely explosive control. Structures may protect buildings, but people outside the buildings must rely on avalanche warnings and closures for safety.

The erratic nature of avalanches, incomplete knowledge about their formation and dynamics, uncertainties about the effect of control measures, and cost make it difficult to apply protection with 100% security. For these reasons, control measures minimize but do not eliminate the inherent residual risk. Often the risk is mitigated by measures that reduce the frequency of large, damaging avalanches, but allow small avalanches that are harmless to facilities (Figure 9.1).

MAKING A DECISION

When a decision must be made about the most effective, practical, and economical avalanche protection at a given site, it is usually necessary to choose from several alternatives. In choosing, the following steps apply:

1. Define objectives and acceptable risk.
2. Delineate the avalanche paths (see Chapter 5).
3. Estimate the nature, frequency, and size of expected avalanches.
4. Define, evaluate, and select optimal protection alternatives.
5. Create a detailed design for the selected alternative.

The primary objectives of avalanche protection are minimizing injury, loss of life, and damage to structures; minimizing interruption of traffic (roads and railways) and utility services; and maintaining safe recreation areas (for example, skiing). Other benefits of avalanche control include more orderly snow removal, modification of snowmelt and runoff, and prevention of damage to forests.

Risk Levels

The acceptable risk level for facilities is strongly related to the frequency (return interval) of damage due to avalanches. For example, the damage threshold may be expressed as the maximum allowable avalanche impact pressure on buildings, the estimated maximum volume and depth of avalanche snow on a road, or the permissible frequency and duration of closures of ski runs and roads. The owner of the facility usually has the responsibility to define acceptable risk considering economics, political and client pressure, and subjective factors. Generally acceptable return periods are determined by experience. Variations will occur based on human usage, importance of the facility, and the local frequency of avalanching. Table 9.1 displays return periods for damaging avalanches, but it may be expected that much shorter return periods will be used in some areas.

Table 9.1 Typical Acceptable Return Periods for Different Facilities

Occupied buildings	200–300 years
Bridges and high-voltage transmission lines	50–100 years
Structures with permissible damage and unoccupied buildings	30 years
Avalanches hazardous to road traffic	5–10 years

Avalanches

For each avalanche path an estimate is made of the types (powder, dry, wet), sizes, and frequencies of each expected avalanche; and the runout position reached by avalanches annually, in 10 to 30 years, and in 100 to 300 years.

Definition and Evaluation of Alternatives

The alternatives are selected from the protective means (including combinations) described in this chapter. The "null" or "do nothing" option (without avalanche or traffic control) is an additional alternative. Evaluation includes:

- *Preliminary design:* Includes the layout and size of structures, the identification of means and placements for explosives, or the location of closure signs and barriers.
- *Residual risk:* Includes the frequency, size, and damage from avalanches that could overcome control measures.
- *Cost:* Includes the capital cost for structures and equipment (guns, weather stations, traffic control

devices). Operating costs include personnel, equipment, ammunition, snow removal, costs of traffic delays, lost business when ski runs are closed, and time lost due to evacuations.
- *Frequency and duration of closures.*

The intangible factors must also be evaluated:

- *Politics:* Local politics may require that a road be kept open continuously despite high cost; or landowners may exert pressure for avalanche control, rather than accepting building restrictions.
- *Psychology:* Personnel at mine or construction sites may feel safer when artillery is applied on avalanche paths, even though rational evaluation shows a very small avalanche hazard.
- *Operation:* Management may not be prepared to commit to the continuous evaluation of avalanche hazards; restrictions to traffic on a forest or mine road would seriously affect the production; or a construction site may operate for only a few winters, so permanent investments are not warranted.
- *Environmental and other hazard considerations:* Structures in the starting zone, track, and runout zones of avalanches might damage forests, cause soil erosion, or affect the aesthetics; the use of explosives might be restricted due to dangers from unexploded shells; stray projectiles may threaten inhabited areas.

Optimization

The best protective measure is the one that meets the objectives, has the lowest cost, and includes acceptable intangibles. Alternatives that do not meet the objectives (adequate protection and acceptable closure times) are rejected in the first step of the selection process.

The cost, benefits, and intangibles are compared in the next step. A cost-benefit analysis may assist, but is not the only criterion. Costs are defined by the sum of annual operating cost and annual depreciation of capital. Benefits may be expressed quantitatively from the estimated reduction of persons and vehicles caught in avalanches and the estimated reduction in monetary damage to structures. The frequency and duration of road and area closures are also reduced and money is saved by preventing death and injury. With respect to the intangibles, Maurice de Coulon's remark about avalanche control decisions applies: "A project which is justified only from an engineering point of view is only half a project."

Detailed Design

The selected optimum alternative is designed in detail and evaluated for effectiveness. The design may include a snow safety plan (procedures for temporary closures of roads and areas) with the following elements:

- Delineation of hazardous areas in a zoning plan and enforcement of building restrictions
- Placement of gun positions and targets for artillery, helicopter bombing, or bomb trams
- Routes and shot placements for hand charges
- Location, dimensions, and design of control structures

PREVENTIVE ROAD CLOSURES

Public and industrial (forestry, mining, construction) roads are closed when avalanches could bury or damage vehicles and during control by explosives. Closures are often the only protection needed for roads with low traffic volume. When avalanches are frequent and the traffic volume is high, closures are applied together with avalanche control.

Experience has shown that closure enforcement must be strict, because drivers are strongly tempted to ignore or defy avalanche hazards. Guidelines for effective road closures include the following.

Access to the closed road should be blocked physically with a strong, locked gate (Figure 9.2). Signs alone

Figure 9.2. Closed gate at a highway. (Photo by P. Schaerer)

and removable barriers are not effective unless they are guarded. On public roads it may be necessary to place a member of the road maintenance staff in front of the gate. His or her function is to guard the gate and inform the traveling public about the reason and the estimated duration of the closure.

The gate should be as close as possible to the avalanche areas. The stopping area in front of the gate should be safe, have a low incline that allows vehicles to start easily, and be wide enough for tractor-trailer units and buses to turn around. Driving around the gate should not be possible.

The standard warning signs PREPARE TO STOP and STOP AHEAD should be placed at the approach, with STOP and ROAD CLOSED signs at the gate. The signs may be mounted permanently; they can be covered or turned to face away when not needed. Painting the gates fluorescent yellow and mounting two or three flashing red warning lights is recommended for visibility during snowfall and at night.

After closing the gates, the road is checked by driving a "sweep" vehicle across. The sweep person attaches a notice (preferably waterproofed) to the windshield of unattended vehicles on the closed road. The notice demands that vehicles are not to be moved.

Potential travelers on a road that may be closed can benefit from information that is posted prior to the closure. Multi-message signs at the exits of the nearest town and junctions where a detour is possible are useful for this purpose. The local staff in the closed area keeps the road maintenance headquarters, the police, and radio stations informed with updated estimates of closure duration.

Often a closure is preceded by a warning of moderate hazard, for example, when small powder avalanches or flowing avalanches could hit the road. Such avalanches may not be hazardous to vehicles and their occupants, but could reduce visibility and block the road. On a high-speed high-volume highway, even small amounts of avalanche debris on the highway can pose a significant traffic hazard and control measures could be warranted.

Effective road closures rely on persons who can evaluate the avalanche hazard. At roads with high potential for avalanche hazard, a technical specialist is often responsible for avalanche hazard evaluation and closure decisions. The road maintenance foreman assumes this task for roads with minor potential hazard. The person in charge of avalanche safety should have adequate training, have the necessary equipment to make weather and snowpack observations, and be fully supported by the management. Road operation manag-

Figure 9.3. Ski area closure sign. (Photo by W. Flann)

ers should make it clear to all other employees that the instructions of the person in charge of avalanche safety must be followed. Avalanche courses are useful to educate the managers about the objectives and operation of protective measures.

Due to the inconvenience and cost to commercial and public traffic, road closures should be kept short. The permissible duration depends on the type and volume of traffic and the availability of alternative routes.

Protection by road closures includes adequate equipment for the safe and quick removal of avalanche snow. Considerations include the type of equipment (bulldozers, loaders), availability of rental equipment, and the difficulty of equipment transport over icy roads.

PREVENTIVE SKI RUN CLOSURES

Temporary Closures

In ski areas, runs are closed frequently when skiers could start avalanches or when they are threatened by avalanches from above. Temporary closures provide low-cost and effective protection when they are kept short. Closures are in effect until the ski patrol has stabilized the snow by skiing or tested (and hopefully stabilized) the slopes with explosives (Figures 9.3 and 9.4).

Figure 9.4. Ski area closure signs.

Guidelines for temporary closures are as follows:

- Closures should be applied only when an avalanche hazard exists. The effectiveness of a closure depends on the decisions and credibility of the avalanche analyst.
- Closures should be short; they should be suspended as soon as the snow is stable. Long closures of attractive slopes invite violation.
- Temporary closures of ski runs should be enforced; violators can be punished by loss of lift ticket or court action, depending on local laws.
- The public should be kept informed by message signs at lift terminals in the valley and on the mountain.
- The boundary of a closed area should follow natural terrain lines, such as ridges, forest boundaries, creeks, or rocks, or it should be at a lift terminal. Barriers to stop skiers should not be placed across a tracked ski slope.

Permanent Closures

For safety, certain slopes may be closed to skiing for the entire winter or during a major part of it. Ski operations tend to avoid permanently closed areas within their boundaries. This is because skiers are tempted to use them sooner or later (in violation of closure signs) without realizing that snow in closed areas has not been subject to avalanche control. Therefore, permanent closures are applied only where the terrain and time would not permit effective avalanche control, or where additional hazards exist (for example, rocks, cliffs, glacial crevasses, open creeks). Closed areas should be well marked, preferably with ropes (Figure 9.5).

Figure 9.5. Permanent closure with sign and ropes. (Photo by W. Flann)

Warning Signs

Warning signs are placed at ski area boundaries or at trailheads (Figure 9.6). They warn travelers when entering uncontrolled terrain where safety responsibility rests with the individuals.

AVALANCHE DETECTION SYSTEMS

Detection systems consist of sensors to detect avalanche occurrences and companion warning devices to stop traffic before it enters the avalanche path.

Successful sensors include horizontal cables and combinations of horizontal and vertical cables, which trip a switch when an avalanche hits and stretches them. Another sensor is radar, mounted either at the side of the avalanche path and looking along the avalanche path, or buried in the ground and looking up. Sensor signals (transmitted either by radio or wire) activate traffic lights at the side of the avalanche path and are sometimes supplemented by a siren and a message sign.

Vibration (e.g., geophones) and sound sensors and photoelectric barriers have not been successfully applied in all cases. The separation of the avalanche signal from other noise is the principal problem. Very good vibration signals have been obtained in cases where good coupling of geophones to the snowpack was available.

Detection systems are used mainly on railways for detection of avalanche snow and rockfall on the tracks. There, the sensors consist of wires along the track; when the wires break, the block signal is activated to warn trains and alert the dispatcher. Usually such systems do not stop trains before avalanches cross the track, but trains are slowed to prevent derailment by avalanche deposits. Derailment in deep snow is a major avalanche hazard on railways.

Detection systems have been applied at roads that contain only one or two avalanche paths because at such locations it would not be economical to apply continuous avalanche hazard evaluation and enforce temporary closures.

Detection systems have several disadvantages. The distance of the sensors from a road must allow ample warning time for vehicles to cross the avalanche path before the avalanche arrives; the width of the avalanche path, speed of the traffic, and the estimated speed of avalanches must be considered in locating the sensor. The difficulty in matching these factors makes the

Figure 9.6. Warning sign at ski area boundary. Note the avalanche behind in which four skiers died. (Photo by N. Wilson)

method impossible at some locations; the most suitable paths are those with a long, narrow track.

Detection systems may issue false alarms either from small avalanches that do not reach the road or from other causes. When traffic has been stopped and avalanches are not observed, road users tend to lose confidence and disregard the signals in the future. Other disadvantages are that powder avalanches may not trigger the signals, and detection equipment requires maintenance (repairing damages, replacing batteries, function checks).

EVACUATION

Evacuation during hazardous times may be a viable and economic safety measure for temporary buildings in construction and mining camps and work sites in avalanche paths. Evacuation is applied in European villages during periods of extreme avalanche hazard. Short-term evacuations may also be necessary as a precaution against unexpected avalanches during avalanche control with explosives.

Evacuation requires reliable evaluation of avalanche hazards and a safety plan that is familiar to potentially affected persons. A good plan includes the following information:

- Designation of hazardous areas subject to evacuation.
- A list of persons responsible for issuing and lifting evacuation orders. Sometimes a committee of ava-

lanche experts, management, and elected officials is in charge.

- Instructions for communication and alarm when an evacuation is necessary. An evacuation order should be preceded by a warning of impending hazard.
- An evacuation procedure with the escape routes, assembly areas, and parking areas for machinery and accommodation for people displaced.
- Procedures for enforcement and checking of evacuated areas.
- Provision to prevent looting.

Implementation of an evacuation plan may be complex. Evacuations disrupt work and interfere with living conditions. Therefore, relying on evacuation for avalanche safety must be considered carefully by estimating evacuation frequency and the size and cost of the operation involved.

LAND-USE RESTRICTIONS

The first consideration when facilities are planned is location in areas unaffected by avalanches. Many problems and accidents in the past might have been prevented with simplified protection if this general rule had

Figure 9.8. The highway at Kootenay Pass, British Columbia, crosses an area with frequent avalanches. A safer route would be the other (left) side of the valley. (Photo by N. Wilson)

been followed during the early stages of planning of buildings, roads, railways, power lines, ski lifts, and ski runs. Planning housing, structures, and other facilities in avalanche-threatened areas requires a thorough study of the terrain and careful estimates of runout distances, speeds, and return intervals of maximum avalanches. Mistakes can result in destruction, loss of life, or overly conservative, impractical restrictions. The evaluations should be reviewed periodically (for example, after 10 years) to plan future developments. Sometimes, relocating structures and roads to safe areas later is an effective alternative when mistakes have been made (Figures 9.7 and 9.8).

Identifying hazardous areas for land-use and applying restrictions to construction is termed *avalanche zoning*. It involves three steps: (1) identification of avalanche paths (see Chapter 5); (2) subdivision of avalanche paths, principally the runout zones, into zones

Figure 9.7. Example of false security deemed to be offered by a small band of timber at the foot of an avalanche path. The circles indicated houses in the development. Two cabins were destroyed and several people were killed by avalanches that overran the development in Stevens Pass, Washington. (Photo by R. Emetaz)

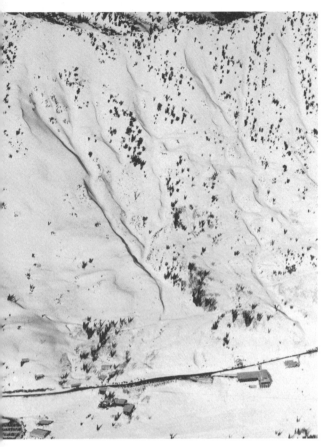

Figure 9.9. Aerial photo of Alta, Utah with avalanche paths above the buildings.

of different hazard levels; and (3) application of restrictions to construction in the various zones (Figures 9.9 and 9.10).

Subdivision of Hazard Zones

The parameters used to quantify hazard level and subdivide areas are frequency of avalanches and their destructive effect. The destructive effect is usually expressed by the expected impact pressure on a wall perpendicular to the avalanche flow. Sometimes, for example, at roads, avalanche size is an additional parameter. Technical experts with a good knowledge of avalanche motion and effects usually delineate the hazard zones. Classes of hazard zones (up to four) are commonly distinguished based on severity (see an example in a later section in this chapter).

Application of Restrictions

The consequences on development and construction in avalanche areas vary with the authority over the land, politics, economic and social pressures, and the applicable regulations. The rules are essentially controlled by governments and the owners. Governments usually enforce zoning laws that define the type and use of structures in hazardous areas. Hazard zone maps are often part of building and zoning bylaws where municipal, district, county, provincial, or state authorities regulate housing developments. Governments also have the power to regulate specific industries under special legislation (for example, mining acts, railway acts, occupational safety regulations). Sometimes difficulties arise when a legal base for enforcement of restrictions in avalanche hazard zones must be created. In other cases (for example, ski areas, forest roads, and electric transmission lines), the owners make decisions about restrictions by considering the risks, costs, and effects on the operation.

Hazard Zones for Building Developments

Avalanche zoning was initiated in Switzerland in 1961 and the hazard zone definitions, methods for determining the zones, and the legislation were developed later. The Swiss hazard zoning, adopted later (with modifications) in France, Austria, Italy, and the United States, defines four zones:

1. *Red Zone = High Hazard:* In the red zone, avalanches are expected that have either (a) an impact pressure of 30 kPa or greater with a return period of up to 300 years, or (b) a return period of 30 years or less regardless of impact pressure.

   No new structures and buildings are permitted in a red zone. Existing buildings must be protected either by control structures or reinforcement, and evacuation plans must be ready.

2. *Blue Zone = Moderate Hazard:* In the blue zone, (a) flowing avalanches are expected with impact pressures of less than 30 kPa and return periods between 30 and 300 years, or (b) powder avalanches are expected with impact pressures of less than 3 kPa and return periods of 30 years or less.

   New residences may be permitted in the blue zone, but they must be protected. No lift terminals, lodges, schools, or buildings that attract large crowds of people are allowed. Avalanche warning and evacuation plans must be prepared.

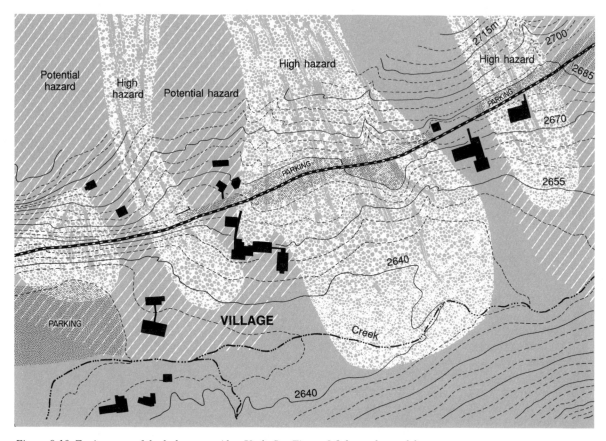

Figure 9.10. Zoning map of the lodge area, Alta, Utah. See Figure 9.9 for a photo of the area.

3. *Yellow Zone = Low Hazard:* In a yellow zone, (a) rare flowing avalanches are possible with an expected return period of more than 300 years, or (b) powder avalanches could produce an impact pressure of less than 3 kPa with a return period of more than 30 years. In the yellow zone, structural measures against powder avalanches may be recommended.

4. *White Zone = No Hazard:* No avalanches are reasonably expected to reach a white zone. No restrictions apply to development.

Hazard Line

The hazard line indicates how far one might reasonably expect avalanches to run within an approximate return period of 300 years. The line defines the boundary between areas where no hazard exists and areas with a hazard. Hazard lines form the basis for developments in Canada and in Norway. In Norway, the line may enclose effects that result from snow avalanches, rockfall, landslides, debris flows, and slush flows.

No restrictions apply outside the hazard line. Inside the line, the hazard and protection must be investigated individually for each structure and type of land use. Since runout distances have a statistical character, a measure of expected errors should be specified if possible.

Hazard Zones at Roads and Ski Developments

For roads, it is very useful to classify the hazard to traffic according to the expected type and size of avalanches and the frequency of them covering the road. The hazard, together with the expected volume and type of traffic, then determines the best applicable control procedure.

Determining avalanche hazards to skiers, lifts, and structures is an essential element of ski development planning. Some ski runs are located in terrain unaffected by avalanches (if possible) and with protective measures for others.

MINIMIZING THE RISK BY DESIGN

Structures

When structures must be built in avalanche paths, guidelines for layout and design can assist with avalanche protection (Figure 9.11). Typical guidelines are summarized as follows:

1. Consider the interaction between avalanches and the structure by accounting for the nature and behavior of avalanches. The best shape for a structure is one that deflects avalanches smoothly around and over the top.
2. Estimate the possible flow directions of avalanches. At a given site, avalanches may come from several directions including deflection by buildings and terrain above the structure.
3. Estimate the speed, density, and flow depth of the *design avalanche*. The design avalanche is the maximum avalanche for a given return period.
4. Design walls and roofs for impact, deflection, and friction forces.
5. Design roofs for vertical loads due to snowfall, moving avalanche snow, and deposited avalanche snow. Consider nonuniform snow deposition in valleys and on upslopes.
6. Consider the damming effect of walls and static snow loads due to deposited avalanche snow.
7. Allow for greater local impact pressure due to hard blocks of snow, rocks, and wood in the avalanches.
8. Consider impact forces from snow falling off roofs.
9. Consider possible suction, uplifting, and vibration forces.
10. Avoid doors on walls facing avalanches; when necessary, design doors against avalanche impact pressure. If doors may be blocked by avalanche snow, other (emergency) exits must be available.
11. Make windows small and strong on walls facing avalanches; shutters may be provided.
12. Avoid eaves, balconies, parapet walls, chimneys,

Figure 9.11. Residence with reinforced walls facing an avalanche path, Tignes, France. (Photo by P. Schaerer)

vents, railings, and other protruding parts at positions where avalanches could impact.
13. Shape the terrain above the structure to prevent avalanches from becoming airborne.
14. Remove trees that could be broken or uprooted by the avalanches and strike the structure, particularly for power line towers.
15. Consider avalanche motion after deflection and how it could affect neighboring structures.

Roads

Ideally, roads should avoid avalanche paths, but any benefits gained from such placement must be weighed against geometric design requirements, soil stability, maintenance, and environmental damage. Relocating a road later around an avalanche path or a greater distance down the avalanche runout zones is sometimes an effective alternative when mistakes have been made (Figures 9.8 and 9.12). When avalanche paths cannot be avoided, proper location and cross-section design can help alleviate the hazard to traffic and snow removal work. Guidelines for road location and design in avalanche paths follow (Figure 9.13):

1. Cross an avalanche path near the tip of the runout zone.
2. Place the road on a fill if possible.
3. Avoid through-cuts by flattening the outside cut slope.
4. Avoid long, steep cut slopes; such slopes could produce avalanches.
5. Make extra wide and deep ditches, particularly at locations with avalanches from short slopes. Such ditches will stop most small avalanches.

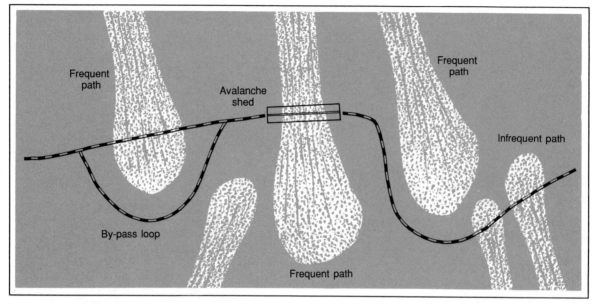

Figure 9.12. Location of mountain highways.

STABILIZATION BY COMPACTION

The strength and stability of a snowpack can be improved by compaction. Compacted dense snow usually retains adequate strength even during melting (see Chapter 3). However, due to terrain steepness, machines cannot usually be applied in avalanche starting zones, and therefore personnel on skis and foot must be used for snow avalanche control compaction.

Ski Stabilization

Ski stabilization (also called ski cutting, control, or protective skiing) involves skiing the avalanche starting zones frequently, releasing small avalanches, and packing the snow in the ski tracks. The effect of ski cutting is confined to surface snow layers; deep, weak layers cannot be compacted and stabilized. Therefore, ski stabilization is best carried out after every light and moderate snowfall. The slopes should be tracked densely to chop up potential starting areas. The distance between tracks should be 1 to 5 m. Caution must be observed: one person at a time on a potential starting area. Normal stability evaluation safety procedures must also be followed (see Chapter 6).

Continuously skied slopes are usually avalanche free except with unskied new snow. It is a good policy to allow skiers to use and ski pack potential avalanche starting zones from the beginning of the winter (Figure 9.14).

Boot Packing

Boot packing involves people walking through avalanche starting zones to make densely spaced footprints (distance about 1 m). Boot packing affects deeper snow layers than does ski stabilization.

Boot packing is generally limited to small, critical areas because of the heavy personnel requirements. It is often applied to strengthen weak snow (depth hoar) that had formed early in the winter before slopes were skied. To prevent avalanche formation, it should be carried out before the weak snow is covered with stronger snow. Packing fresh snow can be very effective for preventing depth hoar formation later.

AVALANCHE CONTROL BY EXPLOSIVES

Detonating explosives in starting zones has two objectives: to release avalanches under controlled conditions and to test the stability of the snowpack (see Chapter 6).

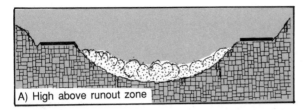

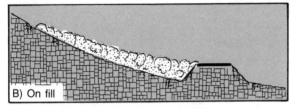

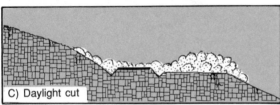

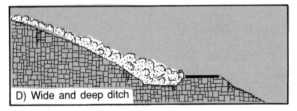

Figure 9.13. Cross section of roads in avalanche paths.

One benefit of releasing avalanches with explosives under controlled conditions is that the avalanche release is chosen when the exposed areas (for example, roads and ski runs) are not occupied. The areas may be opened after avalanches are released; therefore, closures may be kept short. Another benefit is that frequent explosive control usually ensures that snow is brought down in several small avalanches, rather than a single large one. Small avalanches may not reach facilities, and snow removal time on roads can be minimized, making closures short. Also, frequent avalanche release prevents large unpredictable natural avalanches later, for example, with snowmelt.

Effect of Explosions

Explosive charges are used to generate elastic stress waves to initiate shear fracture propagation and dry slab

avalanche release. Stress waves attenuate rapidly in snow, but propagation is more efficient through the air and the ground (Figure 9.15). Explosions above the snow surface stress the snow over a wider area than those in the snowpack; therefore, they are more effective in activating weak spots to produce failure. Stress waves in the ground propagate with little attenuation over long distances, but their impact on the snowpack depends on the quality of the contact between snow and ground. Under favorable conditions, ground shock waves can be very effective. Artillery shells detonated on rocks have released avalanches on adjacent slopes and the opposite side of ridges, but this effect is not very common.

Figure 9.14. Ski-stabilized slope. (Photo by P. Schaerer)

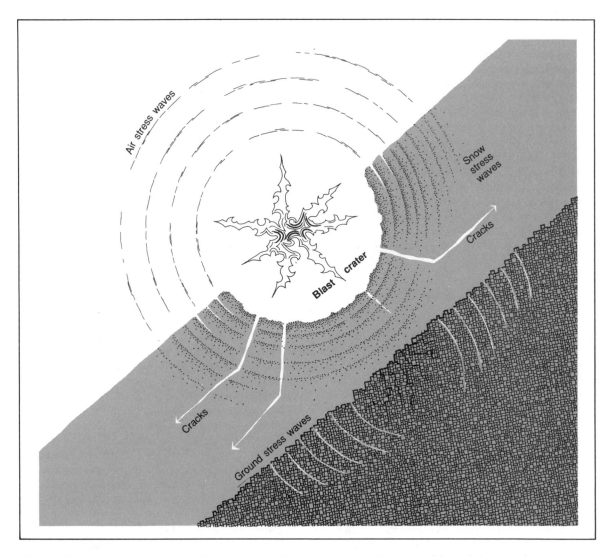

Figure 9.15. Schematic of effects of explosives in generating stress waves in the snow and through the ground.

Successful avalanche release by explosives depends on three parameters: the stability of the snowpack (a function of the strength of the snow and stresses already present), the size of the explosive charge (mass), and the location of the explosion relative to the slope and the snow surface. The parameters may be combined to increase efficiency. For example, when the snow stability is good, a large explosive charge might have to be applied; or an explosion above the snow surface could help compensate if the entire potential fracture zone has not been tested by surface detonations.

Influence of the Snowpack Stability

Explosives should be applied when the snow stability is poor because little additional stress is needed for fracture propagation; if the snow above a weak layer is cohesive enough for a fracture to spread over a wide area and produce a slab avalanche; and before the instability is deep, so that large avalanches are not produced.

Selecting conditions when small avalanches can be produced requires careful evaluation of snow stability and accurate timing. Application of explosives too early during a snowfall might yield little or no avalanche snow; late application might produce avalanches larger than desired. Snow remains unstable for a long time when the temperature is low, but it can stabilize rapidly at moderate temperatures. In this case, the time for successful control may pass in a few hours.

Timing is delicate when the snow loses fracture propagation potential by wetting or due to high temperatures, particularly with the onset of rain on new snow. Generally, explosives are much less effective in wet snow than in dry snow. Field evidence indicates that when the temperature rises there is a short critical time period before the snow stiffness is reduced, but the failure layer is still dry. In such cases, the time for explosive application may be estimated by observing the air temperature increase, solar radiation, and snow temperatures (best).

Influence of Explosive Charge

Numerous types and brands of explosives suitable for avalanche control are on the market. Some manufacturers supply explosives packaged specifically for this purpose. The following guidelines apply for explosives in avalanche work:

1. Explosives with high detonation velocities (5,000 to 7,000 m/s) are most effective for releasing snow slabs when the charge is placed at and above the snow surface.
2. Slower detonation velocities (3,000 to 4,000 m/s) are more appropriate for explosions inside the snow and for cornice removal. Slower explosives are also preferred for buried charges for deep slab release or for large charges used to remove the stauchwall of full-depth avalanches caused by gliding.
3. The explosive and its detonation system should be safe, simple, and not be adversely affected by moisture or low temperatures.
4. Misfires (duds) should be infrequent even though they should become shock-insensitive (disintegrate) with time.
5. Explosives should be reasonably nontoxic under normal handling, and they should be of high density to avoid bulky loads.
6. The ignition system must be reliable. For additional reliability or when duds *must* be avoided, sometimes two fuse and cap assemblies are placed in the same charge. Artillery shells should deto-

nate reliably on impact with a soft snow surface.
7. Electric blasting caps should not be used in avalanche work. Static electricity generated by blowing snow has unexpectedly detonated electric blasting caps.

The effective range of a charge increases with the square root of its mass; for example, a 2-kg charge has a range 1.4 times that of a 1-kg charge. Therefore, the larger the charge the better, but in practice the delivery system limits the size. A 1-kg charge (usual size of hand charges) is generally considered a minimum. Artillery shells carry payloads between 1 and 2 kg. Larger charges (5 to 25 kg or more) are applied with mechanized transport such as on ropeways and helicopters).

Influence of Charge Placement

The best charge locations cover the potential fracture zone. Steep inclines and deep, wind-deposited snow are likely spots. On a specific slope, shot locations may be shifted depending on wind direction. Experience has shown that, as a first guess, explosive charges are best placed about 10 to 20 m slope distance below the expected crown of slab avalanches. Typical crown locations are described in Chapter 5 (see Figure 5.13).

Shots on open slopes (where the shock wave may spread freely) are more effective for releasing snow slabs than on rugged terrain (interrupted by barriers such as ridges and rocks). In narrow, confined terrain (e.g., rock gullies) explosives may start small avalanches that could trigger larger ones below (Figures 9.16 and 9.17).

Explosives detonated above or on the snow surface have a wider range than those exploded inside the snow cover. For optimum effect 1- to 2-kg charges should be detonated at about 1.5 m (4 m for a 10-kg charge) above the snow surface. Artillery shells have the disadvantage of exploding on or just below the snow surface (the cost of proximity fuses would be prohibitive). Sometimes artillery has a better effect when aimed at exposed rocks: The explosion is above the surrounding snow surface and, in addition, it can propagate a shock wave through the ground. Bombs dropped from a helicopter penetrate the snow surface, but some loss of effectiveness results, so charge sizes are often 5 kg or larger.

For deep, hard slabs, buried charges (in close contact with the weakness) appear to be more effective than surface shots even though the effective range is reduced.

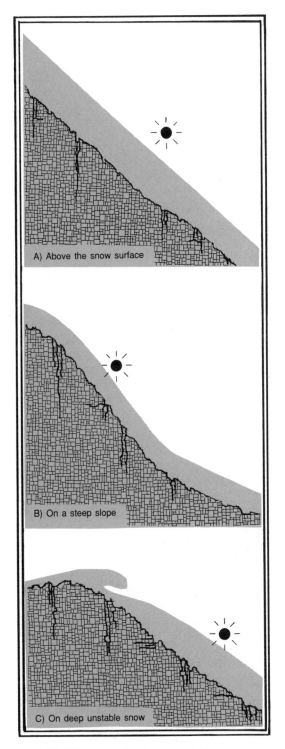

Figure 9.16. Effective application of explosives.

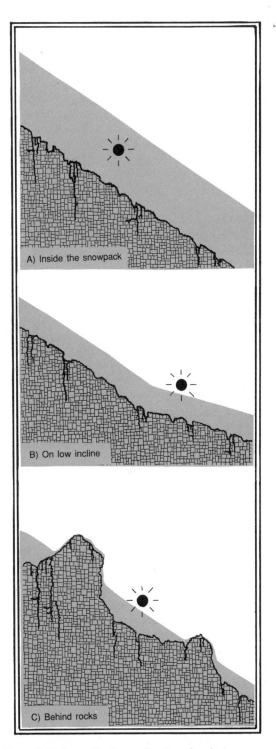

Figure 9.17. Less effective application of explosives.

Safety Measures

Avalanche control by explosives requires strict safety measures because both explosives and avalanches are hazardous. The charges must be stored, prepared, placed, and fired according to established work procedures. Government regulations apply to storeroom design and the storage and handling of explosives. Personnel who supervise shot preparation and application must have a blaster's license.

Safety measures during avalanche control procedures include the following. Exposed areas are closed, roads and railways are made free of traffic, ski slopes are scanned visually, and exposed buildings are evacuated prior to the release of avalanches. In addition, a visual sweep of the exposed area is made before individual charges are fired. In deciding the size of the area to be closed, one should consider that explosives may trigger avalanches on adjacent slopes, and avalanches sometimes take an unexpected path, therefore closures should encompass a generous area. Areas may be opened after the expected avalanches are released. However, it might be necessary to wait several hours if an avalanche has not occurred due to the possibility of postcontrol release (see Chapter 4).

Good communication between the avalanche control team and the traffic control teams (including lift operations in ski areas) is an essential safety element. For all blasting operations, good records of results, explosives used, and time and date need to be kept.

Blasters and artillery crews should be at a location that is safe from all surrounding avalanche slopes. In addition, access to firing positions should be safe. Roped belays should be used whenever necessary, for example, during cornice blasting. Gun position and target locations should be planned with consideration for hazards to occupied areas, particularly when the possibility of overshooting mountain ridges exists.

Unexploded charges and projectiles (duds) require prompt attention because they are a hazard to winter and summer visitors (Figure 9.18). Hand charge duds on ski slopes can often be located and destroyed by placing and exploding a second charge at the side (see the section "Preparation of Hand Charges"). Artillery projectiles usually disappear in the snow and cannot be found before the snow has melted. Their location is recorded in a book, sketch, or photo and the shells are searched for and destroyed as soon as possible. Warnings about unexploded artillery projectiles should be posted near areas with frequent visitors.

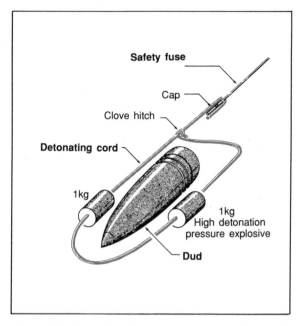

Figure 9.18. Illustration of a method to destroy artillery duds. Approved blasting procedures (varying with government jurisdiction) should be adhered to at all times when dealing with explosives.

Explosives are intended to bring down small avalanches, but there is an inherent risk of releasing large avalanches. Large avalanches may occur for various reasons. Errors in snow stability evaluation, time delays due to equipment breakdown, inaccessibility of firing sites, personnel shortage, or bad weather can allow a large buildup of snow prior to control work. When the optimum time is missed, the person in charge must make a difficult decision about whether to risk releasing a large destructive avalanche (which might not occur naturally) or to wait and risk a large avalanche later. Because of the chance of large avalanches, explosives are not usually applied for the protection of structures. Sometimes the risk of structural damage is accepted for temporary buildings (for example, in a construction camp) or easily replaceable structures (for example, chairlift towers and telephone lines).

Management of Explosive Control

Control by explosives has a low cost and high flexibility associated with it, but it requires skilled personnel, snow stability evaluation, and a safety plan. A safety plan includes descriptions of individual responsibilities, access to firing positions, procedures for closure and evacuation of areas, and communications.

The person responsible for the avalanche control should be skilled in snow stability evaluation and snow tests (including explosives) and also able to make decisions about the time and location of explosive use. He or she should be knowledgeable and responsible about the hazards of explosives and avalanches and be a certified blaster.

APPLICATION OF EXPLOSIVES

The limitations, advantages, and disadvantages of explosive delivery methods are explained in the following sections. No method is ideal for all applications. Technique selection for a given operation and avalanche path involves the following factors:

- Safe access to the avalanche starting zone on foot or ski
- Range, line of fire, and access to firing positions for artillery
- Availability (both short and long term) of artillery for the required firing range
- Capital and operational cost
- Weather and visibility during avalanche control
- Accuracy of shot placement
- Reliability in controlling avalanches and residual hazards
- Hazards from unexploded charges (duds)
- Time and permissible length of facility closures
- Need for skilled manpower and avalanche hazard evaluation
- Legislation for application of explosives and artillery

Hand Charging

A hand charge consists of explosives (usually 1 kg; sometimes larger, particularly with wet snow), a cap, and a fuse. Avalanche control persons often assemble charges at the operations base a short time before use and pack them in to an area near avalanche starting zones. However, many government regulations require assembly at the point of application, therefore, special permission is required to transport them on skis or foot. At safe locations (for example, on a ridge) the charges are ignited with a pull-wire igniter and tossed by hand to a selected shot placement (sometimes attached to an anchor cord). The shot placements may be predeter-

Figure 9.19. Skier on control route. Markers should be made of reflecting material. Ski safety straps are not recommended in avalanche terrain.

mined and the blasting locations marked along set routes with posts (marked with reflectors) for orientation in bad weather and at night (Figure 9.19).

Advantages of Hand Charges

Hand charges are commonly used in ski areas where access to the avalanche starting zones is easy. The cost of hand charges is low; no capital investment for mechanized delivery systems is needed. The application is simple, flexible, and safe when safety guidelines are followed.

Limitations of Hand Charges

Application of hand charges requires safe access to avalanche starting zones and shot placements; hand charges are very difficult to apply when the shot placement is in the middle of a long slope.

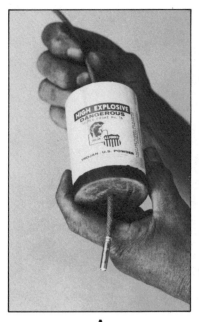 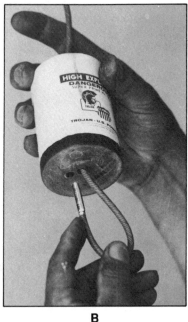 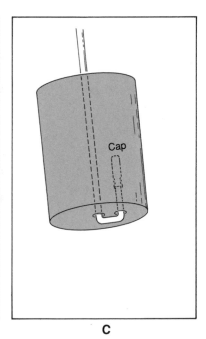

A	**B**	**C**

Figure 9.20. Arming of cast primer.

Because the amount of explosive placed on the snow surface is usually small, it has a limited effective range. Therefore, more than one charge may be required to test the potential fracture zone. (However, these limitations on the effective range can sometimes be overcome by using larger charges.)

The charges may roll down on a hard surface and explode too low on the slope. In such situations the charges may be attached to an anchored cord, which also allows dud retrieval.

PREPARATION OF HAND CHARGES

In addition to the following information about preparing hand charges, remember that explosives safety regulations must be observed as applicable.

The following are the components of hand charges.

Explosive

The most frequently used explosives are either cast primers or gelatin primers. Cast primers are high-density cylinders with a ready-made capwell; some have a second hole to allow a wrap of the fuse (Figure 9.20). Gelatin primers are cartridges wrapped in cardboard or paper; a hole (or holes) must be punched at the side of the cartridge for insertion of the explosive cap (Figure 9.21).

Fuse Assembly

A fuse is a flexible tube containing slow-burning black powder with about a 1-m minimum length and a burning time of approximately 150 seconds (burn time increases with elevation) (Figure 9.22). Note that government regulations allow shorter burning times in some areas, but 70 seconds is considered an absolute minimum. The best fuses are crimped at the factory with a high-strength blasting cap (size 6 preferred), but some operations still crimp blasting caps and fuses together themselves. Blasting caps are explosives and must be treated as such. In some cases, a steel staple connects the blasting cap to the fuse to prevent static buildup.

Pull-Wire Igniter

The pull-wire igniter allows the fuse to be ignited in windy, moist conditions. Igniters must be carried separately from explosives and fuse assemblies to the blasting site. They are attached to the fuse *after* the blaster is in position and ready to throw the hand charge.

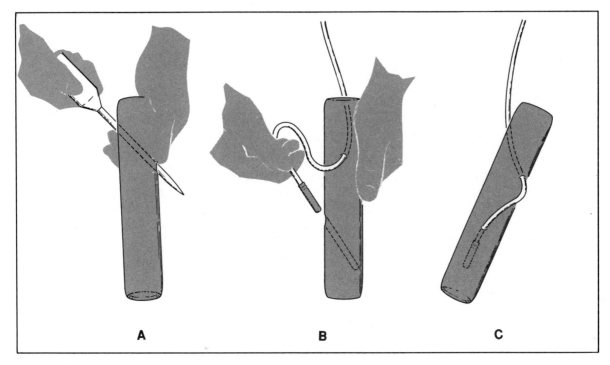

Figure 9.21. Arming gelatin primer by lacing.

Electrician or Duct Tape

Tape wrapped around the explosive and the fuse assembly securely holds the fuse and cap against the explosive (Figure 9.23).

EXAMPLE OF HAND CHARGE PLACEMENT PROCEDURE

An example of hand charge placement procedures is given in Appendix H. Procedures will vary according to local regulations and operational requirements.

ALTERNATIVE HAND CHARGE DELIVERY METHODS

Several hand charge delivery methods (besides tossing) have been developed, and more methods will probably appear. The alternative techniques allow the use of larger charges, or detonation above the snow surface, or the placement of charges lower down the slope. They include the following.

Sleighs

The charge is mounted on a sleigh (or other gliding device), which is lowered into the avalanche starting zone with a rope. The charge may be attached to a disposable sleigh, or suspended from a leaning pole attached to a retrievable sleigh.

Pipes

The charge slides through an inclined, fixed pipe or tube into the starting zone. The device is useful in rugged and treed terrain.

Booms

The charge is lowered to the starting zone from a boom that pivots out from a ridge, similar to a crane or fishing rod. The advantage is placement above the snow surface, but the desired targets must be close to the ridge.

Case Charges

Case charges are large explosive charges (for example, a box of dynamite or large bags of explosive) that

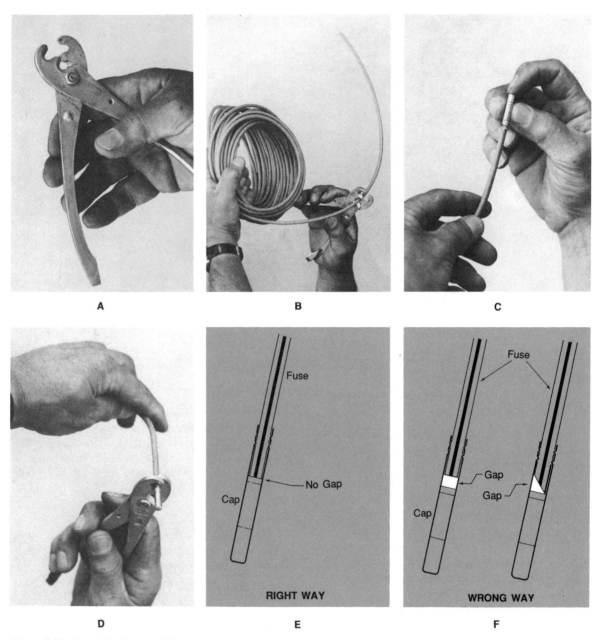

A

B

C

D

E

F

Figure 9.22. Assembly of cap and fuse.

are detonated at an easily accessible location some distance from the avalanche starting zone. The powerful explosive shock traveling through the snow, the air, and the ground can release avalanches at remote locations. The method is useful for control on short slopes above roads.

Artillery

Artillery used for avalanche control consists of military weapons: bazookas, recoilless rifles, howitzers, mortars, and civilian pieces developed specifically for avalanche control work. The choice of a specific artillery weapon depends on required range and availability

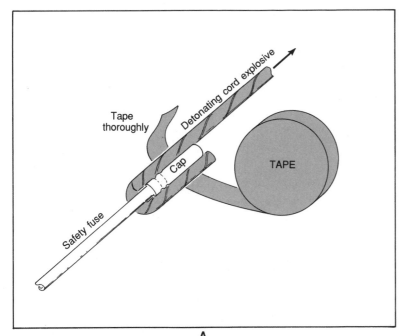
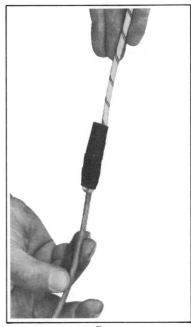

| A | B |

Figure 9.23. Fastening safety fuse to detonating cord.

of weapons and ammunition. In North America, the most commonly used military weapons include the 75-, 105-, and 106-mm recoilless rifles; however, 105-mm howitzers are also used (Figures 9.24 and 9.25). In some countries (e.g., Japan) the use of artillery is forbidden. Availability of ammunition and permission to use these weapons are special problems surrounding the use of military weapons. The maximum ranges of some control weapons are summarized in Table 9.2. For avalanche work, the target distance should not exceed half the maximum range. The range of the weapons will vary depending on the type and size of round used. Safety procedures for use of military weapons follow military

Table 9.2 Approximate Ranges of Avalanche Control Weapons Using High Explosive Rounds (after Perla and Martinelli, 1976)

Weapon	Maximum Range (m)	Payload (kg TNT)
75-mm howitzer	8,800	0.7
105-mm howitzer	11,300	2.3
75-mm recoilless rifle	6,350	0.7
105-mm recoilless rifle	8,600	2.0
Avalauncher	1,000	1.0

Figure 9.24. The 105-mm recoilless rifle. (Photo by S. Walker)

Figure 9.25. The 105-mm howitzer used for avalanche control at Rogers Pass, British Columbia. (Photo by Peter Schaerer)

Avalauncher Procedures

The Avalauncher is a two-chambered pneumatic cannon and is the most popular civilian avalanche control weapon used at present (Figure 9.28). The trajectory of the projectile is varied by altering the firing angle, the elevation, and the pressure of the nitrogen propellant. The principal disadvantages of the Avalauncher are short range and lack of accuracy when the projectiles are subject to strong winds. Since the Avalauncher is widely used by civilians for avalanche control and ammunition is freely available, a sample set of Avalauncher procedures is given in Appendix H. Procedures will vary depending on operational requirements and government guidelines and field manuals, which are published elsewhere and are therefore beyond the scope of this book. Artillery may be fired from fixed positions or deployed along a road at predetermined positions. Targets are usually preselected with the firing data (direction and elevation) predetermined and cataloged (Figures 9.26 and 9.27).

Advantages of Artillery

Some of the advantages of artillery include that the gun allows quick firing at numerous targets and, with predetermined firing data, avalanches can be controlled during poor visibility (snowfalls) and at night. Also, the method is flexible because shot placements may be modified easily, and distant inaccessible avalanche starting zones can be reached.

Limitations of Artillery

Limitations include the fact that the target must be on the same side of the mountain (or ridge) as the gun position, structures and occupied areas should not be in the line of fire, and the charge, detonating on or below the snow surface, has a limited range.

The ammunition does not always ignite on contact; the dud rate is 0.5% to 3%. Also, shrapnel is an environmental and safety concern and shells detonating in the ground can cause an erosional problem. Artillery requires maintenance and ammunition, and spare parts are expensive and not always readily available.

Figure 9.26. Tower with recoilless rifle. (Photo by E. LaChapelle)

Figure 9.27. Sighting for firing artillery.

Figure 9.28. The Avalauncher is a control weapon with limited range utilizing compressed gas. (Photo by P. Schaerer)

regulations. The example in Appendix H can be regarded as one with a minimum set of safety standards.

Helicopter Bombing

Helicopter bombing involves dropping large hand charges while hovering above avalanche starting zones. The bombardier lights the fuse of a prepared charge and drops the charge through the open helicopter door frame (Figure 9.29A). Assistance (optional) is provided by two other qualified blasters: a recorder who selects the targets and records the results, and an explosives handler who carries the igniters (separate from the bombs), places the igniters on the fuse, and hands the charge to the bombardier. In some areas, fewer personnel are used inside the helicopter; in others, more qualified blasters are involved. An example set of procedures is given in Appendix H. The procedures described there assume the (optional) presence of both a recorder and explosives handler. Often, tasks are combined to yield a crew of three including the pilot.

Helicopter flying and explosive transport in mountains are hazardous, therefore, strict safety rules must be adhered to. Procedures include helicopter safety training on the ground, practice flights dropping dummy bombs (of wood), and good communication between the blasting crew, the pilot, and the ground.

Advantages of Helicopter Bombing

Numerous avalanche paths can be treated within a short time. The cost is reasonable if a helicopter is stationed near the area and numerous avalanches paths close together can be controlled during one flight. In addition, the blasters are not exposed to avalanches, and inaccessible starting zones can be reached (not accessible on ground or reachable with artillery).

Figure 9.29A: Helicopter with bombardier dropping a bomb. (Photo by T. Auger)

Figure 9.29B. Control of small cornices by kicking off snow on daily control routes.

Limitations of Helicopter Bombing

Helicopters cannot fly with limited visibility, strong wind, or icing conditions, therefore, avalanches cannot be released during storms. This affects control timing and undesirably large avalanches may result when the

bombing is delayed by storm conditions. Correct placement of the explosive charges is difficult, because the bombardier cannot get the proper feel of the terrain from the air. Another disadvantage is that the explosive charges penetrate the snow and explode slightly below the surface, shortening the effective range. Generally, large charges (5 to 10 kg) are used as compensation for inaccurate shot placement and explosion at depth.

Cornice Control

Removal of cornices has the double benefit of eliminating the danger from a naturally falling cornice and releasing avalanches by the powerful impact on the snow below the cornice. The timing and frequency of cornice control varies but midwinter to spring are generally important times. Surface charges are sometimes used for minor cornice work, and smaller cornices may be kicked off or shoveled off on a regular basis (with climbing rope belays if necessary) (Figure 9.29B).

The accepted method for major cornice control is to plant charges in a line along the ridge (on the cornice roof) and link them together with a detonating cord for

Figure 9.29C. Belay system for cornice control.

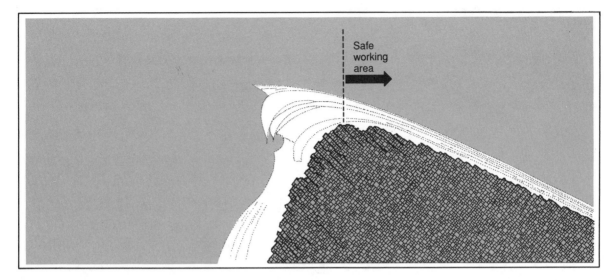

Figure 9.29D. Depiction of safe working area for cornice control.

simultaneous detonation. Charge spacing depends on the snow density and hardness (closer spacing with softer snow; 2 m is typical) and is based on experience.

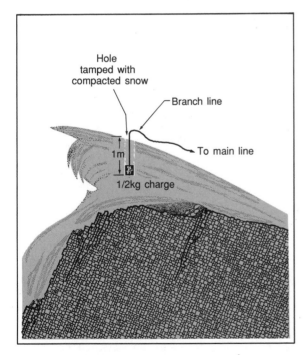

Figure 9.29E. Depiction of buried charges for cornice control.

Slower speed explosives are preferred to take advantage of explosive thrust effects and to force the weight of the cornice to be gradually sliced off to aid further failure. (The analogy to slicing an object with a knife has been used.) Field experience has shown that mature, overhanging cornices provide reasonable chance of success for removal (Figures 9.29C to 9.2G).

Procedures for cornice control work vary with local regulations. An illustrative set of procedures is given in Appendix H. Procedures will vary according to government regulations and operational requirements. The example in Appendix H can be regarded as one with minimum safety standards.

Ropeways

Ropeways deliver charges by means of a permanent ropeway strung across avalanche starting zones (Figure 9.30). Ropeways for avalanche control are also known as bomb trams, avalanche blasting lifts, and CATEX (in France). Ropeways were developed (and are widely used) in countries where military weapons are prohibited for avalanche control (for example, Austria, Germany, and France).

The equipment includes a safe drive and loading station, towers, and a moving wire rope (Figure 9.31). The charges are suspended on the wire rope, driven to the target point, and detonated above the snow surface.

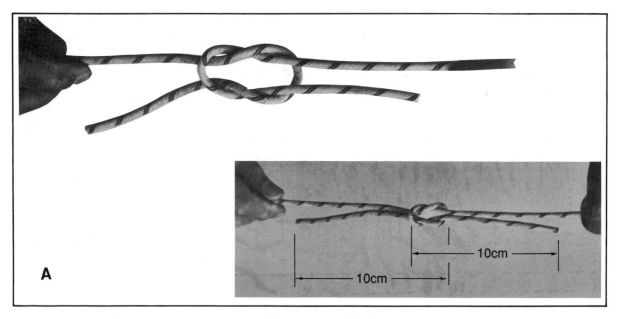

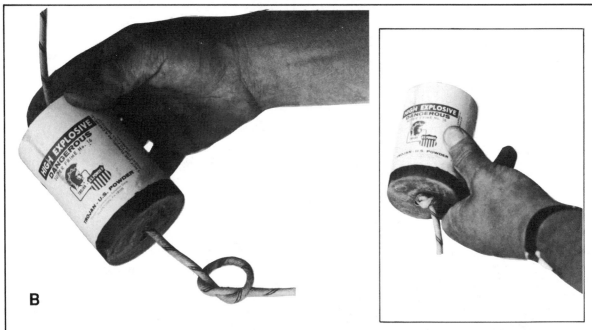

Figure 9.29F. Tying detonating cord to main line for cornice control (A). Attachment of charge to branch line (B).

The sophistication and cost of the systems vary. A ropeway may consist of a short, hand-driven cable strung across one avalanche path with explosives ignited by a fuse, or it may be a computer-controlled system, with radio-controlled ignition and fail-safe features, and run for several kilometers across more than one avalanche path. Long ropeways require professional design in order to perform reliably and safely.

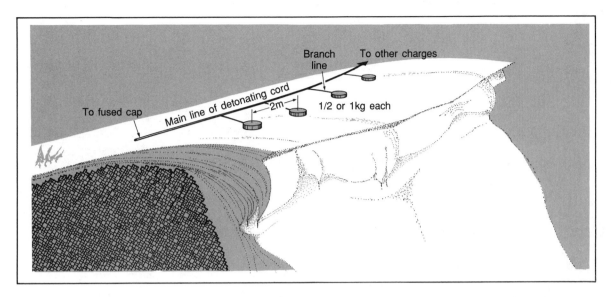

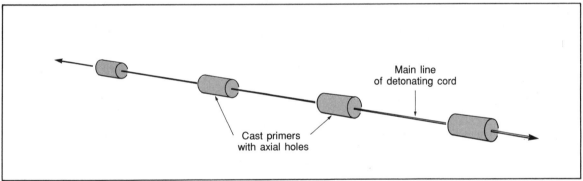

Figure 9.29G . Schematic showing cornice-blasting configurations.

Advantages of Ropeways

Ropeways allow placement of explosives in zones that are inaccessible for hand charging and artillery, or where artillery cannot be used for safety reasons. Other advantages include the following: Avalanches can be accurately controlled independent of visibility, and the effective range of the explosion is optimal because large charges can be detonated above the snow surface. Blasting personnel are assured safe positions during avalanche control, and duds may be retrieved mechanically.

Limitations of Ropeways

With regard to limitations, the capital costs of ropeways are high; the system requires careful planning, because correction of the rope and tower locations is expensive; they have a negative visual impact, because towers are usually placed on exposed ridges; and there is little flexibility in target choice when the snow deposition is unusual.

The systems are also vulnerable to power and mechanical breakdowns and failures due to wind, riming, and lightning. Safety equipment (for example, backup power, de-icing systems) may prevent breakdowns, but the cost increases.

The practical length limit seems to be about 6 km. Longer ropeways require too much time to get the charges to the targets, because the hauling speed of the rope with charges attached is limited.

Figure 9.30. Avalanche area accessed by ropeway, Coquihalla, British Columbia. Avalanche paths and targets are shown. (Photo by S. Walker)

Figure 9.31. Ropeway terminal, Coquihalla, British Columbia. Cut in forest for ropeway ascent is shown in the background. (Photo by S. Walker)

Preplaced Charges

Preplaced charges are installed on the ground at the beginning of the winter, with individual detonation by coded radio signals. Either a single charge at a critical location may be used or, for a wider range, several charges spread across a starting zone may be detonated simultaneously. A radio receiver-decoder, solar panel, and battery are placed at a safe location next to the avalanche starting zone, and cables connecting the explosives are buried in the ground. The charges are best placed on rocky ground to prevent damage to soil and vegetation.

Advantages of Preplaced Charges

The method is applicable in terrain that is inaccessible for hand charging and artillery. Also, avalanche control is fast because avalanches can be released by pushing a button, the application is not affected by visibility and the weather, and the cost is moderate.

Limitations of Preplaced Charges

Detonation is at the bottom of the snowpack, therefore preplaced charges are not effective in areas with deep snow. This disadvantage may be partially compensated for by large charges (5 to 10 kg).

Precautions must be taken to prevent tampering by unauthorized persons, for example:

- Only avalanche starting zones that are difficult to access should be used.
- Charges should be placed as late as possible in the fall.
- Warning signs should be placed.
- All unused charges should be detonated in the spring.
- Since the charges are not in an approved magazine, special permission is required for legal reasons.

Gas Exploders

With gas exploders, the shock is created by igniting a mixture of a gaseous fuel and an oxidant, for example, propane and air. The systems require permanent installations with fuel tanks, oxygen or air tanks, pipes to the blasting site, a mixing chamber, and an ignition system. The mixing of gases and the ignition may be controlled from a remote location. Exploders that direct the blast toward or parallel to the snow surface have proven to be best. Systems using gas explosions at the bottom of the snowpack have not been successful.

Advantages and Limitations of Gas Exploders

Two advantages of gas exploders are that the method is applicable at sites that are inaccessible for hand charging and artillery fire, and avalanches can be released quickly and independently of visibility and weather. On the other hand, the capital costs are high and there is no flexibility in target choice.

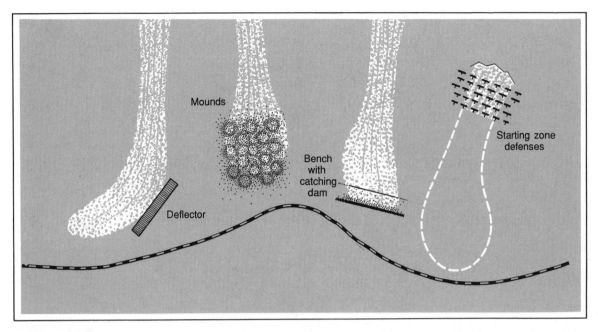

Figure 9.32. Defense structures for protection of mountain highways.

OTHER AVALANCHE TRIGGERING METHODS

Explosives are the common method for the controlled release of avalanches. However, other methods include test skiing, which is discussed in Chapter 6, and loading with snow, in which snowpackers and bulldozers are used to push snow from ridge tops to start avalanches on the slope below.

ENGINEERING WORKS

Engineering works for avalanche protection are permanent structures and earthworks (Figure 9.32). Their functions are avalanche prevention and deflection; facility protection, because avalanches can pass over or under; and deceleration and stopping of avalanches.

Engineering works operate independently of daily avalanche hazard forecasts and operational commitments. Their principal disadvantage is high capital cost. Other disadvantages are inflexibility when operational conditions change, the need for land, and a lack of aesthetic appeal (Figure 9.33). Therefore, engineering

Figure 9.33. The left side shows supporting structures in avalanche starting zones. In the center of the picture, mounds and arrester dikes are visible. (Photo by E. Wengi)

Figure 9.34. Modern supporting structures. (Photo on left by Wagner and Hopf; photo on right from Frutiger and Martinelli)

works are generally used only as follows:

- For the protection of structures such as buildings, bridges, power line towers, and lift towers
- Where high traffic volume or important traffic does not permit road closures
- Where avalanches run frequently (implying excessive snow removal and frequent closures)
- Where the terrain and weather do not permit explosive control
- At isolated avalanche paths without daily avalanche hazard evaluation and traffic control

Supporting Structures

Supporting structures prevent large avalanches in starting zones by limiting their size. The functions are: to give external support to the snow, thereby limiting avalanche initiation; limit fracture propagation and avalanche size by producing a discontinuity in the snow cover; and stop small avalanches from gaining momentum.

Supporting structures consist of rigid barriers or wire-rope nets that have an angle usually between 90° and 105° with the upslope ground surface. Vertical (line

Figure 9.35. Snow net used as supporting structure. (Photo from Frutiger and Martinelli)

Figure 9.36. Older inadequate supporting structures in the foreground. Modern ones in continuous rows at the back. St. Antönien, Switzerland. (Photo by A. Roch)

of plumb) barriers, however, are also applied. Steel is the preferred material today; older works were built of wood, aluminum, or concrete (Figures 9.34 and 9.35).

The structures are built in continuous rows over the full width and length of avalanche starting zones. Attempts to use posts, narrow barriers, rock piles, and steel tripods to provide a point support to the snow cover have proven to be unsuccessful (Figure 9.36). The distance between rows, which is a function of the slope incline and the snow depth, may vary between 10 and 40 m. The structures are at least as high as the expected greatest snow depth (for a return period of 100 years, this is normally between 3 and 5 m), and they are designed against forces from snow creep and glide and impact from small avalanches. Since the stabilization effect and the design forces increase substantially with snow depth, reliable estimates of the maximum expected snow depths are vital. The Swiss Federal Institute for Snow and Avalanche Research has developed guidelines for the location and the design of supporting structures. Inadequacies of supporting structures in providing protection have been traced to gaps between structures (allowing avalanches to gain high speed), exessive snow depths, damage from rockfall, and poor footings (so that creep and glide forces cannot be resisted).

High cost is the most serious limitation for application of supporting structures. Other limitations are deep snow, unstable soil, and rugged, steep terrain. Due to the high cost, supporting structures are justified only for the protection of heavily used areas and residences, such as in the densely populated alpine areas of western Europe. In areas with low population and traffic density, the expense of supporting structures may be justified only for very small avalanche starting zones and where terrain, environmental, social, and political considerations do not permit other control methods.

Terraces in Starting Zones

Horizontal terraces, either built as cut and fill or with back-filled walls, were built as avalanche control measures in starting zones in the Alps in the nineteenth century. Recent experience in Europe and Japan has shown that they are effective only in the following situations:

- In preventing avalanches that start due to gliding snow
- On slope inclines of 35° and less
- When the snow depth does not exceed 1.5 m
- At locations with negligible snow drifting
- When the width W of the terrace is at least 1.5 times the depth H of the snow (Figures 9.37 and 9.38)

Deflectors

Deflectors are dikes and walls that intercept avalanches and redirect the flow. They may also be built parallel to the avalanche flow direction to confine the flow in a narrow channel. Most deflectors are built as earth banks but they may be made of reinforced earth, gabion walls, cribs, concrete, or steel. Stone masonry was used in the past when other materials were not available. Deflectors are usually 6 to 12 m high, but some up to 20 m high have been built. The cost of deflectors is reasonable when local soil can be used (Figure 9.39).

Principal considerations for the location and design of deflectors are as follows:

1. The deflected avalanche must have enough space to run out harmlessly (Figure 9.40).
2. The terrain and the natural direction of avalanche motion should be considered for deflector location. If possible, a deflector should reinforce the natural terrain, for example, by elevating the side slope of a natural channel.
3. Avalanche deflection should occur gradually, otherwise the avalanches will overflow the works. Preferably, the angle α between the direction of an avalanche and the deflector should not exceed 20° (30° maximum).

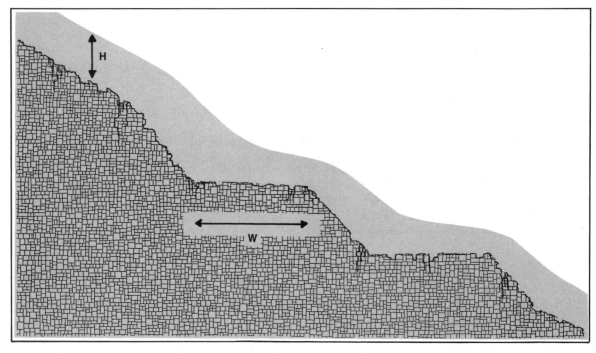

Figure 9.37. Terraces in starting zone. The terrace width W, *is at least 1.5 times the snow depth,* H.

Figure 9.38. Terraces in avalanche starting zone. (Photo by H. Frutiger)

Figure 9.39. Deflector built of earth materials. (Photo by P. Schaerer)

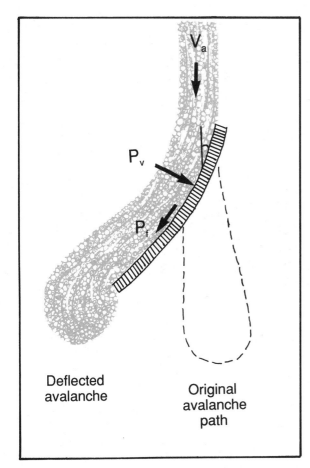

Figure 9.40. Location and forces on a deflector. The initial deflection angle should be less than 20° if possible.

4. The design height H_d of the deflector can be calculated roughly by the relationship (Figure 9.41):

$$H_d = H_s + H_a + H_v$$

where

H_s = depth of snow deposited by snowfall and previous avalanches

H_a = flow depth of the design avalanche

$H_v = (V_a \sin\alpha)^2/2g$ = minimum runup height from flowing snow. Since H_v is derived only from simple energy considerations based on the assumption that the avalanche moves as a point mass, the expression given here must be regarded as a minimum estimate only (Hungr and McClung, 1987). (In practice, H_v may also be larger depending on the details of the avalanche and geometry of the runout zone.)

V_a = approach speed of the design avalanche

α = deflection angle

$g = 9.81$ m/s²

5. The height H_d of the deflector may be extended partially by excavating the soil in front of the dike. Temporary deflectors are sometimes built during the winter by bulldozing snow into a ridge.

6. The ground behind a deflector should be smooth and free of trees, large boulders, or hummocks. The deflector face should be as steep as possible without sharp corners. The terrain should be surveyed with the location staked out precisely prior to construction.

7. Walls should be designed for avalanche impact

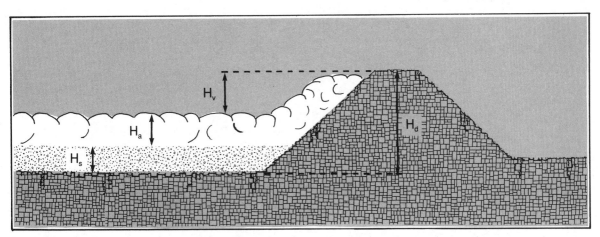

Figure 9.41. Schematic for calculating height of deflectors.

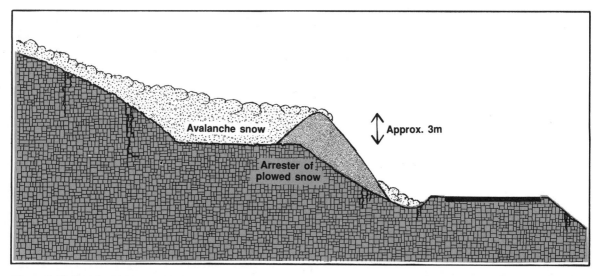

Figure 9.42. Bench with snow arrester.

Figure 9.43. Flow retarders of steel in Japan. (Photo by R. Decker)

forces P_v and friction forces P_f (Figure 9.40). Earth dikes built of granular soil found at avalanche paths usually have adequate stability, but the stability should be checked when high dikes are constructed and when poor soils are suspected.

8. Usually, deflectors are ineffective against powder avalanches; the flow depth of powder avalanches is much higher than the works.

9. The runup H_v may be excessive for high-speed avalanches and large deflection angles. For this reason, deflectors are usually applied fairly near the end of avalanche paths, for example, in the lower track, where slope angles are low and avalanche speeds can be moderate.

10. Deflectors should not be applied at locations with high accumulations of blowing snow or frequent and deep avalanche deposits; these reduce the effective height.

Arresters

Arresters are catching dams, walls, or trenches constructed perpendicular to the avalanche flow that are designed to slow or stop avalanches (Figures 9.42, 9.43, and 9.44). Adequate height for stopping the avalanches and adequate storage capacity behind are both design considerations of arresters. Temporary arresters may be built by forming a ridge of snow at the edge of benches above a road.

The height required to stop an avalanche can be determined roughly with the equation used for calculat-

Figure 9.44. Arrester. (Photo by H. Frutiger)

ing the height of deflectors by setting $\alpha = 90°$. It can be seen that arresters must be unreasonably high when the avalanche speed exceeds 10 m/s. Thus, arresters are applied either against small avalanches with low speed or near the end of the runout zone of large avalanches. It can be effective to reduce avalanche speed by first placing retarders (see later section in this chapter) during the approach to an arrester.

The uphill space behind the arrester must allow for snow deposition—often a surprisingly large amount. Storage capacity can be improved by snow removal between avalanches.

Wide and deep road ditches, high curbs, and temporary walls of snow can retain small avalanches that would stop on the road if they were not controlled. The

Figure 9.46. Splitter with concrete walls. (Photo by P. Schaerer)

effectiveness of ditches may be estimated by comparing the mass of expected avalanches with available ditch storage volume. The following guidelines assist in estimating the available storage volume (Figure 9.45):

• The ditch width is governed by the terrain (values from 2 to 5 m are typical).
• The deposit density of avalanche snow may be as-

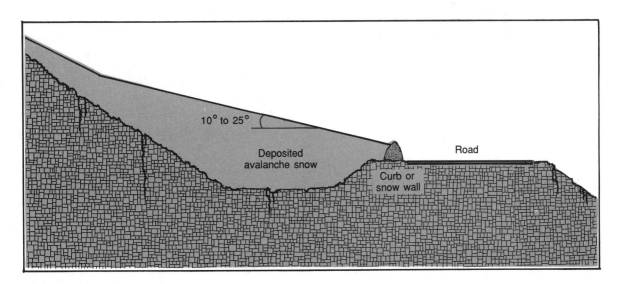

Figure 9.45. Ditch used to arrest snow.

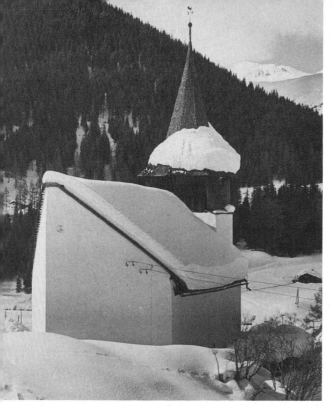

Figure 9.47. Splitter used to protect the Davos-Frauenkirch church. (Photo by E. LaChapelle)

sumed to be 250 kg/m^3 for dry snow and 400 kg/m^3 for wet snow.

- The surface angle of the deposit snow varies between 10° and 25° depending on deposit characteristics.
- Snowfall and plowing require additional ditch capacity but the effectiveness may be maintained by periodic snow removal.

Splitters

Splitters are wedge-shaped dams or walls, earth mounds, or pillars. They are placed directly in front of a single object, for example, a building, a power line tower, or a chairlift tower, to direct the avalanche flow around the structure (Figure 9.46). Splitters can also be incorporated into the structure. For example, a building may be built with a reinforced wall facing the avalanche, or the base of a tower may be encased in concrete or earth (Figure 9.47).

Splitters may also be placed at a strategic location in an avalanche path to divide the avalanches into several small arms. The arms have reduced mass and a shorter runout distance, and they may be controlled easier by

retarders than the concentrated avalanche flow.

The flow direction of usual and erratic avalanches should be determined carefully when a splitter is located. The apex of a wedge-shaped splitter should face the principal direction of flow, and the wings should be long enough to cover the object. The apex of the splitter usually has an angle of 60°. The height of splitters and the design forces are determined in a manner similar to that for deflector design. Splitters cannot be built high enough to control powder avalanches. Therefore, when power line and chairlift towers must be protected, a splitter serves to deflect the dense core component, and the tower structure above is designed against forces from the powder component.

In making decisions about the use of splitters, one should be aware that splitters protect only the objects behind them; traffic and other structures downslope and at the sides are still exposed to the deflected flows.

Snow Sheds

Snow sheds (also called *galleries*) are roofs designed to allow avalanches to pass over the object. They are applied on railways and highways and sometimes incorporated into building design (Figure 9.48). Concrete, steel, wood, and combinations of these materials are used. Temporary snow sheds have been built of snow blocks (igloo-style) and by tunneling into deep avalanche deposits.

Figure 9.48. Snow shed used to protect highway traffic. (Photo by P. Schaerer)

Figure 9.49. Snow shed with dikes that prevent spreading of avalanches. (Photo by P. Schaerer)

Snow sheds are expensive so careful consideration is required for their need, benefits, and alternatives. Sometimes a rock tunnel or a structure in a cut and fill may be a less expensive solution.

A snow shed should be long enough to cover the width of the avalanche path. However, sheds are frequently built shorter with avalanches being allowed to spill over under extreme conditions (for example, once in 10 or 30 years). The length can sometimes be reduced by building guiding dams on top of the shed to prevent spreading of avalanches, but this is not always successful (Figure 9.49). When several avalanche paths are close together, it is often more economical and practical for later operation to build one continuous shed, rather than several short ones.

The following *design forces* are considered:

- Vertical force (weight) of a design avalanche moving over the shed
- Dynamic friction of a design avalanche moving over the shed
- Static weight of snow deposited on the shed from snowfall and avalanches (The weight of deposited avalanche snow at the end of the winter can be very high—comparable to dynamic loads—for snow sheds in the runout zone of frequent avalanches.)
- Dynamic forces if avalanches strike the shed directly due to a sharp transition of slope between the snow shed and the terrain

Figure 9.50. Earth mounds to retard flowing snow at the end of a runout zone. (Photo by P. Schaerer)

- Horizontal snow pressure from avalanche snow deposited adjacent to the snow shed
- Impact, friction, and uplift on protruding roof parts from avalanches that come from the opposite valley side

Not all forces occur simultaneously; each design value must be determined from careful estimates of maximum conditions.

Other considerations for design and operation of snow sheds are that snow sheds reduce the visibility and vertical clearance on roads, and the ground inside the snow shed generally is colder than outside: Ice forms readily on the pavement, creating hazardous driving conditions. Frost action on foundations, retaining walls, and pavement should be considered.

Also, creeks (usually present in avalanche paths) must be diverted to the side, channeled across the shed, or contained in a culvert underneath. The drainage and waterproofing of the roof require special attention, and the shed roof might have to be protected against rockfall (usually with a layer of soil).

Figure 9.51. Earth mounds in a runout zone. (Photo by H. Frutiger)

Retarders

Retarders are obstacles located in avalanche paths to reduce the runout distance by dissipating motion energy of avalanches. Retarders dissipate energy by spreading the avalanches over a wider area (Figure 9.43). This results in reduced flow depth and greater contact area with the ground. They also create friction against forward motion to slow the moving snow. For example, two rows of earth mounds may reduce the runout distance of avalanches by 20 to 30 m (Figures 9.50 and 9.51).

The effect of retarders is limited and it depends crucially on the type of avalanche snow and avalanche motion. Retarders are most effective when the avalanches are slow and contain dense snow (for example, wet snow avalanches). Retarders have little effect on rapidly moving, dry snow. Above a road, the retarders may reduce the number of avalanches and the amount of avalanche snow on the road, but they must not be counted on to eliminate the hazard to traffic.

Earth mounds built from local soil are low in cost and are, therefore, the most common type. Rock piles, concrete blocks and wedges, cribs, and tripods of steel or concrete (open and covered with wire nets) have been applied.

The following guidelines apply to the *location and design of earth mounds:*

- Mounds are best built on terrain with a slope incline not greater than 15° to 20°.
- Mounds should be built in the avalanche runout zone.

One should plan for a storage capacity of more than one avalanche.
- Mounds should be spaced laterally, as close together as possible, with the toe of each mound meeting the toe of the adjacent one.
- At least two rows of mounds in a checkerboard fashion should be built.
- The optimum height is 5 to 6 m, but heights up to 8 m might be needed in areas of deep snow or where more than one avalanche is to be expected. Mounds should be about 2 m wide at their top (across the avalanche path).
- The stability of mounds built from sand-gravel-boulder material (usually found in avalanche runout zones) is adequate against avalanche forces. Surface erosion by avalanches is negligible but planting shrubs and grass helps provide protection against rain erosion.
- Creeks should either be diverted around the mounds or be carried in a culvert underneath mounds. Open creek channels through the mound pattern can provide weak spots.

FOREST CONTROL

Forests control avalanches by preventing large avalanches and retarding avalanches in motion (see Chapter 5). The loss of a forest due to fire, careless cutting,

Figure 9.52. Young trees on an avalanche slope in Switzerland with creep and glide control structures. (Photo by H. Frutiger)

Figure 9.53. Progressive reforestation in avalanche terrain. Left, taken in 1907, shows masonry terraces for protection of planted forest; middle photo taken in 1938; right photo in 1957. (Photos from Swiss Federal Institute for Snow and Avalanche Research with the permission of Rhätische Bahn)

excessive explosive control, disease, or acid precipitation can produce avalanches where none had occurred before (refer to Figure 5.11).

Regrowth of a forest in an avalanche path is difficult, expensive, and slow because the young trees are damaged continuously by avalanches, snow glide, and snow creep. Often reforestation must be combined with supporting structures (Figure 9.52). Supporting structures (often temporary) with a life span of about 50 years are used (100 years for slow-growth conditions and species). Because of the possible damage and the difficulty of repair, logging plans on steep terrain should consider whether new starting zones might be created.

Avalanche paths are usually subject to harsh growing conditions including poor soil, a short growing season, wind and drought conditions, steep ground (which promotes erosion), and persistence of deep snow (which promotes snow mold fungi). Fast-growing native species should be planted whenever possible. Some attempts will have to proceed in stages with the initial use of fast growing successional species (for example, willows and alders). These species have good root systems and they also fix nitrogen (fertilize soil) to provide the

Figure 9.54. Snow fence on a ridge to collect blowing snow. (Photo by H. Frutiger)

environment for the later growth of the final, or climax, species.

Harsh conditions also mean that new seedlings are lost, requiring several replantings to complete reforestation. (Seedling survival rates vary from more than 90% under ideal conditions to near 0% under harsh conditions.) In some cases, sites must be prepared (terraces built), fertilizers used, and even supplemental water provided.

The time commitment and difficulty of reforestation serve to make the method applicable only when the need for avalanche control is severe. Many villages in western Europe owe their existence to forest protection; reforestation of avalanche terrain is less common in North America but it has been applied more often in landslide-scarred terrain (Figure 9.53).

CONTROL OF WIND-TRANSPORTED SNOW

Wind has a significant influence on avalanche formation due to the loading of lee zones of terrain obstacles. However, control of drifting snow affects only avalanches caused by wind and not those that form due to heavy snowfall without wind or high temperatures. The changing and unpredictable directions of the wind and the large surface areas affected are other difficulties with blowing snow control. For these reasons, control of wind-transported snow in avalanche protection is limited to three applications: cornice prevention and control, prevention of deep snow at supporting structures, and reduction of avalanche frequency at short slopes, for example, above a road.

Control by Collector Snow Fences

Collector fences, located on the windward side of a ridge, collect and store the snow before it can reach the ridge. Collector fences prevent cornice formation and reduce the amount of wind-deposited snow on the downwind side of ridges for a maximum distance of about 100 m from the ridge (Figure 9.54).

Collector fences are used on open, windward slopes of low inclines (typically less than 15°). In steep terrain, they are less effective and subject to forces from creeping and gliding snow. The distance from the ridge should be about 20 to 30 times the height H of the fence (Figure 9.55).

Since large amounts of snow must be dealt with on mountain ridges, fences must be higher than those at valley roads and on prairies, but 4 m is a practical maximum. A second fence at a distance of 20 x H to 30 x H in downslope front may be built if the space is available.

For optimal effectiveness, fences should consist of about 50% solid surface and 50% openings, with a gap

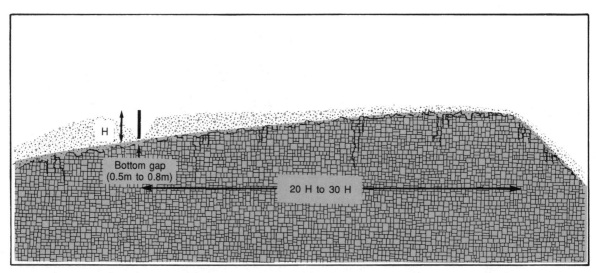

Figure 9.55. Collector fence on windward side of a ridge reduces starting zone accumulations. The influence as a function of snow depth is shown.

0.5 to 0.8 m high at the ground. Strong anchoring by means of bracing and guy wires is required against wind forces; both wood and metal are used as building materials.

A series of solid fences (without openings) may be built at a distance from the ridge about 10 times the fence height if space is limited. The length of drift behind a solid fence is about half that of an open fence, hence the catching capacity is lower.

Control by Blower Fences

Blower fences (also called *jet roofs*) are inclined panels that accelerate the wind and direct it into the slope below (Figure 9.56). The high-velocity wind scours snow from positions where cornices would normally form. A blower fence does not reduce snow deposition on the slope; it merely moves the snow farther downslope. In addition, snow transport by winds opposite to the prevailing ones may result in drifting, making the roofs ineffective and in need of maintenance.

The terrain determines the location and dimensions of blower fences. Fences should face the prevailing wind direction, and the incline of the roof should be parallel or slightly inclined toward the ground on the downwind side. The roof may be solid or have slats (openings). A solid roof is aerodynamically more effective, but it may collect snow and it requires more material.

Control by Vegetation

Forests and high shrubs on the windward side of ridges act similar to collector fences by forcing wind-transported snow to be deposited. It is important that the area in front of the ridge be covered with trees and shrubs; a single line of trees on the ridge top only would produce deep snow deposits on the downwind slope.

The consequences of removing trees on the windward side of ridges (for example, for a ski run) should be considered carefully. A forest or shrubs may be replanted, but it may take a long time before vegetation becomes effective because the climatic conditions on a windward ridge site are usually very unfavorable for tree growth.

References

Brugnot, G. 1987. Avalanche zoning, dynamics, and control. Recent work done in France. *Avalanche*

Figure 9.56. Jet roof used to carry snow beyond the starting zones. (Photo by H. Frutiger)

Formation, Movement and Effects. IAHS Publication No. 162, pp. 521–536.

Brugnot, Gerard, and Francois Rapin. 1989. Recommendations for the safe use of ropeways carrying explosives in avalanche blasting. *Annals of Glaciology* 13: 20–21.

Bundesamt für Forstwesen. 1984. Richtlinien zur Berücksichtigung der Lawinengefahr bei raumwirksamen Tätigkeiten (Guidelines for consideration of the avalanche hazard with land use–related activities). Bern, Switzerland: Eidgenössische Drucksachen und Materialzentrale, 21 pp + appendix.

Dawson, K. L., and T. E. Lang. 1979. Evaluation of jet-roof geometry for snow-cornice control. *Journal of Glaciology* 22(88): 503–511.

Eidg. Oberforstinspectorat. 1968. Lawinenverbau im

Anbruchgebiet (Avalanche control structures in the starting zone). Richtlinien des Eidg. Oberforstinspektorates für den Stutzverbau. Mitleilungen des Eidg. Institutes für Schnee- und Lawinenforschung, No. 29. Davos, Switzerland: Swiss Federal Institute for Snow and Avalanche Research.

Everts, K., and B. Laidlaw. 1978. Research and development of avalanche control methods in Banff National Park. Associate Committee on Geotechnical Research Technical Memo 120. Ottawa: National Research Council of Canada, pp. 30–41.

Freer, G. L. and P. A. Schaerer. 1980. Snow-avalanche hazard zoning in British Columbia, Canada. *Journal of Glaciology* 26(94): 345–354.

Gubler, H. 1977. Artificial release of avalanches by explosives. *Journal of Glaciology* 19(81): 419–429.

Hungr, O., and D. M. McClung. 1987. An equation for calculating snow avalanche run-up against barriers. IAHS Publication No. 162, pp. 605–612.

Institute Federal pour l'Étude de la Neige et des Avalanche. 1984. Directives pour la prise en consideration du danger d'avalanches lors de l'exercice d'activités touchant l'organisation du territoire. Bern, Switzerland: Office Federal des Forêts, 36 pp. (See also title in German.)

International Union of Forestry Research Organizations. 1978. *Mountain Forests and Avalanches: Proceedings of the Davos Seminar,* September 1978. Davos, Switzerland: Swiss Federal Institute for Snow and Avalanche Research, 358 pp.

Ives, J. D., and Plam, M. 1980. Avalanche hazard mapping and zoning problems in the Rocky Mountains, with examples from Colorado, U.S. *Journal of Glaciology* 26(94): 363–376.

Mears, A. I. 1981. Design criteria for avalanche control structures in the runout zone. General Technical Report RM-84. Fort Collins, CO: USDA Forest Service, Rocky Mountain Forest and Range Experiment Station, 28 pp.

Mears, A. I. 1992. Snow-avalanche hazard analysis for land-use planning and engineering, Bulletin 49. Denver: Colorado Geological Survey, 55 pp.

Norem, Harald. 1985. Design criteria and location of snow fences. *Annals of Glaciology* 6: 68–70.

Perla, Ronald I., and M. Martinelli, Jr. 1976 (revised 1978). *Avalanche Handbook.* USDA Agricultural Handbook 489. Washington, DC: U.S. Government Printing Office, 238 pp.

Swiss Federal Institute for Snow and Avalanche Research, 1961. Avalanche control in the starting zone: guidelines for planning and design of permanent supporting structures. Stn. Paper 71, 1962. Translated by Hans Frutiger of Lawinenverbau im Anbruchgebiet. USDA Forest Service, 60 pp.

Thommen, R. A. 1986. Research and development pertaining to steel wire rope net systems for the prevention of avalanches. *Proceedings of the International Snow Science Workshop,* Lake Tahoe, California, October 22–25, 1986. Homewood, CA: ISSW Committee, pp. 201–206

APPENDIX A

SI UNITS

Basic Units

In this book, the metric system of units known as Système International d'Unités, abbreviated SI, is followed as closely as possible. The SI system is used universally in science, industry, and commerce throughout the world.

The main features of SI are as follows:

1. There are five basic units, as given in Table A.1. The meter and the kilogram are used instead of the centimeter and gram of the older c.g.s. metric system. Whenever possible, these five basic units should be used by themselves or in combination.
2. The unit of force is the newton (1 N = 1 kg m/s^2) and is independent of the earth's gravitation. The kilogram-force should not be used, if possible.
3. The unit of energy (including heat) is the joule (1 J = 1 N m) and the unit of power is the watt (1 W = 1 J/s). Units involving calories should not be used.
4. Multiples of units should be restricted to steps of a thousand and fractions to steps of a thousandth. The symbols used for fractions and multiples are given in Table A.2.

Table A.1 Basic SI Units

Physical Quantity	Name of Unit	Symbol for Unit
Length	Meter	m
Mass	Kilogram	kg
Time	Second	s
Temperature	Degree Kelvin	K
Amount of substance	Mole	mol

Table A.2 Fractions and Multiples

Fraction	Prefix	Symbol	Multiple	Prefix	Symbol
10^{-1}*	deci	d	10*	deca	da
10^{-2}*	centi	c	10^2*	necto	n
10^{-3}	milli	m	10^3	kilo	k
10^{-6}	micro	μ	10^6	mega	m
10^{-9}	nano	n	10^9	giga	g
10^{-12}	pico	p	10^{12}	tera	t

* These fractions and multiples should not be used if possible.

In addition to the basic units, some important derived SI units have been given special names. These are listed in Table A.3.

Table A.3 Derived SI Units with Special Names

Physical Quantity	Name of Unit	Symbol	Definition
Force	newton	N	kg m s^{-2}
Stress or pressure	pascal	Pa	kg m^{-1} s^{-2} = N m^{-2}
Energy	joule	J	kg m^2 s^{-2}
Power	watt	W	kg m^2 s^{-3} = J s^{-1}
Frequency	hertz	Hz	Cycles per second
Temperature interval	degree	°	No specification of C or K necessary
Angle	radian	rad	2π radians = 360°

There are also a number of important units that are used in snow and avalanche work because of convenience and which are recommended even though the strict rules of SI units are not followed. These are listed in Table A.4.

Table A.4 Other Units Commonly Used in Snow and Avalanche Work

Physical Quantity	Name of Unit	Symbol	SI Equivalent
Time	hour	h	3,600 s
Time	day	d	86,400 s = 24 hr
Time	year	a	In terms of earth's rotation around the sun
Mass	tonne	t	10^3 kg
Customary temperature	degree Celsius	°C	t (°C) = T (°K)– 273.15
Angle	degree	°	$\pi/180$ rad
Length[a]	centimeter	cm	10^{-2} m
Speed[b]	km/h		
Volume[c]	liter	l	10^{-3} m^3
Pressure[d]	bar	b	1 bar = 10^5 N/m^2 = 10^3 mb

[a] The use of centimeters for length is discouraged except in measuring snow depth where it is a convenient unit.

[b] The use of km/h for speed is discouraged for describing speeds of avalanches or wind speed; the preferred unit is m/s. Since mountain weather forecasts still prescribe wind speeds in km/h, the use of this derived unit will not disappear.

[c] The use of liter is discouraged in very accurate work.

[d] Pressures in weather forecasts are now commonly given in kilopascals (kPa).

Conversion of Units

Derived units may be converted to equivalent ones by cross-multiplication. Two examples follow.

Example 1. Convert 10 m/s to km/h.

Solution:

$$\frac{10 \text{ m}}{\text{s}} \times \frac{(1 \text{ km})}{(10^3 \text{ m})} \times \frac{(3,600 \text{ s})}{(1 \text{ h})} = \frac{36 \text{ km}}{\text{h}}$$

Example 2. Convert 700 mb to kPa.

Solution:

$$700 \text{ mb} \times \frac{(105 \text{ N/m2})}{(1 \text{ bar})} \times \frac{(1 \text{ bar})}{(10^3 \text{ mb})} \times \frac{(1 \text{ Pa})}{(1 \text{ N/m}^2)} \times \frac{(1 \text{ kPa})}{(10^3 \text{ Pa})} = 70 \text{ kPa}$$

Force Measuring Devices

The preferred unit of force is the newton (N). However, force (or weight) measuring devices are calibrated in units of kilograms or grams instead of newtons. Therefore, devices such as spring scales measure a force (called a kilogram-force) but the results are commonly expressed in kilograms or grams. The weight given on the scale may be converted to newtons by multiplying by the acceleration (numerical) value due to gravity (normally 9.81 m/s^2). The conversion factor is:

Weight (N) = Scale Reading (kg) x 9.81

It is rarely, if ever, necessary to do the conversion in practice. This confusion does not arise in the English system of units because scales are directly calibrated in pounds (the unit of force).

It is common in engineering practice to express avalanche impact pressures in t/m^2. Properly speaking the units are tonnes-force/m^2. As an example, 1,000 kPa pressure may be converted to t/m^2 using the formula above.

Solution:

$$1,000 \text{ kPa} =$$

$$10^6 \text{ Pa} \times \frac{(1 \text{ N/m2})}{(1 \text{ Pa})} \times \frac{(1 \text{ kg-force})}{(9.81 \text{ N})} \times \frac{(1 \text{ t-force})}{10^3 \text{ kg–force}}$$

$$1,000 \text{ kPa} = \frac{10^3}{9.81} \times \frac{\text{t}}{\text{m}^2} = 102 \text{ t/m}^2 \approx 100 \text{ t/m}^2$$

EXAMPLE OF SNOW AND WEATHER OBSERVATIONS

This appendix gives an example set of procedures to form a basis for snow and weather observations to aid avalanche forecasting. The description is based on observations with minimal equipment and with measurements taken manually. Computerized data retrieval with radio-linked telemetry and use of cellular phones is common in snow and weather data collection, but a discussion of the vast set combinations used is beyond the scope of this book. Data taken (including symbols), procedures, and observation times will vary between countries. Variations in symbols used will be great, with most computerized operations preferring to choose symbols from the extended ASCII character set.

Objectives

Snow and weather observations are a series of meteorological and snowpack measurements at a properly instrumented study plot (Figure B.1). Taken at regular

Figure B.1. Study plot and snow measurement equipment. (Photo by D. McClung)

intervals, the data provide the basis for recognizing changes in the stability of the snow cover and for reporting the state of the weather to the weather office. On a long-term basis, the observations are used to improve the ability to forecast the avalanche hazard and to increase knowledge of the climate in the area. The observations should be made regularly, be complete, accurate, and recorded in a uniform manner.

Types of Observations

Observations taken at regular daily times are referred to as *standard observations*. Preferably, they should be carried out twice daily at 0700 and 1600 hours, but the type of operation and availability of observers might require different frequencies and times.

Observations between the standard times are referred to as *interval observations*. They are taken when the snow stability is changing rapidly, for example, during a heavy snowfall. Interval observations may contain a few selected observations only or the complete set of those made during standard observations.

Equipment

A study plot usually contains the following equipment:

- Screen for housing thermometers (height adjustable)
- Maximum thermometer
- Minimum thermometer
- Two snow boards (about 400 x 400 mm), one designated as a new snow board and one as a storm board

- Snow stake; a snow depth marker, graduated in centimeters, with a leveling stick
- Ruler, graduated in centimeters
- Snow sampling tube and weigh scale, graduated in grams, or a precipitation gauge
- Knife or plate for cutting snow samples
- Field book of water-resistant paper

The following additional equipment is useful:

- Hygro-thermograph with screen
- Recording precipitation gauge or rain gauge
- One to three additional snow boards
- First section of a ram penetrometer
- Barograph (in the office) or barometer-altimeter
- Anemometer (including windvane) at a separate wind station with radio or cable link to a recording instrument
- Box as shelter for the equipment
- Small broom
- Snow shovel
- Tilt board and shear frames for shear tests

Procedure

Record the location and elevation of the study plot at the top of the field book page, or on the title page. A sample form for field notes is shown in Figure B.2.

Sampling Tube Area __42__ cm²

Location	SNOW	BOUND	CAMP	EL.	1670 m	
Observer	R.M.	R.M.	K.E.L.	K.E.L.	K.E.L.	K.E.L.
Date 1992	02-09	02-09	02-10	02-10	02-10	02-11
Time	0700	1600	0700	1140	1600	0700
Sky	① H	①	⊕	⊕	⊕	○
Precipitation	NIL	*-1	*1	*3	LR	NIL
Max. Temp. °C	-5	-3	-3	-1.5	+1	0
Min. Temp. °C	-8	-6	-4.5	-4	-4	-11
Pres. Temp. °C	-6	-3	-4	-1.5	0	-10
Thermograph °C	-6	-3	-4	-1	0	-10
Temp. Trend	↗	→	↗	↗	↗	→
Humidity %	80	85	95	100	100	65
Interval cm	0	T	10	12	4	0
New Snow cm	0	T	10	12	15	0
Storm cm	0	T	10	20	21	19 GL
Snowpack cm	223	222	231	239	241	239
Weight New g	—	—	33.6	42	67	—
Water Equivalent mm			8	10	16	
Density kg/m³			80	83	110	
Precipitation Gauge mm	60	60	67	77	82	82
Foot Penetration cm	37	35	43	52	51	45
Ram Penetration cm	40	39	47	55	55	48
Surface Condition	V	ΦD	ΦD	ΦD	Φw	~
Wind Base	E LIGHT	CALM	S MOD	S LIGHT	SW LIGHT	E LIGHT
Wind High	S MOD	S MOD	—	—	—	NE LIGHT
Barograph Press. kPa	104.5	103	100	99.5	101	102.5
Barograph Trend	↘	↘	↓	→	↗	→

Figure B.2. Sample of field notes for snow and weather observations.

Carry out and record the observations in the sequence listed below. Wear gloves when touching the instruments.

DATE

Record year, month, and day.

TIME

Record the time of observation on the 24-hour scale (for example 5:10 P.M. is 1710).

SKY CONDITION

Classify the amount of cloud cover and record it with one of the following symbols:

Class	Symbol	Description
Clear	○	No clouds
Scattered clouds	①	Partially cloudy; the sky is half or less covered with clouds
Broken clouds	⊕	Cloudy; more than half but not all of the sky is covered with clouds
Overcast	⊕	The sky is completely covered
Obscured	⊗	Surface conditions (for example, fog or snowfall) prevent the observer from seeing the sky

Add the letter "H" to the symbol when the sky is covered with thin clouds.

Comment: The amount of clouds and not the opacity is the primary classification criterion. Thin clouds forming a hazy sky are classified as clouds; for example, a sky completely covered with thin clouds is recorded as ⊗ H.

PRECIPITATION TYPE AND INTENSITY

Note the type and rate of precipitation at the time of observation. Record the rate of snowfall in centimeters of snow accumulation per hour.

Symbol	Description
NIL	No precipitation
*-1	Continuous snowfall that accumulates at a rate of less than 1 cm/h
*1	Snow accumulates at a rate of about 1 cm/h
*2	Snow accumulates at a rate of about 2 cm/h
*3	Snow accumulates at a rate of about 3 cm/h

VLR   Very light rain

LR   Light rain; accumulation of up to 3 mm of water per hour

MR   Moderate rain; accumulation of up to 3 to 8 mm of water per hour

HR   Heavy rain; accumulation of 8 mm of water per hour or more

FR   Freezing rain

*R   Mixed snow and rain

AIR TEMPERATURE

Read first the maximum and then the minimum temperature from the thermometers to the nearest 0.5°C. Read the present temperature from the minimum thermometer (Figure B.3). Record the results.

Read and record the temperature on the thermograph to the nearest 1°C. Read the temperature trend shown on the thermograph over the preceding 3 hours and record it with an arrow.

Symbol	Description
↑	Temperature rising rapidly
↗	Temperature rising slowly
→	Temperature steady
↘	Temperature falling slowly
↓	Temperature falling rapidly

Remove any snow that might have drifted into or accumulated on top of the screen.

Reset the thermometers after the standard observations.

RELATIVE HUMIDITY

Read the relative humidity to the nearest 5% from the hygrograph.

DEPTH OF SNOWFALL

Using a ruler, measure the snow depth on boards previously placed on the snow surface. Average several measurements and record to the nearest centimeter. Record "T" (trace) when the depth is less than 0.5 cm. Treat surface hoar on the boards as snowfall.

After sampling for the weight of new snow (when required), remove the snow from the appropriate boards and reposition them on the surface.

Comment: The snowfall should be measured on a new snow board and a storm board. Additional boards (for example, interval, 24-hour, or shoot boards) may be used as required by the operation.

Definitions for the boards follow.

Interval

The accumulation of snow on the board refers to periods shorter than the time between standard observations. The board is cleared at the end of every set of observations.

New Snow (HN)

New snow is the depth of snow that has been deposited since the last standard observation. The board is cleared at the end of each standard observation.

24-hour

The 24-hour board holds the snow that has been deposited over a 24-hour period. It is cleared at the end of the morning standard observation.

Storm

Storm snowfall is the depth of snow deposited since the beginning of a storm. The storm board is cleared at the end of a standard observation prior to the next storm and after useful settlement observations have been obtained. The symbol "CL" is added to the recorded data when the storm board is cleared.

Shoot Board

The board holds the snow accumulated since avalanches were last controlled by explosives.

DEPTH OF SNOWPACK (HS)

Observe the total depth of the snow cover on the ground by reading the calibrated, permanent stake to the closest centimeter (Figure B.4). If necessary, level settling cones, wells, and drifts around the stake.

WEIGHT OF NEW SNOW

Determine the weight of new snow when the depth is greater than 3 cm. With a sampling tube, cut a sample of snow vertically from the new snow board and weigh it. Record the net weight of snow in grams (g).

Take a sample from the interval board for interval observations.

Figure B.3. Stevensen screen with maximum and minimum thermometers and hygro-thermograph. (Photo by S. Walker)

Figure B.4. Snow boards and snow depth stake in a study plot. (Photo by D. McClung)

Make a note of the cross-sectional area of the sampling tube at the top of the page or on the title page of the field book.

DENSITY OF NEW SNOW

Calculate the density of new snow in kg/m³. The density (in gm/cm³) is the weight of new snow (in grams) divided by the volume of the sample in cm³ (product of the sample tube area in cm² and the new snow height in cm). According to international standards, SI units are used so the result must be multiplied by 1,000 to give the result in kg/m³.

New Snow Density (kg/m³) =
[Weight New Snow (gm) / Sample Volume (cm³)] x 1,000

WATER EQUIVALENT OF NEW SNOW (HNW)

Calculate the water equivalent of the new snow in mm. The water equivalent is calculated by multiplying the new snow density by the height of new snow in cm

and the result is divided by 100 to yield an answer in mm (Figure B.5).

HNW (mm) =
[New Snow Density (kg/m³) x New Snow Height (cm)]/100

Comments:

1. The water equivalent is the depth of the layer of water that would form if the snow on the board were melted. It is equal to the amount of precipitation.
2. The water equivalent of the new snow can be obtained either by melting a sample of snow and measuring the amount of melt water—for example, with the aid of the rain gauge—or by weighing a snow sample. Weighing is commonly applied for avalanche operations because of its ease. The simplicity of conversion is an additional advantage because 1 cm³ of water weighs 1 g.
3. Meteorological standards require that snow depth be recorded in centimeters (cm) and water equivalent of snow, as well as rainfall in millimeters (mm).

Figure B.5. Instruments for measuring water equivalent of snow on boards and crystal forms. (Photo by S. Walker)

Figure B.6. Gauge for recording total precipitation in water equivalent. (Photo by S. Walker)

RAIN

Measure the amount of rain accumulated in the rain gauge in millimeters and tenths.

Comment: The rain gauge should be placed on the ground or on the snow surface when rainfall is likely to occur.

PRECIPITATION

Record the amount of precipitation accumulated in the recording precipitation gauge to the nearest millimeter (Figure B.6).

Comments:

1. Precipitation gauges collect snowfall, rainfall, and other forms of precipitation and continuously record their water equivalent.
2. The amount of precipitation that has fallen since the last observation is the difference between the present reading and the last reading.
3. When utilizing heated precipitation gauges, care must be taken not to overheat the mixture; otherwise evaporation will reduce the accuracy.

SURFACE PENETRABILITY

(See Chapter 6 for further details.)

Foot Penetration

Step into undisturbed snow and gently put the full body weight on one foot. Measure the depth of the footprint to the nearest centimeter.

Comment: Footprint depths vary between observers. It is recommended that all observers working on the same program compare their foot penetration. Observers who consistently produce penetrations more than 10 cm above or below the average should not record foot penetrations.

Ram Penetration

Let the first section of a standard ram penetrometer (40-mm cone diameter and approximately 1-kg mass) penetrate the snow under its own weight. Read the depth of penetration in centimeters.

Comment: Ram penetration is preferred for observations of penetrability because it produces more consistent results than foot penetration.

SURFACE CONDITION

Classify the type of snow on the surface. Use one of the following symbols:

Symbol	Description
ØD	Loose dry snow
ØW	Loose wet snow
✿	Wind crust
▽	Crust from rain, sun, or melt-freeze; deposition from rime
V	Surface hoar

WIND

Observe and record the wind direction and speed in the vicinity of the observation plot. When visibility allows, observe and record the direction and speed at high elevation near the avalanche starting zones.

Note the direction from which the wind blows with respect to the eight points of the compass: N, NE, E, SE, S, SW, W, NW.

Classify the wind speed by observing the motion of trees, flags, and snow.

Class	Speed m/s	km/h	Description
Calm	0	0	No air motion; smoke rises vertically
Light	1–7	1–25	Light to gentle breeze; flags and twigs in motion
Moderate	8–11	26–40	Fresh breeze; small trees sway; flags stretched; snow begins to drift
Strong	>11	>40	Strong breeze and gale; whole trees in motion; snow drifting

Comments:

1. The description of wind speed effects are rules of thumb; observers should develop their own relationships specific for the area.
2. Wind speeds should be averaged over 1 minute.

BAROMETRIC PRESSURE

Read and record from the barograph, barometer, or altimeter the barometric pressure in hectopascals, kilopascals, millibars, millimeters, or inches (depending on instrument). Classify the level of pressure as "high," "medium," or "low" when the reading of units of pressure is not possible. If possible, record the pressure trend with an arrow representing the pressure change in the preceding 3 hours.

Symbol	Description
H	Air pressure high
M	Air pressure medium
L	Air pressure low
↑	Barometer rising rapidly
↗	Barometer rising slowly
→	Barometer steady
↘	Barometer falling slowly
↓	Barometer falling rapidly

Field Book Notes

In the notebook, write "—" (dash) when no observation was made. Write "0" (zero) when the reading is zero, for example, when no new snow has accumulated on the new snow board.

APPENDIX C

ADVANCED SNOW CRYSTAL CLASSIFICATION SYSTEMS

This appendix contains two systems for classifying snow crystals on a level with more detail than is used in most operational avalanche work.

1. *Magono and Lee's (1966) system for classifying newly fallen snow:* This system is based on field observations and contains 80 categories, including rimed classes. It is complete enough to include perhaps 99% of all snow crystals that reach the earth's surface without resorting to an irregular class. It requires detailed work and sophisticated equipment (for example, a microscope). The system has not been used to date in publications on avalanche work but it has been applied in visibility studies in blowing snow. Table C.1 depicts the system.

2. *ICSI system for classifying seasonal snow:* The ICSI (Colbeck, et al., 1990) gave a process-oriented system to supplement the basic system for classifying snow grains given in Chapter 3. The system is given below in a series of tables along with comments given by ICSI: Table C.2, dry forms; Table C.3, wet forms; and Table C.4, surface forms and crusts. Photos of examples of many of the crystals important for avalanche work are found in Chapter 3.

References

Colbeck, S., E. Akitaya, R. Armstrong, H. Gubler, J. Lafeuille, K. Lied, D. McClung, and E. Morris. 1990. *The International Classification for Seasonal Snow on the Ground.* International Commission on Snow and Ice, 23 pp. (Available from World Data Center on Glaciology, University of Colorado, Boulder, CO.)

Magono, Choji, and Chung Woo Lee. November 1966. Meteorological classification of natural snow crystals. *Journal of the Faculty of Science, Hokkaido University,* Sapporo, Japan, Series VII (Geophysics), II(4): 321–335.

N1a Elementary needle	**P1b** Crystal with sectorlike branches	**P6c** Stellar crystal with spatial plates	**R2a** Densely rimed plate or sector
N1b Bundle of elementary needles	**P1c** Crystal with broad branches	**P6d** Stellar crystal with spatial dendrites	**R2b** Densely rimed stellar crystal
N1c Elementary sheath	**P1d** Stellar crystal	**P7a** Radiating assemblage of plates	**R2c** Stellar crystal with rimed spatial branches
N1d Bundle of elementary sheaths	**P1e** Ordinary dendritic crystal	**P7b** Radiating assemblage of dendrites	**R3a** Graupel-like snow of hexagonal type
N1e Long, solid column	**P1f** Fernlike crystal	**CP1a** Column with plates	**R3b** Graupel-like snow of lump type
N2a Combination of needles	**P2a** Stellar crystal with plates at ends	**CP1b** Column with dendrites	**R3c** Graupel-like snow with nonrimed extensions
N2b Combination of sheaths	**P2b** Stellar crystal with sectorlike ends	**CP1c** Multiple capped column	**R4a** Hexagonal graupel
N2c Combination of long, solid columns	**P2c** Dendritic crystal with plates at ends	**Cp2a** Bullet with plates	**R4b** Lump graupel
C1a Pyramid	**P2d** Dendritic crystal with sectorlike ends	**CP2b** Bullet with dendrites	**R4c** Conelike graupel
C1b Cup	**P2e** Plate with simple extensions	**CP3a** Stellar crystal with needles	**I1** Ice particle
C1c Solid bullet	**P2f** Plate with sectorlike extensions	**CP3b** Stellar crystal with columns	**I2** Rimed particle
C1d Hollow bullet	**P2g** Plate with dendritic extensions	**CP3c** Stellar crystal with scrolls at ends	**I3a** Broken branch
C1e Solid column	**P3a** Two-branched crystal	**CP3d** Plate with scrolls at ends	**I3b** Rimed broken branch
C1f Hollow column	**P3b** Three-branched crystal	**S1** Side planes	**I4** Miscellaneous
C1g Solid thick plate	**P3c** Four-branched crystal	**S2** Scalelike side planes	**G1** Minute column
C1h Thick plate of skeleton form	**P4a** Broad branch crystal with 12 branches	**S3** Combination of side planes, bullets, columns	**G2** Germ of skeletal form
C1i Scroll	**P4b** Dendritic crystal with 12 branches	**R1a** Rimed needle crystal	**G3** Minute hexagonal plate
C2a Combination of bullets	**P5** Malformed crystal	**R1b** Rimed columnar crystal	**G4** Minute stellar crystal
C2b Combination of columns	**P6a** Plate with spatial plates	**R1c** Rimed plate or sector	**G5** Minute assemblage of plates
P1a Hexagonal plate	**P6b** Plate with spatial dendrites	**R1d** Rimed stellar crystal	**G6** Irregular germ

Figure C.1. Classification of new snow crystals according to Magono and Lee (1966).

DRY SNOW FORMS

BASIC CLASSIFICATION	SYMB	SUBCLASS	SYMB	SHAPE	PLACE OF FORMATION	CLASSIFICATION	PHYSICAL PROCESSES	DEPENDENCE ON MOST IMPORTANT PARAMETERS	COMMON EFFECT ON STRENGTH
		MORPHOLOGICAL CLASSIFICATION			PROCESS-ORIENTED CLASSIFICATION		ADDITIONAL INFORMATION ON PHYSICAL PROCESSES AND STRENGTH		
DECOMPOSING AND FRAGMENTED PRECIPITATION PARTICLES /	2								
	a	Partly decomposed precip. particles /	dc	Partly rounded particles, characteristic shapes of precip. particles still recognizable	Recently deposited snow	Initial rounding and separation	Decrease of surface area to reduce surface free energy at low temperature gradients	Speed of decomposition decreases with decreasing snow temperature and decreasing temperature gradient	Strength decreases with time; felt-like arrangement of dendrites has modest initial strength
	b	Highly broken particles /	bk	Packed, shards or rounded fragments of precipitation particles	Saltation layer	Wind-broken particles; initially fractured then rapid rounding due to small size	Fragmented particles are closely packed by wind; fragmentation followed by rounding and growth	Fragmentation and packing increase with wind speed	Quick sintering results in rapid strength increase
ROUNDED GRAINS (MONOCRYSTALS) ●	3				Dry snow				
	a	Small rounded particles ●	sr	Well-rounded; particles of size <0.5 mm often well bonded		Small equilibrium form	Decrease of specific surface area by slow decrease of number of grains and increase of mean grain diameter; equilibrium form may be partly faceted at lower temperatures	Growth rate increases with increasing temperature and temperature gradient; growth slower in high density snow with smaller pores	Strength increases with time, density and decreasing grain size
	b	Large rounded particles ●	lr	Well-rounded particles of size >0.5 mm		Large equilibrium form	Grain-to-grain vapor diffusion due to low to medium temperature gradients; mean excess vapor density remains below critical value for kinetic growth	Same as above	Strength increases with time and density and decreasing grain size
	c	Mixed forms ●	mx	Rounded particles with few facets which are developing		Transitional form as temperature gradient increases	Growth regime changes if temperature gradient increases above critical value of about 10°C/m	Grains are changing in response to an increasing temperature gradient	De-sintering could decrease strength
FACETED CRYSTALS ☐	4				Dry snow				
	a	Solid faceted particles ☐	fa	Solid faceted crystals; usually hexagonal prisms		Solid kinetic growth form	Strong grain-to-grain vapor diffusion driven by large temperature gradient; excess vapor density above critical value for kinetic growth	Growth rate increases with temperature, temperature gradient, and decreasing density; may not occur in high-density snow because of small pores	Strength decreases with increasing growth rate and grain size
	b	Small faceted particles ◩	sf	Small faceted crystals in surface layer; <0.5 mm in size	Near surface	Kinetic growth form at early stage of development	May develop directly from 1 or 2a due to large, near-surface temperature gradients	Temperature gradient may periodically change sign but remains at a high absolute value	Low-strength snow
	c	Mixed forms ⌂	mx	Faceted particles with recent rounding of facets		Transitional form as temperature gradient decreases	Faceted grains are rounding due to decrease in temperature gradient		
CUP-SHAPED CRYSTALS; DEPTH HOAR ∧	5				Dry snow				
	a	Cup crystal ∧ ▲	cp	Cup-shaped, striated crystal; usually hollow		Hollow or partly solid cup-shaped kinetic growth crystals	Very fast growth at large temperature gradient	Formation increases with increasing vapor flux	Usually fragile but strength increases with density
	b	Columns of depth hoar ⋋	dh	Large cup-shaped striated hollow crystals arranged in columns (<10 mm)		Large cup-shaped kinetic growth forms arranged in columns	Intergranular arrangement in columns; most of the lateral bonds between columns have disappeared during crystal growth	Snow has almost completely recrystalized; high recrystalization rate for long period at low snow density and high external temperature gradient facilitates formation	Very fragile snow
	c	Columnar crystals ☰	cl	Very large, columnar crystals with c-axis horizontal (10-20 mm)		Final growth stage of depth hoar at high temperature gradient in low-density snow	Evolves from earlier stage described above; some bonding occurs and new crystals are initiated	Longer time required than for any other snow crystal	Some strength returns

Figure C.2. ICSI classification for dry snow crystals.

WET SNOW FORMS

BASIC CLASSIFICATION	MORPHOLOGICAL CLASSIFICATION				PROCESS-ORIENTED CLASSIFICATION		ADDITIONAL INFORMATION ON PHYSICAL PROCESSES AND STRENGTH		
	SYMB	SUBCLASS	SYMB	SHAPE	PLACE OF FORMATION	CLASSIFICATION	DEPENDENCE ON MOST IMPORTANT PARAMETERS		COMMON EFFECT ON STRENGTH
							PHYSICAL PROCESSES		
WET GRAINS	6				Wet snow				
	a	Clustered rounded grains	cl	Clustered rounded crystals held by large ice-to-ice bonds; water in internal veins among three crystals or two-grain boundaries		Grain clusters without melt-freeze cycles	Wet snow at low water content, pendular regime; clusters form to minimize surface free energy	Meltwater can drain; too much water leads to slush; freezing leads to melt-freeze particles	Ice-to-ice bonds give strength
	b	Rounded poly-crystals	mf	Individual crystals are frozen into a solid polycrystalline grain; may be seen either wet or refrozen		Melt-freeze polycrystals	Wet snow at low water content; melt-freeze cycles form poly-crystals when water in veins freezes	Particle size increases with number of melt-freeze cycles; radiation penetration over time restores 6a; excess water leads to 6c	High strength in the frozen state; lower strength in the wet state; strength increases with number of melt-freeze cycles
	c	Slush	sl	Separate rounded crystals completely immersed in water		Poorly bonded, rounded single crystals	High liquid content; equilibrium form of ice in water	Water drainage blocked by impermeable layer or ground; high energy input to snow cover by solar radiation, high air temperature or water input	Little strength due to decaying bonds

Figure C.3. ICSI classification for wet snow grains.

SURFACE FORMS AND CRUSTS

BASIC CLASSIFICATION	SYMB	SUBCLASS	SYMB	SHAPE	PLACE OF FORMATION	CLASSIFICATION	PHYSICAL PROCESSES	DEPENDENCE ON MOST IMPORTANT PARAMETERS	COMMON EFFECT ON STRENGTH
				MORPHOLOGICAL CLASSIFICATION		PROCESS-ORIENTATED CLASSIFICATION	ADDITIONAL INFORMATION ON PHYSICAL PROCESSES AND STRENGTH		
FEATHERY CRYSTALS	7								
	a	Surface hoar crystals	sh	Striated, usually feathery crystal; aligned; usually flat, sometimes needle-like	Cold snow surface	Kinetic growth form in air	Rapid kinetic growth of crystals at the snow surface by rapid transfer of water vapor toward the snow surface; snow surface cooled below ambient air temperature by radiational cooling	Increasing growth rate with increased cooling of the snow surface below air temperature and increasing relative humidity of the air	Fragile, extremely low shear strength; strength may remain low for extended periods when buried in cold snow
	b	Cavity hoar	ch	Striated, planar or feathery crystals grown in cavities; random orientation	Cavities in snow; same form might grow in very low density snow with extreme temperature gradient	Kinetic growth form in cavities	Plate or feathery crystals may grow in high-temperature gradient fields in large voids in the snow, e.g., in the vicinity of tree trunks, buried bushes or below sun crusts		
ICE MASSES	8								
	a	Ice layer	il	Horizontal ice layer	Buried layers in snow being melted and refrozen	Icy layer from refreezing of draining meltwater; usually retains some degree of permeability	Rain or meltwater from the surface percolates into cold snow where it refreezes; water may be preferentially held by fine-grained layer such as a buried wind crust	Depends on timing of percolating water and cycles of melting and refreezing; more likely to occur if snow is highly stratified	Ice layers are strong but strength decays once snow is completely wetted
	b	Ice column	ic	Vertical ice body	Within layers	Icy column from refreezing of draining meltwater	Water within flow fingers freezes due to heat conduction into surrounding snow at T<0°C	Flow fingers more likely to occur if snow is highly stratified; freezing greater if snow is very cold,	
	c	Basal ice	bi	Basal Ice layer	Base of snow cover	Ice forms from freezing of ponded meltwater	Water ponds above substrate and freezes by heat conduction into cold substrate	Formation enchanced if substrate is impermeable and very cold, (e.g., permafrost)	Weak slush layer may form on top
SURFACE DEPOSITS AND CRUSTS	9								
	a	Rime	rm	Soft rime: irregular deposit; Hard rime: small supercooled water droplets frozen in place	Surface	Surface rime	Accretion of small, supercooled fog droplets onto surface grains	Increases with fog density and exposure to wind	Thin breakable crust forms if process continues long enough
	b	Rain crust	rc	Thin, transparent glaze or clear surface layer	Surface	Frozen rain water at snow surface	Results from freezing rain on snow; forms a surface glaze	Droplets have to be supercooled but coalesce before freezing	Thin breakable crust
	c	Sun crust, firnspiegel	sc	Thin, transparent glaze or surface film	Surface	Refrozen meltwater at snow surface	Refrozen surface layer partially melted by solar radiation; shortwave absorption in the glaze is decreased; cooling of the glaze by long-wave radiation and evaporation; greenhouse effect for the underlying snow; water vapor condenses below the glaze; may develop into smooth, shiny layer of clear ice at surface	Builds during clear weather (long-wave cooling), air temperatures below freezing and strong irradiation (not to be confused with melt-freeze crusts); melting can occur below the crust in clean snow	Thin, often breakable ice crust
	d	Wind crust	wc	Small, broken or abraded, closely-packed particles; well sintered	Surface	Wind crust	Fragmentation and packing of wind transported snow particles; high number of contact points and small size causes rapid strength increase through sintering	Hardness of crust increases with wind speed, decreasing particle size and moderate temperature	Hard, sometimes breakable crust
	e	Melt-freeze crust	mfc	Crust of recognizable melt-freeze polycrystals	Near surface	Crust of melt-freeze particles	Refrozen layer (e.g. wind crust) which was wetted with water at least once	Particle size and density increases with number of melt-freeze cycles	Hardness increases with number of melt-freeze cycles

Figure C.4. ICSI classification for surface forms and crusts.

APPENDIX D
SNOW AVALANCHE SIZE CLASSIFICATION

When avalanche events are reported, an estimate or measure of their size should be included. If a simple, consistent method of sizing avalanches can be found, obvious benefits can be derived. For example, data from different storm cycles, years, or areas can be compared. People such as avalanche forecasters, observers, or consultants, as well as skiers, stand to benefit once a good method is established.

Unfortunately, in most cases there is no visual record of the avalanche as it falls. The observer is left with only a few measurable factors after the event. Some of these are mass, runout distance, path dimension, depth and spatial extent (volume) of the deposit, and water content of the debris. In addition, other variables may be estimated such as area swept out by the flowing avalanche, degree of path confinement, and damage to structures or vegetation. Proposed measures such as volume of snow moved, avalanche mass, and estimated kinetic or potential energy seem inadequate to describe avalanche size when taken individually because of the inherent complexity of the phenomenon of avalanches in motion. Since there is no international standard for reporting sizes of avalanches, a summary of systems is given below.

Size Systems in Use or Proposed

RECOMMENDATIONS OF ICSI WORKING GROUP ON AVALANCHE CLASSIFICATION

In a comprehensive paper on avalanche classification (de Quervain et al., 1973), the ICSI recommended that a set of length measurements be recorded when reporting events. Those measurements relevant to avalanche size are width and thickness of fracture, length and width of avalanche path, and dimensions and volume of the deposit.

The data recommended by the ICSI are potentially very useful in determining avalanche size. However, some essential elements such as density of the deposit are not specified so that avalanche mass, for example, cannot be calculated. In addition, no scheme is presented to combine the measurements into a size factor. Thus, the ICSI recommendations do not constitute a size classification system although the format prescribed is used internationally for reporting destructive avalanches.

U.S. REPORTING SYSTEM

In the United States, avalanches are classified using five sizes. The sizes are based on an estimate of the volume of snow transported down the avalanche path. The five sizes (Perla and Martinelli, 1976) are:

- Sluff or snowslide less than 50 m (150 ft) of slope distance [approximately 25 m (75 ft) vertical] regardless of snow volume
- Small, relative to path
- Medium, relative to path
- Large, relative to path
- Major or maximum, relative to path.

The important feature of the system is that sizes "small" through "major" are related to the path in question. By relating avalanche size to the path, the implication is that size depends on location. Specifically, the same avalanche may have a wide variation in size according to the path on which it falls. As it stands, the system is subjective and it yields data that may be not particularly meaningful to anyone unfamiliar with the paths in question. The system does, however, give information relative to how large a given event is with respect to the historical record of occurrences on a given path.

SYSTEMS PROPOSED IN JAPAN

Several systems have been proposed in theoretical papers by Japanese researchers. None of these, however, appears to be used systematically for reporting avalanche events.

Shoda (1965) proposed a logarithmic scale based on avalanche potential energy, $\log_{10} MgH$, where H is the vertical drop, M is avalanche mass, and g is acceleration due to gravity. An advantage to Shoda's system is that M and H are measurable. Furthermore, the concept can be applied to any avalanche even though falling avalanches are subject to nonconservative frictional forces.

Shimizu (1967) proposed two additional systems: (1) $\log_{10} M$ and (2) a scale based logarithmically on destructive kinetic energy, $\log_{10} 1/2MV_t^2$, where V_t is the avalanche terminal speed. One problem with the latter system is that the terminal speed is very seldom known due to measurement difficulties. None of these systems is used in practice.

SYSTEMS USED IN SWITZERLAND

Researchers in Switzerland have proposed a variety of specific systems in various research papers. None of these is used systematically in practice.

De Quervain (1975) proposed a two-class system based on the objects that avalanches affect. Those affecting people were designated "tourist" while those affecting villages were designated "catastrophic." Föhn (1975) used a similar system in which he established the following classes: sluff, slope avalanche, and valley avalanche, with the latter two designations used as synonyms for tourist and catastrophic.

Föhn et al. (1977) related size to the area covered by the avalanche in a three-class system: small (sluffs), medium, and large (50,000 m²).

None of these systems makes use of all important measurable variables. Also, it would seem that there are not enough size classes to discriminate adequately in most cases.

CANADIAN REPORTING SYSTEM

The system used in Canada is based on estimated potential destructive effects. It is an extension of the system originally introduced by Atwater in the United States (USDA, 1961, revised 1968). Perla introduced the system into Canada and it was adopted by the Canadian Avalanche Committee in 1977.

The basic idea of the system is to estimate the potential destructive effects of avalanches. The five sizes are listed in Table D.1, along with suggested values for typical associated factors. In Table D.1, the size of the objects affected increases with size classification, so there is a strong relation between size, avalanche mass, and area swept out by the falling avalanche.

The Canadian system attempts to integrate all observable variables associated with the events into a simple estimate of size. The disadvantage of such a system is that there is some subjective judgment involved. This is the primary reason why only five classes are used. Only approximate estimates are necessary to classify events in the system. Field experience shows that observers with a reasonable amount of experience will generally agree on the size of a given avalanche.

The principal advantage of the system is to provide easy communication between the observers themselves

Table D.1 Canadian Snow Avalanche Size Classification System and Typical Factors

Size	Description	Typical Mass	Typical Path Length	Typical Impact Pressures
1	Relatively harmless to people	<10 t	10 m	1 kPa
2	Could bury, injure, or kill a person	10^2 t	100 m	10 kPa
3	Could bury a car, destroy a small building, or break a few trees	10^3 t	1,000 m	100 kPa
4	Could destroy a railway car, large truck, several buildings, or a forest with an area up to 4 hectares	10^4 t	2,000 m	500 kPa
5	Largest snow avalanches known; could destroy a village or a forest of 40 hectares	10^5 t	3,000 m	1,000 kPa

and others (not necessarily observers) who may wish to use approximate data for describing recorded events.

The factors listed in Table D.1 for the Canadian size classification system are determined from data and theoretical analysis. Only approximate values for each size are given. In practice, operational people often use half sizes.

References

Föhn, P. M. B. 1975. Statistiche Aspekte bei Lawinenereignissen. Congress "Interpraevent 1975." Klagenfurt, Austria: International Society of Research "Interpraevent," pp. 293–304.

Föhn, P., W. Good, P. Bois, and C. Obled. 1977. Evaluation and comparison of statistical and conventional methods of forecasting avalanche hazard. *Journal of Glaciology* 19(81): 375–387.

McClung, D. M., and P. A. Schaerer. 1981. Snow avalanche size classification. Canadian Avalanche Committee, Ed. Proceedings of Avalanche Workshop, Nov. 3–5, 1980. Associate Committee on Geotechnical Research. Technical Memorandum 133. Ottawa: National Research Council of Canada, pp. 12–27.

Perla, R., and M. Martinelli, Jr. 1976 (revised 1978). *Avalanche Handbook.* USDA Agricultural Handbook 489. Washington, DC: U.S. Government Printing Office, 238 pp.

Quervain, M. de, L. de Crecy, E. R. LaChapelle, K. Losev, and M. Shoda. 1973. Avalanche classification. *Hydrological Sciences Bulletin* XVIII(4): 391–402.

Quervain, M. de. 1975. Avalanche formation. In *Avalanche Protection in Switzerland.* USDA Forest Service General Technical Report RM-9 (translation of Lawinenschutz in der Schweiz, Buendnerwald, Beiheft Nr. 9, 1972), pp. 6–18.

Shimizu, H. 1967. Magnitude of avalanche. *Physics of Snow and Ice. International Conference on Low Temperature Science,* H. Ôura, Ed., Sapporo, Japan, August 14–19, 1966. Sapporo: Hokkaido University, Vol. 1, Part 2, pp. 1269–1276.

Shoda, M. 1965. An experimental study on dynamics of snow avalanches. International Association of Hydrological Sciences Publication No. 69, pp. 215–229.

USDA Forest Service. 1961 (revised October 1968). *Snow Avalanches.* USDA Handbook No. 194. Washington, DC: U.S. Government Printing Office, 84 pp.

RECORDING AVALANCHE EVENTS

The following list contains information that is usually recorded. The first six items are basic information and are applicable for any operation. Whether or not the other items are recorded depends on the type of operation, accessibility of the starting zone, and visibility. Schemes for reporting avalanche events have not been standardized on a worldwide basis; some size systems used in various countries are discussed in Appendix D.

List of Recorded Information

1. Date and time of occurrence. Even when the time is not known exactly, it is better to make an estimate than not to include this information.
2. Identifier for the avalanche path by name, number, aspect, and/or elevation.
3. Size of the avalanche. Numerical classification systems, qualitative descriptions (for example, large, medium, small), the volume, the average length, width, and depth of the deposit, or the mass are applied for size description. See Appendix D for a description of size classification systems used in various countries.
4. Content of liquid water in the avalanche snow at the time and location of deposition. Commonly the terms "dry," "moist," and "wet" are used.
5. Location of the tip of the avalanche in the runout zone. The location is described either by terrain features (sometimes in code form) or the estimated distance from creeks, roads, or terrain breaks.
6. Additional relevant information. Examples are associated accidents, property or trees destroyed, contamination with rock, soil, or wood.
7. Type of avalanche trigger. Examples are natural avalanche, release by hand charge, release by artillery, started by a skier.
8. Location of slab avalanche crowns or the starting point of loose snow avalanches. The location may be described by terrain features (for example, below cornice, toe of rock band, middle of slope), elevation, and/or aspect.
9. Type of snow failure. The avalanche is classified either as a loose snow avalanche or a slab avalanche.
10. Position of the sliding surface within the snow cover and thickness of the snow slab that failed. Examples of sliding surface position are in new snow, in old snow, on the ground.
11. Crown width of slab avalanches.
12. Length of road or railway covered by avalanche snow.
13. Average and maximum depth of deposited avalanche snow.

EXAMPLES OF SNOW STABILITY RATING SCALES AND AVALANCHE HAZARD RATING SCALES

Stability Rating Systems

This appendix contains examples of stability and avalanche hazard rating scales. There is no international agreement with respect to either kind of scale. A stability scale should focus on stability of the snow cover, whereas a hazard scale should include the effects on people and property. This simple rule is not followed in all countries.

UNITED STATES

The system adopted for public warnings in the United States contains four classes. It is a stability rating, but the term hazard is used to describe the categories. It has been suggested that the term *hazard* should be replaced with *instability*.

- *Low hazard:* Mostly stable snow. Avalanches are unlikely except in isolated pockets on steep snow-covered slopes and gullies.
- *Moderate hazard:* Areas of unstable snow. Avalanches are possible on steep snow-covered open slopes and gullies.
- *High hazard:* Mostly unstable snow. Avalanches are likely on steep snow-covered open slopes and gullies.
- *Extreme hazard:* Widespread areas of unstable snow. Avalanches are certain on some steep snow-covered gullies. Large destructive avalanches are possible.

CANADA

In the Canadian stability rating system, the probability of avalanche release is described in four classes.

Along with the rating, an explanation with aspect and elevation may be included. The Canadian system attempts to define classes that can be verified by observation, data, or experiments.

- *Good stability:* Natural avalanches are not expected. Skiers or explosives could trigger small avalanches on very steep terrain (gullies, cliffs).
- *Fair stability:* Natural avalanches are not expected. Skiers could start avalanches on steep slopes. Explosive charges are required to start avalanches on other slopes.
- *Poor stability:* Natural avalanches can start with small triggers such as loading from blowing snow or new snowfall or a rise in temperature. Skiing and explosives will usually trigger avalanches.
- *Very poor stability:* Natural avalanches run. Skiing and explosives will produce avalanches.

FRANCE

The French rating system is based on the probability of avalanche release and the spatial extent of the instability. Again as with the U.S. and Swiss systems, the word *instability* may be properly substituted for the word *hazard* in the classification nomenclature.

- *Minimum hazard:* Very low hazard, but always keep in mind safety rules, because hazard is inherent in mountain terrain.
- *Low hazard:* Snowpack generally stable. Low hazard related to local and/or temporary weak instability.
- *Local accidental hazard:* Low probability of natural release. Local accidental hazard due to marked local latent instability.

- *General accidental hazard:* Still low natural hazard. Very marked accidental hazard due to widespread latent instability.
- *Moderate natural hazard:* Likely natural release of limited avalanches. Accidental hazard is high.
- *High natural hazard:* Unstable snowpack. Natural release of avalanches will occur.
- *Avalanche situation:* High instability. Large local accumulations. Numerous and sometimes large avalanches.
- *Extreme avalanche situation:* Numerous avalanches. Due to huge accumulations, exceptionally large avalanches are expected.

SWITZERLAND

The Swiss system has seven classes; four of these describe localized hazard (instability) and three are for widespread hazard (instability).

- *Very low widespread:* Stable snowpack. The only spontaneous avalanches would be sluffs. Triggered avalanches occur only in isolated areas with high stresses required as a trigger.
- *Moderate local hazard:* Although snowpack is generally well bonded, there are isolated steep slopes with triggered potential of aspect and elevation. Avalanches are possible in other areas with high load, such as a group of skiers standing together.
- *High local hazard:* Although the snowpack is moderate to generally stable, most steep slopes of aspect and elevation have low strength. Both spontaneous and triggered avalanches are expected. Any disturbance may make the slope fail.
- *Elevated widespread:* Snowpack in general is insufficiently bonded. While spontaneous avalanches are expected only in isolated areas, human and explosive triggered avalanches are expected on many steep slopes.
- *High widespread:* Snowpack in general is weakly bonded. Spontaneous avalanches are possible on all steep slopes without additional loads.
- *Very high widespread:* Unstable snowpack. Expect numerous spontaneous and large avalanches. Avalanches may also occur in moderately steep terrain and in sparse forests.

Hazard Ratings

Hazard ratings include the effects on people and property once avalanches start. They refer specifically to the objects threatened. For comparison two examples are given.

SWITZERLAND

The Swiss system rates hazard to highways, railways, villages, and ski lifts. The snow stability (from the stability rating scale) is included in the description.

- *Very low widespread local hazard:* No hazard.
- *Moderate local hazard:* Spontaneous slides are small but in rare cases, triggered avalanches could be large.
- *Elevated local hazard:* Rare damage at exposed areas.
- *High local hazard:* Mostly large avalanches expected. Some exposed structures or roads are at risk.
- *Elevated widespread hazard:* Avalanches cover large areas. Some exposed structures or roads should be protected by control and closures.
- *High widespread hazard:* Large slides on known paths. Evacuation of roads and buildings is advised.
- *Very high widespread hazard:* No description given.

CANADA

The Canadian rating for avalanche hazards to road traffic follows:

- *Low:* No avalanches are likely to run on the roadway.
- *Moderate:* The snow stability is poor. Avalanches affecting the road are expected to be small. Powder avalanches could cross the road.
- *High:* The snow stability is very poor. Avalanches hazardous to traffic are expected.
- *Extreme:* Numerous large avalanches are expected to affect the road.

Since hazard rating scales are potentially much more complex than stability rating scales, more variations may be expected between them from country to country. In Canada and Switzerland, scales for hazards to backcountry skiers have been proposed that are of a very general nature.

INTERNATIONAL AVALANCHE CLASSIFICATION

A system for classifying observable features of avalanche events was published by the International Commission on Snow and Ice (UNESCO, 1981) and is shown in Table G.1. The system is in two parts: morphological and genetic. The morphological portion refers to those properties of the avalanche that are directly observable and help one to classify the type of avalanche that has taken place. The genetic portion refers to the processes and conditions that cause avalanches or are responsible for their effects. Of these two classification systems, only the morphological one is used operationally. Furthermore, the morphological system is generally only a guideline for what to observe or record; it has not been adopted verbatim by any country and the proposed codes are not used in practice. The morphological classification takes into account three zones: origin, transition, and runout, which are called the starting zone, track, and runout zone in North American usage.

Reference

International Commission on Snow and Ice. 1981. *Avalanche Atlas. Illustrated International Avalanche Classification.* Paris: UNESCO, 265 pp.

Table G.1 International Morphological Avalanche Classification

Zone	Criterion	Alternative Characteristics, Denominations, and Code	
Zone of origin	A Manner of starting	A1 Starting from a point (loose-snow avalanche)	A2 Starting from a line (slab avalanche)
		A3 Soft	A4 Hard
	B Position of sliding surface	B1 Within snow cover (surface-layer avalanche)	B2 New-snow fracture
		B3 Old-snow fracture	B4 On the ground (full-depth avalanche)
	C Liquid water in snow	C1 Absent (dry-snow avalanche)	C2 Present (wet-snow avalanche)
Zone of transition	D Form of path	D1 Path on open slope (unconfined avalanche)	D2 Path in gulley or channel (channeled avalanche)
	E Form of movement	E1 Snow dust cloud (powder avalanche)	E2 Flowing along the ground (flow avalanche)
Zone of deposition	F Surface roughness of deposit	F1 Coarse (coarse deposit)	F2 Angular blocks
		F3 Rounded clods	F4 Fine (fine deposit)
	G Liquid water in snow debris at time of deposition	G1 Absent (dry avalanche deposit)	G2 Present (wet avalanche deposit)
	H Contamination of deposit	H1 No apparent contamination (clean avalanche)	H2 Contamination present (contaminated avalanche)
		H3 Rock debris, soil	H4 Branches, trees
		H5 Debris of structures	

EXAMPLES OF COMMON EXPLOSIVE CONTROL PROCEDURES

This appendix contains four illustrative examples of avalanche control procedures: (1) hand charging, (2) helicopter bombing, (3) cornice control, and (4) Avalauncher (see Chapter 9 for further details). In all cases, qualified licensed blasters must apply the procedures with approval granted by local government regulators. The procedures given here should not be taken verbatim and then used operationally. In most cases, procedures must be submitted to regulatory agencies for approval. The procedures given here are included only as illustrative examples that might be used as a baseline to achieve a minimum safety standard. It is hoped that these examples are improved on before usage.

Example of Hand Charge Placement Procedures

Safety procedures will vary according to local government regulations. The following example is only an illustration, which provides a *minimum standard* of safety.

1. Patrol personnel should proceed on hand charge routes as directed by supervisor of control operations; minimum team of two persons.
2. Travel to hand charge sites is usually on skis. Safety measures should be exercised as in standard mountaineering procedures. Each member of the control team should carry an electronic rescue transceiver, avalanche probe, and shovel. Each hand charge team should be equipped with a radio, but it is preferred that each member have a radio.
3. Charges should be removed from the pack only

when needed, for example, when in position above the avalanche slopes.
4. One member of the team should place him- or herself in a position from which to toss the hand charge while the other observes from a safe position (well removed from the edge of the slope.)
5. When the blaster is in position to toss the charge, approximately 2 cm of fuse should be clipped off using the cutting edge of the cap crimpers. This will provide a fresh powder train.
6. The blaster should check to see that the area in question is clear of persons.
7. *Only* when the blaster is in position to toss the charge should the pull wire igniter be placed on the fuse; then the igniter can be pulled to light the fuse.
8. Trail the end of the fuse in the snow to ensure it is burning (telltale blackening of the surface) or confirm burning visually; then toss the charge onto the slope using an underarm action.
9. Yell clearly, "Fire in the hole." All members of the team should move to an area safe from the burning explosive (i.e., with a terrain barrier between the team and the hand charges).
10. After detonation, check and record the results on the slope then move on to the next site.
11. If a dud occurs, contact your supervisor and inform him or her of the problem. Any area containing a dud should be closed to entry for all personnel. A search for the dud should be made after waiting a minimum of one-half hour and with consideration of the snow stability. If conditions make it impractical or dangerous to retrieve a dud

promptly (for example, with continued avalanche hazard), the search should be conducted as soon as conditions permit. When searching for a dud on uncontrolled slopes, good mountaineering practices must be followed. After the wait, the charge may be approached, but it should be checked for burning and it should not be touched. Carefully place a second charge next to the dud and ignite the second charge. Remove yourself to a safe position and await detonation. Following detonation, return to the site to ensure that all the explosive materials have been destroyed. Dud rates should be less than 0.1%.

12. *Under no circumstances* should hand charges be dismantled once prepared. If necessary, extra charges should be detonated in a safe area well removed from persons or structures.

Example of Helicopter Bombing Procedures

An example of helicopter bombing procedures is given below for illustrative purposes. Variations will depend on local government regulations. It is assumed that normal closure of the blasting area is carried out (including a sweep) prior to application of the procedures to ensure no one is in the danger area. In the description below, a crew of four including a pilot is assumed: bombardier, shot preparer, recorder, and pilot. Often duties are combined to yield a total crew of three: bombardier, shot preparer/recorder, and pilot.

PREPARATION OF EXPLOSIVES

Hand charges are prepared as per standard procedures with the exception that fuses are cut to expose a fresh powder train prior to loading in the helicopter. Explosives are transported in an aluminum wood-lined container (approximately 50 x 40 x 25 cm); maximum load 25 kg.

NOTE: Pull-wire igniters are carried by the shot preparer separate from explosive charges or in a separate container if the shot preparation blaster is left on the ground.

PROCEDURES

1. Pilot removes a rear door from the helicopter. The left rear door (behind the pilot) is preferred since this ensures that the pilot and bombardier share the same view of the slope.
2. Pilot ensures correct function of intercom.
3. Prior to flight, crew familiarization regarding procedures and equipment is conducted.
4. Explosives and personnel are loaded aboard helicopter.
5. Bombardier wears spotter's harness. Seat belt secured.
6. Intercom system and stopwatch checked.
7. Helicopter proceeds to avalanche sites, with the recorder navigating (directing pilot). Target inspection is made and a dummy run is carried out. Navigator informs bombardier of approach to target.
8. As helicopter is on final approach to avalanche target, bombardier makes visual sweep of blasting area and requests charge.
9. Shot preparer places igniter on fuse and passes charge to bombardier. Shot preparer does not wear gloves so that a hot fuse can be felt. Shot preparer does not "snug" igniter on fuse.
10. Bombardier directs pilot into correct postion.
11. Bombardier snugs igniter onto fuse.
12. Bombardier ignites charge directing igniter toward open door (to direct any possible sparks outside the helicopter).
13. Bombardier drops charge toward slope. The following dialogue is used:

Bombardier: "First shot is lit."
Recorder: "First shot is lit, stopwatch started."
Bombardier: "First shot is away, second shot is away," and so on.
Recorder: "Time." (1.5 minutes maximum from ignition of first fuse.)

14. Circle back, observe, and record results in the blaster's log from a safe altitude.
15. Ground personnel are informed of the results.
16. The blast area is reopened as soon as it is safe.

SAFETY PRECAUTIONS

1. *Bombardier: Under no circumstances* can the shot be released behind his/her seat position, above his/her seat position, or underneath the machine (out of the pilot's view). Bombardier's hand *must be on top* of the shot, i.e., *thumb below the shot* and when released the shot *should be pushed down and forward.* Bombardier may jettison explosives

if a malfunction in the system is suspected; the pilot must be informed of such an action.

2. *Pilot:* Should machine trouble develop, the pilot will say whether or not to jettison the box of explosives. The pilot will make the decision regarding weather conditions and if it is safe to fly. He or she also communicates with base operations.

3. *Recorder:* Carefully observes time of burning fuses. Informs crew and directs pilot to safe area during detonation periods. Ensures and records proper detonation of charges.

4. *Shot Preparer:* Carries igniters separate from explosives container. Places igniters on fuses on request of bombardier. Assists bombardier should it become necessary to jettison explosives.

Example of Cornice Control Procedures

Refer to Figure 9.29 in Chapter 9 for illustrations of these cornice control procedures:

Safety Measures:

1. Temporary closure of the corniced area and its potential runout zone must be maintained throughout the operation (post guards if necessary; radio contact is required).
2. Persons working on cornices must be protected by secure belays using 11-mm mountaineering rope.
3. The work is restricted to favorable weather conditions.

Blasting Procedures:

1. The team leader selects the number of charges, spacing, and line of placement according to cornice geometry, properties, and configuration of the ground cover.
2. Prepare a secure belay for the person working on the cornice.
3. Prepare the required shotholes (a number of drilling techniques are available depending on cornice size and properties). Sometimes single charges are suspended over the cornice face on a detonation cord used in combination with drilled charges.
4. Run a trunk line of detonating cord along the safe working line.
5. Place charges in the shotholes, stem the holes, and tie each with its branch line to the trunk line using a clove hitch. (Girth hitches have caused duds due to kinking of the line and they are *not* recom-

mended.) The charges are prepared prior to placement by lacing them each with a short length of detonating cord called the *branch line,* about 2.0 m in length. Cast primers with one or two holes and about 0.5 kg are favored.

6. Align branch lines approximately 90° to the main line and check the layout to minimize the risk of branch lines being cut.
7. When all charges and lines are correctly in place, tape a blasting cap and fuse assembly (90 cm minimum) to a free end of the main line. The free (explosive) end of the cap must point down the main line toward the charges.
8. Check by radio (guards, etc.) for clearance. Ensure cornice team is in a safe position. Ignite the fuse, check for proper ignition, and move to a safe position.
9. After detonation, check for cutoff charges. Perform cleanup patrol or dud recovery operations as necessary.
10. Record results in blaster's log.
11. The area is reopened as soon as it is safe.

Example of Avalauncher Procedures

The following equipment is needed for explosive control using an Avalauncher:

- Stable truck, snowcat, trailer, or tower with Avalauncher securely mounted
- Compressed nitrogen
- Pentolite boosters (or equivalent); 2 lb or 1 kg
- Approved caps
- Avalauncher tail fin assemblies and nose cones
- 10-in. crescent wrench
- $5/16$-in. T wrench or chain pipe vise grip, depending on Avalauncher type
- Range cards
- Record book and pencils
- Ear protection devices
- Portable radio
- Avalauncher repair kit

The Avalauncher crew consists of a gunner and an assistant. The gunner is responsible for the following:

- Safety of the entire operation
- Transportation of the explosives
- Ensuring that the area closure is complete

- Setting and checking the required pressures, elevations, and angles
- Handling the safety lever pressure release valve
- Firing the gun

The gunner's assistant is reponsible for the following:

- Transporting the equipment
- Handling the nitrogen cylinders
- Handling the barrel
- Loading the projectiles
- Removing the cotter key rings and pins
- Visually checking that the area is clear
- Recording the observations

Both gunner and assistant are responsible for projectile preparation and equipment preparation.

Explosives are prepared in a tower or at the shooting location. The following procedures are used:

1. Unpack the required number of tail fin assemblies, ensuring that they are in proper working order.
2. Unpack the required number of cast explosives, ensuring that they are in good condition.
3. Properly attach the nose cones to the explosives, taping if necessary.
4. Count the number of caps needed.
5. Place a cap on a tail fin assembly shot gun primer or ferrule.
6. Assemble the explosive and tail fin assembly, forming the projectile (the projectile is now primed). Tape nose cone and tail fin assembly.
7. Place the projectile in the approved holding container.
8. Repeat steps 5 to 7 until the required number of projectiles is assembled.
9. The projectile-holding container must be firmly attached to the tower or vehicle transporting it.
10. Projectiles shall only be primed at the Avalauncher shoot location.

PROCEDURES

Procedure for Avalauncher Preparation

1. Place the safety valve in the closed position.
2. Ensure that the gun opening is free of obstructions.
3. Ensure that both supply hose valves are closed.
4. Attach the gas supply hose to the nitrogen cylinder.

5. Check the level of test pressure in the gun.
6. Open the nitrogen cylinder valve.
7. Check the gun for changes in pressure level. **Do not proceed further unless gas pressure level in Avalauncher is steady.**
8. Attach the barrel loading tray to the gun and tighten the securing nuts (assistant).
9. Fit the barrel into the loading tray, seat firmly, and tighten the securing clamp (assistant).
10. Ensure that the blasting area closure is complete and that the area has been swept (gunner).
11. Bring the gun test pressure to 50 psi (gunner).

Procedure for Test Firing

Procedure	Crew	"Command"
Check gun for pressure leakage	Gunner Assistant Gunner	
Check visually that surrounding area is clear	Assistant Gunner	All clear
Open safety valve	Gunner	Safety off
Open fire valve	Gunner	Fire
Close safety valve	Gunner	Safety on
Pressurize gun to test pressure	Gunner	Test pressure

Procedure for Firing Projectiles

Procedure	Crew	"Command"
(*Note:* Test pressure from test firing.)		
Position to target	Gunner	Target elevation?
Reference data card	Assistant Gunner	Target elevation
Set elevation scale and read back	Gunner	Elevation
Re-reference data card	Assistant Gunner	Correct/no
Position to target	Gunner	Deflection?
Reference data card	Assistant Gunner	Deflection
Set deflection scale and read back	Gunner	Deflection
Re-reference data card	Assistant Gunner	Correct/no

Open barrel	Gunner	Ready to load
Present round for loading	Assistant Gunner	

Check:
  Base plate
  Bore pin safety wire
  Safety pin
  Bore rider pin
	Gunner	Projectile OK

Place projectile in loading tray	Assistant Gunner	Half load
Response	Gunner	Half load
Remove safety pin from projectile (retain pin)	Assistant Gunner	Pin out
Response	Gunner	Pin out
Move projectile to final position	Assistant Gunner	Full load
Response	Gunner	Full load
Close barrel	Gunner	Barrel down
Response	Assistant Gunner	Barrel down
Lock barrel	Gunner	Barrel locked
Response	Assistant Gunner	Barrel locked
Read elevation off gun	Gunner	Elevation
Re-reference data card	Assistant Gunner	Correct/no
Read deflection off gun	Gunner	Deflection
Re-reference data card	Assistant Gunner	Correct/no
Reference data card for pressure	Assistant Gunner	Pressure
Pressurize Gun	Gunner	Read back pressure; ready to fire
Re-reference data card	Assistant Gunner	Correct/no
Visually check that surrounding area is clear	Gunner	All clear?
Visually check that surrounding area is clear	Assistant Gunner	Clear to fire
Open safety valve	Gunner	Safety off
Open fire valve	Gunner	Fire
Close safety valve	Gunner	Safety on
Watch projectile in flight	Assistant Gunner	Base plate off
Pressurize gun to test pressure	Gunner	Test pressure

Procedure for Shut Down

- Inform closure control personnel of the termination of the shoot.
- Return the unused explosives and caps to their respective magazines.
- Secure the Avalauncher.

SAFETY PRECAUTIONS

- No persons or explosives will be forward of the Avalauncher loading tray when firing is occurring. Only authorized personnel shall be within the immediate area.
- No talking other than shooting sequence commands shall occur during or immediately preceding firing.
- Cotter keys and pins shall be shown to the gunner to ensure that the projectile firing train will not be unnecessarily blocked.
- Projectiles shall not be loaded into the Avalauncher when it has less than 50 psi in the pressure vessel.
- Cylinders of compressed nitrogen must be transported such that they are secured from movement with their protective caps in place.
- Hearing protection will be used when the Avalauncher is fired.

APPENDIX I
GENERAL REFERENCES

Armstrong, B. R., and Knox Williams. 1992. *The Avalanche Book,* revised ed. Denver: Colorado Geological Survey, 240 pp.

Avalanche Research Centre, NRCC, and Canadian Avalanche Association. 1989. Guidelines for weather, snowpack, and avalanche observations. Associate Committee on Geotechnical Research Technical Memorandum 132, Publication NRCC 30544. Ottawa: National Research Council of Canada, 49 pp.

Bader, H., et al. 1939. Snow and its metamorphism (Der Schnee und seine Metamorphose). Translation January 1954. Snow, Ice, and Permafrost Research Establishment, U.S. Army, 313 pp.

Brown, R. L., S. Colbeck, and R. N. Yong, Eds. 1982. Procedures of a workshop on the properties of snow. Special Report 82-18, Hanover, NH: U.S. Army CRREL, 135 pp. [See also 1982, Reviews of Geophysics and Space Physics 20(1).]

Canadian Avalanche Committee, Ed. 1981. *Proceedings of Avalanche Workshop,* November 3–5, 1980. Associate Committee on Geotechnical Research Technical Memorandum 133. Ottawa: National Research Council of Canada, 248 pp.

Colbeck, S., E. Akitaya, R. Armstrong, H. Gubler, J. Lafeuille, K. Lied, D. McClung, and E. Morris. 1990. The international classification for seasonal snow on the ground. International Commission on Snow and Ice, 23 pp. (Available from World Data Center on Glaciology, University of Colorado, Boulder, CO.)

Daffern, Tony. 1992. *Avalanche Safety for Skiers and Climbers,* 2nd ed. Seattle: Cloudcap, 192 pp.

Fraser, Colin. 1978. *Avalanches and Snow Safety.* New York: Charles Scribner and Sons, 269 pp. (Originally published by John Murray as *The Avalanche Enigma,* 1966.)

Fredston, Jill A., and Doug Fesler. 1988. Snow sense: a guide to evaluating avalanche hazards, 3rd ed. Anchorage, AK: Alaska Mountain Safety Center, Inc., 48 pp.

Gallagher, Dale, Ed. 1967. The snowy torrents: avalanche accidents in the United States 1910–1966. Wasatch National Forest: USDA Forest Service, 143 pp.

Gold, L. W., and G. P. Williams, Eds. 1970. Ice engineering and avalanche forecasting and control. Associate Committee on Geotechnical Research Technical Memorandum 98. Ottawa: National Research Council of Canada, 163 pp.

Hobbs, P.V. 1974. *Ice Physics.* Oxford: Clarendon Press, 837 pp.

International Association of Hydrological Sciences. 1966. *International Symposium on Scientific Aspects of Snow and Ice Avalanches.* Publication No. 69. Gentbrugge, Belgium: IAHS Press, 424 pp.

International Association of Hydrological Sciences. 1975. *Snow Mechanics Symposium.* Publication No. 114. Dorking, UK: IAHS Press, 424 pp.

International Snow Science Workshop Committee, Ed. 1983. *Proceedings of the International Snow Science Workshop,* Bozeman, Montana, October 1982.

International Snow Science Workshop Committee, Ed. 1985. *Proceedings of the International Snow Science Workshop,* Aspen, Colorado, October 24–27, 1984, 218 pp.

International Snow Science Workshop Committee, Ed.

1987. *Proceedings of the International Snow Science Workshop,* Lake Tahoe, California, October 22–25, 1986. Homewood, CA: ISSW Committee, 248 pp.

International Snow Science Workshop Committee, Ed. 1989. *Proceedings of the International Snow Science Workshop,* Whistler, British Columbia, October 12–15, 1988. Vancouver, BC: Canadian Avalanche Association, 303 pp.

International Snow Science Workshop Committee, Ed. 1991. *Proceedings of the International Snow Science Workshop,* Bigfork, Montana, October 9–13, 1990, 337 pp.

International Snow Science Workshop Committee, Ed. 1993. *Proceedings of the International Snow Science Workshop,* Breckenridge, Colorado, October 5–9, 1992, 385 pp.

LaChapelle, E. R. 1985. *The ABC of Avalanche Safety,* 2d ed. Seattle, WA: The Mountaineers Books, 112 pp.

Lawinenhandbuch. Herausgeber Land Tirol. Innsbruck-Wien, Austria: Tyrolia-Verlag, 224 pp.

Mellor, M. 1968. Avalanches. Cold Regions Science and Engineering, Part III, Section A3D. Hanover, NH: U.S. Army CRREL, 215 pp.

Ôura, H., Ed. 1967. *Physics of Snow and Ice. International Conference on Low Temperature Science,* Hokkaido University, Sapporo, Japan: Institute of Low Temperature Science, Vol. I, 711 pp.; Vol. II, 1414 pp.

Perla, R. I., Ed. 1978. *Avalanche Control Forecasting and Safety: Proceedings of a Workshop,* Banff, Alberta, November 1–4, 1976. Associate Committee on Geotechnical Research Technical Memorandum 120. Ottawa: National Research Council of Canada, 301 pp.

Perla, R. I., and M. Martinelli, Jr. 1976 (revised 1978). *Avalanche Handbook.* USDA Agricultural Handbook 489, Washington, DC: U.S. Government Printing Office, 238 pp.

Salm, B. 1982. *Lawinenkunde für den Praktiker.* Bern, Switzerland: Schweizer Alpen Club, 148 pp.

Salm, B., and H. Gubler, Eds. 1987. Avalanche Formation, Movement and Effects. International Association of Hydrological Sciences Publication No. 162. Wallingford, UK: IAHS Press, 686 pp.

Schaerer, P. A. 1987. Avalanche accidents in Canada III. A selection of case histories 1978–1984. Publication

NRCC 27950. Ottawa: National Research Council of Canada, 138 pp.

Stethem, C. J., and Schaerer, P. A. 1979. Avalanche accidents in Canada I. A selection of case histories of accidents, 1955–1976. National Research Council of Canada, Division of Building Research, Paper No. 834. Ottawa: National Research Council of Canada, 114 pp.

Stethem, C. J., and Schaerer, P. A. 1980. Avalanche accidents in Canada II. A selection of case histories of accidents, 1943–1978. National Research Council of Canada, Division of Building Research, Paper No. 926. Ottawa: National Research Council of Canada, 75 pp.

Swiss Federal Institute for Snow and Avalanche Research. 1989. Schnee und Lawinen in den Schweizer Alpen Winter 1987/88. Winterbericht No. 52. Switzerland: Weissflujoch/Davos, 148 pp.

Symposium on Applied Glaciology. *Journal of Glaciology* 19(81), 1977, 686 pp.

Symposium on Applied Glaciology II. *Annals of Glaciology* Vol. 4, 1983, 314 pp.

Symposium on Snow and Glacier Research Relating to Human Living Conditions. 1988. *Annals of Glaciology* Vol. 13, 1989, 303 pp.

Symposium on Snow and Ice Processes at the Earth's Surface. 1984. *Annals of Glaciology* Vol. 6, 1985, 329 pp.

Symposium on Snow and Snow Related Problems. 1992. *Annals of Glaciology* Vol. 18, 1993.

Symposium on Snow in Motion. 1979. *Journal of Glaciology* 26(94), 1980, 527 pp.

USDA Forest Service. 1975. *Avalanche Protection in Switzerland* (translation of Lawinenschutz in der Schweiz). Translated by US Army CRREL. General Technical Report RM-9, Fort Collins, CO: USDA Forest Service, Rocky Mountain Forest and Range Experiment Station, 168 pp.

Williams, Knox. 1975. The snowy torrents: avalanche accidents in the United States 1967–1971. General Technical Report RM-8, Fort Collins, CO: USDA Forest Service, 190 pp.

Williams, Knox, and Betsy Armstrong. 1984. The snowy torrents: avalanche accidents in the United States 1972–1979. Jackson, WY: Teton Bookshop Publishing Company, 221 pp.

INDEX

ABOUT THE AUTHORS

David McClung heads the avalanche research group at the University of British Columbia and is Associate Professor in the Departments of Geography and Civil Engineering. His early studies in geophysics with Professor Ed LaChapelle at the University of Washington lead to 20 years of avalanche research and consulting in Canada, the United States, and Norway. McClung has published almost 70 papers on snow and avalanches. An active skier and mountaineer with expedition experience in the Himalaya, Andes, and Alaska, he lives in Vancouver, British Columbia.

Peter Schaerer's Swiss and Canadian experience with avalanches spans more than 40 years. He spent most of his career as a senior research officer and head of the Avalanche Research Center of the National Research Council of Canada. Schaerer was instrumental in forming the Canadian Avalanche Association and in setting up professional avalanche training programs in western Canada. A Vancouver resident, he is active as an avalanche consultant and is an avid backcountry skier.

THE MOUNTAINEERS, founded in 1906, is a nonprofit outdoor activity and conservation club, whose mission is "to explore, study, preserve, and enjoy the natural beauty of the outdoors...." Based in Seattle, Washington, the club is now the third-largest such organization in the United States, with 12,000 members and four branches throughout Washington State.

The Mountaineers sponsors both classes and year-round outdoor activities in the Pacific Northwest, which include hiking, mountain climbing, ski-touring, snowshoeing, bicycling, camping, kayaking and canoeing, nature study, sailing, and adventure travel. The club's conservation division supports environmental causes through educational activities, sponsoring legislation, and presenting informational programs. All club activities are led by skilled, experienced volunteers, who are dedicated to promoting safe and responsible enjoyment and preservation of the outdoors.

The Mountaineers Books, an active, nonprofit publishing program of the club, produces guidebooks, instructional texts, historical works, natural history guides, and works on environmental conservation. All books produced by The Mountaineers are aimed at fulfilling the club's mission.

If you would like to participate in these organized outdoor activities or the club's programs, consider a membership in The Mountaineers. For information and an application, write or call The Mountaineers, Club Headquarters, 300 Third Avenue West, Seattle, Washington 98119; (206) 284-6310.

Send or call for our catalog of more than 200 outdoor books:
The Mountaineers Books
1011 SW Klickitat Way, Suite 107
Seattle, WA 98134
1-800-553-4453